# Out
## *of the*
# Noösphere

— • ▲ ■ —

## *ADVENTURE, SPORTS, TRAVEL, AND THE ENVIRONMENT: THE BEST OF OUTSIDE MAGAZINE*

*Compiled by the Editors*

*A Fireside Book*

*Published by Simon & Schuster*

*New York    London    Toronto    Sydney    Tokyo    Singapore*

**FIRESIDE**
Simon & Schuster Building
Rockefeller Center
1230 Avenue of the Americas
New York, New York 10020

FIRESIDE and colophon are registered trademarks
of Simon & Schuster Inc.

Designed by Chris Welch
Manufactured in the United States of America

1 3 5 7 9 10 8 6 4 2

Library of Congress Cataloging-in-Publication Data
Out of the noösphere : Adventure, sports, travel, and the Environment:
the best of Outside magazine / compiled by the editors [Mark Bryant].
p. cm.
"A Fireside book."
1. Outdoor recreation. 2. Outdoor recreation—United States.
3. Outside (Chicago, Ill.) I. Bryant, Mark, 1956–   . II. Outside
(San Francisco, Calif.)
GV191.6.O94   1992
796.5—dc20                                        92-16584
                                                      CIP

ISBN: 0-671-75466-1

# CONTENTS

*p a r t*

II

—

THE **H**OME FRONT

*p a r t*

III

—

THE **N**ATURAL WORLD

*p a r t*

IV

—

THE WORLD OUT THERE

# INTRODUCTION

*"The ferrets must have a full mouth o' teeth,"* Reg Mellor said as
he fiddled with his belt. *"No filing of the teeth, no clipping. . . .
You must be sober, and the ferret must be hungry."*
—Donald Katz, "The King of the Ferret Leggers"

Sometime in the winter of 1982 we waffled, winced, and finally published an article concerning a 72-year-old British gentleman, a pair of
baggy trousers, a ferret or two, and the obscure and indelicate sport of
"keepin' 'em down." In considerable hindsight, the experience probably
taught us a good deal about editing, and about *Outside*.

I say "winced" because even among a group of editors who liked to
think of themselves as a broad-minded, irreverent lot, Don Katz's "The
King of the Ferret Leggers," funny as it was, seemed a bit, well, much.
"Sure, it has its moments," noted one editor, "but I was grimacing *all
the way through*. Tell me, is that good or bad?" Don must have picked up
on the jitters, for he fired off this little missive: "As to why *Outside*
shouldn't fear an entertaining and true story like this, I can come up
with 30 or 40 good reasons. And as raw as the sport may be, I do think
I handled it with some taste. I think you have a sophisticated audience
that responds to a good read—and maybe a laugh—as well as to visions
of the great outdoors."

Respond they did. "Katz's article was a definite withdrawal from your
usual standards," wrote a reader from Florida. "Any animal can be turned
into a viscious beast by trapping it in someone's stinking britches." Our
critic was not alone, but almost. "I know a brilliant writer when I read
one," went a more typical letter. "If Katz suggests an article about staring
at blank walls, for pete's sake see that he gets a good advance and all
expenses paid." Indeed. In the ten years since its publication, "The King
of the Ferret Leggers" has achieved something like cult status around
here. Our editors have bumped into readers everywhere from the finish
line of the Tour de France to the most genteel of dinner parties who

say, "So you're the people with that unbe-*lee*-vable story about the ferret-legging guy? A friend sent me a copy, and I photocopied it for 30 more of my closest friends." Katz himself is still occasionally called upon to pull out his photographs and prove to cynics that the story is true; just recently his physician asked him, "I've been wondering, you aren't the same Don Katz who wrote that ferret piece, are you?"

And to think that first we waffled, and then we winced. This and other examples of what we've come up with in our better moments are offered in this book.

TO REASSURE our friend from Florida, "The King of the Ferret Leggers" isn't the usual stuff of *Outside*. But when you define your magazine as one that covers "the people, places, activities, art, literature, and politics of the outdoors," you've mapped out a lot of territory in which to operate. And as stories like Katz's continue to remind us, we're not doing our jobs if we're not exploring and celebrating all that's out there. Which, of course, means taking a few risks.

When the magazine started out, there wasn't much to go on in the way of literate outdoor writing, at least in magazines. There was certainly the grand literary tradition of Cooper, Twain, Melville, London, and Conrad—great writers who had tromped through what Wallace Stevens called "the wild country of the soul." But back in 1977, there was little or no such soul to be found in periodicals. There were the well-established fishing and hunting journals. There were some fine magazines that concerned themselves with articles on how to dehydrate carrots or how to identify the call of the fulvous whistling duck (a slurred *ka-whee-oo!*). And growing up, there had been the "men's adventure magazines," a unique genre thought to push the hot buttons of virile American males. With titles like *Action for Men, Amazing Men's Stories,* and (naturally) *Adventure for Men,* these magazines published "truelife tales" featuring blood-crazed bikers, blood-crazed cannibals, rabid wild animals, and sex-crazed "nymphos." Fun reading, I guess, if you go for that sort of thing.

Needless to say, the people putting the magazine together in those early days were anxious to raise the level of it all. There would be some timely where-to-go and how-to-do-it articles in *Outside*, certainly, but when it came to its own pieces on adventure or wild animals or "the natives," they would be executed by people who were writers first and foremost, and they would be published for people whose sensibilities were very much like those of the staff. Through essays, profiles, and reportage, the writers would aim to tell stories that went beyond the obvious subject at hand and dealt with what your English professors called "the human condition." In other words, stories that would be more emotionally valid for the reader than what might be suggested by such titles as, "I Was Buried by a Killer Avalanche for Eight Long Days—and Lived!"

So adventure writing could be a good deal more than pompous chest-pounding or silly platitudes. Nature writing didn't have to be fusty and academic or fuzzy and dripping syrup. *Outside*'s readers deserved better, the editors argued. As Tim Cahill, one of the founding editors, a longtime columnist, and now our editor at large, saw it, the magazine's mission was to "give people back their dreams," dreams that get tucked away when the responsibilities of career and adulthood intrude.

David Quammen, the magazine's Natural Acts columnist for the last 11 years, is perhaps driving at something along these lines in his essay "Thinking About Earthworms," which is reprinted here. He writes of the Jesuit philosopher and paleontologist Pierre Teilhard de Chardin and his notion of the *noösphere:* "the sphere of reflexion, of conscious invention, of the conscious unity of souls." Bad idea, says Quammen, who invites us to join him in the good "battle against homogenization of the mind, the battle to preserve a cacophonous disunity of souls." Quammen is of course thinking of bigger things than a magazine, but he also seems to sum up pretty neatly what *Outside* set out to do—and to avoid. No homogenization, no pasteurization; just the world as it is and as we seldom get a chance to see it.

At the outset, however, the editors weren't exactly sure who was going to appreciate their noble efforts. One San Francisco newspaper columnist apparently didn't think *anyone* would. "The outdoor market, as far as he was concerned," wrote Cahill in *Outside*'s tenth anniversary issue, "consisted of illiterate hermits, ecological zealots, and gun-toting louts. Did such people really want to read great articles by National Book Award nominees?

"What if," Cahill wondered, "there was no one else on earth remotely like us; what if we were alone in the universe, nincompoops?"

AS IT TURNED OUT, Tim and his friends were not alone. Not nearly. In the 15 years since that first issue, *Outside* has attracted a smart, diverse, and loyal following, has seen its pages and audience grow, and has won a couple of National Magazine Awards. We editors like to pat ourselves on the back for things like that, but the truth is, much of our success is owed to the magazine's writers, and we take enormous pleasure in being able to work with them.

These people share not so much a style of writing (what we sometimes hear referred to, somewhat alarmingly, as "the *Outside* style") but an attitude—about themselves and the world at large. It's one that's sometimes irreverent and almost certainly independent, but also warm and inclusive. We generally like writers who don't take themselves too seriously, who come with a healthy dose of humor and an even healthier sense of irony. Writers who aren't afraid to portray themselves as screwups out in the big yonder, because there's plenty to screw up, and after all, bum luck or incompetence in otherwise competent hands can make for a fine story. We like writers who revel in simply being out and about and whose enthusiasms are infectious. We like writers who are keenly aware that what they see and do outside is all part of that thing called life, who don't pack their various experiences and passions into neat compartments as soon as they get home. Perhaps most of all, we like writers who aim for something more. Who write not just for the sake of an entertaining read on the subject at hand—travel, endurance sports, natural science, whatever—but to explore our values, our behavior, our judgments, the dreams we find or lose and, if we're lucky enough, find again. Thomas McGuane's "The Heart of the Game," then, is as much about being alive in the world as it is about hunting; Geoffrey Norman's "Mel Fisher's Morning After" is as much about the importance of the quest as it is about finding treasure and getting rich; Annick Smith's "The Importance of Dunes" is as much about growing up and meeting life as it is about the pleasures of summertime on the shores of Lake Michigan; David Roberts's "Moments of Doubt" is as much about coming to terms with death as it is about climbing; and Randy Wayne White's "Costa Rica, the Twig Syndrome, and the World Record that Got Away" is, suffice it to say, not much about a world fishing record.

And so on. The people in these pages know how to see and listen and tell a story. Many have their own collections, which you ought to check out, for choosing one or two pieces by them is a frustrating task. Many other fine *Outside* writers aren't represented here, which is perhaps even more frustrating, for they deserve to be. Too bad; we'll all have to wait till the next collection. In the meantime, enjoy the rare folks represented here—they give us the goods.

JUST AS RARE are good editors. These are people who understand that editing a magazine like ours is a wonderful license to be curious. They believe in intuition and fear the doctrinaire. They want the unconventional narrative and won't settle for the formulaic. They value good old-fashioned journalism and the kind of intelligence and grace and wit that sometimes seem in short supply. They know when to push or cajole a writer and when, as one of our founding editors, Terry McDonnell, once said of Cahill, to "let the big horse run." All of them smile at Jim Harrison's observation in "Going Places": "If you were really smart, you probably wouldn't be doing this. You would be in an office or club, acting nifty." Many say, *Those writers, they get to have all the fun.* And then they get back to work. It's a natural tension, we desk people tell ourselves, that makes for a better magazine. We all want to dream right along with the readers.

That said, abundant thanks go to Larry Burke, our publisher and editor-in-chief, for his inspiration, willingness to take risks, and unconditional support all these years; to John Rasmus, *Outside*'s longtime editor, with whom we learned and shared a lot; to Will Hearst, Terry McDonnell, Harriet Fier, Michael Rogers, and (of course) Tim Cahill, who helped get the magazine on its feet and give it a voice; to Laura Hohnhold, Dan Ferrara, Greg Cliburn, Donovan Webster, Lisa Chase, Dan Coyle, Kathy Martin, Margaret Davis, Brad Wetzler, Will Dana, Andrew Tilin, Marilyn Johnson, David Schonauer, Michelle Stacey, Susan Campbell McQuilkin, Michael McRae, Elizabeth Kaufmann, Craig Vetter, Alison Carpenter Davis, Todd Balf, Lisa Twyman Bessone, Wendy Anderson, Marshall Sella, Matthew Childs, Rob Story, Mike Grudowski, Michael Kiefer, Barbara Rowley, Joe Crump, Carolyn Arden Bresler, and others who have lent us their talents.

Not long ago, David Quammen—who, I'd better make clear, loves his work—dropped us this cover note to a manuscript. "My sense of literary despair," he wrote, "like the Angel of Death, has narrowly passed by. Every month, it seems, I'm out there frantically painting our gateposts with blood. Sometimes I use a roller."

Reg Mellor, and every writer in this collection, knows what he means.

Mark Bryant,
Editor, *Outside*

part

I

# THE
# PEOPLE

# COWGIRLS
## ALL THE WAY

*We want you to remember that the contestants here don't care much for the pajama parties or cosmetics lectures. These beauty queens are special.*

———————— ● ▲ ■ ————————

### E. JEAN CARROLL

· 1 ·

There is a horse auction establishment on South MacArthur in Oklahoma City. It is a big white building with a dirt arena inside. Actually, there are two arenas, a large one where the horses are exercised and a smaller one that has a stage with seats around it. I mention this place because it was there that the 50 Miss Rodeo America contestants made their first public appearance. They ate the barbecue in the large arena, and then were introduced by state in the small arena with the seats. In the large arena there was an open bar, but the contestants were not allowed to drink.

"They should let us," said Miss Rodeo Pennsylvania, "to see who gets crocked and who doesn't." Then Miss Rodeo Utah introduced herself.

She had on a baby-blue western suit with white leather piping down both pant legs. Her jacket had four white arrows on the back, pointing at her bottom. She had on baby-blue boots, a white ruffled blouse, and a baby-blue cowboy hat. She wore Merle Norman's Boston Blue eyeshadow, and two hearts held her rodeo sash. She clasped her Miss Rodeo Utah purse in her baby-blue gloves.

"You look like you've won a lot of beauty contests," I said. "Have you ever entered one?"

"No," she said, "I'm a cowgirl all the way!"

· · ·

IN 1975 MISS RODEO COLORADO was bucked off in the grand entry of the Miss Rodeo America Contest and was rushed from the arena to the hospital with fractured vertebrae. In 1976 a horse fell on Miss Rodeo Arizona and broke her back. In 1978 Miss Rodeo Kansas, who later became Miss Rodeo America, pivoted her horse to avoid hitting a contestant who had just run over a spectator in the arena. She caught her foot in the gate, was jerked off backwards, and broke her arm. It's a rugged kind of competition—no cakewalk.

Before leaving the horse auction building, a man came up to me and said he was from Springdale, Arkansas, "the chicken-pluckin' capital of the world." Said he was "with the chamber of commerce there" and was on the Miss Rodeo Board. Then he said, "I'm not a cowboy, but I believe in this crap."

I want to pass along these notes so you'll know what he meant by that. A lot of people are dubious about these contests. The banner on the bosom, the high-heeled hobble, the ramble down the runway. But in a very particular way, this pageant can tell you something special about these women and the way they grew up, about what someone taught them once, about a certain way of life. I mean there are things here that can cloud the issue, and it can all make for a clash in styles. But you should remember that these rodeo queens have roared into the arenas of Ranger, Texas; Ringling, Oklahoma; Roundup, Montana; and Rifle, Colorado, on the foulest, greenest, dumbest, and rankest of horses, shot their salutes to the crowd, and raced out to standing ovations. I want you to remember that Miss Rodeo America 1980 laid a leg over 200 head of weirdo horses and ran the rail in 300 rodeo performances. "Ah, the arena is a little wet, ma'am," they told her in Oregon. "The rain has made it a little *slick*. And that horse there don't like to see his reflection in no mud puddle. Makes him *hoppy*."

"Hand me the reins," said Miss Rodeo America, and half a minute later she exploded out of the gate in a gallop, her crown sparkling in the spotlights, her hips flaring over the saddle, her horse snorting and sliding, her salutes popping like cherry bombs.

I want you to remember that Miss Arkansas is a bull-riding champion and that Miss Wyoming was raised on a 5,000-acre ranch and rounds up cattle; she ropes, wrestles, brands, implants, and inoculates the calves, and runs the buck rigs, hay rigs, tractors, and stackers. I want you to remember that the queens in this contest have won barrel-racing championships, pole-bending championships, team-roping championships, and all-round cowgirl championships. I want you to recall that these queens raise, ride, race, rack, rope, rein, run, rub, breed, and sleep horses. I want you to remember that when Miss Utah was still in a baby-blue bib she took her afternoon nap in the barn on the back of a palomino. "Wasn't your mother terrified you'd fall off and get trampled to death?" I asked her.

"Well, of course, she'd put a *saddle* on him *first,*" said Miss Utah, mortified that anyone would speak ill of her mother.

I want you to remember all these things because I am about to introduce you to Dorothy Alexander, the pageant coordinator.

· **2** ·

Dorothy Alexander came out of her room in a leopard-skin polyester negligee and said, "You girls have so much pep, I want you to do this all week, OK?"

The queens applauded. Dorothy had confessed to me earlier that she was once Miss University of Montana "a thousand years ago."

The queens had changed from the three-piece suits they had worn all day to their nightgowns. They were seated on the floor in the hall in front of the elevators on the third floor of the Lincoln Plaza Hotel.

"You're the best horsewomen in America," Dorothy said, "and you've got a lot of pep!" More applause.

Dorothy had told me that the queens rode like "real ladies" but that she thought the personality competition was the most important. "We can't have a dunce for Miss Rodeo America," said Dorothy. "This is *not* a bawdy pageant!"

The elevator doors opened a few minutes later, and a television crew got off to take pictures of the "best horsewomen in America" wearing their nighties.

· **3** ·

A cowboy was once fined $200 by the Professional Rodeo Cowboy's Association for making a pass at a queen.

"Now listen," said Tom Poteet, general chairman of the pageant, "tonight you girls are going to be with the cowboys a little while. I know I can count on you to be ladies. I know I don't have to worry about any *problems,* OK?" The queens were then led into an empty room, where a buffet had been prepared for the cowboys, contestants in the National Finals Rodeo. The queens were asked to fill their plates and then were directed to four tables in the furthermost corner of the room. When the last queen was seated and had her lap covered with a paper napkin, the doors were thrown open and one hundred rodeo cowboys swaggered in.

There was a pause. A hush fell. The lone figure of Hawkeye Henson, former world champion bronc rider, emerged from the clutch of men. He started across the room, his black silk shirt pulled tight across his chest, his neckerchief arranged with the point hanging down the front, his black hat cocked, his famous eagle feather at an upward angle, his spurs softly jingling on the tiles. As he neared the queens, Miss Kentucky looked him up and down and said, "I wonder if this is the beginning of the end?"

· 4 ·

WORKING COWHORSE PATTERN
Ride the pattern as follows:
Begin work to the right,
First figure eight,
Second figure eight; proceed to rail,
Begin run,
Sliding stop,
Turn away from rail; begin second run,
Sliding stop,
Turn away from rail; make short run,
Sliding stop,
Back up,
Quarter turn to right or left,
Half turn to opposite direction,
Half turn opposite.

That is one of the horsemanship patterns printed in the *Miss Rodeo America Official Rule Book*. The book is a white paperback with 24 Xeroxed pages, and it begins with the question: "What are we looking for in a Miss Rodeo America? Answer: An attractive, intelligent girl . . . a girl who has never been, is not now, or who will not become pregnant during her reign . . . a well-dressed girl who can ride a horse with showmanship and skill, and promote the great sport of rodeo." In other words, a beautiful, big-breasted, barrel-racing, flag-waving, fashionable *virgo intacta* with an IQ somewhere above the persons who composed the *Official Rule Book*.

The book provides a section on "dress wear for horsemanship," supplies a list of equestrian skills the queens are scored on, and concludes with two pages of diagrams illustrating the Miss Rodeo America Horsemanship Patterns Numbers 1 and 2. There is one omission, however, one fact the *Rule Book* committee neglected to Xerox: The horses in the contest are green. The Miss Rodeo America Pageant is produced in the Cowgirl Capital of the World during National Finals Rodeo Week, when the finest stock in America is stabled in the city limits, and the queens get green horses. (They are supplied by local saddle and bridle clubs, riding schools, stock contractors, and "interested individuals.") That is to say, the *Official Rule Book* tells a queen that she must wear a "form-fitting western blouse or shirt with long sleeves, any color with yoke, and shirttail tucked in" while she performs her figure eights, proceeds to the rail, begins her run, slides to a stop, turns from the rail, begins her second run, slides to a stop, turns from the rail, makes her short run, slides to a stop, and backs up; but it does not tell her that her horse might blow up.

The *Official Rule Book* was composed by persons who yearn to merge Miss America with Dale Evans, who burn to combine "The Star-Spangled Banner" and the barnyard; the breast and the breast collar. What do these people care about green horses when what they are looking for is Phyllis George Evans, her hair flashing in the floodlights and her ass fastened on anything that nickers? Next to nothing.

## • 5 •

7:30 A.M. TO 9:30 A.M. BREAKFAST. SPEECHES BY ONE-THIRD OF THE CONTESTANTS ON THEIR RESPECTIVE STATES.

Miss Rodeo Hawaii walked to the front of the room, smiled—she had a mouthful of spectacularly large, dazzlingly white, splendidly shaped teeth with beautiful crimson gums—delivered the first paragraph of her speech, and stopped dead. "I'm sorry," she said, smiling. A half minute passed. "I'm sorry," she said, her smile disintegrating completely, and sat down.

"Our next contestant will be Miss Nebraska!" sang Dorothy Alexander. 10:00 P.M. PAJAMA PARTY. ONE THIRD OF THE CONTESTANTS GIVE GIFTS.

Illinois passed out popcorn balls; Colorado, Coors T-shirts; Iowa, crocheted booties; and Tennessee, 50 bottles of Jack Daniel's.

"But you *cannot drink them!*" yelled Dorothy. She was now wearing a Mediterranean-blue peignoir set. "Listen to mother," said the television producer, who was there with his crew again.

"I'm going to come in *every* room tonight and check," giggled Dorothy.

"Hey, Texas," yelled the television producer, "hold up that bottle. Hey! Hold up that bottle."

"No pictures!" cried Dorothy.


A MEMBER OF THE PRESS and a pageant official were at the gate when Miss Idaho entered the arena in the first go-round of the horsemanship competition. "This horse turns nice," said the official. The horse ducked off the wrong way four times toward the alley in the figure eight. "He's nice on the turns, though," said the official. The horse lunged at the rail, made two bounds, and blew up into a ticking gallop on the run. On the slide, he reared, nearly fell over backwards. "Miss Idaho should sit more on her crotch," said the official. In the second run, Miss Idaho worked the reins, kept the horse's head low, corrected the cross-firing of his back end. On the slide, he reared again. "It's *all* in Miss Idaho's crotch," said the official. The third run was smooth—the slide was second-rate, but no rearing. "Boy, wait till you see this guy turn," said the official. Miss Idaho backed the horse, reined him to the right for the pivot. The horse stood like a post. Miss Idaho calmly worked the reins. The horse sucked in his breath, became a statue. "Where did you find this piece of crap?" asked the member of the press. The nine judges looked on in silence. Miss Idaho removed her foot from the stirrup and heeled the horse in the right shoulder with her boot. The horse swung to the right. The crowd applauded. "He's fantastic!" shouted the official. The horse spun left. The crowd cheered. Miss Idaho rolled him right, shot her salute, and cantered out of the arena to an enthusiastic ovation. The official shouted even more excitedly, "Oh, he's just fantastic! Fantastic, fantastic!"

## · 6 ·

"You girls are out on horses all day. In the gunk. In the muck. In the manure. That's what causes blackheads."

The queens were listening to this in the hotel conference room. The room had rows of seats ascending in tiers, and on the ceiling there were the sort of circles of tiny fluorescent lights that make people who sit under them look funny. The lights in the room could be turned high or low, but either way the queens looked weird. They looked especially weird in the light because they were wearing little pink ruffs around their necks and had little pink plastic makeup trays with mirrors in front of them, and masks on their faces. It was the afternoon of the coronation, and the Mary Kay consultants were meeting with them in the conference room for a "cosmetic session."

"Have any of you dried?" asked the head consultant, at a lectern in the front of the room. The assistant consultants walked up and down the rows checking to see if any queens were dry. If they were, they were handed hot washcloths.

"Since the masks are taking some time," said the head consultant, "why don't I just give you a little history about how Mary Kay got started. Well, there was this old tanner of hides . . ." At this point Miss South Dakota ripped off her ruff, put her head down on her tray, and went to sleep.

"I SEE YOU ARE DRESSED for the coronation," I said.

"Yes, but I don't look as good as some of the girls."

"Do you mind if I write down what you have on?"

"No. Go ahead."

"All right. You have on gold-and-silver collar tips with your initials."

"Right."

"You have on a blue silk scarf with your initials set in diamonds pinned across the knot."

"Right."

"Your buckle is gold and silver with rubies and diamonds."

"Right."

"You have blue—what are those?"

"Eel."

"Blue eel boots. Black hat. Black pants. Blue jacket."

"You forgot the buttons."

"The, ah, buttons are silver circles with raised gold flowers with rubies in the middle."

"Right."

The person I was speaking to was Joe "Sandy" Boone, president of Miss Rodeo America.

· 7 ·

There is a sound that barrel-racing horses make when they are in the alley and ready to run. It's a rapid, thumping sound of hoofs hitting dirt. The air is thick with dust, and the noise of the hoofs sounds richer in the dust, and when the dirt clods hit the iron chutes as the horses rear back and dig out, there is also a ringing sound. These were the sounds in the state fairgrounds arena alley the night of the coronation. The horses were rank, and they didn't have 50; and each queen had to race into the arena, fire her salute, and then gallop out the gate and dismount so that the next could ride in. But it was, as a matter of fact, the finest time of the pageant.

The ten finalists had been named. The four runners-up had been named. The reigning Miss Rodeo America had taken her last royal roar around the arena. Six rodeo clowns had competed in a bullfighting championship. And the winner of *that* had been named.

"Well, folks," said Hadley Barrett, the rodeo announcer, to a crowd that could have been larger, "is there anything else we have to do tonight?"

"I can't *stand* it any longer," said Diana Putnam, the reigning queen.

"May we have the envelope, please?" said Hadley. There was a drum roll. "Who will wear the crown next? If you're too nervous to open that envelope I'll—Oh! You got it. Ladies and gentlemen, we are going to ask Diana to name her successor. Diana, we want *you* to name the 1981 Miss Rodeo America."

Diana looked down at the card in her hand, then shouted, "Miss Rodeo Colorado!"

Screams from the contestants.

Kathy Martin, five-foot-six, 120 pounds, dark eyes, flashing hair, a public relations major whose hobbies were "equine evaluation, training quarter horses, dancing, jogging, sewing, and trail riding," made her way toward her precursor. The band struck up "The Most Beautiful Girl in the World." Diana removed the crown from her hat and placed it on Miss Colorado's hat. The queens were screaming.

"There she is, ladies and gentlemen!" said Hadley. "The 1981 Miss Rodeo America!"

Miss Colorado walked down the steps: no train, no tears, no toppling tiaras, no scepters, no roses, no ermine. All that awaited her was the top reining horse in the country, dancing at the end of a rein held by a cowboy in white.

*April/May 1981*

# JOHN BACHAR HANGS ON

*He threw away his ropes a long time ago*
*—so what's tugging at him now?*

•  ▲  ■

CRAIG VETTER

It's not that the question haunts John Bachar, exactly, but it does follow him around, and at the end of last summer in Yosemite, a young climber pestered up to him with it. Bachar was getting ready to climb Midnight Lightning, the infamous little boulder problem that sits in Camp Four as if to separate those who ask such questions from those whose answer might be taken seriously. "Who's the very best rock climber in the world, you think?" said the kid.

Bachar stood there with his shirt off, scrubbing the tiny lower holds with a toothbrush, trying to think up an answer that was neither arrogant nor stupidly modest. I was eavesdropping with particular interest because I'd just spent several days watching him climb, and at a certain point I'd asked him the same question. He'd given me the long answer, full of ifs and althoughs, full of names, but it looked here as if he were searching for a short way to make the same point, and after a minute he found it.

"It's a tough question," he said, "because there are so many different skills to it, and like one guy might be best at this and another guy best at that." Then he took his chalky hands and used them on each other. "It's like that old game, you know the one, where rock breaks scissors, scissors cut paper, and paper covers rock—so that each is the best in its way." The kid nodded, but the Zen answer wasn't what he was after, so he took another tack. "Do all these young guys trying to knock off a piece of your reputation ever bother you?"

"Oh yeah," said Bachar. "I'm still awfully competitive."

When I joined him last September in Yosemite, all that was left of the waterfalls were long, shiny streaks on the rocks, and it was *hot*. He was living with his wife, Brenda, in a house in Foresta and was just back from Spain, where he'd spent two weeks at the factory that makes Fires, the current hottest of climbing shoes. Bachar and a pal are Fire distributors, an enterprise that is likely to earn each of them something like $100,000 this year. The morning we met in the Camp Four parking lot, he pulled up in his brand-new Toyota pickup with the cab full of reggae. He was in shorts, a T-shirt, and jogging shoes, and as we talked about where he wanted to climb I couldn't help thinking to myself that this was just another day at the office for John Bachar. Taking journalists out on the rocks has become a familiar exercise for him.

Newspapers and magazines have profiled and photographed him as if he pitched for the Mets, and in fact, during the telecast of the 1985 World Series you couldn't go more than a couple of innings without watching him mantle and pendulum around the rock in a commercial for razor blades that featured him as the "essence of climbing," the way another ad for the blades used George Brett for the essence of hitting. Because, although the question of who is the best all-around climber will never be entirely settled, John Bachar is certainly the most famous rock climber in the history of the sport, and all he had to do to become that was to leave his gear in camp, begin climbing without ropes or chocks or carabiners, without any protection at all. Free soloing, they call it.

Bachar decided it was too hot to climb in the valley itself, so we drove to Tuolumne Meadows and the Polydomes in the cooler high country about an hour away.

On the way we talked about his notoriety. He's a little prickly about it. Rock climbers have always been suspicious of publicity, perhaps because they've so often seen the death-defying, crazy-ass moments of their sport puffed all out of proportion while the subtle heart and spirit of what they do is missed completely. In Yosemite the grapevine ethic that has passed from generation to generation is that you do not climb to become famous or to make a living. You climb to climb, and if you do it with intensity, the rewards are deep and private. At its purest, you go alone, and when you get back, you might not even say where you've been or what you've climbed.

"I've never tried to toot my own horn," said Bachar. "I didn't mail my name to the magazines." He did, however, offer $10,000 to anyone who could follow him free solo up routes he chose, which is a louder sort of crowing than usually goes on around Camp Four. Even so, for a rock climber, there is something a little embarrassing about being followed from station to station on the boulder circuit by a Japanese group so large that their camera clicking overwhelms the sound of the birds, the sound of everything, or by a posse of German climbers who offered him $100 to climb Midnight Lightning while they videotaped it. Bachar did it, and they filmed him, but when they huddled up to ask questions afterward, he literally snatched the money from the leader's hand and bolted into the woods.

Other climbers grumble about what all this means. They worry about where Bachar's free-solo media blitz is pointing the sport. Some say Bachar is casting a dangerous, irresponsible image that young climbers and even some veterans are reaching for at their peril. He hears stories of broken bones suffered by free soloists who have fallen from places just past the limits of their strength and experience, and the stories affect him; but philosophically his line is tough. "I don't feel any responsibility in that way," he told me. "I don't feel I'm taking the sport in that direction, either. I'm just doing what I like to do. If it happens that people emulate me, that's far out, because that means they're doing what *they* want to do."

Finally, of course, the publicity has led to his living, has allowed him to become the first purely professional rock climber, to make good money at it without teaching, or taking pictures, or wanting to pay the way. His deal with Fire (pronounced Feeray) came out of that, after a couple of Spanish journalists brought the first pair of the sticky-soled shoes into the valley. They asked Bachar if he wanted to test-drive them. Better than EBs, the French climbing shoe he was using, they said. Bachar was skeptical.

"I'd heard that I don't know how many times," he said. "But I said, 'Sure, I'll try anything.' So I take them out and they're floppy, a half-size too big and worn out. I tried them on my bouldering circuit in camp, and I was sure they were going to pop off a hold somewhere, but they didn't—not even on Blue Suede Shoes, which is pretty edgy. So I took them over to Midnight Lightning because I was sure they'd pop on that lip, but they didn't even come close to popping. When they asked me how I liked them, I said I wanted ten pair just for my personal stash. That's when they asked me if I wanted to distribute them."

.   .   .

IT'S NO SURPRISE that Bachar used Midnight Lightning as the acid test for the shoes. In many ways this 25-foot, 12-move route up the northwest side of the Columbia Boulder is the linchpin of the ambitious and fiercely competitive climbing career that he brought to Yosemite 12 years ago. It was 1974, and he was 17 years old, new to Yosemite, and hungry to knock off pieces of the reputations that had preceded him. Back then all the new boys climbed in the shade of the big-wall heroes like Royal Robbins, Warren Harding, Yvan Chouinard, and Chuck Pratt, and it wasn't at all clear how or if the hungry young climbers were ever going to do anything in this valley that would seem brilliant or daring. But they were working on it: going without jumar or bolts on routes that had only been climbed by mechanical aid before, seeking out terrible corners and horrific overhangs that required whole new levels of gymnastic talent and conditioning. John Bachar and Ron Kauk, another young valley hotshot, stood out immediately. They were the same age, good friends, and they began authoring terrifically difficult little routes all over the valley.

The old heroes, grumbling some about the new style, called it "sport climbing," as if it were not so much a life anymore, but somehow closer to gymnastics or wire walking. And because they used gymnastic chalk, one of the old timers gave the Bachar/Kauk bunch a nickname that had a sort of feminine spin to it: They think it was Harding who started calling them "the powder-puff boys."

But it was Midnight Lightning that made them the monkeys to chase. It sits almost in the middle of Camp Four, but none of the great rock athletes who had ever come to Yosemite and walked past it a hundred times had ever put their climber's eyes on the overhanging side of the rock and imagined a way up it. Then, one evening, Ron Kauk looked at the nasty little pitch and said he thought he saw a route: ten or 12 moves of insane difficulty, including a crux near the top that he rated a 15.3 (at that time the highest degree of difficulty in rock climbing), where whatever strength and energy you had started with would be all but gone.

Kauk and Bachar began working on it like two dogs on one bone: falling off it, over and over, from February to May of 1976. Each coached the other from the ground, tried to root the other over the 5.13 move near the top, then winced as he came exploding off it like some gymnast in a wild emergency dismount. Kauk remembers the day he got it: "So I mantle over and creep up on it like this, then I reached, grabbed it, and I couldn't even believe it at first. I almost fell off just from the excitement. Bachar was watching and he was really funny; he was going 'Come on, come on,' and then I made it, and he told me later he went, 'Oh, no!'

"It was the full prize," Kauk says, and it should have gone into the valley lore simply and cleanly. But the friendly competition between him and Bachar, which had pushed both of them to the incredible levels they were reaching, now began—by a fluke—to pull against their camaraderie.

Bachar continued to work for the second ascent, and during one of his tries a crucial nubbin broke off. Kauk watched him whip violently off the rock and says now that he's amazed Bachar wasn't hurt. At the same time, Kauk realized the subtle implications of the event: The climb had been changed; only slightly he thought, but he knew he'd have to do it again. When Bachar tells the story, he says it was more than a slight change, the implication being that another first ascent was possible up the route in its new form. Kauk left the valley for a while, and not long after that, Bachar made it. When Kauk returned and tried to repeat the ascent, he couldn't. He says it took him a couple of weeks to get it again; Bachar remembers it being more like a couple of months. And although Bachar never claimed to have made the first ascent, the broken nubbin put an asterisk in the story that has confused the oral history enough so that he sometimes gets credit for doing it first. Nubbin or no nubbin, however, the little climb was stunning: It was six years before anyone but Kauk and Bachar put mind and muscle in shape enough to pull themselves over the same lip.

JOHN BACHAR HAD BEGUN CLIMBING at 14 on practice rocks around Los Angeles, and it was a timid beginning as he describes it. He stayed on the easy climbs, and used every piece of safety equipment you could buy then, including a helmet. He and a friend tinkered on the rocks every weekend, and during the week he thought about it, read about it, and sat through his classes at Westchester High daydreaming about it. He says he didn't think he'd ever be particularly good; he just liked it.

After his high school graduation Bachar spent the summer at Yosemite—on roughly a hundred dollars. "Some of the best days of my life," he told me. "I was so poor. But I did my first 5.11 that summer, New Dimensions."

That fall he went off to U.C.L.A. as a math major, but after the first year he had a conversation with himself. "I knew I wanted to, but I thought, I can't just quit college and go climbing 'cause that's crazy, but deep in my mind I just started smiling. From then on I dedicated myself completely to climbing. It had nothing to do with making a living."

For the next seven years he spent his summers climbing in Yosemite or teaching climbing in Colorado, and his winters working construction or on the loading docks in Los Angeles. Battling through, month by month, he calls it now. "If I had $500 in my bank account, I felt like a millionaire."

His move into free soloing could hardly be called timid, but it wasn't exactly bold either. John Long had to talk him into it. For years most of the best climbers, including Long, had now and then gone without protection up short climbs that they knew well, mostly for fun. In a way it was a sort of hairy bouldering: 5.12 climbers on 5.8 routes. Nobody talked about it much, and they didn't think of it as a real branch of the sport. The first time Bachar soloed, he and Long were in Joshua Tree, and as they got ready to climb a 5.8 crack called Double Cross, Bachar says, he assumed they'd rope up.

"We're going to do it without a rope," Long told him.

"I don't think I can do that," said Bachar.

"Think of it this way," said Long. "If you climbed this route a hundred times, how many times would you fall off?"

"Never," said Bachar.

"Then let's go," said Long.

"Makes sense," said Bachar, and they went.

By 1979 Bachar was free soloing all over the valley, harder and harder routes, and when he wasn't on the rocks, he worked out like an Olympian. He designed and built a 70-foot rope ladder, hung it from a pine, and climbed it hand-over-hand two and three rungs at a time. He did set after set of fingertip pull-ups with 50-pound weights hanging between his legs. He worked on a boxer's speed bag, practiced karate kicks and spins, walked a slack wire for balance. For aerobic conditioning, he speed climbed 5.8 and 5.9 routes like 600-foot Manure Pile Buttress, racing his friend Rick Cashner to the top until the two of them could do in 11 or 12 minutes what good roped climbers did in an hour. All in all it was a training regimen that had never been seen among climbers before. It was cool-headed, scientific, relentless, and it came together in a stroke that not only caught the public's attention but also astounded every climber who heard about it (though none remembers now exactly when it happened). Bachar returned to New Dimensions, the soaring, 400-foot dead-vertical crack that had been his first 5.11 climb years before, and this time he climbed it alone and without protection, as if it were some camp boulder he could jump free of if things got tough.

It was the kind of performance that changed the sport. For other climbers, it meant that no matter how difficult and beautiful their new routes, if they used a rope to protect themselves, their commitment seemed somehow less than total. And for the public, what had always been an arcane jumble of hardware, ropes, and technical vocabulary was now reduced to an exercise of beautiful, terrifying simplicity: You pull yourself up by hand and foot—you fall, you die.

THE FIRST CLIMB in Tuolumne that September morning was called Pot Luck, a 25-foot, overhanging 5.11 corner that sat a quarter-mile off the road through a stumpy grove of pine.

"It's a little sequency, a little strenuous," Bachar said as he put on his shoes. "But I don't know why they call it 5.11." Then he put crack-cleaning tools—a toothbrush and some nail clippers—in his teeth, strapped his chalk bag around his waist, and began to climb.

It looked like 5.11 from where I was standing, or worse, with its overhangs and fingernail purchases, and as he stemmed and hung and drew himself up, there was no sound except for his breathing and the occasional rustle of his hand in the chalk bag. It's hypnotizing to watch Bachar climb. There is such strength and flow to the way he takes a rock. He talks about his style sometimes as being like T'ai Chi, and that's exactly what he makes it look like. Nothing about this dance jerks or strains or overreaches. There are pauses, but there is no hesitation. While he climbed, the muscles in his back became as particular as a Leonardo drawing, and it wasn't until he topped out, shook his arms, blew some air, and rubbed his left elbow that I remembered he was climbing hurt.

It's not his first injury. He's had tendonitis in his fingers for years, but he says it's never bothered him much. When it gets bad, he stops climbing for a while and plays the tenor saxophone he taught himself; he says he can tell when he is ready to go back by the way his fingers feel on the horn. But about two years ago, while he was working out, climbing the ladder that now bears his name in the Chouinard Equipment catalog, his elbow went. At first the doctors thought it was tendonitis, but it was finally diagnosed as capsulitis, which heals more slowly, is more likely to recur, and which prevents him from locking his arm into certain hanging positions. Since then he's worn a big ice bag on it after his climbs and workouts, and has carefully trained himself back to what he calls 90 percent. There are still a couple of boulder problems and climbs he can't do anymore, but he thinks he can eventually get back all that he's lost. He wasn't that optimistic when it happened, though. "For a long time it was a big bummer for me to try to deal with it. It was my life, and I was crying every day."

We went from Pot Luck to Lembert Dome. Phil Bard, the photographer-climber with us, wanted him to do something called Oz, but Bachar resisted quietly—said he'd rather do Water Crack. It was the first sign of a moodiness, a reluctance to be pointed here and there, a weariness, I thought, at being led like a one-trick pony from show to show.

There were four other climbers on the steep, slippery golden granite of the dome. They were well roped and working hard, and as they watched Bachar glide by ropeless, they stared at him the way refugees on a hard road might watch a limousine that was passing them slowly, squinting at windows through which they couldn't see, wondering who in the hell was in there. He did two routes for the photographer before either of the roped teams made it to the top.

The next day we stayed in the valley, and Bachar's mood had deepened. It was too hot to climb at the Cookie Cliff, he said, even if Crack-a-Go-Go made dramatic photos. He just didn't feel like it. It was too greasy, his pinkies were stressed. He wanted to do one of the shadier climbs. Bard argued against those because of the poor light. Bachar finally said OK, but there was enough petulance to it that I got him aside to talk just before we made the walk to the base of the Cookie. I told him that if he didn't feel right about going up Crack-a-Go-Go, 150 feet of 5.11 directly in the sun, he shouldn't do it. I said I understood that as many times as he'd done these climbs before, there was still always the chance that something would go wrong and he'd die. Even monkeys fall out of trees sometimes. I told him I didn't want him to think I took what he was doing for granted.

Others do, he said. He overhears climbers talking about what Bachar can do, about what Bachar's done. Sometimes he hears the legend outrun the reality.

"When is he going to do Astral Man?"

"I thought he already did that."

"They want me to do more and more outrageous stuff," he said.

He decided he'd do Crack-a-Go-Go. "One *last* shot," he said. Then he stepped from a tree branch into a crack most climbers can't do with a rope and went up it something like smoke rising from a campfire. Then he did a nearby 5.11 called Catchy Corner, just as vertical, just as sweaty. Then he said he wanted to do New Dimensions, still a favorite of his, and in the shade at that point.

BARD RAPPELLED partway down the 400-foot cliff with his camera; I watched through binoculars from a couple of hundred yards away, which added chill to the perspective. These are just big rocks, I thought, until man gets on them. Then they take on truly monstrous proportions, and up against them you see the human speck for the infinitely strange and curious character he is. And when Bachar talks about being up there alone, you get some sense of just how personal and even spiritual the whole exercise really is.

"When you're doing it properly," he'd told me earlier, "you don't even know how far off the ground you are. You're just in this little shell of concentration where you're looking at your hands and feet, and that's it. You don't see anything else. You don't see the ground—I mean, you know it's there, peripherally you see it—but if it's right, you're working on the moves, working on being smooth, and just having a great time moving.

"I like to feel I'm in complete control up there. Every now and then I get a little scared, a little strung out, and have to do some moves I don't want to do, and that's not good. I like to feel supersolid, like I could just throw a little ballet on top of the whole thing. I can say I soloed this 5.12 or something, but that's not what really counts. It's how it felt. Some of the hard climbs I've soloed were maybe impressive from the outside, but inside I might not feel that great about them, because I was maybe only 90 percent in control, and that's less than I want when I solo, because one move . . . I mean, you blow it once . . . ." He'd hesitated, and I finished his sentence for him: ". . . the punishment is severe."

He laughed. "Way severe," he said.

Later we drove to Foresta to the hand-built workout area behind his friend Rick Cashner's cabin. Bachar goes there three or four times a week to work through a carefully designed two-hour routine of fingertip pull-ups, one-armed pullups, bag punching, and rope walking. His 70-foot ladder is rigged to the upper reaches of a ponderosa, and he climbed it that afternoon, though he says he doesn't do it much these days with his elbow the way it is. I watched him do set after set of things most athletes can't do one of, and at one point, as he added weight to his belt for more pull-ups, I remembered something he said when we had talked about the saxophone and John Coltrane, his favorite player. "All the heroes I have," he said, "I admire for their dedication."

When I asked if he was going to be able to get back into top form, he told me he thought so. "We'll see," he said. And when we talked about what he wants to be doing ten years from now, he said, "Just what I'm doing now. Climbing, living in the valley."

Right after sunset, when I left him, he was still at it, warming down, hanging by his fingertips in the fading light, head back, eyes closed.

THE NEXT MORNING in Camp Four I met Ron Kauk to chat and to watch him climb. Bachar was there, taking a day off, sitting around on the logs in the parking lot with various others of the dusty trolls to whom this camp is home.

Kauk was there to be photographed on Midnight Lightning, and as he laced his shoes, he said, "No matter what, when you get ready to do this problem, your heart starts pumping."

Bachar asked if he could watch, and Kauk said sure, but the fact that the question had been asked at all was a small, clear sign of the stiffness that has grown into the friendship. It was also a sign of respect from Bachar—paper, scissors, and rock—and an acknowledgment that Kauk is justly famous in his own right. A few weeks before, he and Jerry Moffett had climbed Lost Arrow Spire on a live telecast for "ABC's Wide World of Sports," and Kauk, who teaches at the Yosemite Mountaineering School, has his television commercial, too, for Ford Bronco. His roped climbing is as difficult as any that's ever been done—as astounding in its own way as Bachar's free soloing.

When Kauk talks about the cool between him and Bachar, there's more regret than bitterness in it. "When John first started soloing, I thought it was kind of neat. Then, with all the sensational press coverage, the whole thing got real shallow and started to misrepresent the sport,

I thought. Then the money started coming. John says things change as you grow up, but still, to me having friends is one of the most important things . . . and it's kind of changed my whole feeling for things around the valley in a lot of ways. There used to be a really neat friendship, camaraderie, whatever you want to call it. . . ."

The first time up the rock that morning, Kauk came off at what they call the Lightning Bolt Hold, a hanging switchhands move that is about as far as even the best climbers ever get. He made it on the second try, and when he came down, he held out his shaking hands for us. "I always feel like that on top," said Bachar.

Kauk made the climb again so the photographer could get each move in sequence, and while he did, Bachar took his wife Brenda's mountain bike a few yards away and started making speed runs at a dirt hump to see how much air he could get.

At one point he yelled over, "Remember when we used to do this, Ronnie?" Kauk turned to me and said, "Look at that. You gotta love John. I guess he's just got a lot more on his mind these days."

*April 1986*

# RECKLESS

## *Bill Johnson is unsafe at any speed.*

● ▲ ■

### LAURENCE SHAMES

Last winter, on a mountain called Bjelasnica, William Dean Johnson of Van Nuys, California, cannonballed into history by way of a downhill sprint that lasted exactly one minute, 45 and 59/100ths seconds. In the same brief interval, the skier made the heady transition from cocky unknown to celebrity bad boy, a role he donned as rakishly as if it were a custom-made fedora. He mugged for the cameras, made outrageous statements, won some hearts, and made some enemies, then receded in a blur of speed and fame. Billy Johnson, like the media machinery around him, had been a master of the short take that winter; one wondered if, through the hot, distended summer months, he was yet beginning to think in terms of longer increments of time. It seemed the right season to talk to him.

As it turned out, though, I wasn't the only person hanging around a launch ramp on Lake Powell, in the middle of the Arizona desert, waiting to meet up with Billy Johnson on a 100-degree Sunday. The park rangers were waiting for him, too. They had walkie-talkies and guns. They weren't there to ask for his autograph . . .

On February 16, 1984, in Sarajevo, Yugoslavia, Billy Johnson had triumphed by the perilous but straightforward means of trajecting himself from the top of the hill to the bottom faster than any of the other skiers there assembled.

He did this, basically, by keeping his vital organs closer to his skis than any other downhill racer has ever dared to do. Careening down a mountain in one of his clinging candy-striped jumpsuits, Johnson resembles nothing so much as a giant Easter egg out for a lunatic sleigh ride. He holds the tuck on turns, amid the hissing violence of edges cutting runnels into grainy snow. He holds the tuck in midair, when bumps are pushing him one way and gravity is pulling him the other, conspiring to stretch him like a piece of melting cheese. He holds the tuck on straightaways where, at 80 miles an hour, there is an understandable tendency to pull one's face an extra inch or two up from the mountain. What enables Johnson to keep himself in that efficient ovoid form is a blend of ferocious concentration, great power in the haunches, and a reckless moxie that makes him spiritual cousin to the kamikaze. "Win or fall" is the way he describes the only two acceptable outcomes of a race. Johnson's moxie on Bjelasnica earned him an Olympic gold medal, the first gold medal ever gleaned by an American male in an Olympic alpine event, and the first medal of any kind that an American male had ever taken in the downhill. It was a grand achievement, perhaps the grandest of the entire Winter Games, yet it had to some degree been smudged in advance by the controversy and plain dislike surrounding Johnson.

Twenty-three and talkative, he had been daring people to hate his guts practically from the minute he hit the Continent. Considered not even a serious contender at Sarajevo, let alone the favorite, he announced after a single training run that "This course was designed for me, and everyone else is here to fight for second place." His cocky persona seemed modeled on that of Robert Redford's handsomely obnoxious loner in *Downhill Racer*—a movie that Johnson has reportedly seen no fewer than seven times—and, like his cinematic alter ego, Johnson managed to alienate almost everybody. The ordinarily mild-mannered Franz Klammer, winner of the '76 gold, was annoyed enough to call him a "nose-picker." The capper, though, came when the new champion was asked to describe the personal significance of his glorious triumph; he fixed the camera with an immodest grin and, in a jubilation of ecstatic and unabashed avarice, said, "Millions. We're talking millions."

This time he had gone too far, and the media responded with righteous gusto. Bill Johnson, to do what he does on the sides of mountains, must have preternaturally fast reflexes; but those golden synapses couldn't fire fast enough to keep up with the process that got rolling the instant he'd won the gold. It was a process that moved much faster even than the speeds that Johnson was used to—as fast, in fact, as microwaves bouncing off satellites—and it caught the skier unprepared. He'd spent his whole life getting superbly good at one thing. Now, moments after having shown the world the result of that driven single-mindedness, he was being called upon to be *other* things as well: a paragon, a charmer, an example to the young, a master at the vocabulary of fame. But he wasn't ready; he was blowing his lines. The more he said, the worse he sounded. It was just like taking a fall on a slope, and the press examined the tumble with a similar, slightly ghoulish fascination. One American reporter predicted that Johnson's was "one gold medal that's going to end up in a pawnshop." Johnson left Sarajevo with a trinket in one hand telling him he was the world's best downhill skier; in the other hand he had a stack of press clips, the consensus of which was that he was a washout as a human being.

One thing no one had been able to say about Johnson, though, was that he was a whiner. He didn't complain much about his treatment by the press, and he didn't let it change him much either; he acted as if the criticisms didn't hurt him. That part was a bluff. They hurt like hell.

ON SUN-SHOT LAKE POWELL, guys in cowboy hats and women with hairdos were launching motorboats from the Wahweap Marina at the rate of about three a minute. They did this in teams. The girlfriend would back the pickup axle-deep into the lake, and the guy would finesse the boat motor in reverse until the craft slithered off the trailer with the melancholy of a fat man pushing backward from the dinner table. Meanwhile, the rangers and I kept a lookout for Billy Johnson's yellow Sea-Ray, the one equipped with the 307 Chevy engine.

It seems that the day before Johnson had a small and inconclusive disagreement with a ranger over (fittingly enough) attitudes toward velocity. On water as on snow, Johnson delights in going fast. The ranger, on the other hand, was sworn to enforce a policy of no wake close to port, which meant, *ipso facto,* going slow. Johnson allegedly tooled into the Dangling Rope Marina cutting a definite wake, and the ranger confronted him on the dock to inform him of the infraction. This discussion, however, did not long hold Johnson's interest, and he purportedly suggested changing the subject to a consideration of the ranger's "tin badge, tin gun, and silly hat." At this point the ranger opined that Johnson was being "disorderly and abusive," whereupon the gold medalist apparently offered to wrap up the colloquy by throwing the ranger in the lake. The ranger withdrew, pending advice from his colleagues.

"So you gonna arrest him?" I asked the rangers as we stood looking

out over the lake. The slammer is a lousy place to do an interview. You
end up with these dungeonlike echoes on your tapes, and you don't get
a suntan.

"Nah," said one of the officers. "We just wanna talk to him about
this attitude he's got on him."

The ranger scanned the marina through his Ray-Bans, took in the guys
loading cases of Bud onto speedboats, the kids filling bright yellow tanks
at the gas dock. "It's a damn shame he can't learn how to behave himself,"
he said sadly. He made a vague, inclusive gesture toward the lake. "He's
a hero to these people."

This was Johnson's natural constituency, all right, meat-and-potatoes
Americans who might not know or care very much about the art of
skiing, but who reveled in the dual freedoms of going fast and raising
hell. They loved Billy Johnson because he'd beaten the foreigners and
done it in his own way. They weren't leaning on him to be a model
citizen.

"I don't think he's really asking to be anybody's hero," I said to the
ranger.

"Ain't a question of asking to be," he answered. "It's a question of
*is*."

"LOOK," SAYS BILLY JOHNSON, drinking in the air-conditioning in my
room at the Wahweap Lodge, "if you want the truth, I just never thought
of it in terms of skiing for America or whatever. I was out there racing
for myself. Bill Johnson wants to get ahead in the world, too, you know,
and he's just out there doing the best he can. That's how I felt. But OK,
if people want to build me up into some kind of national figure, that's
all right by me. I'd just as soon be their American hero as some other
jerk."

He's been camping, and this is his first time indoors in about ten days.
His hair is bleached almost white, his skin is the color of rosewood, his
accidental beard is just making the passage from down to stubble. He's
wearing a beat-up, slept-in pair of tennis shorts, and he's plunked himself
languidly down and across the bed, having slipped the rangers by simply
running his boat up onto the desert instead of parking it at the dock.
Now and then he sticks a finger in his ear and wriggles it around while
shaking his head; now and then he yawns.

"They call it the U.S. ski team," he goes on drowsily, "because you travel together. But that's about it, as far as being a team goes. You ski alone."

Johnson skis more alone than most. He's camping here with his father and his sister; he has a conspicuous shortage of friends. He's never been popular with his teammates, and he has never tried to be. He's been thrown off teams for fighting; he's been pegged with the nickname Hatchet Man. He takes criticism from coaches the same way he takes it from park rangers. In 1981, he was bounced from the national squad for coming to training camp out of shape and then refusing to do dry-land drills. It would be easy to dismiss Johnson as just one more grating if attractive misfit, one more self-wasting brooder of the James Dean school, were it not that he somehow manages to wring from his anger, his unacknowl-edged sadness, and his pigheadedness a level of performance that edges on the sublime.

He was born in Los Angeles and brought up in Oregon, near Mount Hood. He was on skis by the age of six. The youngest of four kids, he realized only gradually how poor his family was. On a recent four-hanky episode of *This Is Your Life,* Johnson's mother testified that there were times when funds were so scarce that a choice had to be made between buying food and continuing Bill's skiing lessons. Bill's father, Wally, worked in computers. Now, you might think it would take a special kind of guy not to do well in computers in those go-go days, and in fact Wally Johnson is a thoroughly self-styled human being. What he really likes to do is hang out with his boy. He does this while wearing a straw hat with a pinkish-red band that, considered of itself, might appear effeminate. This effect is totally undercut, however, by Wally Johnson's grinning, feisty stance toward the universe. His entire being exudes the message: *Oh yeah? What of it?* Bill describes him as "my best friend."

Some years ago, Wally Johnson got out of the computer business temporarily and started building houses. For a while the family was relatively flush, but then, as Bill tells it, "things went sour because of a few bad judgments, and suddenly we were poor again." At around the same time, when he was 16, his parents' marriage also went sour, and they divorced. Bill started playing hooky to go off skiing by himself. He also started breaking into houses and stealing cars, and shortly before his 18th birthday he was arrested for laying claim to someone else's Chevrolet. He spent three days in jail. Then, in an instance of judicial clemency by now well known to TV viewers, he was let off with a warning on the condition that he attend the Mission Ridge Academy up in Washington and get serious about his racing.

If skiing kept Billy Johnson out of the hoosegow, it didn't make his life a bed of roses. He still had the politics and economics of so-called amateur skiing to contend with. Skiing isn't like, say, boxing; it is not a logical extension of life at the bottom, nor does it have any tradition whatsoever as a means of redistributing wealth. It is an elite pastime, and as Bill Johnson observes with undisguised bitterness, "If you've got a parent pumping money into the organization and sitting on a committee, you're gonna get certain preferences. It's as simple as that."

In 1979, feeling that he'd get a fairer shake away from the close-knit Northwestern ski establishment, Johnson won a scholarship to the Alpine Training Center at Lake Placid. It was there that the full extent of his talent started showing through—when he wasn't tripping over his personality. Johnson is a spray hitter. He gets mad about different things at different times. If you look past his sheer orneriness, however, you see that his targets are quite often the right targets; the things he's so cussedly stubborn about often turn out to make a great deal of sense.

"Like this business with the videos," he says. He feels strongly enough about the subject to raise himself up on one elbow to discuss it. "Coaches up at Placid thought I was arrogant because I didn't want to watch myself while they pointed out what I was doing wrong. But look, at the time there were guys in the world who were skiing a lot better than I was—so why should I watch myself doing things wrong when I could watch them doing things *right?* I saw how they did it, and I went them one better."

Johnson pauses, basking in the unquiet satisfaction of the outsider who is in midprocess of showing them all. He shuffles his bare feet against the bedspread, luxuriating. "So now it's *their* turn to go to school," he says. "Yup, they'll be looking at a lot of videos come fall. And you know who they're gonna be looking at now."

WHILE THE OTHER DOWNHILLERS are studying what makes Johnson run, he will be doing something for which he is not widely known: training. That the gold medalist is bearish on conditioning, that he catnaps in the sunshine while others grunt and groan, is an integral part of his bad-boy image; it is also plain not true. The world is full of slouchers who try to look as if they're working hard; a guy who works hard but hates letting on remains something of an oddity.

"I train plenty," he says, almost annoyed, as if a slightly unsavory admission were being weaseled out of him. "But I happen not to believe in making a spectacle of it. I'd rather run an eight- or ten-mile loop around my father's house and lift weights in my basement than do it at some rah-rah camp with a lot of other guys. I train because it's part of what I have to do to make it through the long season without getting racked up or killed—not so somebody'll stick a gold star on my forehead."

God forbid that anyone should ever come after Johnson with a gold star. He fends off that ignominy with a stance that goes beyond his pretended sloth to include, in the off-season at least, *cerveza fria* for breakfast, an unabashed appetite for cigarettes, and the occasional lewd remark about the opportunities for thrills and spills with the female enthusiasts along the World Cup circuit. In fact, however, Johnson's life from December through April is little short of monastic, "like the Army," as he puts it, "except that hardly anybody speaks the same language as you do, even to shoot the breeze." For solace, he does little that is more scandalous than hurrying back to his girlfriend stateside—a girlfriend who would like to be married to him. But even here, Bill is a lean and self-insistent drifter.

"She wants a total commitment," he complains, shaking his head as if he were being asked to walk a tightrope to the moon and bring back a sliver of green cheese, fingering water out of his ears as he contemplates the sheer egregiousness of the request. "But hey—who wants to commit to anything?"

THE ASPHALT PARKING LOT was melting in the sun, and Billy Johnson had no shoes. He scampered across as if he were in that Army drill where they smash your ankles between bamboo poles if you don't hop fast enough. He was looking down at his feet. He didn't see the rangers convened around his yellow boat.

"Bill Johnson?" one of them said.

So they gave him a little talking to. Suddenly it was high school, the same corked fury, the same embarrassment about getting yelled at in front of another kid, the same thin line determining how face-savingly defiant you could look without making more trouble for yourself. Billy Johnson, working-class hero, let the scolding wash over him while watching the horizon, squinting into the glare. When it was done he said, "Yeah, OK."

Downhill skiers express themselves through the muscles of their legs. Johnson's were twitching as he grabbed onto the bow of his Sea-Ray and pushed it into the lake. He sulked until we were out of the harbor. Then he popped a Bud and threw the top into the back of the boat along with the crushed packs of Marlboro and ketchupy McDonald's wrappers and a special summer issue of *Mad* magazine. "I never said he had a tin badge," he protested, in the tone of one who has been disgracefully wronged. Then came the grin. "I said he had a plastic badge."

"WHATEVER YOU DO," yells Billy Johnson's sister, Vicki, "don't freeze."

Sound advice, I'm sure, but tardy. I am halfway up a bluff overlooking Padre Canyon, coming to a fresh appreciation of why they call it sandstone. Rock is crumbling to powder under my fingernails. The sweat on my feet is turning the mountain muddy under my toes.

Up ahead, Johnson himself is traversing the hill like a Navajo. He crouches low, never hesitating, bare feet padding silently along, arms dangling at the ready but almost never being used. He seems to stick out from the hill at impossible angles, like in those old cartoons of people standing upside down in China, and yet he clings. He's not big—maybe 5 feet 9 and 160 pounds—and out of action he doesn't look like a world-class athlete; even the thighs that hold that remarkable tuck don't have the definition you might expect. But in the midst of effort there is a superb congruence between his body and what his body is doing. Some guys climb a hill; Johnson becomes that which is doing the climbing. We're not talking mystical union with the mountain here; it's just that his muscles, mind, aspiration, and sense of play all seem to be in register. Maybe this containment has something to do with growing up short on sporting goods, in the absence of rackets and bats and other toys that extend the body beyond its outline. Johnson stays tucked within his own exertions. He is his own toy.

Later, back at camp amid the sagebrush and the lizards, we talk about the future. Or try to. There is a daunting disparity between the glyphic simplicity of the accomplishments that have made Johnson remarkable in the eyes of the world and the fine-print *mishigas* that lie ahead for him as a famous person. What Johnson has done so far is win three ski races. (Aside from the Olympics, he's won the only two World Cup downhills ever taken by an American—at Wengen, Switzerland, before Sarajevo, and at Aspen afterward.) You could say those races took a lifetime, or you could say they took five minutes; in either case, they hinged on things as simple, desperate, and pure as gravity and time. What Johnson has to deal with now, by contrast, are matters as contrived as legalese and as byzantine as the mysteries of amateur standing. He's got to figure out, for example, whether he's allowed to perform and get paid for the skiing sequences in a TV movie that CBS is planning to do about his life. He's got to haggle with the U.S. ski team about what its cut will be if he is asked to enthuse about a mouthwash, a soft drink, a brand of underwear. Johnson is no softy in these negotiations; he knows the strength of his position. "I'm the only gold medal winner they've got," he says. "For the next four years, I'm supposed to be the cash cow." On the other hand, the ski team has some leverage, too; by an illogic worthy of Swift, a skier has to play by the amateur rules to get the sort of exposure that translates into serious money. "I've always said I'm gonna cash in big on this," avows the unrepentant Johnson, "and that's what I intend to do. The only question is, What's the best way to do it?"

It's a fatiguing question, less fun than skiing, and just before dusk Bill Johnson decides he wants to take a toodle around the canyon. He jumps in the lake. His sister brings the boat around and tosses him the slalom ski. He sits there, bobbing in his yellow vest as she idles away to the length of the towline. Then he shouts, she guns it, and for a moment he disappears behind a wall of water. The light has gotten very red by now, and when he emerges, still shaking droplets from his hair, his skin looks almost purple and his tennis shorts are tinted orange. He leans far back against the rope, as relaxed as a lady in a beach chair, and then he starts to play. Back and forth across the wake, his knees gobble up the bumps like a thousand-dollar turntable. Now and then he digs a heel and a geyser sprouts around him as he turns, so close to the canyon walls that the spray stains the pink rock garnet. He points a finger straight ahead, begging for more speed, and Vicki opens up full throttle, the bow as high as a cresting marlin, Billy whiplashing behind, the buttes swinging crazily over his shoulder, the water scooped into hollows where he's plowed it. He leaps, he leans; he defies the pull of the boat and skis away from it. Then, as in a lover's farewell, he gives in to the attraction and comes sweeping back across the ripples. You know his arms are beginning to ache by now, that his fingers are going stiff around the grips; even those world-beating knees and ankles are getting used up by the water. Still, when Vicki looks back at her brother, he grins and makes a circular motion with his hand.

The gesture says: Take me around again. The one single thing I want from life right now is to go around again.

*November 1984*

# "I DID NOT KILL CHICO MENDES"

## *João Branco, Amazonian cattle baron, wants you to understand some things.*

●  ▲  ■

### BOB REISS

"Look into my eyes and you will know the truth," said João Branco. "I did not kill Chico Mendes. You'll write it. Other people will write it. And after a while everyone will know. I had nothing to do with the murder."

I had come to Rio Branco, capital of the state of Acre in far-western Brazil, to learn about ranching, not murder. Chico Mendes, the leader of the rubber tappers' union, had been dead for months. Suspects were in prison, a trial was scheduled, a witness was in protective custody, shielded by fearful police. But it seemed that wherever I went, people said that the man behind the killing was João Branco, rancher, newspaper owner, lawyer, and, at the time of Mendes's death, regional head of the União Democrática Rural, the ranchers' right-wing political organization and the group many blame for a rash of executions along the Amazon frontier.

Two days earlier, for instance, we'd ridden to a ranch outside of town. The taxi driver joked with João Branco the whole way. But the second Branco stepped from the cab, the driver whispered to me, "He was in on the murder."

On another ranch the owner had said to me, in front of his friend João Branco, "Pretty brave guy, hanging out with the man who killed Chico Mendes." Both of them laughed.

And every evening when I strolled through Rio Branco, around the plaza, past the governor's palace and the war monuments, I saw graffiti. Huge black letters, scrawled for yards: THE DEATH OF CHICO MENDES WILL NOT BE WHITEWASHED. The Portuguese word for white, *branco*, was underlined.

Now João Branco and I were relaxing at the airport bar, watching girls go by in the late afternoon light and sipping Antarctica beer. In Rio Branco, the ranchers hang out at the airport. They meet for espresso before breakfast, for steak at lunch, for coffee another five times a day.

João Branco poured a fresh beer. "You're the only journalist who's even asked me about this." he said. "People think I was involved, but no one ever asks."

"Why not?"

He laughed. "Maybe they're afraid of me."

ACRE IS RUBBER COUNTRY, some of the richest in the world. For more than a hundred years the economy has been fueled by *seringueiros*, rubber tappers who live deep in the forest. They spend their days walking jungle trails, slitting rubber trees and collecting the milk-white sap. The sap is dried, packed out on mules, and loaded onto boats that bring it down the Amazon.

Rubber is why thousands of Brazilians came here in the first place, in the 1800s, when Acre belonged to Bolivia. Rubber is why the Bolivians tried to tax these newcomers, causing them to rebel. Rubber is why, in 1903, Brazil annexed the state after four years of unrest.

For a hundred years, Acre's rubber business ran on the patron system. Rich landowners reigned over vast tracts of jungle called *seringais*. Tappers living in the seringais sold all their rubber to the owners and bought all their tools, food, and medicines from them. During rubber booms the landowners lived in Acre and took a closer interest in their land. During busts they moved away, and the seringueiros lived in the forest on their own.

The system worked until the 1970s, when Brazil began encouraging colonization in the Amazon. All over the region—58 percent of the country—governors tried to attract settlers. In Acre that meant cattle, a perfect business for opening up a frontier. Cattle didn't need roads to get to market. They could walk. And land was cheap. The federal government even offered special land concessions, loans, and tax incentives. People moved west.

But in order to establish ranches, they had to cut down the forest. "In Brazil," a 1988 World Bank report said, "cattle ranching is the leading cause of deforestation." According to LANDSAT satellite information, by 1985 only about 5 percent of Acre had been burned. But the fear was that with the rate of deforestation soaring, Acre would go the way of

Rondônia, the state just to the east, where as much as 25 percent of the forest had been lost.

For thousands of rubber tappers, ranching meant the end. Some made deals with the new owners, selling their meager rights for cash or a small piece of property. Some were driven away by hired *pistoleiros*. They moved to towns or across the border to Bolivia. They became gold miners along the rivers in Rondônia.

Then, in one part of Acre, Chico Mendes began to organize the seringueiros. He developed the idea of peaceful standoffs called *empates*. When ranchers sent workers into the jungle to clear land, hundreds of rubber tappers and their families would materialize out of the forest, women and children in front. They would ask the workers not to cut the trees. After the outnumbered workers left, Mendes and the rubber tappers would continue the fight in court. Sometimes the land title was unclear, the judicial system worked, and the rancher lost.

Another new plan electrified environmental organizations around the world. Environmentalists had been looking for ways to prove that rainforests, left standing, could provide more sustainable income than pasture. In five or ten years, ranches turned into wasteland that might need decades to recover. The only way the ranchers really made money, the environmentalists argued, was through enormous government incentives and land scams. Then Mendes came up with a proposal: Zone the forest by setting up "extractive reserves." Deforestation inside these areas would be prohibited. Tappers could live as they always had, harvesting rubber from March to November, Brazil nuts in the off-season. Even in the short run, the land would prove more profitable.

In October of 1988 the governor of Acre established the world's first extractive reserve in the Seringal Cachoeira, the forest where Chico Mendes grew up. Two months later, Mendes was shot as he left his house in Xapuri, going out back to take a shower.

To João Branco's assertions that he had no prior knowledge of the murder, citizens of Acre had lots of questions. Like how come days earlier a columnist in João Branco's newspaper, *O Rio Branco,* had predicted that soon "a bomb of 200 megatons" would explode in Acre? How come reporters from the paper were said to be on the scene within an hour and a half of the murder, although it takes between two and a half and four hours to get there from Rio Branco? And how come the next day João Branco left town for a while on his private plane?

Like most ranchers around Rio Branco, however, João Branco says he doesn't understand what all the fuss is about. The UDR, he says, was just a lobbying organization, the murder the outcome of a personal dispute between Mendes and a rancher named Darli Alves. João Branco said that part of a ranch Alves owned was seized for an extractive reserve. Then Mendes tried to get Alves and his brother Alvarino arrested for a murder in another part of Brazil. Darli Alves's son had confessed to killing Mendes. "The outcry about a plan to kill him," João Branco says, "all lies."

"Chico Mendes wasn't a real ecologist," he says. "He was a political leader, a syndicate leader. On the day he became a false ecologist, he was killed."

LIKE MANY LOCAL RANCHERS, João Branco lives in town, in a one-story home with flowers and a low wall in front: it is across the street from the former mayor, down the block from the military police, and a five-minute stroll from the governor's palace. He is a rich man. Between his two ranches he owns 13,000 acres and 1,400 head of cattle. He owns half of *O Rio Branco*. He's a partner in the biggest concrete company in the state. A lawyer by training, he travels around Brazil representing ranchers whose land has been seized by the government. Last year he took a trip to the United States to help a friend buy a horse for $50,000. This year he's considering sending his daughter to school in Paris, where his sister lives.

"I want to show you the three most important things to me about being a rancher," João Branco said. "If you don't understand these things, you'll never be able to understand what I do."

We were in a maroon Volkswagen taxicab, pitching our way east along BR-364, Brazil's controversial highway across the Amazon. It is the road Brazilians dream will link the country to Peru and the Pacific. It is the road environmentalists fear will mean the end of the western Amazon. In 1983 after BR-364 was paved as far as Pôrto Velho, 200 miles to the east in Rondônia, hundreds of thousands of settlers poured in. They chopped and burned forest, contracted malaria, started ranches, swelled slums. Sixty percent abandoned their land within three years. The soil lacked the nutrients for growing crops. But no one told the settlers that beforehand.

The road from Pôrto Velho to Rio Branco is scheduled to be paved by mid-1991.

Satellites spinning over BR-364 produce the kind of pictures that strike terror into the hearts of environmentalists: a long, meandering strip of deforestation hugging both sides of a thin line that forces its way through the massive Amazon green. But from the road the view was peaceful. Rolling pasture. Grazing cattle. The tops of high Brazil-nut trees floated above the Georgia-red dust thrown up from the road. Mercedes trucks materialized out of the distance, their wooden sides swaying like accordions. The air filled with a horrible stink; we were passing the brand-new slaughterhouse.

"*Love of land,*" João Branco said, leaning toward me. He was not a physically large man, but there was something in his manner, in the dark flowing hair, the thick black mustache, the billowy shirts, that made him seem powerful. Sometimes he wore reading glasses, the kind that make judges look stern.

João Branco said he had spent part of his childhood on his grandfather's ranch. Had gone on to become the first Branco in the family's 300 years in Brazil to graduate from law school. "I was a broker in Rio," he said. "I lived in Ipanema, on the beach. I had girls. Cars. Everything a young man would want. But something was missing."

Land. Land was missing. At Christmas in the eastern state of Minas Gerais, the family would sit around eating beef and telling ranching stories. The story of how João Branco's grandfather wooed his bride. Of how his father, a truck driver, married into this ranching family and went to work with an ax. Of how his grandfather was never the same after selling the ranch.

As João Branco spoke, I was reminded of the opening of the top-running Brazilian soap opera. An odd, mystical scene in which a man, poor and in rags, walks resolutely across a field, then a farm, then a futuristic city. As the music continues, the man keeps walking, getting smaller, finally stepping into outer space, until he is gone. "The farther away from the land you go," say the words to the music, "the farther you go from God."

I realized that the rubber tappers had used the same words as João Branco: "If you want to understand us, understand love of land."

"In 1973 I was invited to Rio Branco by a real estate company here, asked if I wanted to be their lawyer," João Branco said. "I fell in love with Acre. I quit my job and moved here within a month. I worked for eight years to buy my land. I didn't borrow money from the government. And I had my land tested before I bought it. Acre land is the filet mignon of the Amazon. That's why people fight over it. Would you fight over an ugly woman? No. You fight over a beautiful woman."

The taxi turned up a red dirt driveway, past lush pasture, toward a cookhouse on a beautiful ranch. Nelore cattle grazed on gently rolling slopes. There were tall, wide-canopied Brazil-nut trees and a small finger-shaped lake. There was no evidence of burning, or cutting, or forest destruction. No blackened stumps. No cut brush.

"How do you like our desert?" João Branco bragged. "Go ahead. Write it's a desert."

On quarter horses we toured the grounds. The ranch belonged to Alemão, a friend who ran a farm-machinery company in town and a 30,000-acre ranch in southern Acre. Alemão had owned this ranch for 16 years, João Branco said. He attacked the notion that ranches always failed because the land was bad for cattle. Alemão made a good profit, João Branco said. And Alemão wasn't a land speculator or he would have sold out long ago. All the ranchers around here worked to make their places as beautiful as Alemão's.

João Branco wasn't alone in his thinking. At EMBRAPA, a federal agricultural institute near BR-364, I had met some scientists who thought there might be profit in cattle, too. They were growing new kinds of grasses to protect the soil. They were testing kudzu and peanut plants as cattle fodder. They were experimenting with garlic, oranges, pineapples, peppers, lemons, and coffee. "Anyone who says anything about what percentage of the Amazon is unproductive is guessing," Judson Valentim, one of the scientists, had said. "We need more research to develop nationally."

João Branco knelt down and put his hands on the earth, then ran them through the grass. He stood up and struck himself, once, over the chest.

"*Land,*" he said.

THE BISHOP of Acre, Dom Moacyr Grecchi, was a quiet-looking man in a short-sleeved cotton shirt and horn-rimmed glasses. An accountant, you might guess, or a social worker. A small electric fan hummed on his desk. Behind him on the wall was a Byzantine icon of colored tiles depicting Jesus Christ. The bishop smiled gently and gestured at an empty chair.

"The ranchers are assholes," he said.

The day after conducting the funeral mass for Chico Mendes, the bishop said, he had received another of many *anúncios,* or death threats.

In an hour, he was scheduled to lead a memorial mass for Mendes. Mendes had been dead for six months, but more than a thousand people were expected to crowd into the church. Printed prayer-sheets were piled and waiting for use in the chapel. They included lines like, "The tyrants take land, profit, kill. These are their plans."

"When I arrived here in 1972 there were 32,000 people in Rio Branco," Dom Moacyr said. "Now we have almost 200,000. Most of them came from the forest. They left because they were threatened. They couldn't exist there anymore. Sometimes they were so frightened they left pigs, hens, chickens."

Downstairs in another office I'd noticed a poster showing a peasant climbing over a barbed-wire fence. It said, WITHOUT AGRARIAN REFORM YOU DON'T HAVE DEMOCRACY. There was also a photograph of Chico Mendes sitting on the floor of his house, eating a simple meal and looking with joy at his young son.

"João Branco is right when he says there was no strife between ranchers and seringueiros until seven years ago," the bishop says. "Until seven years ago, the seringueiros would run away. Nowadays it happens less. There's organization."

He looked at his watch. It was almost time for the mass. He explained how Chico Mendes had devised his ecological strategies in conjunction with the Church and the leftist Workers Party. He told a story of a rancher who had altered the deed to his own land, so that he owned a thousand times more land than he really did. Then he sold the land he didn't really own and kept the money. "The ranchers," the bishop said, "get land illegal ways."

I knew there were many who said deforestation would never stop until land reform was instituted. In the early 1980s, thousands of the peasants who crowded into the region had lost their small farms in southern Brazil when banks and large agricultural concerns took over the land. One percent of the population owns 46 percent of the country's arable land.

"Brazil has 12 million families without land," the bishop said. "I'm talking about people who live on the land but don't own it. That's 50 million people."

Dom Moacyr said that Chico Mendes was the 83rd union leader to be murdered in Brazil in 1988. I thought of how the rubber tappers had joked that UDR stands for *Usamos Dinero e Revolveres:* "We use money and revolvers."

The bishop's office was a five-minute walk from João Branco's house.

All you had to do was walk outside, down a hill, across the main square, past the war memorials, and onto Branco's block.

I asked the bishop if he had ever met João Branco.

"No," he said.

AT 3 A.M. the phone rang.

There was drunken laughter in the background. Then João Branco's hoarse, familiar voice said, "Want to go to a party tomorrow, fellow? It's the second thing I want to show you. Good friends."

The next morning he picked me up at the hotel in a new Ford pickup, and we set off south toward Xapuri, where Chico Mendes had lived. The road was paved, but João Branco preferred driving on the rough dirt shoulder. "It's more fun," he said.

We passed cocoa farms and rubber farms. And, as always, ranches. The road ran parallel to the Bolivian border, a few miles away. After a while it started drizzling, and João Branco pulled the truck over to help three hitchhiking women. They were carrying a baby and were grateful for the ride. Ten miles later two got out, but the third rode awhile more. When she got out, near a small thatched farmhouse, she leaned back into the cab and gave a huge smile. She wanted to thank the driver properly, so she asked his name.

"João Branco," he said. The woman's smile dropped. She turned, the door still open, and staggered off. She never looked back.

"Funny people," João Branco said. "They don't even say thanks."

Soon we reached the Santa Lucia ranch, which belonged to one of João Branco's best friends. Arisbeu Medeiros was a tall, lean man in Ralph Lauren jeans and a peaked cap that said DIESEL POWER. Aragão Silva, the other friend, was shorter, stockier, and famous. Only a week before, I'd seen his picture in *Manchete,* Brazil's version of *Life* magazine. In the photograph he was instructing workers on how to clear jungle for pasture. Aragão said he had gotten a license to clear the land.

The party turned out to be a celebration of castrating young bulls. We sat in the cab of a Caterpillar bulldozer and drank beer from long-neck bottles. Drunken cowboys wheeled horses in a corral, lassoed their targets, and castrated them. They dabbed medicines on the wounds to clean and keep flies from nesting in them. They were a little too rough with the first bull, and they broke its leg.

"How are you going to tell your story?" Arisbeu asked in friendly challenge. "Will you write about this?" he said, meaning the green, rolling pastures, the well-tended fences, the fat cattle. "Or *this,* " he said, meaning the drunken cowboys. "Ecology?" he said. "Yes. Ecologists? Shit."

Aragão then asked if I wanted to see some rainforest being cut. His ranch was down the road, and his crews were in the jungle today. In two cars we headed back onto the highway, a lazy Saturday among friends, a stop at a roadside stand for cheese pastries and soda. When we reached the Três Marias ranch, there was lots of activity. Cowboys herded cattle into new corrals. Bare-chested men with machetes strapped to their waists pounded fenceposts into the earth. In a jovial mood, we accompanied Aragão on a tour of his property. The housing he had built for 27 families. The school he had constructed. Arisbeu and João Branco made admiring comments, appraised pasture, tested new doors on the cattle chutes. Then it was time to see the forest cut.

Brazilian law mandates that only 50 percent of a ranch can be deforested, and Aragão said he had not reached his limit yet. On foot, on a dirt road, we walked into the rain forest. The pasture disappeared, and huge trees rose around us. Strangler vines wrapped buttresses. A macaw flew overhead. We reached an area where the brush had been cut and lay in piles at the foot of the larger trees. Branco explained that when you burn rainforest, it is necessary to chop the small plants first and allow them to dry. Otherwise the big trees fall on them, trapping the moisture, and the forest won't burn.

Smoke rose around a bend. As we got closer I saw cans of motor oil scattered on the ground. Then a migrant-worker camp. Two open-air shelters with thatch for roofs and hammocks hanging inside. Fires going to dispel insects. Men playing dominoes on wooden cartons. A woman breastfeeding a baby. A little girl clutching an empty beer bottle as a doll.

The workers had quit for the day, but in honor of my presence they would cut a little more. Aragão gave instructions to a shy-looking man with a gap in his front teeth. The man picked up a chain saw and waded through the drying brush, deciding which tree to cut. He pulled the starter and the scream of the engine filled the forest. I glanced at my watch. I was curious to see how long it would take the man to end the life of a tree. I had heard a tree could be cut down in ten minutes. He selected an average-size tree, two feet in diameter, and I guessed ten minutes would be about right.

The blade bit into the wood; the tree tilted. Two adjacent trees blocked its fall. Smoothly, the worker swung the chain saw and the blade sliced through all three. They fell together. A hole broke the forest canopy, gray sky where green leaves had been a moment before.

"How long?" João Branco asked. I didn't realize the others had been timing it, too.

"Forty-five seconds," Arisbeu said.

Aragão smiled up at me. "No more forest."

"The Brazilian frontier is a lot like the old American frontier," Kenton Miller, a program director at the World Resources Institute in Washington, had told me. "You had thousands of poor people moving west. The only difference is that we have chain saws, not axes."

Back at the cook-house, Aragão's cook grilled us fresh steaks from the ranch and served them with rice and beans. The friends drank whiskey and told jokes. "You can fuck my wife," João Branco said, reaching the punch line of a story, "but don't fuck me." Arisbeu was laughing so hard he had trouble breathing. He gasped, fumbling with his shoelaces. "Did you ever see the way Portuguese people *tie their shoes?*"

At that moment these weren't tyrants or murderers. They were just three guys telling jokes. It was pleasant, and dusk was falling in the Amazon. There was a cool mist outside. The rainy season was over. João Branco said the mist would last three days, as would the cold. Afterward, the dry season would begin. It was as if all the moisture of the jungle was being sucked out of the ground, dissipating in white smoke from the sky.

When I got back to my hotel, I glanced at Rio Branco's other newspaper, the one João Branco did not own. Aragão Silva's name caught my eye. Investigators were looking into his term as mayor. It seemed that, during his term, much of Rio Branco's education funds had disappeared.

COLONEL ROBERTO FERREIRA DA SILVA was not what I'd expected. He was a tall, lean man wearing Gandhi-like wire-rimmed glasses. He gave me an autographed picture of beautiful Amazon flowers. The inscription read, "You are my friend. This makes me happy." Colonel Roberto, as he was called, was the commander of the Acre military police.

Soccer trophies lined the office walls. Armed guards stood at doorways. Outside the barracks, platoons of teenage boys in uniform marched in a courtyard flanking Rio Branco's main square. They were Colonel Roberto's urchin corps, delinquent boys he gave jobs to so that they could better their lives.

I explained to Colonel Roberto that I had not come to Acre to write about Chico Mendes. I added that this must sound odd, since I was asking about him. But it seemed impossible to talk to anyone about João Branco without the subject coming up. I said I had heard that the colonel had a witness in custody who had linked João Branco to the killing, and Colonel Roberto nodded pleasantly and said this was true.

He turned more serious when I asked if I could see the witness, a 15-year-old boy named Genésio. Genésio had been held in protective custody in these very barracks the night before, but even with all the guards he had not been safe, and he had been moved. He was being moved every day. Genésio didn't want to talk to reporters, Colonel Roberto said. He added that he himself could not talk about a pending case, but he agreed to answer yes/no questions, to confirm or deny information I had heard in town.

I asked, "Did Genésio work on Darli Alves's ranch? Did he say that Alves was a killer and that the ranch itself had been payment for murders he carried out for ranchers?"

Colonel Roberto considered. "Yes."

"Did Genésio say that eight people had been murdered on the ranch and that their bodies had been burned?"

"Yes."

"That two of these victims were drug smugglers? That one had wanted to marry Alves's daughter? That two of them were seringueiros?"

Colonel Roberto nodded.

"Did Genésio tell you that João Branco had been on Darli Alves's ranch for a period of five days, drinking whiskey with Alves? That the murder of Chico Mendes had been discussed by the men present?"

"Yes."

"Did he say that Alves asked Branco, 'What will happen if I kill Chico Mendes?' Did he say that Branco replied, 'Nothing, like the others. And if something does happen we will help you'?"

"Yes."

"Was Genésio supposed to be in the room when this happened? Or did he hear it from other men on the ranch? Did he say he actually heard it?"

"Yes."

"Are you sure I can't meet with Genésio?"

Colonel Roberto smiled.

"Colonel," I said, "you're a policeman, and you have experience with people telling lies. You've talked with Genésio. Do you believe what he said?"

He blinked from behind his spectacles. Even the bishop, who hates the ranchers, had told me that the colonel was a good man.

Colonel Roberto looked unhappy. "I don't know," he said.

SOON JOÃO BRANCO invited me to see the third thing he loved about ranching: buying more cattle. Once again, we were off to a friend's ranch. This one was almost 25,000 acres, with 2,000 head of cattle and plans for 8,000 more. The owner looked like Martin Sheen except that he wore shorts with cuffs and backless slippers, even when he rode a horse.

João Branco had come to buy 200 head of cattle. We stood on platforms above the corral and watched as bucking livestock were herded and shouted, one by one, into a chute. Holding a red-hot iron with both hands, the owner leaned down and pressed metal to flesh. Smoke rose, and João Branco's 2J brand appeared in black on the animal's right-rear flank. This was a tradition, the seller applying the buyer's brand to the cows, as if they were a gift.

"You have a good life here," I said to João Branco.

"Ha ha ha!" he laughed. "Certainly."

It was July, the middle of the dry season, and all over Acre forest was being cut. In September the big burning would begin, but already in the afternoons you could see funnels of gray smoke rising over the trees, or blackened patches along the roads. Looking content, João Branco talked of his vision of the future, of what Acre would be like in ten years. There would be no more seringueiros. Their way of life was doomed, he said, not only by ranches but by simple market logistics. Soon huge rubber plantations would start up in southern Brazil, the government would stop price hikes on imported Asian rubber, and the seringueiros would lose what little income they had. They would have to move away.

There would be more ranches, João Branco said. Lots of ranches. More cattle. More roads. More jobs for settlers. "They want work," he said generously. "We have it." Why, in the old days, the butcher had been the most powerful man in Rio Branco. Once a week a plane would fly in with beef from Bolivia, and in between deliveries the butcher would receive all kinds of favors from hungry citizens. Was that any way to live, from week to week?

There would be no more labor problems. Or environmentalists. "The concern about the Amazon is a fad," João Branco said. "People will realize it isn't in danger. You can fly all the way to Manaus. Forest! All the way to Lima. Forest! People will turn to something else."

In fact, João Branco said as we headed back to town, many ranchers were purposely not burning this year, waiting for world attention to flag, waiting for the press to get bored and move on to Africa or Beirut or wherever those lightweights would gravitate to next. Then the ranchers would be able to get on with things.

In October, big fires would be burning all over Acre. Staffers at the state environmental institute had told me that the smoke would be so thick the airport would close. People would rush home after work, close their doors, and turn on air conditioners.

"There is no other way, no better way to clear land than to burn it," João Branco said, lighting another cigarette. "If the developed world wants to help us, that is something to discover, a way of clearing forest without burning it. But for the time being, the burning will not stop."

I told João Branco that when people at home in the United States see those massive sweeping blazes on TV, they see genocide of species, they see global warming, they see death. I asked João Branco what the fires meant to him.

The pickup rocked over the hard red earth. Rio Branco was coming up in the distance. I caught sight of the airport, where they were heading to drink coffee, to joke with the other ranchers, to see who was coming and going out of town.

"When I see fires," João Branco said, "I see beauty. I see transformation."

*March 1990*

# CHUCK JONES, ALONE AT THE EDGE OF HUMAN ENDURANCE

*So far, so good*

— • ▲ ■ —

### JOHN BRANT

Chuck Jones's breakfast is as normal as his name: a Denver omelet, wheat toast, and coffee at a freeway Denny's near Grass Valley, California. And Jones looks normal enough—six-foot-two and a deep-chested 170 pounds, with wide-set, clear, brown eyes, tangled shoulder-length hair, and a buccaneer's beard. A shade scraggly for a city man, but not at all wild for these Sierra foothills, home since the gold rush to sourdoughs, gamblers, drifters, and dreamers. No one at Denny's—not the kindly coffee-slinging waitresses or the leather-faced guys squinting over their smokes—takes Jones for anything out of the way. A nice kid, they'd say, noting his work-swollen fingers and hard palms, his wide shoulders and seasoned jeans. A Cat driver or logger or bush chipper, probably, and if he's any kind of athlete, a river guide or bull rider or former high school quarterback.

They wouldn't take Jones for a runner, and certainly not for the runner that he is: the nation's premier trail racer, a master of some of the most arduous footraces ever devised. An athlete who, in one season, redefined the limits of his sport. A man who very probably runs longer and harder and more faithfully than anybody else on earth.

Jones forks in a mouthful of omelet, washes it down with a long pull of coffee. He clears a spot on the table and spreads out a map of Australia. "Now the race begins here," he says, stabbing at the map with a horny-nailed finger, "in Sydney, and runs all the way to Melbourne." His eyes glint with the thought of it. "That's almost exactly 650 miles. The part where I should kick in is along here." He rubs his thumb along an empty spot midway through the continent. "That's the hilliest, gnarliest part.

I've tried to break the race down into four-hour blocks. A marathon every four hours. Twenty-three of 'em, one after the other, with about 30 minutes' rest between each one."

THE MOMENT IS distinctly hallucinatory—Jones, over breakfast in California, discussing a six-day footrace across Australia as blithely as travelers at other tables speak of driving from Fremont to Reno. But the Australian race, now two weeks away, seems no less surreal than Jones's accomplishments last summer. In a 90-day period he pulled off one of the unlikeliest—and least-noticed—quinielas in recent sporting history, winning the 100-mile Western States Endurance Run in California, finishing second in Colorado's Leadville 100, and then winning the Wasatch 100 in Utah. The difficulty of each of these races—totaling 300 miles of the most spectacular but forbidding terrain in North America—cannot be overestimated. Merely completing any one represents a major achievement for even the most experienced ultramarathoner, the culmination of a year or more of training. To finish another in the same year is exceedingly rare; to seriously compete in more than one annually is unheard of; winning two, and nearly winning the third, is the stuff of fantasy. "Jones single-handedly blew a myth out of the water—that it was all anybody could do just to finish one of these races," comments Dan Brannen, chairman of the Ultrarunning Committee of The Athletics Congress and secretary general of the International Association of Ultrarunners. "To be able to hold that level athletically and psychologically, and combine it with an absolutely incredible rate of recovery—it's astounding. He's almost reached legendary status within one year."

Jones sandwiched the three races between shifts as a counselor at a group home for delinquent children, twice driving all night on his motorcycle to make the starting lines. He bracketed his ultra season with a near win at the prestigious Levi's Ride & Tie in June and a 15-day, 20-person relay across the United States in September. But these feats are no more staggering than the regular 200-mile training weeks that made them possible. . . .

The numbers and miles mushroom out to the edge where asceticism drops off to perversity. There's something Bunyanesque about Jones's accomplishments, but something terrible, too, for we know them to be actual rather than legendary. When we consider his case, the comforting limits that channel and codify our endeavors shimmer, warp, and gradually dissolve. He's a self-educated man whose conversation is larded with terms such as "resonance," "frequencies," and "vibrations"—concepts we'd quickly dismiss if Jones didn't so stubbornly and inconveniently demonstrate their utility. He's also fond of the word "balance," which might be the most critical term of all. For if Jones is able to pursue his seemingly shattering vocation in a manner that's physically and emotionally wholesome—if his prodigious running in fact forms the foundation of a balanced life—then his career is more exemplary than eccentric.

"A lot of things will go by the wayside in the next 15 or 20 years," says Jones when asked about his motives. "And I just want to bypass them. Just the way we look at everything. I want to pursue what I'm doing and not be affected too much by what other people think." He sits back in his booth, tosses off the last of his coffee, and, characteristically, struggles to find the right words. "I just tell everyone I'm into human development."

The main arena for Jones's development is the hundreds of miles of foot trails and logging roads honeycombing the high country near his house in Malakoff Diggins State Park, 15 miles of twisting road from Nevada City. His work today will be about average: 32 miles at altitudes ranging from 3,000 to 5,200 feet, totaling five to six hours of running.

He starts out in the early afternoon, just as the first cold drops of a late-winter rainstorm lash the branches of the giant oak in front of his house. Jones wears blue tights and a white sweatshirt; his hair is tucked into a red baseball cap. His training companions—a laconic, philosophical Rhodesian Ridgeback named Sri Lanka, and a skittering, grinning young dalmation named Rascal—are leashed beside him.

He turns right on the dirt road and begins a sharp milelong descent through the ghost town of North Bloomfield. All that remain are a half-dozen restored clapboard buildings—a schoolhouse, a general store, an assay office that in the summer serves as a museum and ranger station. But through the 1880s, North Bloomfield—first named Humbug in 1857—was home to 1,800 miners working the nearby Malakoff Diggins, one of the biggest and richest excavations of the Sierra's mother lode.

Cutting through the middle of town, Jones waves to a woman bending over a bank of mailboxes. As the road narrows and flattens on the village outskirts, his stride gradually loosens and lengthens. Jones runs in a relaxed, muscular swing—very efficient, but unlike the willowy, light-footed strides of most distance runners. His style is tailored to the demands of ultra- and trail running, which require strength and superior coordination, as well as stamina and speed.

Over the past decade this combination of qualities has been developed by a group of elite trail runners that includes Sally Edwards, Bjorg Austrheim-Smith, Skip Hamilton, Doug Latimer, Jim Howard, and Jim King. These athletes (all from Northern California except Hamilton, a Coloradoan) demonstrated that a hundred-mile backcountry run not only could be endured, it could be *raced*. Building upon their work, Jones has raised the ante by proving that trail ultras can be raced consistently, and that extraordinarily high mileage can be maintained perhaps indefinitely.

"A lot of people, myself included, were real skeptical about his mileage," says three-time Western States winner King, who like most other ultramarathoners has never consistently run more than 120 miles a week in training. "Chuck's kind of broken a barrier by being able to handle that kind of training."

After another quarter-mile, Jones comes to the Diggins, a sculpted, milelong divot scooped out of the golden-red earth. To the east the snow peaks of the high Sierra poke against a gray, brooding sky. Jones stops to unleash the dogs, and when he begins again, it seems as though he's been freed, too. Clearly, running is a delight and relief for him. At rest, he's a slow-talking, even-tempered man who could pass for five years older than his actual 28. But while running he looks younger and lighter, his voice rises and clears. Forty minutes into a three-hour run, Jones seems as lucid and articulate as another man might be in his office or living room.

The more time one spends watching Jones, the more difficult it becomes to judge the wisdom or folly of his undertaking. A quote attributed to New Zealand ultramarathoner Ziggy Bauer comes to mind: "Ultrarunning is a natural sport. Man was built for endurance, not for speed." But then there's the growing mass of contrary opinion, the grim stories of excess and addiction, the increasing conviction that, for most people, the most healthful miles are the ones not run.

"It wouldn't be right for everybody—running 20 or 30 miles a day —but I just like to do it," says Jones. "It depends on what you view as natural. I like to look at it more as something being healthy or unhealthy. If I'm thinking and growing through doing this, then I'd say my running is something healthy." He carries on for a few hundred yards, moving to the rhythm of the panting dogs, his soles lightly slapping the dirt and rock, his breath chuffing at the thin air redolent of pine and rain. "I guess I have a love/hate relationship with pain," he says thoughtfully. "But what really drives me is a sense of wonder at what I can do, about how far I can go. My body's like a laboratory, I guess, and I'm just like a kid let loose in it."

PERHAPS JONES is enjoying this second youth so much because his first was filled with difficulty and conflict. He was born near Phoenix, the second-youngest of 14 children. His father was a failed dairy rancher who turned to drinking when he lost his land. Eventually the man abandoned his family, and his wife's plight was such that she landed on the "Queen for a Day" TV program. One of her prizes was a reunion with her husband, who had drifted to the Sierra foothills. After this improbable Dickensian meeting, the father moved the family to California with him. There, his periods of employment as a carpenter and construction worker were intermittent, as was his drinking.

The bottom was sounded one afternoon when Jones was 11. He and his sisters were in the living room, peeling pears. Their mother was at work, and their father was languishing in his bedroom when he turned a gun on himself. "The damn bullet came right through the staircase," Jones remembers. "He used a thirty-thirty hunting rifle. The bullet carried right through the stucco and sheetrock and ricocheted all around the room. A piece of flying plaster cut my sister's face."

His 18-year-old brother took charge, rushing back to the bedroom. He took one look inside and shut the door, but not before Jones and his sister had gotten a look, too.

"That gave me a sense of being chickenshit about being motivated," Jones says of his father's suicide. "When I was younger than that, I used to push a lot harder. But after that it was hard to take a lot of things seriously. After that I wasn't as peer-influenced—I didn't give a shit about what my peers or others thought about me. From that point on I didn't want others to decide or influence the way I thought and felt about things."

Jones's fierce sense of independence took him in various directions. There was some petty theft and shoplifting done more for the thrill than for bragging rights—he liked to work alone. But after he was caught breaking into a house, he started pursuing his freedom by other means. His thirst for solitude led to a love for long rambles in the fields and woods and hills. He discovered that he could walk and jog and bicycle for hours without tiring. He started playing the drums. When he was 16, he graduated from high school and filled the time before joining the Air Force by installing swimming pools with his brothers in Phoenix.

"I didn't feel like I was really in tune with myself or the environment," says Jones. "I was worried about handling the stress I knew I'd catch in the Air Force. I like to be by myself, and there wouldn't be a chance for that in the military. There wouldn't be anyplace to escape. I heard about meditation and how it involved being quiet twice a day. It sounded like something I needed."

Jones meditated all through his four-year Air Force enlistment, often indulging in lengthy sessions while stationed in Germany. After his discharge he lived briefly in Alaska and then returned to Grass Valley and the foothills, where he combined meditation and other spiritual investigations with a series of odd jobs. Employed as a tree trimmer, he delighted his boss and intrigued himself by being able to work longer and harder than his coworkers. "I was feeling really good about my body," he says. "I began realizing that I could probably expand this with nutrition. I immediately got interested in extending physical limits and consciousness. I'd never really dedicated myself physically, put out 100 percent."

Another thread in Jones's thickening web of interests was children. He enrolled in psychology classes at a community college, and those led to an internship and job at Northstar Academy, a residential school and treatment center for troubled children. At this point, Jones was pursuing myriad paths—social work, meditation, parapsychology, nutrition, the outdoors—that might have canceled one another, might have led to one or another dilettantish, neohippie dead end. Instead, he decided to start running.

"IT WAS DEFINITELY premeditated," says Jones. "I didn't know anything about it, didn't know about any local runners or races, but I knew I was already in pretty good shape. I saw running as a way to explore physical limits. I was really interested in endurance."

In February of 1982, Jones took his first run: three miles. Within six weeks he was running 100 miles a week and going as far as 45 miles in a single workout—training levels reached only by professional or semi-professional marathoners with years of experience. The simplest explanation would be that he was a latent prodigy, but Jones thinks otherwise.

"I might have a psychological gift, but not a physical one," he insists. "When I discovered I could run five or ten miles without much trouble, I knew it could be extended. The possibilities were jumping right out at me. I was prepared through meditation. I was able to recover faster."

Jones explains that during deep meditation the metabolic rate is actually slower than during deep sleep. Thus, through meditation, the body's regenerative powers are magnified. He further bolstered the healing processes by ingesting a daily pharmacopoeia of vitamins, minerals, and food supplements.

Predictably, Jones's first race was a marathon, a remarkable 2:56 run over a hilly course just four months after he'd begun training. Local runners were incredulous, but Jones was exultant. He felt strong at the finish and knew immediately that running 26.2 miles wouldn't be enough for him. The next month, still completely on his own, Jones took off one Saturday and ran 80 miles around Lake Tahoe. He'd run ten miles, stop at a store for a soda, and run ten miles more. The trip took 14 hours, and hooked Jones irrevocably on ultradistances. In September he again ran around Lake Tahoe, but this time while competing in an organized ultramarathon. He finished third in a field of 80. "I knew I was on my way," Jones recalls. "It was a matter of time until I was on top."

After his meteoric start, Jones plateaued over the next three years. In the spring of 1984 he entered his first major ultra, the American River 50 in California, and finished a disappointing 40th. He made a few strong showings at local 50-mile trail races, but his entry for the 1984 Western States wasn't accepted, and he failed to finish the race in 1985. He got a full-time job at Northstar and moved from house to house in the foothills, gaining increasing access to the area's bountiful trails. By 1986, Jones had become an avid student of distance running. "The competitive aspects opened me up to a lot of new techniques," he says. "I started talking to a lot more people about running, but they just couldn't understand the miles I was putting in. They felt that putting in more than a hundred miles a week was just pissing in the wind. Relaxation and my environment became very important. I learned that running megamiles definitely has to be a life-style. You have to respect your psyche and rest your body. But other runners just couldn't understand how I was holding up."

Their bafflement seems eminently understandable. For despite Jones's explanation of meditation and nutrition, the sources of his endurance remain a tantalizing mystery. It seems that he harbors a secret formula, one based upon metaphysics as much as sweat. It involves concepts he calls "frequencies" and "vibrations," terms that Jones seems reluctant to discuss because he knows how loony they might sound. When the subject rises, the spaces between his words grow wider. He repeats questions. A pained expression falls over his face as the questioner, sniffing a truth about to be revealed, leans closer, badgering him.

"It's resonant qualities," he stammers, "trying to tap into resonance. Some of my meditation gave me insight into frequencies and resonances. It's a matter of being in tune with the trail. It's like a continuous art form. It's monitoring yourself and your environment with just as much alertness as you can. It's a heightened awareness of all your senses—your breathing and what's going on in your mind. You want to be aware of the different smells, the different sounds. Balance is what it is—your equilibrium kicks in. It's like you're walking on a tightrope, and trying to make everything smooth.

"I'd already developed this state through meditation, but it took a few months to have it come out through running. Now it's a conscious thing, a tool. I don't use it constantly. Sometimes now, when I'm on a trail, I can run without even looking at the ground. It's like my feet can feel their own way, and kick rocks out of the way."

JONES TAKES the last steep hill in a long, surging charge, the dogs panting behind him, and turns into his yard at a little past five, just as the light, thin all day, begins to retreat up the steep ridges of sugar and ponderosa pine. He checks the thermometer, waters and feeds the dogs, then lets them into the kitchen. They immediately layer themselves in front of the space heater. Jones carries a moderate post 20-mile glow, but he's hardly depleted. His breathing is normal, his face is dry, no salt rimes his beard. He pours himself a single tall glass of cranberry juice, slices a wedge of store-bought pie, and begins boiling water for coffee. Jones resembles nothing so much as a man coming home from a ho-hum shift at the lumber mill.

The small, drafty farmhouse Jones caretakes was built before 1910. The place is thick with the effluvia of a bachelor outdoorsman. A dozen or so pairs of neatly arranged running shoes sit in front of the sofa. Cross-country skis lean in a corner. Trophies and plaques are displayed beside a giant TV and stereo hookup.

The house fell to Jones at just the right concatenation of events. He was committing himself to being the best trail runner in America, was narrowing his goals to the Western States, and was solidifying his job at Northstar. He was also realizing that his life was all of a piece and that his love of solitude formed the basic building block of his ultramarathoning. "I'm really isolated up here," he says, sitting down at the scarred picnic table that fills one end of the big kitchen. "I like to think that I'm not that aloof or hermetic, but I guess that I am. I know I couldn't live in the city and do the training that I do. I'd feel too closed in. I wouldn't feel right. I need to control when I'm with people and when I'm not. . . ." He pauses again. The dogs snuffle in front of the heater. The water ticks on the stove. Outside, the mountain silence seeps around the house in the dying light. "How would I put it? Social contact is really important, you need that interaction, that criticism, or whatever. You have to be able to deal with the world. That balance is very important to me because I train alone 99.9 percent of the time."

FOR THE PAST TWO YEARS, Jones has been remarkably successful at hammering out his private equilibrium. In early 1986 he began putting in regular 58-hour weeks at the school, and consistently running alternate weeks of 130 and 200 miles. Most nights he'd get off work at 10 or 11 and run home on the twisting 23-mile dirt road, which rises 2,000 feet in its climb from Grass Valley. He'd get to Malakoff at three in the morning, take a friend to work back in Grass Valley at 5:30, return home and sleep until 11, eat breakfast, and then take off running again.

All the work began to pay off in April of 1986, when Jones won the American River 50, which annually draws more than 300 runners, the biggest field of any American ultra. In June, just a week before Western States, Jones and his partner finished 22nd out of 225 teams in the Levi's Ride & Tie. ("It's speed, it's dirt, it's Western," Jones says of the event. In the warm months he rides horseback 30 miles a week.)

At Western States, Jones drew upon all of his mental, physical, and spiritual resources to seize the lead from Jim Pellon at 82 miles, and later, in the last ten miles, to stave off Pellon with a series of withering sub-6:30 miles. His 16-hour, 37-minute victory earned him $3,000, the only money he's ever gotten for running. He celebrated with a cheeseburger and a milk shake. The next morning, he was up at 5:30, back into his routine. "I couldn't sleep anyway," Jones recalls. "The next two or three nights I kept waking up and saying, 'I did it!' "

Jones had been planning to try the Leadville 100 in Colorado on August 23. Immediately after Western States he returned to work and training, battling through the inevitable letdown to get back to 160-mile weeks. In the last week before the race he ran 200 miles. "If there ever was going to be any overtraining in my life," says Jones, "that would have been it."

The Leadville 100 is run at 10,000 feet, over the highest range in the American Rockies. Jones ran strongly, but couldn't overtake winner Skip Hamilton, who regularly trains at that altitude. Jones finished second in 20:48. At 4:30 on the morning after the race, he hopped on his motorcycle and drove the 1,000 miles home without stopping. "I got back here around midnight, ten minutes faster than it took me to run 100 miles," says Jones. "To go that fast after going so slow is a real high."

Jones had already completed an impossible season of running, but the Wasatch 100 kept tugging at his mind. He forced himself back to another 160-mile week. On September 5, his 28th birthday, he mounted his motorcycle at 3:30 in the morning, blew across Nevada, and arrived at the Wasatch race headquarters in Salt Lake City at five in the afternoon. By this time his legend had preceded him. Race officials took one look at his motorcycle and said, "You must be Chuck Jones."

Jones had never seen the course before, and hadn't arranged for a support crew. But the next day he ran 100 miles across the Wasatch Mountains in 20:39, winning the race and breaking the course record by 53 minutes.

That's not all. Jones crossed the Wasatch finish line at 12:30 Sunday morning, slept until ten, jumped on his bike at 8:30 that evening, and drove all night through the desert, arriving home at noon on Monday. He went to work on Tuesday, and on Wednesday morning got a phone call from a friend wanting to know if he was interested in running across the United States, starting the next Monday. Jones said sure.

That cross-country trip, launched in support of an antidrug program, included 20 runners, ages 17 to 70. Jones and the other top runners covered 20 to 25 miles a day, most of them at a sub-six-minute pace. "It was a hell of an experience," says Jones, "seeing the country at eight miles per hour."

AN HOUR HAS PASSED, the light has died at the window, and the rain and cold have thickened. The coffee and pie have disappeared, and Jones has further stoked himself with a couple of peanut-butter-and-jelly sand-wiches. "I still feel pretty strong," he says, stretching. "I think I'll go out for another 12."

The thought of running 12 more miles through the pitch-black rain revives the original questions: Is Jones a freak or a visionary? A quirky aberrance or a world-class athlete? A crackpot or an unusually sane and rational man?

"It's tough to think about," Jones acknowledges, changing into a dry shirt. "I know I've always been a little bit eccentric. I've always been out there in my ideas and views." He pauses, turning the words over in his mind, knowing the ones he chooses will inevitably fall short of the truth he's trying to express. "I just think there's a lot of reality out there, and we've only seen bits and pieces of it. I think it's possible that I've seen a little more than most people, that I'm a little more in tune."

And then it's time to run again, and Chuck Jones is free. His evening workout will take him up the mountain instead of down; climbing six miles, past 5,200 feet, where the slashing rain will give way to sleet, then snow. Where the wind will howl and Jones will be alone to commune with his visions and vibrations, running toward his fierce, precarious balance.

*September 1987*

# HE IS CRAZY AND HE IS FEARLESS

*He is Redmond O'Hanlon, the most unlikely adventurer in the English language.*

● ▲ ■

BILL BRYSON

Redmond O'Hanlon greets you at the door with a glass of champagne, seats you in a plump chair, and almost immediately starts barging. He barges off into the next room, mumbling about something he wants to show you. You can hear what sounds like books being taken from shelves and discarded with backward flings, and then with an "Aha!" he returns bearing an old textbook called *Principles and Practices of Rectal Surgery,* by W. Gabriel, and passes it on for inspection. "His students called him the Arse Angel Gabriel," O'Hanlon says fondly. "You can't look at the pictures for more than a few moments without starting to feel ill."

Abruptly he barges off again—you look at the book; he's right about the pictures—and soon reemerges from some dark recess of the house with the rest of the champagne and two fresh bottles of wine. He begins to uncork one of the bottles but, seized by the sudden thought of something else you might like to see, barges off again. Redmond O'Hanlon barges a lot. He is a wonderfully odd person.

He is also probably the finest writer of travel books in the English language, and certainly the most daring. He specializes in going to strange and uncomfortable places—Borneo, Amazonia, central Africa—and writing books about them that are at once serious (well, pretty serious) accounts of the nature and anthropology of exotic climes and also wildly hilarious adventure stories. Eric Newby, the dean of British travel writers, called O'Hanlon's first book, *Into the Heart of Borneo,* "the funniest travel book I have ever read." His second, *In Trouble Again,* is even better.

When not exploring, O'Hanlon, who is "43 and almost dead," lives with his wife, Belinda, and two small children, Puffin and Galen, in a gloriously cluttered cottage on the edge of the Cotswolds near Oxford. Books, mostly from the nineteenth century, are everywhere—stuffed onto ceiling-high shelves, stacked in unsteady piles on every flat surface, strewn open around the floor. Every other space groans with odd and exotic treasures: a pair of human skulls, a stuffed pelican in a glass case, photographs from O'Hanlon's expeditions, souvenirs from three continents, and, somewhere, his anticandiru device.

This, designed in consultation with a leading medical authority in Oxford, is a jockstrap with a metal tea-strainer sewn into the cup to thwart the notorious candiru, a toothpick-shaped Amazonian fish that darts up the unwary bather's urethra, extends its spiny fins, and becomes agonizingly undislodgable. "Nothing can be done," O'Hanlon writes in *In Trouble Again*. "The pain, apparently, is spectacular. You must get to a hospital before your bladder bursts; you must ask a surgeon to cut off your penis."

This is the sort of thing Redmond O'Hanlon would have you think of before you travel in the tropics.

NOTHING ABOUT O'HANLON suggests a tough and adventuring spirit. Behind his wire-rimmed glasses he looks scholarly, monkish, benign, almost diffident. (One English newspaper has called him the Mild Man of Borneo.) He speaks softly, tends to shamble, and looks like he has just gotten out of bed. It is all but impossible to imagine him abseiling down cliff faces, wrestling with crocodiles, or indeed doing anything more taxing than wandering a Thames towpath with a butterfly net.

Wisely, he has made a virtue of this. His books are filled with engagingly heartfelt expressions of alarm at the prospect of real physical exertion. Here he is, for instance, in Caracas and about to set off on an expedition, seeking advice from a true he-man explorer named Charlie Brewer-Carías:

"Care for a session in the gym?" said Charlie, stroking his enormous drooping moustache.

"Certainly not," I said, panicking. "Couldn't we talk over a bottle or two?"

"That would be very bad for you. A very bad idea. You must stay away from drink altogether. The Indians have not adapted to it. You must not take it with you. The Amazonas, Redmond, is not a kind place."

"Look here—I haven't been to a gym since school."

"Now's the time," said Charlie, getting up. "You must fight that belly. Everyone should go to a gym."

He picked up an athlete's bag from the paving stones, swung it onto his muscled shoulders, and pointed to a leather pouch on the table.

"Bring that," said Charlie, "and give it to me if there's trouble. Come on. We can get in a full hour before lunch."

The pouch was extraordinarily heavy. I half-undid the zip and looked inside. It was a large, black Browning automatic.

"Jesus," I said.

Not exactly Indiana Jones, what? Nonetheless, O'Hanlon is firmly embedded in a long line of English explorer-adventurers—Charles Darwin, Sir Richard Burton, Alfred Russel Wallace, and many others in this century and last. What sets him apart is that things are wonderfully apt to go wrong on his trips: rivers prove unnavigable, dangerous animals are inadvertently antagonized, expeditions get lost and spend days wandering in circles, native guides threaten mutiny in the middle of nowhere, tempers unravel. You find yourself racing through his books not simply because the writing is so engrossing, but because you are becoming genuinely concerned about this crazy, likeable, hopelessly optimistic Englishman plunging ever deeper into the jungle.

"He is crazy and he is fearless. Those are the two things that you have to understand about Redmond," says Lary Shaffer, an American biologist and longtime friend who recently spent two and a half months in the Congo with O'Hanlon. "He is also the quintessential English gentleman traveler. He lives in the nineteenth century, you know, and has this odd Victorian code of conduct. In Africa he came down with malaria so bad that I seriously thought he might die, and yet when we were invited to this Congolese man's house, Redmond insisted on coming with me. He even drank a glass of palm wine—which is like the world's most revolting drink, believe me—because he didn't want to offend the man. This is a guy who the day before had been racked with chills and, as far as I could tell, was *dying*."

"He's like two different people," says Simon Stockton, who partnered O'Hanlon on the rancorous South American journey that became the 1988 book *In Trouble Again*. "At home, he's this droll, amiable bloke who's a lot of fun to get drunk with. Then you get to the jungle, and he becomes another person altogether. Not only was he no longer amiable and witty, he didn't even talk. He went to bed at six o'clock every evening and didn't reappear until six the next morning, and the rest of the time he was in this world of his own, just taking notes. He was the most boring company I've ever had. But yeah"—a tone of reluctant admiration comes into Stockton's voice—"he does write good books."

Considering that he does it so well, O'Hanlon came late and more or less accidentally to travel writing. He was born in 1947 in Dorset, the son of a Church of England vicar, and was dispatched at a young age to Marlborough, a leading private school. It was there that he discovered the works of Charles Darwin. "It was just electrifying," he says of his first reading of *On the Origin of Species*. "Darwin is still my great hero." O'Hanlon visibly regrets that he wasn't born in the nineteenth century. His bibliographies are full of entries like "*The Expedition to Borneo of HMS Dido for the Suppression of Piracy, with Extracts from the Journal of James Brooke Esq*, 2 vols, London, 1846," and in his books he constantly compares his progress with that of nineteenth-century explorers like Alexander von Humboldt. A hundred years ago, not only was the most interesting work being done, but there was still lots of planet to explore. "Now all that's left is mostly swamp," O'Hanlon says unhappily.

Had he not become a travel writer, O'Hanlon would have enjoyed a distinguished career as a naturalist and academic. Before embarking on his first popular book, he had already been a research fellow at Oxford, been appointed natural history editor of the *Times Literary Supplement,* and published respectable monographs with titles like "Changing Scientific Concepts of Nature in the English Novel, 1850–1920" and *Joseph Conrad and Charles Darwin: The Influence of Scientific Thought on Conrad's Fiction.*

Yet O'Hanlon's progress through the higher realms of academe was not without its setbacks. In 1966, aged 19, he was expelled from Oxford for writing a scatological novel that fell into the wrong hands. It took him a year to persuade the authorities to give him a second chance. Supported by his new wife, whom almost everyone describes as "the saintly Belinda," O'Hanlon spent most of the next decade "sleeping and working intermittently on my doctorate, but mostly sleeping."

After receiving his M.Phil. (as it is called at Oxford) in Nineteenth-Century English Studies with distinction, O'Hanlon took a post teaching at the university's Hertford College. This proved disastrous, however, when it was discovered that he had been teaching his English literature students the wrong century.

"It was awful, awful," he says. "I mean, really, it is quite devastating to discover that you have fucked up in such an unusual and comprehensive way. It was literally disastrous for some of the students. I had a letter in the top drawer of my desk and I don't know if I misread it or what . . ." He trails off, hands aflutter, a huge, sheepish grin across his face.

"IF YOU ARE GOING to interview him, don't whatever you do let him give you a drink," Lary Shaffer warned me by telephone from America. Redmond O'Hanlon has long been known as an inveterate giver and goer-to of parties, and he remains, I am discovering, an extraordinarily gracious host, forever bounding up to top off the wineglass, making sure that we each have at least two drinks on the go at any one time. A radio interviewer for the BBC told me that she once went to his house to do a recording, had a wonderful lunch, and came away remembering almost nothing of the afternoon "except for a hazy recollection of it having been *extremely* pleasant."

O'Hanlon's closest friends include many of the leading lights of British literature—Julian Barnes, Martin Amis, Ian McEwan, the late Bruce Chatwin, and the poets James Fenton and Craig Raine—most of whom O'Hanlon has known since long before they or he became famous. It was in consultation with one of these friends, Fenton, that the idea of making an expedition first arose. They decided in 1983 to venture to Borneo with the intention of traveling up the Baleh River to its source in the Tiban mountains, an area not explored since 1926. O'Hanlon also nurtured vague hopes of encountering the rare Borneo rhinoceros. After two months of traipsing the jungle, O'Hanlon returned home to produce what the London *Evening Standard* called "the most hilarious travel book in many years."

Much of the humor in *Into the Heart of Borneo* comes from O'Hanlon's affectionate descriptions of the imperturbable, Buddha-like Fenton and from his bemused encounters with an alien culture, as when he finds that he has been given, as a mark of honor, a pungent reptilian delicacy, the tail of a monitor lizard: "The flesh was yellow and softish and smelt bad, very like the stray chunks of solid matter in the effluvia one sees in England on an unwashed pavement outside a public house late on a Saturday night."

The trip taught O'Hanlon that traveling in the tropics is exhausting, muggy, lonely, insect-ridden, gastronomically distressing, often tedious, sometimes dangerous, and always uncomfortable. But he also discovered that he loved it. "It's hard to explain," he says. "Partly it's the pleasure of seeing a bird I've never seen before and would never otherwise see. But also there's this odd sense that if you're suffering, somehow the experience must be real.

Upon his return from Borneo, O'Hanlon began to plan a much more ambitious undertaking: a journey along the Orinoco and Rio Negro rivers in Venezuela. He tried to talk Fenton into going with him. "I want you to know," Fenton replied calmly, "*that I would not come with you to High Wycombe.*" Instead, O'Hanlon settled on an old friend named Simon Stockton—a spectacularly inappropriate choice. Stockton worked in a London casino, smoked and drank heavily, bedded women with the ease and fluency of the leading man in a XXX-rated movie, and scarcely ever saw daylight.

Borneo had been exotic and challenging but comparatively accommodating; even in the most remote fastnesses, O'Hanlon and Fenton had encountered people who spoke passable English and wanted to know the latest disco steps, and on one notable occasion they even found a jungle store selling cans of beer and Green Giant sweetcorn. There would be nothing like that in Amazonia.

Such people as they encountered would be likely to want to kill them, and for the rest there was nothing but vast, uncharted jungle aswarm with living things for which the opportunity to sting, suck, cling to, or otherwise feast upon human flesh was not to be missed: vicious wasps, scorpions, spiders, piranhas, electric eels, giant catfish with jaws capable of taking a swimmer's foot off at the ankle, leeches, ticks, fire-ants whose stings make the bitten appendage feel as if it has been plunged repeatedly into a flame, botflies whose larvae bore into the host's skin and emerge 40 days later as wriggling maggots, swarms of blackflies so dense that they fill the mouth and nostrils and make life literally unbearable, snakes that strike at the speed of light and leave you dead in minutes. All of these, O'Hanlon and Stockton would discover, are as endemic to the tropics as houseflies on an Indiana porch door in August.

Moreover, they were entering an area so remote that its highest mountain, Neblina, wasn't "discovered" until 1953, even though it is the loftiest peak in South America outside the Andes.

The result is a book that is far darker than *Into the Heart of Borneo.* O'Hanlon's chronicle of Stockton's spirited disintegration in this hostile environment manages to be both hilarious and disquieting. "It's different for you, all this," the wild-eyed Stockton tells O'Hanlon at one point. "You've got no taste buds at all. You think everything's wonderful [and] you're manic on top of it. You get excited every time you see a new bird. Whereas me, in all honesty, Redmond, to be totally frank with you, I just think, well, *there goes another fucking bird*." He abandons the expedition before it is half finished and returns to England, promising to settle down, marry his girlfriend, work "like a shitcake and never ever complain about anything ever again."

"Which," O'Hanlon adds, tossing back yet another drink, "is more or less precisely what he did." More or less. Stockton did return to England, married his girlfriend, and gratefully took back his job at the casino, but he didn't stop complaining. One of the things he complained most bitterly about was his depiction in the book.

"It was complete and utter character assassination," Stockton says. "If he hadn't been such a good friend, I'd have sued him for all he was worth. I don't mind being portrayed as mildly obnoxious or crude—I'm the first to admit I sometimes am—but it did hurt me to see myself portrayed as a wimp or a moron. A lot of the things that I am purported to have said or done in the book just didn't happen, at least not in the way they are described.

"What hurt even more was that Redmond showed me the manuscript, and when I told him the things I didn't like or agree with, he said to each one, 'OK, I'll change that, no problem,' and when the book came out he hadn't changed a bloody thing. I felt betrayed and didn't talk to him for six months. But we're friends again now. Like I say, he's a different person when you get him out of the jungle."

Whatever the degree of veracity—and O'Hanlon insists that his is a faithful account of the trip as he saw it—the book remains vivid literature.

Bereft of his compatriot, O'Hanlon pressed obsessively on with his Indian guides in search of a rumored tribe of Yanomami Indians, a people said to be so violent that their idea of a good time was to take turns hitting each other over the head with a sort of tropical pool-cue. When they were angry, which was often, they shot each other with lethal, curare-tipped arrows. This, the guides assured O'Hanlon, was almost certainly what the Yanomami would do to them.

With supplies nearly exhausted, forced to subsist on greasy rodents and tiny fish that offered little more than a mouthful of bones, his guides restive and constantly threatening to abandon him, O'Hanlon experienced a kind of disintegration of his own. One evening, after the guides had been out hunting, he looked into his food bowl to find the boiled head of a monkey floating there. "I picked it up, put my lips to the rim of each socket in turn, and sucked. The eyes came away from their soft stalks and slid down my throat." His descent into the outer fringes of savagery is recorded with a matter-of-factness that is surreal and at moments terrifying.

O'Hanlon did eventually find the Yanomami and, as you will have gathered, lived to tell the tale, but it was hairy and it was close. To say any more would be to spoil it for those who haven't read the book. He says he is immensely proud to have made a genuine contribution to anthropology with the trip and, after filling my glass and a small section of tabletop with claret, goes off for several minutes and returns with a long article from *The New York Times* about a recent expedition, undertaken by his friend and Amazon mentor Charlie Brewer-Cariás and an American anthropologist with the jaunty name of Napoleon A. Chagnon, into the same area. "Good, huh?" he says proudly.

O'Hanlon recently completed his third expedition, accompanied by Lary Shaffer, now a professor at the State University of New York at Plattsburgh, but a close friend of O'Hanlon's since they were graduate students together at Oxford. They traveled together in the far north of the People's Republic of the Congo, before O'Hanlon pushed on to Lake Télé.

"We were looking for a dinosaur called Mokele Nbembe, which was rumored to be surviving there," O'Hanlon says. "In fact it's extinct." The trip was not a barrel of laughs. "I had this bout of malaria, which slowed us down, and there was a lot of disease, including AIDS, among children, which was rather depressing. And it was expensive and difficult. The whole trip cost £19,000, mostly in bribes. Every uniformed official in the country expects a payoff. We got out by lying to the soldiers at the airport and telling them we were coming back soon with a television crew and that there would be *lots* of money then."

Shaffer agrees that the trip was often uncomfortable and occasionally frightening, but unlike Stockton he has nothing but praise for O'Hanlon as a traveling companion. "I know Simon had some problems adapting to Redmond's behavior patterns in the jungle," Shaffer says. "And it's true, he does become a different person on these trips. For one thing, he doesn't drink. And he takes the work very seriously. But I was impressed by that. A villager would tell Redmond a story, for instance, and Redmond would go around checking it with as many people as he could because he seems to feel he has this duty to get things exactly right. But I wouldn't say that he was ever boring company, not in my experience. I'd go again with him tomorrow—but then, of course, I haven't seen what he's going to write about me yet."

O'HANLON COMPOSES his books in an upstairs study that is even more impossibly cluttered than the rooms below. He takes me there very late in our evening together, clutching a bottle of port in case of emergency. You don't so much walk into O'Hanlon's study as wade in, clearing a path through books, manuscripts, charts, maps, and other assorted detritus. He works with monumental slowness, writing longhand in a neat, almost Victorian script, which he then passes on to a typist.

He expects the Congo book to take three, maybe four years. But then there are a lot of distractions. For one thing, the house next door is lived in by young nurses who have the habit of wandering around their backyard naked when the weather is fine. "Makes it a bit difficult to concentrate," O'Hanlon muses, topping up my glass for the fourth time in ten minutes and then, ever the naturalist, embarking on a lovingly detailed and evocative description of the 19-year-old female form.

A faraway look comes over him, and he abruptly points at a map of Asia. "Might go to New Guinea next," he says. "There's a thing there called the Wallace Line, named for Alfred Russel Wallace, who discovered that there are two islands just 30 miles apart but on which all the birds and animals are completely different. We know now that it's because it's where two of the earth's plates meet. Anyway, there's a swamp there that looks as if it might be interesting." He looks astonishingly clear-eyed and sober. I, on the other hand, can no longer stand without the aid of a wall.

A distant sense of duty tells me that I should ask him the name of the swamp, but O'Hanlon is already barging off toward the stairs, looking for brandy or whiskey or more probably both.

*February 1991*

# MEL FISHER'S MORNING AFTER

*What happens when you've found what you're looking for?*

● ▲ ■

GEOFFREY NORMAN

**B**y the time Johnny Carson had left Key West, there was a hurricane off Cuba, threatening to blow into the Gulf. It was mid-August, storm season, so all the boats had come in off the site of the wreck and tied up at a pier not far from the old Navy building where Mel Fisher's treasure is on display.

Fisher's is a decrepit-looking fleet, and one or two tourists who had found their way to it to take some pictures shook their heads in wonder. *These boats found 400 million, one of them was saying. Back in Jersey they wouldn't make it as garbage scows.* A couple of wharf rummies, filthy and bearded, were enjoying an afternoon cocktail on the dock. An old Navy bomb— the barnacles making it look more seedy than lethal—was propped up against the side of a building, forgotten. It was hot, but the low pressure in the Gulf was drawing air off the Atlantic. There was a stiff wind.

The divers, half a dozen of them, were idling around the boats. Drinking beer, reading *Playboy,* wrestling. They were young, most of them. And they were not end-of-the-roaders, a breed common to the Keys. The ones who were most eager to talk were from the Midwest, and they looked implausibly clean and cheerful and innocent. The salt water and the tropics had not gotten to them yet.

I talked to some of them, passing time. They described the great find in living detail. I asked one of them what the mood was like afterwards, that night out in the Gulf.

"The quietest I can remember," one of them says. "Everyone had a beer and went to bed. I guess everyone was thinking the same thing."

What was that?

"They were thinking, 'Shit, now I gotta get a *job!*' "

WHEN THE BIG MOMENT CAME at last, Mel Fisher himself was out. He had been shopping for a mask and fins, then stopped for a drink at one of the bars in Key West. It was a Saturday morning, and Fisher knew that the time was near. For 16 years he had been saying "today's the day," but how was he to know that this time it really was?

Some 40 miles west, Fisher's son, Kane, had anchored an unsightly, ungainly, old coastal rig called *Dauntless* over a spot in the Gulf of Mexico. Something was down there, Kane thought, and the instrument readings confirmed it. He had lowered two large sections of pipe, bent like elbows, from their stern mountings into the water. The pipes carried the turbulent water from *Dauntless*'s props straight down so that it blew away the sand and other bottom covering. Anything buried by the sand would be exposed and visible to divers.

When the large elbow joints of pipe, called "mailboxes," had done their work, the divers went over. They were in a little less than 60 feet of water, warm enough in July that none of them wore wet suits. One of them carried a hand-held metal detector. None of them expected anything remarkable from this dive, though it was always possible. Not two months earlier, on Memorial Day, other divers working for Fisher had found 13 bars of gold about two miles from this site. You just never knew. You never did.

When they finished their descent, the divers looked into the crater that had been blown by *Dauntless*'s mailboxes. They saw silver coins, heavily encrusted with black oxide after three and a half centuries on the bottom. They had been finding coins for the past several days, and it had added to the divers' conviction that they were near their goal. This was Kane's trail, his hunch, and it was paying off with coins and artifacts that had been on their way to Philip IV of Spain before a hurricane grounded—and then sank—the vessel that carried them, the *Nuestra Señora de Atocha*.

Silver coins had become almost routine, and anyway, they weren't going anywhere in the next few minutes, Greg Wareham thought. He had bottom time enough to take a look around first and then pick them up later. Maybe he would find something more interesting or valuable.

(This was the prerogative of the diver, the man on the scene. He could play a hunch, too.)

So Wareham swam away from the crater to see what he could find. In a few minutes, he was back motioning to Andy Matroci to follow him. They swam off together to look at what Wareham had found. One glance and Matroci knew what it was, just as Wareham had known. It was a mound, rising out of the mud bottom. A mound of stone and copper some 70 or 80 feet long and perhaps half that wide. There were dark bars the shape of bread loaves scattered on the bottom around this mound of stone and copper. These bars were, they knew, solid silver, weighing about 70 pounds each. They also knew that the stone mound had been ballast and the copper the freight in the hold of *Atocha* and that it had been there for 350 years. They had found what they had all been looking for for so long. This was it. The mother lode.

They surfaced together, screaming with inarticulate delight to Kane Fisher and to the other divers still on the boat. "I don't remember what I said," Wareham says. "I don't even know if it made any sense. I was just yelling." In minutes, Kane Fisher was on the radio calling Key West and the headquarters of his father's company, Treasure Salvors, Inc. "You can put away the charts," he said. "We've found it."

The word went out all over Key West. Mel Fisher, call your office. Finally, Fisher was located and taken back to his headquarters where a champagne party was already in progress and a statement was being released to the press.

The next day Fisher himself went out to the site to inspect the find. All four of his salvage boats had converged on the *Dauntless*. They were tied up alongside each other. There was a celebration in progress there, too. Also some work, as divers loaded 200 silver bars carried by the *Atocha* into wire baskets, and the people topside hauled them aboard and stacked them into neat piles.

Jimmy Buffett was a few miles away in the Marquesas shooting pictures for the cover of his next album. He came out to the site and joined the party. He sang a few numbers from the flying bridge of the *Magruder,* including "Pirate Looks at Forty," one of his best songs and one that some of Fisher's people say was inspired by him.

"It was a great party," one of the divers remembers. "A really great day and a great party. I could hardly believe it was happening. Any of it."

Within days, Fisher was on the morning television circuit telling his story and showing samples of what he had found. Reporters dropped everything and went to Key West for the story. One left his high school reunion, another a family wake. Movie companies called frantically to find out if the story had already been optioned.

Fisher, meanwhile, graduated from Jane Pauley and David Hartman to the absolute final certification of celebrity in the United States—the Johnny Carson show. Johnny made some jokes about how long Fisher's treasure would be able to finance Carson's alimony (a couple of months) and others about a device that Fisher claimed was a recovered Spanish enema tube (it wouldn't be "The Tonight Show" without a proctology joke). Fisher was a charming guest, and Carson asked him if he could come dive on the site. Fisher said, as he had said to other rich men who could help him over the years, "Sure, come on down."

Back in Key West, one of Fisher's oldest associates watched the show and said, "It was great. Just great. I haven't seen Mel *up* like that in 10 or 11 years."

After two weeks, the intensity of the press coverage in Key West began to ebb a little. Still, people from *Paris Match* were over; *National Geographic*'s television division had a very thorough crew down. Others drifted in and out. Bleth McHaley, a vice president of Treasure Salvors and an old associate of Fisher's, said that a major movie deal would be announced any day.

Then, on a weekend in early August, Johnny Carson flew into town in his Lear jet. Carson dove both days with Fisher. Had his picture taken with the crew. Signed autographs, one on a ballast stone one of the divers was keeping for a souvenir. Film was made of Carson and Fisher and Fisher's attorney loading silver bars into a wheelbarrow that they pushed around the bottom of the Gulf of Mexico. When the second dive was over, Carson went back to shore and flew out of Key West.

Ten days later, Carson told the story and ran the film on "The Tonight Show." Fisher was flying high. All over the country there are people who crave celebrity and would walk to Burbank on their knees for a few minutes on the same studio stage with Carson. But Johnny had come to *him*.

You know what they say about Johnny Carson—that nobody has a better feel for the root nerve of the American psyche. Wise men in the time of Watergate knew that Nixon was finished when Johnny started making jokes about him. His touch is absolutely sure. If he says Mel Fisher is big, then he is big. But what is it about this story that makes it so compelling? What is it about Mel Fisher and his gold?

FISHER DOES NOT EXPLAIN himself or his reasons well, partly because he is not an articulate man and partly because he sees things in self-evident terms. He hunts for gold because it is gold he is hunting for. He began his life at 40 years of age as a treasure hunter, and the search for the *Atocha* became the entire point of his life. The only thing more durable than gold fever is gold itself. When it is found on the bottom of the sea, it glitters just as brightly as it did the day it went down.

Fisher began looking for the *Atocha* 19 years ago, starting in the Atlantic, off Islamorada in the Middle Keys. Several other treasure hunters were looking there as well, but Mel Fisher was easily the most famous. Here was a former California chicken farmer who had sold everything and come across the country by car with his family to find millions—and did it, by God. He'd hit big off Vero Beach. When he came to Islamorada, he had money and a reputation. He expected—as did many of his rivals—that he would find the *Atocha* almost right away. But he also had the wrong ocean.

Fisher alone might never have discovered his error. His rivals persisted in looking in the wrong ocean for ten years after he had moved to Key West and the Gulf. They relied, as he once had, on the research of a Spanish woman with access to remarkably thorough documents of Spain's empire. According to her reading, the *Atocha* went down off Matecumbe Key, near the present-day town of Islamorada. But Fisher had an American friend, Eugene Lyon, who was working on his Ph.D. in Spain, and he asked him to find any additional archival information on the *Atocha*. Fisher promised payment of $10,000 if Lyon could put him within a quarter of a mile of the wreck.

Lyon's research was deeper and more thorough than the Spanish woman's—and luckier. Lyon, who later wrote a book about the search, found records in Seville that convinced him the *Atocha* had gone down off the Marquesas Keys, 35 miles west of Key West, in the Gulf of Mexico. Fisher accepted his conclusions, and while his competitors continued to search the Atlantic off Matecumbe, he moved his operation to Key West. This was in 1970. So, the first important discovery, one upon which so much of Fisher's later success depended, was Lyon's.

Though Fisher had narrowed the search area to manageable proportions, he still had to search it. And modern treasure hunting is expensive. It takes equipment. Vessels large enough to work in the open seas. Captains to run the boats. Divers to go down off of them. Equipment and food for the divers. Fuel for the boats. Spare parts for machinery used hard in the salt water and salt air. By the end of the search, Fisher had 70 or so salvors on the payroll and an annual payroll of nearly half a million dollars.

Fisher's tactics were more or less standard. A relatively small boat would drag a magnetometer—an instrument designed to indicate the presence of metal—across the water in a methodical pattern. The boat would "mag" an area and record the hits, marking them with buoys and on a radio navigational system that reads out precise coordinates—Loran in the earlier days, recently the more accurate Delnorte system.

Once a hit had been recorded, divers were sent down immediately to conduct a visual "circle search," or to go over the area with hand-held metal detectors. If they didn't find anything on the surface, a larger boat would maneuver into place over the site of the hit, drop several anchors, and lower the mailboxes.

The area Fisher was searching was not only large—after so many years, the treasure had certainly been spread out by the currents over many square miles—but also it had been heavily trafficked over the years. Sound procedure called for a careful investigation of every hit, and there were hundreds. Among other things, the divers found a pickup truck, the remains of other ships that, sadly, had not been carrying treasure, and scores of Navy bombs and depth charges. The site was also adjacent to a training range for aviators out of Key West. Many of the bombs were still live. Some were leaking bubbles. No one was ever sure what that meant.

Fisher had money when he arrived in Key West. But every investigation of every false hit drained more of it away. The two methods open to him to raise more were: to sell the treasure that he had found on the Vero Beach wrecks, or to convince people with money to invest in the search.

Fisher tried both methods, and both got him into trouble. For a long time, in fact, the world's greatest treasure hunter was much better at finding trouble than he was at finding gold.

Fisher's legal problems—which were eventually argued all the way up to the Supreme Court—would have been enough to discourage most people. But he persevered because . . . well, because he was looking for gold. Fisher knew there was gold on the *Atocha* because Eugene Lyon had found the ship's manifest, and that document said the *Atocha* carried at least 256 troy pounds of gold. And that was only the legal cargo. Spain was a corrupt empire, and the passengers and crew of every galleon smuggled their own treasure back to the mother country. The contraband often exceeded the legal cargo.

In 1970, the state of Florida claimed title to the treasure in the area of sea bottom where Fisher believed the *Atocha* had gone down. The state was willing to give him a salvage permit on the condition that any treasure he found would be split: 25 percent to the state (it took first pick, of course, and got the choicest items) and 75 percent for the salvager. The state would hold all treasure until the salvage was completed. The split came before costs were figured. In movie terms, the state got a percentage of the gross, not the net. It was a sweet deal.

Fisher agreed because he didn't think he had a choice. Seventy-five percent of something was better than 100 percent of nothing. And if he found the mother lode, there would be plenty for everyone.

BUT FIRST FISHER found trouble. The Securities and Exchange Commission did not like the way he was enticing investors, and to avoid prosecution, Fisher had to hire an expensive law firm. They finally cut a deal with the government in which Fisher did not exactly plead guilty but promised to quit doing what he'd been doing. The lawyers he hired fixed it so that he couldn't do business anymore, and then they charged him an arm and a leg and threatened to take him to court if he didn't pay. He had no money and no way of getting any. So he hired another lawyer, a local one this time, whom he met in a Key West bar. David Paul Horan was two years out of law school, and his practice in Key West involved, for the most part, representing fishermen and shrimpers who were being harassed by people in state agencies Horan calls "ecoholics." Fisher promised to pay Horan in treasure . . . when he found some. A standard Fisher business tactic. Horan, who had a family, said he could not afford to work on a contingency. But he liked Mel, and probably he was seduced just a little by the complexity of the case and the glitter of the gold. He would cut his fee from $75 per hour to $50, if Fisher would agree to pay on time. Fisher agreed.

"He made the first payment on time," Horan says. "And that was the last one he made on time in 11 years."

Horan's battles in court were long and complex, beginning with his realization that Florida's claim to the wreck site could be successfully disputed, and ending with Horan, seven years later, arguing in front of the U.S. Supreme Court. These were not dry legal contests. At one point the state of Florida actually had Mel Fisher arrested and thrown in jail for attempting to work a wreck site without having a state official on the premises. Another time, Fisher appealed to the chief of the state's antiquities division by saying, "You are acting like you think you're God."

The man replied, "As far as you are concerned, Mel Fisher, I am God."

Even after the state had lost in court, its lawyers refused to return treasure that Fisher had found. Horan had to get a court order, and still the state's principal lawyer threatened defiance. Horan called a federal marshal, who called the judge, who threatened the lawyer and another Florida official with arrest. They turned over the treasure.

"We had to go out and round up some U-Hauls to get it out of Tallahassee and back down to Key West," Horan says. "But it was a sweet moment."

The state's argument was that Mel Fisher and those of his ilk are neither competent to excavate wrecks of archaeological and historic importance nor interested in doing it. What they are interested in is the money, and they will go to any lengths—including dynamite—to get it. Fisher's detractors say that he and his methods are destructive of the environment and the priceless archaeological treasures he salvages. One man, a world-famous marine archaeologist named Peter Throckmorton, has called Fisher the "Attila the Hun of the Seas." On the other hand, according to himself, his lawyer, and his supporters, Fisher is the embodiment of free enterprise and the American way. Through initiative, resourcefulness, and pluck he has accomplished what he set out to do. In a regulated, restricted, state ownership situation, he says, the Atocha would never have been found.

In any case, none of the lawyers or bureaucrats or academics had ever sunk all of their savings into a boat, pleaded with investors for funds, or put on a diving suit and gone to the bottom of the sea to look for lost Spanish gold. And none had risked their lives in storms, had a boat capsize under them, or seen a son and daughter-in-law die during the search.

·  ·  ·

THE STORY IS THIS: In July 1975, a boat Fisher owned was anchored over one of the scattered sites of the *Atocha*. This was a time of excitement in the search. Dirk Fisher, Mel's oldest son, had found bronze cannons, and they had been confirmed as having come from the *Atocha* by Eugene Lyon who had brought microfilmed records back from Spain. This was virtually the first conclusive proof in all the years he had been searching that Fisher was actually above the *Atocha*. Excitement ran high. The people around Fisher expected to find the mother lode any day.

The boat over the site was a Mississippi River tug. Old, ungainly, and in bad repair. Fisher had picked it up cheap when he was, as always, low on money. The boat was one of two. Its sister ship nearly sank on the run across the Gulf from New Orleans. According to Horan, aside from installing mailboxes, Fisher and Treasure Salvors had done little to improve the vessel or make it more seaworthy. It leaked, and its bilges had to be continually pumped. There were no watertight bulkheads. Sometimes a fitting on the marine head would come loose, and water would pour into the bilge.

Early on the morning of July 30, while crew members were attempting to close down a leak, the old tug capsized, turned turtle, and then sank. Dirk Fisher and his wife, Angel, were trapped in their cabin and drowned. A diver also drowned. The other divers survived and were rescued after sunup.

Under English law, Peter Throckmorton suggests, the owner of an unseaworthy vessel might have gone to jail for criminal negligence. "He was the owner of record, and that vessel should not have been at sea," Throckmorton says.

No charges were filed. There are stories, still told around Key West, that the Coast Guard investigator found five pages worth of safety defects in the boat and wanted to prosecute.

But Fisher had lost his son.

These were not the only deaths that resulted from the search. The 11-year-old son of a *National Geographic* photographer was sucked into the prop of one of Fisher's boats while it was blowing a hole with its mailboxes. The boy bled to death.

And then, according to a former business associate of Fisher's, there was a day in 1971 when the captain of the magnetometer boat decided to go off on his own, into deep water. He found something and put divers over. "Fisher rarely had real professionals working for him," the man says, "because he couldn't pay enough, in the first place, and his operation was too slipshod, in the second. I had a man working for me who was a trained commercial diver, a real pipeline walker, former Navy Seal and the whole bit. He was sort of on loan to Fisher, even though I was paying his expenses. We got some stock from Mel so we'd be rich when he found the treasure, right?

"Well, the deal was my man was supposed to do any heavy diving if there was a call for it. Some of Fisher's guys had never even been to school. My diver said that Fisher would put 'em in a wet suit and tanks, throw 'em over a couple of times, and that was it. They were divers.

"Well this day, when two of them went over in deep water, something went wrong below a hundred feet. A regulator. These two guys got in a fight over the good regulator. One of them drowned and the other one got badly bent. He spent 11 hours in the decompression chamber. After that, I got out, and I stayed away from Fisher. That kind of work is dangerous enough if you do it right. He's *never* done it right. I can't believe he put his own son out in a boat like the one that sank on him."

FOR THE NEXT TEN YEARS, Fisher kept searching—and trying to keep his operation going. There were persistent rumors, reported even in Robert Daley's admiring biography of Mel Fisher, that when the funds were low, Fisher kept his investors' spirits up with rigged treasure hunts at the site. And there have, of course, been disgruntled investors left in his wake. One of Fisher's methods is to sell shares in limited partnerships that last for one year. Investors are entitled to a share of any treasure recovered that year. The temptation is there, of course, to leave something on the bottom if it is found near the end of a profitable year and pick it up in the next year.

But most of Fisher's investors are in it for a write-off or a shelter or just for the hell of it. (The greatest flaw in Fisher's free-enterprise armor, according to one thoughtful critic, is that he lives by the tax laws. If treasure hunting were a straight-up investment, nobody would get in.) Fisher's investors and former investors are everywhere. And they will almost always say, "Oh yeah, I put a little money into that thing. Mel's a hell of a fellow. No businessman, but a hell of a fellow."

A general practitioner from Natchez, Mississippi, told me that he met Fisher in Canada at one of those seminars where doctors go to learn how to handle their money. Fisher had a booth set up outside the hall. He was showing film and displaying treasure and selling $10,000 units in that year's limited partnership. His best-selling strategy, according to the G.P., was to drape a gold chain around the neck of some doctor's wife and then tell her that if they invested, and he had the kind of year he thought he might have, she could own a chain just like that one.

The G.P. bought in. He also asked Fisher if there was any chance he could dive the wreck site. Fisher said, "Sure, come on down." The doctor found a silver coin on his very first dive.

At the end of the year, the partners assembled in Key West, and Fisher distributed their shares of that year's find. The doctor's share was some 30 pieces of eight. One gold doubloon. A gold bar. A partially corroded silver wash basin. A "beautiful dagger." And a cannonball. After the division of treasure, and a party in Key West, he returned home. Three different museums appraised his treasure at $60,000. He could have donated it and taken the write-off, but he chose to keep it.

"I didn't invest again. It was just a lark, and I had my fun. I liked Mel enormously. He's just a big, slow, kind fellow. Very keen on treasure, but no businessman. I suppose I'll wish I had invested now, though. What do the papers say this new find is worth? Four hundred million?"

That is indeed what the papers said.

"I'LL TELL YOU, it was really a thrill that day," one of the young divers on the dock in Key West was saying. "I mean, I don't think I'll ever experience anything like it again. It was pretty special the first time I found some gold. That was before we found the mother lode. I was feeling around in the bedrock after the mailboxes had blown the sand away, and I felt something with my hand. I gripped it and started to lift it out of this little crevice, and then I felt how heavy it was, and I said to myself, 'Uh oh. This is it.' I just held onto it and didn't pull it out for a minute. Because, man, I knew it was gold."

"I just can't describe," another one says, "what it is like to go down there and actually find treasure. There just isn't anything like it. Here's this stuff that people have been looking for all these years, that people have died for, man, and you've found it, and you are holding it in your hands. After a while, you start to get a little used to it. 'Oh yeah,' you'll say to yourself, 'silver coins.' Like it is just another day at the office. But then something will shake you out of it. Like the other day we found a chest of gold."

A real chest? Even a journalist can still work up a small spasm of excitement for one of those heavy old chests with the rounded tops, packed full of gold.

"Well, not a chest so much as a crate. You know, like they ship oranges in. The wood was still intact and it held 13 bars of solid gold."

Oh. For some reason it isn't the same when it comes in an orange crate. But no reaction to pirate gold is very rational.

When the divers are asked if they make good money, they laugh happily. "You gotta be kidding. But with Mel, it's a great thing if you are getting your check on time."

Did they get a big raise?

"I dunno. Is five percent big?"

"And we got these T-shirts," one of them says. He models it. The standard Treasure Salvor's 1080 is silk-screened on the chest, with Mel Fisher's profile dominating. Also his war cry: TODAY'S THE DAY.

The word "crew" is printed on the shirt, and the date of the great find is on the sleeve, July 20, 1985 (ten years, to the day, from the date of Dirk Fisher's death).

"Good looking, huh?" the diver modeling the shirt says.

Very sporty.

" 'Course they docked me $4.50 in this week's check."

"But we all got a $200 bonus," another man says.

" 'Course none of us got to talk to the press or Johnny Carson. We're just the guys who found it, you know. We're not as important as the people who answer the phones up at the office."

For a while the divers indulge in a little bitching. Guys at the front talking about how nobody appreciates them and how the guys in head-quarters have it so easy and so on and so forth.

But are any of them disgruntled enough to quit?

"You gotta be kidding, man. Quit? And go to work? The fun's just starting."

FOR FISHER HIMSELF, it is slowly running down. He left Key West the same day Carson did. This time to appear on "Larry King Live." He is due to return early the next morning to accept an award from the Key West Chamber of Commerce. He does not report to the office in the morning, and nobody knows if he has even made it back to Florida soil. If he does not show up at the awards lunch, Bleth McHaley is prepared to accept the award in his behalf.

But he is there at Casa Marina, an improbably big, modern, prosperous, sterile resort hotel on the very southern end of the United States. There were no such resorts on shabby old Key West when Mel Fisher first arrived. If there had been, he may not have been allowed on the island. Fisher looks tired and beyond tired. Closer to exhausted. Wasted.

He sits at a table in the little banquet room, eyes not focusing on much of anything, obviously not hearing anything that is being said around him. While the salads are still being served, he leaves the room and steps outside to find a bar. He orders a rum and Coke, stares across the bar while he drinks it, the eyes behind his glasses not taking in much of anything. He is a big man with big bones. But he also has a big belly, which is not totally concealed by the shirt he wears outside his pants. But you can tell he must have been strong, 20 and 30 years ago, when he was first diving and first looking for treasure, when diving was a new sport and considered high adventure all by itself. When divers did reckless things, such as play with sharks, because diving itself was a reckless thing. Something only fearless and free spirits did seriously.

When Fisher is asked by a reporter if he can answer a few questions, he mumbles, "Better wait till tomorrow, in the morning. I'm wiped out right now. Been traveling. Haven't stopped for a month."

He finishes his drink and goes back inside to accept his award which, it turns out, is one of about two dozen given that day. This is the Venture Award. In the presentation, Fisher is thanked for finding the *Atocha* in the summer, and for "bringing people here to see your gold at a time when they wouldn't otherwise be coming to Key West."

Fisher smiles, shakes a hand, has his picture taken, and sits back down. The *National Geographic* people pack up their cameras. "Really knocked themselves out, didn't they?" one of the sound men says.

The next morning, Fisher is in the office catching up on calls and correspondence, talking with some investors. Another photographer is pestering him for a picture. He puts her off very gently and with genuine regret. It is plain he hates the office, has never mastered it or the art of delegating. He's got 40 guys out guarding the site of the wreck, but he spends 15 minutes at the Xerox machine, running off his own copies. Every time he passes the photographer, he smiles and says, "Just a few more minutes and I'll be with you."

Around noon, he excuses himself to shave. Then when he reappears, he asks the photographer if maybe it wouldn't be better to have him with a gold chain around his neck. She says yes, it probably would be.

He steps into his museum, where the tourists mingle, admiring the things he has recovered, takes a gold chain from one of the exhibits, and reappears.

He drives his new Cadillac down to the dock, which is about 500 yards away. Two men who have also been waiting for him all morning come along for the ride. They are agents but not the kind Fisher is accustomed to dealing with. These are talent agents from New York. They name their agency. "We represent people like Arnold Palmer," one of them says. "Well, I guess I need an agent," Fisher says, "even though up to now, I've been getting along pretty well without one. I didn't have an agent when I got on the Carson show."

The men from New York nod.

Fisher is a cooperative, helpful subject, and the photographer thanks him. "Thank you," he says in a courtly way.

On the way back to the office, another visitor asks what he'll do next. "I've got the records," Fisher says, "of every treasure ship that ever went down along this coast."

So he'll go looking for another one?

"Yeah, sure. We're just getting started. There's treasure all up and down this coast."

So it is his life. When you've looked for something long enough, the fear is that you will find it, not that you won't. And gold does that to people. The Indians made a culture of extracting it from the ground, and the Spaniards based an empire on plundering it from them. It was, of course, one of the briefest and most inconsequential empires in all of history. England was probably lucky to settle where there was no gold. The real curse of El Dorado is that it makes everything else seem unimportant. Eugene Lyon broke new ground in the archives. David Paul Horan broke new ground in the law. And Mel Fisher, the greatest treasure hunter of them all, found the gold . . . and went on the Carson show.

*November 1985*

# HIGH PRIEST
## OF THE LOW-FLOW
## SHOWER HEADS

*From the hills of Colorado, energy guru Amory Lovins can hear America conserving. Efficiency in excelsis!*

● ▲ ■

**CHIP BROWN**

If character can't be quantified, maybe evangelical passion can. Amory Lovins traveled more than 200,000 miles last year, spreading the gospel of energy efficiency. His Honda CRX gets 60 miles to the gallon in the mountain air of Colorado; it's white, which saves about one-fourth of the cooling load on the air-conditioner. His third-generation Hewlett-Packard 15 C calculator rides in his shirt pocket like a sidekick, always ready to discombobulate foes with a fusillade of brilliance. Even friends sometimes find the heavy technical flow (of watts and joules and units of primary energy consumed per dollar of GNP) a little overwhelming.

"Talking to Amory is like trying to drink water from a fire hose," says his wife, Hunter, who serves as executive director of the Rocky Mountain Institute, the nonprofit educational and research foundation they started in 1982; she's also a member of the Basalt Volunteer Fire Department and a veteran of the Colorado rodeo circuit, and on Tuesdays she moonlights as a bouncer at a cowboy bar. The Lovinses' house in Snowmass, at 7,100 feet, also serves as RMI headquarters and as a showroom of energy-saving technologies. It is one of the most innovative and efficient lairs in America by a factor of—well, what could make the point better than the banana tree growing under the argon-filled R-5 Heat Mirror windows in the greenhouse? Lovins claims the world's altitude record for passive-solar bananas and a household electric bill of $5 a month. More than 30,000 people have stopped by to see the low-flow shower heads (which use 1.5 gallons per minute, compared with the usual four to seven), and the Swedish Ifö toilet (which flushes with three liters of water instead of 20). The two iguanas in the bougainvillea, Iggy and Juana, are no more energy efficient than standard pet-store models, but they make an arresting sight, linking the Triassic Period of the dinosaurs with the Soft Path future of superefficient toilets.

Even at 27 pages Lovins's resume doesn't tell the whole story. He composed his first piano music when he was seven, received a patent on nuclear magnetic resonance technology when he was 17, and did work reported in the *Journal of Chemical Physics* (his first publication) long before he could vote. He has clients and contacts and friends in more than 30 countries. He's met with eight heads of state. He never graduated from college but has six honorary degrees. He can get around in a dozen languages. He earns $7,500 per speech; if the cause is congenial, he'll lecture for expenses, mixing esoteric technical terms with vivid analogies: Aircraft carriers get 17 feet per gallon, and the rain in the eastern United States can be as acidic as tomato juice. He's universally credited with the line that heating your house with electricity is like cutting butter with a chainsaw, but he didn't say it first, and every time he runs into Doug Kelbaugh, a professor at the University of Washington, he apologizes. Lovins did make what may have been the sharpest op-ed point of the Gulf War, succinctly asking, "Are we putting our kids in 0.56-mile-per-gallon tanks because we didn't put them in 32-mile-per-gallon cars?"

In 20 years of number-crunching Lovins admits to making only a handful of mistakes—three, actually. The worst was on the day he testified on behalf of some clients at a hearing in Ontario, when he was wrong by a factor of 8,766. He was embarrassed, quickly traced the genesis of the boo-boo, and waived his fee. His prescience, debating skills, powers of synthesis, vast network of contacts, catholic curiosity, and ability to slice across intellectual boundaries are unrivaled in the energy field. He is a walking *Whole Earth Catalog* of technical resources, but he eats meat, reveres market forces, and sometimes wonders if he's a Republican. "If you had to list the top ten energy experts in the world," says his friend and fellow energy analyst Charles Komanoff, "Amory would have the first five spots."

In many ways the energy debate in America can be divided into two periods: Before Lovins and After Lovins. The moment of demarcation came 15 years ago when, at the age of 29, Lovins published an article in *Foreign Affairs* that changed the world.

"GOOD MORNING, Merry Sunshine," says Amory Lovins, ambling into the kitchen on this, a faultless Colorado morning in July, the third morning we've met to talk. (It's best to catch him early before he pumps up the

pressure in his fire hose with a mug of jasmine tea.) In college he was a
whey-faced, 119-pound rail; now, at 43, he has bulked out to a portly
172. A black mustache offsets the hair that has vanished up top. He has
warm, brown eyes behind 20/2,000 glasses. His manner in middle age
seems almost cherubic, with no trace of what his critics used to call a
haughty air. He always carries a whistle, a knife, and a piece of string
(he once invented a new knot, a cousin of the Eskimo spear-lashing).

Proselytizing, teaching, launching forays against the old thinking, Lovins
is still in the vanguard of the energy debate, leading the revolution from
the hills. He does not have all the answers, much less pride of place
among policymakers. (The Bush administration's new energy plan, he
says, is "the most cretinous we've had in a long time.") But today many
of his former adversaries in the utility industry provide his bread and
butter in the form of consulting work, and with the calculator that sleeps
lightly in his right shirt pocket he is still defining and shaping the frontiers
of energy policy.

"Have you had your back cracked?" he asks.

Suddenly he is hoisting me onto his back, supporting the full burden
of my body on his faulty knees. Lovins has always been helpful to journalists, but this seems beyond the call.

As he's pretty much been dreaming up ideas, estimating the potential
of technical "fixes," and researching and writing letters, reports, and
books for 12 to 18 hours a day, seven days a week, for the last 20 years,
it's no exaggeration to say that his life is his work. He's gone to great
length to marry the two, in fact. Lovins's morning commute is as energy-
efficient as they come. He lives in the west wing of the 4,000-square-
foot, scalloped-stone "bioshelter" he and Hunter built for half a million
dollars with the help of a hundred volunteers. The Rocky Mountain
Institute, where floor-to-ceiling bookshelves hold one of the world's most
comprehensive energy libraries, is lodged in the east wing. The north
wall of the building is backed with earth, and the sun-facing south side
commands a handsome prospect of pasture, range, and mountains up the
valley of Snowmass Creek Road. A large greenhouse under a canted glass
roof serves as the building's solar furnace. The house is so quiet that
Lovins designed a waterfall to provide a wash of white noise and to help
irrigate the indoor garden. A Japanese waterfall tuner adjusted the stones
in order to change the splash frequency from the range of beta waves to
the more restful frequency of alpha waves.

After the impromptu chiropractic adjustment, my back feels better. Lovins brews his morning tea. He's recovered from the injury he suffered in New York last month when he tore a shoulder ligament. His speech on efficient water use before a gathering of Hudson River activists at the American Museum of Natural History was but one stop on a typical multicity tour. As usual, he was hauling some 45 pounds of low-flow shower heads, compact fluorescent light bulbs, and recent publications in a shoulder bag. Torn ligaments are one of the occupational hazards of the crusade.

"Have you seen our new paper on electrical efficiency in *Scientific American?*" he asked. "And here's one from *Fine Homebuilding* on energy-efficient technologies for the home. Here's one on abating air pollution at negative cost with energy efficiency. This one's on the negawatt revolution, and this one's on making markets in resource efficiency. It's very interesting now: Utilities are realizing they can treat negawatts, or electricity they save and don't have to make, as a commodity, like copper or pork bellies, and trade them with other utilities."

He handed me a few more papers. If he'd thrown in one of his Heat Mirror glazing samples, one of *my* ligaments would have torn. By now he was surrounded by admirers, acquaintances, and people with questions about architectural fee reform, fluorescent dimmers, and the optimal pitch of sewer pipes. He fielded them all. When the crowd dispersed, Lovins whipped out a wallet photo and asked, "Have you seen my daughter?" It was a picture of a dog—Nanuq, his beloved white bull terrier.

Now Nanuq is snoozing by the baby grand piano. Visitors are constantly comparing her to Spuds MacKenzie, which seems to pain Lovins a little. He has calculated that when Nanuq runs around she emits enough radiant heat energy to raise the indoor temperature by a fraction of a degree. Sometimes he uses her to get a reading on a stranger. My first day at the house, he'd plunked "the beastoid" on my lap and given me the "beastoid compatibility test." Nanuq entertained my pleasantries with mild disdain before allowing herself to be ceremoniously returned to the floor.

There are in Lovins vestiges of the gifted but socially awkward adolescent, eager for contact but not sure of what behavior is appropriate. He's always giving his staff spur-of-the-moment shoulder rubs, but most everyone who knows him says he is incapable of small talk. A few nights earlier we'd attended a barbecue thrown by the Aspen Institute. It was after a seminar on energy policy, and we were standing in a clearing of tall spruces with Roger Sant, a former Ford administration official and the first person in the history of the U.S. government to head an energy conservation department. James Schlesinger wandered over. He'd been secretary of energy under Carter when Carter was quoting Lovins's work; Carter had arranged for Schlesinger and Lovins to meet. If they'd ever had a common wavelength, it wasn't evident, because a certain tension seized the conversation. Somehow the awkward chitchat lighted on the subject of hell, and Lovins piped up: "I once calculated a theory showing the thermodynamic properties of Dante's Inferno. If hell's entropy is decreasing and you assume that hell is infinitely hot and stays that way, then there are between hell and us a number of discontinuities with the properties that Dante ascribed to the intermediate rings."

There was a long pause. Everyone seemed at a loss for words. Except Schlesinger. He eyed Lovins with a mixture of skepticism and amusement and asked, "Has this work been published?"

"No," said Lovins. "Where would you suggest?"

"*Modern Language Quarterly*," said Schlesinger.

SINCE THE OIL EMBARGO of 1973, American energy policy has been gripped by the politics of scarcity. We have been told, often in apocalyptic tones, that the country has an energy problem. We're running out of energy. Demand is outstripping supply. We're going to freeze in the dark.

The solution proposed time and time again has been to increase the supply. For years it made sense. Primary energy consumption rose in lockstep with the country's gross national product; it got to be an article of faith that economic vitality depended on increased energy supply. Demand for primary sources, such as oil and coal, and for more highly-processed forms of energy, such as electricity, had to be met, however great.

Take the example of electricity, which now accounts for about 36 percent of fuel burned in the United States. In the 1950s and 1960s it had been impossible to overestimate future demand, because electricity obeyed the Field of Dreams phenomenon: If you built a power plant, people would come to use it—irrigators, aluminum companies, airplane manufacturers. And thanks to the economics of scale, every time a new plant came on line the cost of electricity went down. Then about 1970 the energy order was jolted by a series of economic, political, and technical shocks. Plans to expand supply ran headlong into new environmental laws, rising interest rates, technical complications, the inflating cost of materials and labor. Increasing supply now meant increasing the price the customer paid; when the cost of a commodity went up, common sense made people look for ways to use less. Suddenly there were terrible penalties for overestimating demand: canceled plants, irate stockholders, even bankruptcy.

But old supply-side habits were deeply ingrained, and many people in government and industry were slow to perceive the changed landscape. Believing that energy use would double in the next 20 years—that it had to double lest our standard of living collapse—forecasters sketched out massive supply expansions. Bechtel, the engineering and construction giant, estimated in 1976 that the country would need 2,000 nuclear plants by the year 2000.

The prospect of a nuke in every county, of vast tracts of wilderness opened for oil drilling and coal mining, of much of the nation's capital tied up in a building program, was staggering. Could we afford to pour more money into what was already the most capital-intensive industry in the country? Did it make sense to use tax money to subsidize schemes like the Synfuels Corporation and the breeder reactor? Already some prudent utilities were canceling nuclear projects as too expensive. (By 1984 they would have lost more than $20 billion on abandoned nuclear plants alone.) Moreover, could we keep excluding from the cost of energy the damage we were causing to the environment—the salmon that died before the Columbia River dams, the growing danger of acid rain and global warming gasses?

Enter Amory Lovins. He was 28 years old and working as the British representative for Friends of the Earth, an environmental group started by David Brower. From his base in London, Lovins had been thinking about energy for five years; FOE had already published several of his books including *World Energy Strategies* and *Non-nuclear Futures*.

Drawing on the Ford Foundation's 1973 Zero Energy Growth scenario and the American Physical Society's thermodynamic end-use efficiency studies a year later, Lovins began questioning the assumptions of the supply doctrine. Would our standard of living really collapse if we used less energy? One study he found showed that Danes used more energy per capita for heating and cooking in 1500 than they did 400 years later. Had the Danes just regained the standard of living they'd enjoyed in the

Middle Ages? Behind the numbers, concluded Lovins, lay the story of a technological shift from peat and wood to coal burned in more efficient stoves, and then to oil and electricity. The connection between energy supply and economic vitality was a fallacy: It didn't say anything about how the energy was used.

What did people want with energy, anyway? Lovins wondered. Was it barrels of oil and watts of electricity, or the services energy could provide: cold beer, hot showers, warm houses, light by which to scrutinize rising electric bills? You might say a fluorescent light bulb went off in his head. When he analyzed energy from the vantage of end use, the country didn't have an energy-supply problem, it had a badly-insulated-house problem. It had a leaky-window problem. It had an inefficiently-designed-refrigerator problem. America was using more energy than any other country in the world, but it was also wasting more energy than any country in the world. Far from preserving the country's economic future, Lovins was convinced that the program and ideology of the supply-side scenarios might well jeopardize it.

In the spring of 1975 Lovins unholstered his calculator, a large, primitive forerunner of the one he has today. He added up the energy lost converting primary fuel to electricity (three units of fuel for every one unit of electricity) and the high costs and transmission losses incurred getting the power from the plants to faraway consumers (then 69 cents of every dollar on consumers' electric bills). He calculated the energy that wouldn't be needed if end users were more efficient. He sketched two curves: One showed energy use climbing drastically as the millenium approached. The other showed it rising as gently as an English moor and then sloping back. When America's energy "problem" was examined from the perspective of how energy was being used—from the demand side, not the supply side—a cheaper and less risky solution seemed to be staring him in the face. And so the Soft Path emerged.

THE HIGH PRIEST of energy efficiency came on line in November 1947, the second child of Gerald and Miriam Lovins. Ukrainian forebears on both sides of Lovins's family had come to America with the massive wave of Eastern European immigrants between 1889 and 1905. Gerald's father arrived alone at age 16, eventually settling in Denver, where he opened a pharmacy. Miriam's Ukrainian parents were first cousins. ("That's supposed to result in imbeciles," she laughs.)

Miriam was a social service administrator, Gerald an engineer who custom-designed and built scientific instruments. They were in their forties when Amory and Julie (now a computer linguist in California) were born. Husband and wife ran Lovins Engineering Company from the basement of a small house in Silver Spring, Maryland, a suburb of Washington, D.C.

Amory's career as a contrarian began shortly after birth. He had severe food allergies. Desperate to find something he could digest, if only to cut down on diapers, his parents finally hit upon a concoction of rice run through the blender. Gerald used a hot nail to widen the hole in the nipple of his son's bottle.

It didn't take long for them to recognize his unusual aptitude. He hardly uttered a word until he was 20 months old, and then out came complete and grammatically correct sentences. "I didn't need to talk. Everybody did everything for me," he explained to his parents. By the time he was three he'd picked up the multiplication tables. By four and a half he was reading on his own from his parents' library. "He became a speed reader," says his father. "He still amazes me on that score." He had taken up the piano at three, and later composed his Opus 1 on the Sohmer upright in the living room: Air in A Minor, 1:15, owed a heavy debt to Purcell, but Amory was only seven. As a teenager he gave children's recitals, including one with a cartoonist who sketched as Amory played from his suite *Morceaux de la Jeunesse,* which featured such numbers as "The Splash-Happy Seal," "The Dainty Hippo," and "General Nuisance March."

Lovins can trace some of his feeling for the land to the maple woods that he slipped through each morning on his way to East Silver Spring Elementary. He skipped second grade, then fifth. Lovins, with his mania for numbers, says his IQ was measured between 180 and 220, but he recalls that the tests "weren't very interesting."

All through early childhood he was besieged by colds and croup; he spent long stretches at home, reading by himself in his room, which he had decorated with portraits of American Indians. Pneumonia nearly killed him at age three and again at eight. It wasn't until he was diagnosed and treated for a gamma globulin deficiency at age ten that he began to gain strength. He suffered in his teens from chronic synovitis; his joints, especially his knees and shoulders, were inflamed, and he was often in considerable pain when he practiced the piano or burned up the keys on the typewriter.

The family moved north in 1955, settling in Upper Montclair, New

Jersey, and a few years later in Amherst, Massachusetts. "I think his interest in physics and in science generally started when we were in Montclair," says Gerald Lovins. "One day when he was around eight he presented me with a diagram of a floor plan of a submarine he'd cooked up, naming all the parts and functions. Then he started designing shaped charges of explosives."

His talents were nudged in a more constructive direction by the table talk in Amherst. "I had joined the League of Women Voters," remembers Miriam. "I'd come home and tell the family about the meetings at dinner. Amory was always interested that there were people out there changing conditions that weren't good for the community. I think he got the idea that you don't just sit still and take it, you do something about it."

At Amherst High he started designing and building nuclear magnetic resonance machines. He also took physics courses at Amherst College. His protected, isolated childhood formed a social style he would deprecate years later as that of a "techno-twit." Some of the lower life forms gave him the business, shoving him down and stealing his briefcase. The abuse ended when Amory, installed as manager of the track team, was befriended by Peter Johnson, a star hurdler who still holds a record at Amherst High.

"Mentally high school was superfluous," recalls Johnson, who now works as a potter and an artist in Whitehall, Michigan. "He went for the socialization. He was a 98-pound weakling, but underneath he had a big desire to see what youth was like."

It was Johnson who took Lovins camping in the Holyoke Range and then to Camp Winona, in Bridgton, Maine, where Lovins spent the first of 15 summers hiking and leading trips. He had overcome some of his physical handicaps with a regimen of special exercises designed to strengthen his joints.

At 16, a National Merit and Presidential scholar, he went off to Harvard. He hustled lunch money playing pool and purging circuit noise from nuclear magnetic resonance machines. The synovitis in his knees kept him out of Harvard his second year; when he returned he took graduate courses and some law. Harvard wanted him to declare a major. He got a one-page application to Oxford, filled it out, and was admitted.

After two years at Magdalen College and aiming toward a doctorate in biophysics, he applied for a scholarship. He was called before a roomful of stone-faced dons in black robes who, he was surprised to discover, were considering him for a post on the faculty of Merton College. He was elected to the plum office of junior research fellow, though dons were supposed to have at least a master's degree and Lovins didn't even have a bachelor's. A special gown with shortened tassels was designed for the degreeless new don, who was, at 21, the youngest faculty member in 400 years.

The good thing about the post was that he had few duties other than reciting grace in medieval Latin when the "senior classical postmaster" was absent. He was free to go tramping in the mountains of Wales, which he had discovered not long after moving to England. His weak knees got stronger, and in those stone climbing huts, those misty cwms, those wind-scoured summits of Yr Wyddfa and Tryfan and Pen-Llythrig-y-Wrach, he met a new side of himself, an energy that had first stirred in the woods of Silver Spring. A muse descended: "These torn stones on which we stand," he wrote, "this blinding fire and the snow on which it casts our shadows high and thin, this freezing air that sears our throats—of these things we are made, and in the grace of an instant and a place we dissolve into them again, single in exaltation. There is no we and no time, nothing but the blazing silent earth. There are no words."

Learning of a mining company's bid to open a copper mine in Snowdonia National Park, Lovins's life swerved from academia. He had taken many pictures of the wild lands in jeopardy. Eventually they found their way to David Brower at Friends of the Earth, who commissioned Lovins's first book, *Eryri,* a collection of photographs and rapturous essays, and a strong indictment of those who would despoil the Welsh wildlands. The copper company tried unsuccessfully to prevent the book from being published and eventually abandoned its efforts to develop the mine.

Brower became Lovins's mentor. After two years at Merton College Lovins had developed a passion for energy policy but was unable to do a doctorate because no such field existed. He was ready to move on. Brower was convinced that Amory and his calculator could be of immense help to the cause. Consider what he proposed to do for the Sierra cup: Lovins sketched some 11 improvements to that classic implement of 1970s backpacking, including a new rim that wouldn't collect dirt, a knurled bottom to keep the cup from sliding, scribe marks on the inside for measuring liquids, and a handle that could be readily grasped in mittens. Brower persuaded Lovins to put aside his education and take up a new position representing Friends of the Earth in Britain.

ONE OF THE MOST frequently reprinted articles ever published in *Foreign Affairs,* that distinguished organ of policy wallahs, is "Energy Strategy: The Road Not Taken?" The paper went through 12 drafts; with a hurricane threatening to knock out power lines in Maine, Lovins stood in a phone booth near Camp Winona for 14 hours, combing galleys.

He made many points, but the main one was that the country had to decide which of two routes it would travel into the future. We could continue down the Hard Path or take a road less traveled. The Hard Path relied on a technical elite to operate huge, centralized power stations; the Hard Path was expensive, rigid, and bureaucratic, and it separated the benefits of power from the costs. (New Englanders, for example, enjoy the benefits of Hydro-Québec; the Cree Indians lose their hunting grounds.) Driven to consume more and more nonrenewable resources, we would be obliged to raid the earth's wild places, despoil the air and water.

Or we could take what Lovins called the Soft Path toward a system of energy that would rely on renewable resources like sun and wind and on the more efficient use of energy already available. Soft Path technologies were "flexible, resilient, sustainable, and benign," and they enhanced democratic values because energy decisions were closer to the people using the energy. Lovins did not foresee the Soft Path immediately solving the energy problem, only keeping it from getting worse. He didn't call for throwing away the power plants already built or for a halt to the burning of fossil fuels. Rather, he envisioned a 50-year transition to a new energy system.

There was little reaction in the first weeks after the *Foreign Affairs* article came out, but a debate began to build as it made its way around the energy community.

"I thought it might make a stir, but I had no idea how much," Lovins recalls. And indeed, were it not for some three dozen critiques, ranging from reasoned rebuttals to ad hominem denunciations, the article might have faded into oblivion. Instead Lovins rode to fame on the outrage of his critics.

"Reckless," they called him. "Myopic." "Irresponsible." Nuclear advocates were beside themselves about Lovins's nonnuclear scenario. The

Soft Path was "a Shangri-la," said General Electric executive Bertram Wolfe. Lovins's ideas were "flaccid and flatulent," said Charles Yulish, a former employee of the Atomic Energy Commission and a public relations consultant for the nuclear industry who gathered ten critiques of the article into a book. The most melodramatic denunciation came from University of Arizona professors Aden and Marjorie Meinel: "Should this siren philosophy be heard and believed, we can perceive the onset of a new dark age."

Lovins was not easily intimidated. Two months after the article appeared, he testified before a congressional committee. What had proved especially controversial was his argument that the two paths were mutually exclusive. He explained to the committee: "In principle nuclear power stations and solar collectors can coexist. But soft and hard paths are culturally incompatible: Each path entails a certain evolution of social values and perceptions that makes the other kind of world harder to imagine. . . . Every dollar, every bit of sweat and technical talent, every barrel of irreplaceable oil, every year that we devote to the very demanding high technologies is a resource that we cannot use to pursue the elements of a soft path urgently enough to make them work together properly."

Over the next two years Lovins parried every critical thrust—time he considers wasted today. Where questions were raised about his numbers, Lovins directed critics to the technical companion paper he presented to the Oak Ridge National Laboratory. After extensive correspondence, Hans Bethe, the Nobel laureate, conceded that a disputed calculation was in fact sound: "Thank you very much for your detailed discussion of seasonal storage with solar heating. I am very much surprised that it works. The figures seemed based on solid statistics."

Where the social implications of his scenario were doubted, Lovins reminded commentators that he had simply launched an experiment as a scientist, exploring what was possible from existing data. He claimed he had not tried to make his numbers fit his values, but rather articulated values only upon obtaining numerical results—results that were, as it turned out, rather congenial.

Where his work had been met with ad hominem attacks, he professed a policy of taking the high road, "lest I approach here the fatuity of the material to which I am responding." Along with his daunting calculator, he had a polemicist's knack for finding ever more subtle ways of patronizing opponents, a cheeky Oxford wit, and an elegant and lucid style. He could be neither outcalculated nor outargued. "This baby-faced expatriate," said *Newsweek* in 1977, "has become one of the world's most influential energy thinkers."

Lovins had struck at a belief system, and the blow was felt at many levels. No less an authority than Margaret Mead later suggested that some of the hostility toward the concept of a Soft Path came from the unmanly overtones of the phrase. Was Lovins not, in essence, urging a phallocentric generation of men who had energized great metropolises with turbines and transmission towers to give up their life's mission and devote themselves to the humble task of retrofitting homes with better insulation and more efficient light bulbs? It was the equivalent of trying to recast John Wayne as a hostage negotiator from the U.N.

TIME FOR MORE TEA. In what seems seconds, the water comes to a boil. Water boils fast at altitude but here in the "bioshelter" it's being whizzed along by an English copper kettle with a heavy coil rim that traps hot gases. Most of the heat is put to work and does not escape up the side. (The fuel saving has been calculated, of course.) After a while in Lovins's company you begin to see waste and inefficiency everywhere; an ordinary house peppered with spendthrift incandescent bulbs is positively offensive.

The night before, he had noticed that his wife had attached a Basalt Volunteer Fire Department tag to the bumper of his Honda—or "Pongomobile" as he calls it, in honor of his beloved orangutans. (Orangutan portraits cover the walls of his bedroom.) The little plate was sticking up into the slipstream. He had calculated the increase on the car's drag coefficient and the waste chafed on his nerves.

Hunter walks in. She works at the house and runs the institute with Amory, but she now has her own apartment down the valley. They were introduced at the Los Angeles airport by the chief economist of Arco. She was a lawyer, a political scientist, an active environmentalist, and an admirer of his work. They were married in September 1979 in an aspen grove in the mountains around Crestone, Colorado: an Episcopal–Zen– Ute Indian ceremony. Amory wore an Indian headdress. Paul Winter played the soprano sax. Are the marital strains that have produced separate living arrangements amenable to a technical fix? Amory is happy to see his wife, and strokes her hand while they talk. Since 1978, they have been inseparable professional partners, coauthoring books and articles, appearing together on "60 Minutes" and in a film about the Soft Path. Hunter is technically Amory's boss.

Hunter says she has to buy a washing machine. "Get a front loader," he says. "It uses half the water and half the energy."

"I don't want a front loader," Hunter says. "You have to bend over to put your damn clothes in."

"You just put the clothes in," he says. (Later he would find that a horizontal-axis top-loader is more efficient and would amend his position.)

RMI now has a $1.4 million budget and employs 39 people. With its goal of fostering the efficient and sustainable use of resources, the institute does policy research in five areas: energy, water, agriculture, security, and economic renewal. The budget comes from consulting work, grants, contributions, and the sale of publications. Many of the so-called RMItes are the sort of bright idealists who might have gone into public-interest work in Washington but were lured to Colorado by the mountain setting and the communal spirit of the nonprofit enterprise. The RMI community also includes a stable of nine horses, two peacocks, three beef calves named Barbeque, Brunch, and Dinner, and Nanuq's sometime adversary Bandit, who is part coyote and who enjoys bathing in the alpha waterfall. Lovins presides over the research staff with an air of benevolent distraction; the best way to get some time alone with him is to take him for a walk—there's a sign-up sheet on a bulletin board. The workplace atmosphere is casual, but the fax machines are always croaking and the in-boxes are stuffed. Several of Lovins's former employees have spun off businesses from their work at RMI; the growing professionalism of the institute is reflected not just in rising budgets but in new marketing efforts. RMI recently hired a publicist, and some of the new brochures feature corporate-report-style logos and velum flyleaves—true evolutionary milestones for what began as a kind of countercultural think tank. Sometimes on Thursday afternoons there's a staff meeting to discuss broad topics such as "Efficiency for What?" People in jeans circle up over trays of cookies and fruit; strawberry hulls are pitched directly into the garden; conversation may halt if Iggy or Juana makes a stir in the bougainvillea.

"Hey, Hunter?" says Amory as she heads for her office. "You know that little fire department plate on the front bumper of the Pongomobile?"

"Yeah."

"We'll have to move it. It's right in the slipstream. I figure it's probably costing us upwards of a mile per gallon."

"Horrors," she says.

TO THE DISTRESS of Amory Lovins, news of the efficiency revolution has not reached Washington, where the political power and PAC money of the supply side are well entrenched. Certainly some of the reluctance to brandish the banner of efficiency comes from the connotation of scarcity and doing-without that energy conservation acquired when President Carter lowered the White House thermostat and donned his infamous cardigan.

President Reagan understood conservation to mean being hotter in summer and colder in winter. In 1980 the Solar Energy Research Institute made the first comprehensive government study of what the country could save with an approach that maximized renewable energy sources and energy efficiency. The draft was finished as Reagan was assuming power, and one of the first acts of his new regime was to try to shut down the study and suppress the results. Staff members stayed all night photocopying the draft and mailing it out before the order could be effected.

"The potential for energy savings was so huge that we had one scenario in which the U.S. could join OPEC," recalls Karl Gawell, former project director for the SERI study and now an energy aide for Senator Paul Wellstone (D-Minnesota).

To Lovins, efficiency never entailed life-style compromises. Efficiency meant doing more with less. Efficiency meant saving money, and it should have appealed to free-market Republicans, except that where energy was concerned, free-market Republicans often behaved, in his words, like "corporate socialists."

It's true that federal policymakers in the Bush administration continue to act as if no alternative exists for eliminating the country's dependence on foreign oil—and the need for further military adventures in the Middle East—but to march full speed down the Hard Path beating a 55-gallon supply-side drum. The Bush energy blueprint is embodied in The National Energy Security Act, which was voted out of the Senate Energy Committee in July. Sponsored by Senators Bennett Johnston (D-Louisiana) and Malcolm Wallop (R-Wyoming), the bill would launch another round of nuclear-power subsidies (now called "incentives"), authorizing "an advanced nuclear reactor," and forgiving the industry's $10 billion debt for uranium-enrichment services. It would open the Arctic National Wildlife Refuge, resume oil exploration and development on the outer continental shelf, weaken the Clean Air Act, and exempt new power plants from emission-control standards.

"We're doing as badly in oil efficiency as we are doing well in electricity," says Lovins. "Technical fixes alone could cut U.S. oil consumption by 80 percent. Each barrel saved would cost you only a few dollars, so it's cheaper to save oil than drill for more, let alone do anything with it if you find some."

"If you want to find the innovation and achievement in efficiency, Washington is the last place to look," says Ralph Cavanagh, energy program director for the Natural Resources Defense Council. "You have to look at state regulatory agencies and the utilities."

Indeed, far from the Beltway, the heresies of the Soft Path are rapidly becoming the by-words of conventional wisdom. Thanks to costly supply-side fiascoes, many utilities have discovered that it is cheaper to save energy than to produce it. Between 1981 and 1987, utilities in the Pacific Northwest spent more than $900 million to buy more energy through efficiency measures. What is called end-use/least-cost planning is now in place or under development in 43 states. That means that before new plants are built, lawyers and experts argue before public utility commissions over the cheapest way to provide energy services. Environmental costs are being factored into the price of power; some states have severed utility profits from sales, removing a major barrier to saving electricity. At least eight states require projects that will add to the supply of electricity to compete in an open auction against programs designed to save power by improving customers' efficiency. About 60 utilities offer rebates to encourage the buying and selling of energy-efficient appliances. Electrical efficiency has become a $4 billion-a-year business.

California, as usual, is leading the way. Pacific Gas & Electric, the nation's largest private utility, plans to meet at least 75 percent of its needs in the nineties with efficiency programs to hold down demand; the other 25 percent will come from renewables. By last year the amount of electricity consumed per dollar of California's gross product had decreased 20 percent, flying in the face of the supply-side assumption that economic growth and electricity use rise in lockstep. Utilities in the Northwest, New York, New England, and Wisconsin are finding the equivalent of new power plants in caulk guns and fluorescent bulbs. In California alone, increased efficiency has already saved $23 billion. (Lovins estimates the United States has spent more than $270 billion on unneeded generating capacity.) Since 1979 the United States has gotten seven times as much energy from saving energy as from increasing energy supply. No coal or nuclear plants are under construction in the western United States. "The future has gone over to the mammals," says Ralph Cavanagh. "The dinosaurs no longer roam the earth."

"The energy problem is conceptually solved, but about 50 years of details remain," says Lovins. "The important elements of the transition are already firmly and irreversibly embedded in the market. Now within the industry, future demand is not fate, but choice. What we had before was a Stalinist planning system where a small group of people would decide how much energy we needed and ram it down our throats whether we needed it or not. The battle's been won in all except a handful of places."

Lovins was once a prophet without honor—utility executives would leave the room when he showed up, and Hans Bethe refused to shake his hand. More recently some of his old adversaries have had second thoughts, and Lovins now has the satisfaction of seeing many facets of energy use unfold according to his numbers. His 1972 estimate of total energy consumption in the year 2000 was, a mere six years later, the industry estimate put forth by Ralph Lapp, one of his staunchest critics.

"I've been reevaluating Amory Lovins," says Charles Yulish. "I think he was very prophetic in many ways and deserves to be revisited. I would not retract 'flaccid and flatulent,' but I should have added that in spite of what he is and the way he says it, there is an irresistible quality to the simpleness of his ideas that ought to be tried."

"We're very close to Amory on the technical potential of efficiency," says Tom Morran of the Edison Electric Institute. "Our disagreement is over the market potential. In our judgment you're still going to have to build a power plant or two."

Lovins himself has grown up some, too. No longer inclined to do the General Nuisance March, he tries to practice what he calls aikido politics, which means that you don't fight with an opponent, you dance with a partner. It's not enough to be right; Lovins wants to get along, to help translate theory into practice. So he spends his days dreaming up ways for utilities to finance investments in efficiency, ways to reform regulations to reward efficient energy use. Perhaps the best tribute both to the wisdom of what was once his heresy and his abiding commitment to the efficiency crusade is RMI's Competitek service—exhaustively researched technical encyclopedias of the latest in energy-efficient lights, motors, air conditioners, heaters, appliances, and office equipment. The series costs $9,000 a throw. And among its many subscribers are more than 70 utilities.

WE SHOULD ALL LIVE as elegantly as Amory Lovins, adding the minimum of noxious gases to the air, treading lightly and economically on the land. Lovins has created a little paradise of his own in which theory and practice are one. Home fits with work as yin with yang. For lunch someone may bring down a pot of beans cooked for free in the solar oven on the roof. Sometimes at night when the waterfall is turned off and the greenhouse glass is full of stars, the proprietor may roam about with gadgets that tell him where heat is leaking, where power is being wasted. To the extent it's possible, Lovins has dominion over his world. Even pests in the garden are controlled by natural insect predators that he has carefully introduced.

A life as elegant as his is bound to acquire an aura of myth, but the truth is that nothing is as exact as a page of numbers. It turns out winters in utopia can be chilly. The energy-efficient appliances extolled in RMI's visitors' guide do not include the two 600-watt space heaters that are occasionally plugged into the grid. The throngs who come on tours do not see the institute staff occasionally donning long johns and fingerless gloves. The solar-heating failure can be explained by the fact that some of the superefficient windows need to be fixed, that the weather stripping never seems to get installed on time, and that the design of the house doesn't take into account that people sometimes forget to close windows or shut doors. Maddening human caprice can ruin the best of calculations. The heaters, explains Lovins, who cannot be beaten in last-word Ping-Pong, "are mostly used by one elderly person with poor circulation."

Tonight there is a rodeo picnic in Snowmass. The archangel of the Soft Path is sitting under a tent with a foam tray of ribs and corn on the cob and powdered lemonade. Children bound about, and good ole boys cut up in a Wild West show, discharging six-guns and dying like hams. Lovins flinches when the guns go off. He seems a little preoccupied, and it's hard to blame him. It's hard not to wonder how he fits in among the clichés of the West, with his cowboy hat and snap-button shirt, with his calculator asleep in his pocket.

The crowd drifts to the wooden bleachers. The dirt in the U-shaped arena is dark and pungent and freshly plowed. Amory always sits at the far end, near the gate, so he can watch when Hunter rides in. On come the bucking broncos and the bawling calves, the lariats and clowns and beauty queens on a stagecoach. Short-legged cow-dogs nip the bulls back into their pens; their life is their work, too.

Lovins looks on with mild interest until Hunter appears, blond hair cascading from under the black brim of her hat. His colleague, his coauthor, his business partner, his wife. She flashes across the dirt, rounds the barrels, and digs for home—alas, not fast enough to win. He seems to suffer her loss.

Sun long gone under an indigo wash, the rodeo winds out under the glare of some homely lights. "Those are old mercury-vapor lights," Lovins says, suddenly brightening. "New high-pressure sodium lights are twice as efficient."

*September 1987*

# THE KING OF THE FERRET LEGGERS

## A true story

● ▲ ■

### DONALD KATZ

$M$r. Reg Mellor, the "king of ferret-legging," paced across his tiny Yorkshire miner's cottage as he explained the rules of the English sport that he has come to dominate rather late in life. "Ay lad," said the 72-year-old champion, "no jockstraps allowed. No underpants—nothin' whatever. And it's no good with tight trousers, mind ye. Little bah-stards have to be able to move around inside there from ankle to ankle."

Some 11 years ago I first heard of the strange pastime called ferret-legging, and for a decade since then I have sought a publication possessed of sufficient intelligence and vision to allow me to travel to northern England in search of the fabled players of the game.

Basically the contest involves the tying of a competitor's trousers at the ankles and the subsequent insertion into those trousers of a couple of peculiarly vicious fur-coated, footlong carnivores called ferrets. The brave contestant's belt is then pulled tight, and he proceeds to stand there in front of the judges as long as he can, while animals with claws like hypodermic needles and teeth like number 16 carpet tacks try their damndest to get out.

From a dark and obscure past, the sport has made an astonishing comeback in the past 15 years. When I first heard about ferret-legging, the world record stood at 40 painful seconds of "keepin' 'em down," as they say in ferret-legging circles. A few years later the dreaded one-minute mark was finally surpassed. The current record—implausible as it may seem—now stands at an awesome 5 hours and 26 minutes, a mark reached last year by the gaudily tattooed 72-year-old little York-shireman with the waxed military mustache who now stood two feet away from me in the middle of the room, apparently undoing his trousers.

"The ferrets must have a full mouth o' teeth," Reg Mellor said as he fiddled with his belt. "No filing of the teeth; no clipping. No dope for you or the ferrets. You must be sober, and the ferrets must be hungry—though any ferret'll eat yer eyes out even if he isn't hungry."

Reg Mellor lives several hours north of London atop the thick central seam of British coal that once fueled the most powerful surge into modernity in the world's history. He lives in the city of Barnsley, home to a quarter-million downtrodden souls, and the brunt of many derisive jokes in Great Britain. Barnsley was the subject of much national mirth recently when "the most grievously mocked town in Yorkshire"—a place people drive miles out of their way to circumvent—opened a tourist information center. Everyone thought that was a good one.

When I stopped at the tourist office and asked the astonished woman for a map, she said, "Ooooh, a mup ees it, luv? No mups 'ere. Noooo." She did, however, know the way to Reg Mellor's house. Reg is, after all, Barnsley's only reigning king.

Finally, then, after 11 long years, I sat in front of a real ferret-legger, a man among men. He stood now next to a glowing fire of Yorkshire coal as I tried to interpret the primitive record of his long life, which is etched in tattoos up and down his thick arms. Reg finally finished explaining the technicalities of this burgeoning sport.

"So then, lad. Any more questions for I poot a few down for ye?"

"Yes, Reg."

"Ay, whoot then?"

"Well, Reg," I said. "I think people in America will want to know. Well . . . since you don't wear any protection . . . and, well, I've heard a ferret can bite your thumb off. Do they ever—you know?"

Reg's stiff mustache arched toward the ceiling under a sly grin. "You really want to know what they get up to down there, eh?" Reg said, looking for all the world like some working man's Long John Silver. "Well, take a good look."

Then Reg Mellor let his trousers fall around his ankles.

A SHORT DIGRESSION: A word is in order concerning ferrets, a weasel-like animal well known to Europeans but, because of the near extinction of the black-footed variety in the American West, not widely known in the United States.

Alternatively referred to by professional ferret-handlers as "shark-of-the-land," a "piranha with feet," "fur-coated evil," and "the only four-legged creature in existence that kills just for kicks," the common domesticated ferret—*Mustela putorius*—has the spinal flexibility of a snake and the jaw musculature of a pit bull. Rabbits, rats, and even frogs run screaming from hiding places when confronted with a ferret. Ferreters —those who hunt with ferrets, as opposed to putting them in their pants—sit around and tell tales of rabbits running toward hunters to surrender after gazing into the torch-red eyes of an oncoming ferret.

Before they were outlawed in New York State in the early part of the century, ferrets were used to exterminate rats. A ferret with a string on its leg, it was said, could knock off more than a hundred street-wise New York City rats twice its size in an evening.

In England the amazing rise of ferret-legging pales before the new popularity of keeping ferrets as pets, a trend replete with numerous tragic consequences. A baby was killed and eaten in 1978, and several children have been mauled by ferrets every year since then.

Loyal to nothing that lives, the ferret has only one characteristic that might be deemed positive—a tenacious, single-minded belief in finishing whatever it starts. That usually entails biting *off* whatever it bites. The rules of ferret-legging do allow the leggers to try to knock the ferret off a spot it's biting (from outside the trousers only), but that is no small matter, as ferrets never let go. No less a source than the *Encyclopaedia Britannica* suggests that you can get a ferret to let go by pressing a certain spot over its eye, but Reg Mellor and the other ferret specialists I talked to all say that is absurd. Reg favors a large screwdriver to get a ferret off his finger. Another ferret-legger told me that a ferret that had almost dislodged his left thumb let go only after the ferret and the man's thumb were held under scalding tap water—for ten minutes.

Mr. Graham Wellstead, the head of the British Ferret and Ferreting Society, says that little is known of the diseases carried by the ferret because veterinarians are afraid to touch them.

Reg Mellor, a man who has been more intimate with ferrets than many men have been with their wives, calls ferrets "cannibals, things that live only to kill, that'll eat your eyes out to get at your brain" at their worst, and "untrustworthy" at their very best.

Reg says he observed with wonder the growing popularity of ferret-legging throughout the seventies. He had been hunting with ferrets in the verdant moors and dales outside of Barnsley for much of a century. Since a cold and wet ferret exterminates with a little less enthusiasm than a dry one, Reg used to keep his ferrets in his pants for hours when he hunted in the rain—and it always rained where he hunted.

"The *world record* was 60 seconds. Sixty seconds! I can stick a ferret up me ass longer than that."

So at 69, Reg Mellor found his game. As he stood in front of me now, naked from the waist down, Reg looked every bit a champion.

"So LOOK CLOSE," he said again.

I did look, at an incredible tattoo of a zaftig woman on Reg's thigh. His legs appeared crosshatched with scars. But I refused to "look close," saying something about not being paid enough for that.

"Come on, Reg," I said. "Do they bite your—you know?"

"Do they!" he thundered with irritation as he pulled up his pants. "Why, I had 'em hangin' off me—"

Reg stopped short because a woman who was with me, a London television reporter, had entered the cottage. I suddenly feared that I would never know from what the raging ferrets dangle. Reg offered my friend a chair with the considerable gallantry of a man who had served in the Queen's army for more than 20 years. Then he said to her, "Are ye cheeky, luv?"

My friend looked confused.

"Say yes," I hissed.

"Yes."

"Why," Reg roared again, "I had 'em hangin' from me tool for hours an' hours an' hours! Two at a time—one on each side. I been swelled up big as that!" Reg pointed to a five-pound can of instant coffee.

I then made the mistake of asking Reg Mellor if his age allowed him the impunity to be the most daring ferret-legger in the world.

"And what do ye mean by that?" he said.

"Well, I just thought since you probably aren't going to have any more children. . . ."

"Are you sayin' I ain't pokin' 'em no more?" Reg growled with menace. "Is that your meaning? Cause I am pokin' 'em for sure."

A SMALL RED HUT sits in an overgrown yard outside Reg Mellor's door. "Come outta there, ye bah-stards," Reg yelled as he flailed around the inside of the hut looking for some ferrets that had just arrived a few hours earlier. He emerged with two dirty white animals, which he held quite firmly by their necks. They both had fearsome unblinking eyes as hard and red as rubies.

Reg thrust one of them at me, and I suddenly thought that he intended the ferret to avenge my faux pas concerning his virility; so I began to run for a fence behind which my television friend was already standing because she refused to watch. Reg finally got me to take one of the ferrets by its steel cable of a neck while he tied his pants at the ankle and prepared to "put em down."

A young man named Malcolm, with a punk haircut, came into the yard on a motorbike. "You puttin' 'em down again, Reg?" Malcolm asked.

Reg took the ferret from my bloodless hand and stuck the beast's head deep into his mouth.

"Oh yuk, Reg," said Malcolm.

Reg pulled the now quite embittered-looking ferret out of his mouth and stuffed it and another ferret into his pants. He cinched his belt tight, clenched his fists at his sides, and gazed up into the gray Yorkshire firmament in what I guessed could only be a gesture of prayer. Claws and teeth now protruded all over Reg's hyperactive trousers. The two bulges circled round and round one leg, getting higher and higher, and finally . . . they went up and over to the other leg.

"Thank God," I said.

"Yuk, Reg," said Malcolm.

"The claws," I managed, "Aren't they sharp, Reg?"

"Ay," said Reg laconically. "Ay."

REG MELLOR GIVES all the money he makes from ferret-legging to the local children's home. As with all great champions, he has also tried to bring more visibility to the sport that has made him famous. One Mellor innovation is the introduction of white trousers at major competitions ("shows the blood better").

Mellor is a proud man. Last year he retired from professional ferret-legging in disgust after attempting to break a magic six-hour mark—the four-minute-mile of ferret-legging. After five hours of having them down, Mellor found that almost all of the 2,500 spectators had gone home. Then workmen came and began to dismantle the stage, despite his protestations that he was on his way to a new record. "I'm not packing it in because

I am too old or because I can't take the bites anymore," Reg told reporters after the event, "I am just too disillusioned."

ONE OF THE FERRETS in Reg's pants finally poked its nose into daylight before any major damage was done, and Reg pulled the other ferret out. We all went across the road to the local pub, where everyone but Reg had a drink to calm the nerves. Reg doesn't drink. Bad for his health, he says.

Reg said he had been coaxed out of retirement recently and intends to break six—"maybe even eight"—hours within the year.

Some very big Yorkshiremen stood around us in the pub. Some of them claimed they had bitten the heads off sparrows, shrews, and even rats, but none of them would compete with Reg Mellor. One can only wonder what suffering might have been avoided if the Argentine junta had been informed that sportsmen in England put down their pants animals that are known only for their astonishingly powerful bites and their penchant for insinuating themselves into small dark holes. Perhaps the generals would have reconsidered their actions on the Falklands.

But Reg Mellor refuses to acknowledge that his talent is made of the stuff of heroes, of a mixture of indomitable pride, courage, concentration, and artless grace. "Naw noon o' that," said the king. "You just got be able ta have your tool bitten and not care."

*February/March 1983*

# A SIMPLE QUEST

*Antarctica is the last good, clean, wholesome place left on the planet. That's why Warren Pearson had to get there.*

● ▲ ■

### MICHAEL MCRAE

In 1981, at age 47, Warren Pearson took stock of his life. He was married to a lovely, talented wife. He held a respectable job teaching college biology. He lived an hour from San Francisco in a comfortable home that the bank did not own. He had close friends. And he felt terribly unfulfilled—as if his life were slipping away without his ever having done something genuinely good.

There was only one solution: make a solitary pilgrimage to Antarctica and spend a winter there, alone and cut off.

His first plan was to buy a beat-up C-47 cargo plane and crashland it on a glacier. After some preliminary research, this seemed to be impractical. However, Plan B—to make the trip by sea and use the boat as an icebound base camp—struck him as eminently more feasible. Never mind that he had never captained a boat, that he wore a pacemaker, that such a voyage was without precedent, and that overwintering in Antarctica without a permit is illegal. Pearson began plotting in earnest and in total secrecy. Not even his wife was to know.

Four years later, on January 7, 1985, still having never piloted a boat a day in his life, Warren Pearson left port at Melbourne, Australia, bound for Cape Denison, a point of land near the south magnetic pole. His dreams had been realized.

This is his story. It is a tale of a spiritual quest and a scientific expedition, a test of limits and a grand political statement—and perhaps a way of salvaging a life of quiet desperation. Warren Pearson would appreciate your reading it. After all, he made the journey on behalf of all of us. And all of us, he would like to think, were with him in spirit on that terrible voyage.

Sipping coffee with him in his kitchen, you'd hardly think Warren Pearson the type to go haring off to Antarctica alone in a 37-foot ketch. Though he has an athletic, six-foot frame and a jaunty red beard, he has a gnomishness about him, and a shy reserve in his voice and manner. Warren Pearson is the guy next door: a somewhat colorless, scrupulously precise, rational, industrious man, not especially given to risking his life on foolhardy adventures. But if you listen to his story long enough, the pieces start to fall together, and the whole gambit begins to make perfect sense. Almost.

Pearson and his wife, Barbara, have a life of normalcy in suburban Benicia. He has taught at nearby Diablo Valley College for nearly 20 years. As well as teaching biology, he instructs nurses in human anatomy and has gained a reputation for his deftness in dissecting cadavers. His wife is a psychologist and artist, and teaches art to disturbed adults. Their home, which he built in his spare time, is a vision of California living: a dramatic, all-wood two-story, with a cavernous, mosaic-tiled spa, decks all around, and a magnificent view of the Carquinez Straits, the eastern gateway to the San Francisco Bay. The house is full of art: Pearson's whimsical junk sculptures made of brass fittings, his collection of penguins, Navajo rugs, Barbara's flamboyant, surrealistic canvases. The driveway harbors a decrepit 1955 Chevrolet sedan and a '57 Chevy pickup he is restoring.

If the Antarctic voyage has a genesis, it was probably Pearson's heart attack in 1979, which he says grew out of a long squabble with the college. In 1973 he took a paid sabbatical to study public health at the University of California at Berkeley, but when several courses were canceled he substituted a natural history field seminar in the Amazon. It was a time of high adventure and intellectual stimulation: He flew to Leticia, Colombia, deep in the Amazon Basin, with a scientific team, and documented the expedition with a professional-quality Ariflex 16mm camera that he had taught himself to use. It took ten years to finish the half-hour documentary, but it was well received by his students. "It was not some bullshit thing," he says.

The college, however, was not impressed and sued him for the $12,000 in sabbatical salary. "It was Kafkaesque." he says, "six years in litigation." The stress led to the heart attack, but Pearson emerged from the ordeal a new man: "Material things became less important. It was as if I'd entered a spiritual phase of my life. Touching a part of nature that was dying—the rainforest—I became moved enough so that my perspective changed. My attention was directed to Antarctica. It was a pure place, and it hadn't been destroyed by man as the Amazon had."

He immersed himself in the literature of Antarctica, and finally the urge to go there overcame him. Over the new year of 1981–82 he booked passage on the Lindblad *Explorer*. He had invited his wife, but she decided to spend the holidays with her daughter from an earlier marriage and new granddaughter. The three-week Antarctic cruise cost $6,000, and because the college would not approve the trip as a sabbatical, he had to hire substitute teachers for his classes.

But the trip was worth every cent. Antarctica was a fantasy land, novel and unsullied. He brought his Ariflex and could hardly stop shooting. What struck him particularly was the air—so clear that mountains hundreds of miles distant would seem only half a day's walk away. There were other marvelous anomalies. Because of the absence of bacteria, food left out in a hut used by Sir Douglas Mawson's expedition was just as it had been left in 1914. The icebergs were more enormous than he imagined possible; the sun never set during the austral summer.

For all its difference and remoteness, though, Pearson felt at one with the strange new environment. The profusion of wildlife displayed an affecting innocence. "It's the damnedest thing to walk up to a penguin four feet high, and it isn't the slightest bit afraid of you," he recalls. "It's like walking in a primeval place of which you're a natural part, accepted into the community of living things."

In the book *Beyond Cape Horn*—one of Pearson's favorites—author Charles Neider discusses the syndrome of Antarctic addiction that struck a number of polar explorers, including himself. Pearson's sojourn seems to have affected him similarly, and he sits forward in his chair when he talks about his visit: "It casts a spell on you; it's so damn neat—like going back in time. Five million years ago it was the same as it is today. Talk about a wilderness experience, hey, that's it in spades.

"It's such a clean, innocent, symbolically pure, idyllic place that when you leave it and get back in the noisy, dirty city and see the human condition and the consequences of humanity, it makes you want to turn and go right back." This is pure hyperbole; Benicia is one of those all-American cities where a wino would appear as incongruous as a Martian.

Nevertheless, Warren Pearson's Lindblad homecoming was less than joyous. And so he began to plot his return.

FROM THE OUTSET Pearson knew he would have to mount his own expedition. He stood no chance of qualifying for a National Science Foundation research grant, thus attaining eligibility for government transportation. Even if he had had a valid project, his pacemaker probably would have disqualified him. Not that he wanted help. Under the 1959 Antarctic Treaty each of the nations with voting power over activities in Antarctica—"The Club"—must be given advance notice about any expedition. That meant, as Pearson wrote in his three-volume journal of the expedition, "the countries would 'rescue' me against my will. My plans are meant to keep this from happening, if secrecy is not broached prematurely."

Pearson was vague with his wife about his plans, saying only that he intended to take a year off to sail the South Pacific. By doing so he kept his options open—he could have abandoned the Antarctic trip at any time—and spared her undue worry. The two interpret their marriage pact as allowing each other to be individuals. "I have a right to take a year off, to do any damn thing I want to," he says, "and so does she." Barbara Pearson, for example, once went to Huautla, Mexico, to visit a friend and wound up taking magic mushrooms in a ritualistic ceremony performed by a female shaman.

Barbara Pearson is fascinated by the school of Jungian myth interpretation, which explains human behavior in terms of mythological archetypes, and she saw his supposed island sojourn as a "spiritual quest, a seeking for the Holy Grail." She and Pearson share a private language that is charged with the symbols of medieval romances: grails, magicians, knights on white horses, unicorns—the same icons that inspire Californians from George Lucas to computer hackers with Dungeons and Dragons on the brain. Had she known his real plans, she would have despaired.

After abandoning the absurd C-47 crash-landing scheme, Pearson decided to buy a steel-hulled fishing trawler and motor his way south from Melbourne, Australia. If he succeeded, he reckoned, he would be the first man to make a solo voyage to the continent itself. (From 1972 to 1974 David Lewis, a retired physician living in Australia, sailed alone in a 32-foot sloop, the Ice Bird to the Antarctic peninsula and back to South Africa. "But that was the peninsula," Pearson explains. "It's farther north and much warmer there. Hell, on the mainland they refer to it as the 'Banana Belt.' " Lewis, whose boat was capsized and dismasted several times in waves cresting 60 feet, would probably scoff.)

In his journals, Pearson describes his expedition in terms far more grandiose and romantic than his wife's. He refers to Antarctica as "a wilderness emperor's palace" where his soul began to awaken, and "a Camelot" where good things happen and happiness reigns.

His heroic quest was to be a struggle with "the white soul of the planet. . . . It could be deadly but I am going to fight my guts out once in my life." The struggle, he was sure, would earn him "blessings from every god, king, savior, and spiritual force that ever existed in the minds and hearts of wellmeaning people." This adulation would be deserved because of the primary goal of the voyage: to publicize the value of Antarctica. It was this loftier motive that was to elevate the expedition above "self-indulgent escapism" and, he hoped, persuade the authorities to forgive his illegal scientific station.

In our kitchen conversation, Pearson became animated when he elaborated on his higher goal: "Antarctica brings out the best in people, and it's a hell of a nice example of people working together cooperatively. It's so easy to be hopeless about international relations, but the Argentines and the British would give each other the shirts off their backs down there. I wanted people to know that things are working for the collective good there, and that maybe it's possible to make it work elsewhere. I wanted to say that Antarctica is an unspoiled wilderness. It's important to know that there's a good, clean, wholesome place left. When people feel down and hopeless, just the mere knowledge of that is uplifting.

"My job is to be an informer. This was going to be an elaborate lecture to as many people as possible, and the message was: 'Antarctica is a good thing. Don't screw it up. Pat yourself on the back. You've done a good thing. We all have.' In a world full of negativity, that message was significant enough for me to risk my life."

NOT LONG AFTER he returned from the Lindblad trip, Pearson began working 14-hour days, substitute teaching and taking on night courses. The expedition would be expensive, and he intended to settle all his debts and have his insurance policies paid up before leaving. Between classes, he either worked on his Antarctica documentary or buried himself in the library. He read every book on Antarctica he could find and studied navigation, oceanography, meteorology—anything that might be useful on the voyage.

His first actual commitment came in December 1982 when he ordered 925 cloth patches that read HONORING THE SPIRIT OF ANTARCTIC INTERNATIONAL CO-OPERATION—CAPE DENNISON BASE 1985 (Antarctic teams collect and trade such emblems like baseball cards.) Pearson had them printed in each of the four official languages of the Antarctic Treaty: English, French, Spanish, and Russian. On each version, *Denison* was misspelled with two n's.

He had chosen Cape Denison with good reason. Though his vessel would be steel-hulled, pack ice that forms in the austral winter could easily crush the boat, as it did Ernest Shackleton's ship *Endurance* in 1914. One way to prevent this is to anchor in a narrow inlet, where the pressure of the ice cannot build up as much as it does in the open sea. Denison offers such an anchorage, and it is one of the few places on the ice-choked coastline accessible to a small boat. Perhaps more important, though, Pearson had stopped there on his Lindblad trip to visit the Mawson hut and to explore, and he had a deep sentimental attachment to the cape.

Unfortunately, that particular section of coastline has some of the harshest weather on the planet. Frigid air pouring off the continent's 10,000-foot-high central plateau creates 200-mile-per-hour winds there—the so-called katabatic winds. "They would have been a bitch," Pearson says, "but I would have dealt with them."

Had his boat's hull become crushed anyway, Pearson could have sought refuge from the otherworldly winter cold in the Mawson hut. (The lowest recorded Antarctic temperature is minus 88.3 degrees Celsius, minus 126 Fahrenheit without the wind.) Then, in the spring, he could have walked overland to DuMont d'Urville, the French outpost 80 miles away, and caught a supply ship home. In any case, he was aiming for another first: the only man to overwinter alone since Byrd in 1934 ("and he had major government support and maintained regular radio contact").

In spite of all his planning, Pearson never developed more than a vague idea of what he would do once he reached Antarctica. He wanted to film another documentary, do some creative writing, conduct modest research (perhaps collect meteorites or investigate sexual differences in the brain anatomy of dead or injured marine mammals). "Specifically I had no definite program," he says. "I wanted to expose myself to influences of an unforeseen nature—jumping out into the flow of life, experiencing the unknown. Why did Hillary want to climb Everest? The reason I wanted to go to Antarctica was to see what happened when I got to Antarctica.

"I also wanted to experience the inner changes I felt. If I died, that would have been part of the experience. I would have hoped if I had died that my 'lecture' would have gotten out, in which case my life would have had some meaning."

By the summer of 1984 Pearson had amassed almost $40,000. He had been so meticulous in putting his affairs in order that he had even written newspaper advertisements so that his wife could sell his cars if he were to die. To ensure that his lecture got out, he prepared a sealed box that she was to open March 31, 1985, three months after his projected departure date. By then, he figured, he would be either icebound and unreachable, or shipwrecked and dead. Inside were letters to the U.S. ambassadors of the 16 nations in The Club and to major newspapers in those countries. Each envelope also contained a number of patches. Barbara was to trundle these down to the Benicia post office and drop them in the slot, one by one: The Hon. Anatoly F. Dobrinyn, *Pravda, Le Monde, The London Times, El Mercurio, The New Zealand Herald* . . .

Another envelope contained an article—already typeset—for *Artwell* magazine, a guide to Benicia's annual spring art fair, which perhaps a thousand people might read. His wife would be editing the magazine in late March, and the piece would be her first inkling about his real destination.

Titled "Performance Peace," it presents his expedition as a kind of performance art in which the readers could participate by simply wishing him Godspeed. His only hope for success, he wrote, lay in "dancing with the forces of nature" and using the "supportive spiritual force coming from all humanity," whom he represented. "Without this force, or my belief in it," he wrote, "I would never undertake such an odyssey and doubt that I could survive it."

IN LATE JULY, on a break between semesters, Pearson flew to Melbourne to find a boat. He had chosen Melbourne for its size and its proximity to Antarctica. Hobart, Tasmania, would have been closer, but a man buying a boat and tons of supplies in such a small city would arouse suspicion. In Melbourne he could maintain secrecy.

It was winter down under, and the day he arrived was gray and blustery. He checked into a modest hotel downtown. While the room was being prepared he took a walk, hoping to get his first glimpse of the Southern Ocean. His path led him to a lonely wharf, and when he looked over the edge, there at his feet, bobbing in the choppy, gray water, was a scruffy 37-foot steel-hulled cruising ketch: the *Finegold*. She was perfect.

Though the *Finegold* did not have a for sale sign on her, her owner was willing to give her up for $16,840. "When Cinderella put her foot in the shoe, it not only fit her perfectly but it was a moment of joy that I know about," Pearson wrote in his journal after closing the deal. Adding to his sense of predestination, the owner's name was Alan Pearson, and he had the same heart condition as Pearson did. Alan Pearson had bought her with his brother, intending to sail around the world, but his cardiac arrhythmia sabotaged the plans. Besides having a steel hull, the *Finegold* had a nearly new six-cylinder diesel engine; an insulated, self-bailing cockpit; and an enormous ballast, which would help prevent her from capsizing and right her if she did go over. Then there was the added feature of sail power.

"A.W. Pearson almost had another heart attack when J.W. Pearson walked up and bought his boat *without even stepping on it* or knowing if it had an engine," Pearson wrote gleefully back at his hotel.

For the next two weeks, with the start of the next semester rapidly approaching, Pearson worked like a madman. He figured he could motor all the way to Antarctica, but decided to rerig the *Finegold* with small, heavy-duty sails that would be easy to handle. Knowing little about rigging or sailing, he bought six books. ("So much to learn.") When he was not studying or working on the boat, he was building equipment: a ship's radio, compass and sextant, charts, flares, an emergency position-indicating radio beacon (EPIRB), used sails, hardware. He rode streetcars, and between stops, scribbled private thoughts in his journal. Little did the commuters around him know that the tan book contained a message to them:

"I am a wisp of love drifting through your life, an insignificant medium through which your kindness is rewarded. My destiny is to carry a torch of hope to the white kingdom for you. Your godly spirits will keep me from faltering in our journey, and I pledge my life that I will stay a worthy messenger."

For those four weeks in August, Warren Pearson was totally absorbed and content—an anonymous man on a top-secret mission for mankind. It was finally happening. Back home in California, Pearson's secret anticipation of weighing anchor for the "magnum opus" of his life carried him through the routine of teaching the fall semester.

In December Pearson left Benicia—for the last time, for all he knew—without even waiting for Christmas. On Christmas Eve, instead of carols and a crackling fire at home, he spent a solitary night aboard the *Finegold* in Melbourne. Short of cash until the banks reopened, and with his gear still in transit on a freighter, he washed up in a bucket of water heated on the stove, soaping up with some detergent and drying himself on old drapes. Afterward he went out to order sheet-metal hatch covers, wandered into a church, and sat alone listening to the choir and sermon. "Merry, merry. My soul has been fed," he wrote before going to sleep on a bunk without sheets.

It was not a melancholy time, however. He had concluded months earlier, with a curious logic, that by eliminating his sense of self-importance, he would not feel lonely. "I will realize a kind of joy by being as unimportant as a grain of sand on a storm-tossed beach," he rhapsodized in his diary. "Sadness, loneliness, and pain should remind me of my unimportance and then I might get a glimpse of that illusive thing I am seeking: a transcendent communion with myself as an infinitesimal fragment of the whole." Pearson was more put off by his lack of hair conditioner and towels than of companionship.

On Christmas morning he opened his present from Barbara: a tiny crystal chalice ("My grail!"); a letter opener with a unicorn on the handle, his sword; a hand harp; and a book titled *We*. The thin volume, by a Jungian analyst, recounts the epic story of Tristan and Iseult and explores the dynamics of romantic love. In one of Tristan's two voyages, he is "sick unto death" and drifts with only his harp, trusting the sea to bring him his cure. His inner journey eventually brings him to Iseult the Fair. Gazing at the chalice, Pearson felt a surge of warmth. Then, unaware of the symbolism of the letter opener, he opened a can of beans for breakfast with it and went straight to work rigging the mainsail.

PEARSON PUSHED himself during the next two weeks in Melbourne, resuming his 14-hour schedule. He made a canvas retainer for his bunk, rigged the tiller in the aft cockpit so that he could steer from there or the cabin, studied his navigation books. Unable to find propane tanks for sale ("Just rentals, mate"), he bought a small wood stove in which he planned to burn leftover coal from Mawson's expedition for heat or, if necessary, seal blubber.

On January 4 he cleared through customs the ton and a half of equipment he had shipped and transferred it to his boat in a rental van. Sitting amid the jumble, he took stock. Though he claimed to have transcended materialism, you would never know it from the inventory: Chouinard ice-climbing equipment (for self-rescues from crevasses), a Wilderness Experience Everest suit, a wet suit, Koflach Ultra Extreme mountaineering boots, vapor-barrier systems for himself and his sleeping bags, a mountain of polypropylene and wool clothing, a year's supply of survival rations supplying 6,000 calories a day, medical supplies, 8,000 feet of color movie film, his Ariflex, a 4-by-5 camera, two Canon A-1s, a 650-watt generator, a 13-foot Zodiac and outboard motor, 180 gallons of diesel and 40 of gas, and 10 propane tanks he had tracked down. He had spared no expense—nor bothered to keep track.

With his departure looming, his excitement gave way briefly to worry: "There has been so much frantic activity that I've had little time to realize the implications of what I am about to do," he wrote. But the timetable he had set for himself allowed no time for reflection and he plunged on, working each day until he dropped. On January 5 he filed customs clearance forms, listing Bluff, New Zealand, as his next port of call and January 24, 1985, as his arrival date. He felt some guilt over the deception, but wrote it off as a white lie: "If all goes well, I will arrive in Bluff on Jan. 24, 1986."

His real plan was to conduct his shakedown cruise on Port Phillip Bay below Melbourne and then streak to Kings Island off northwestern Tasmania, usually a three-day sail across the Bass Strait, notorious for its unpredictable weather. Just a week earlier, the Sydney-to-Hobart race over the strait had been a disaster. Only 40 boats in the field of 150 had finished; the rest had been disabled. Pearson wanted to put this part of the trip behind him as soon as possible. Not only is the weather generally miserable and the swells horrendous, the winds could drive him aground in the Furneaux Group, a cluster of islands off northeastern Tasmania. Once clear of Tasmania, there was nothing to run into for the next 1,500 miles. All he had to worry about were killer storms and rogue waves in the Roaring Forties, Furious Fifties, and Screaming Sixties—and, of course, the icebergs. But they would come later.

From the log of the *Finegold:*

"Monday, Jan. 7, 12:45 P.M.—Am now *sailing!* Lee helm, all canvas up. Light breeze. Bearing 220 degrees. Talk about excitement!"

The 60-mile shakedown cruise across the bay was marred only by a broken oil line—easily fixed—and a navigation blunder that put him aground in the shallows. "*Stupid, stupid, stupid,*" he berated himself in his journal. That evening, the rising tide freed him and he motored off toward the inlet of the bay, a treacherous spot called The Rip. A full moon rose over Melbourne and a dolphin jumped next to the boat—good omens. The evening was lovely, the papers had forecast fair weather, and Pearson decided to run The Rip.

"Mistake. Big mistake," is the next log entry. Huge swells beat the *Finegold,* turning the cabin into a tumble dryer full of flying gear. Twenty miles into the Bass Strait, with the swells still thrashing the boat, the engine quit. Pearson was terrified of being blown ashore, but took to his bunk. "Boat did crazy bobbing all night. Bad ass. Thought I was dead, really."

Tuesday morning, with the engine running again, a cup of coffee in him, and the sun shining, Pearson motored on. The wind subsided and he put up the main. "Really cooking with both sails and engine!" he wrote. The engine sputtered and died intermittently through the day, and the winds rose steadily, but he took heart that the *Finegold* was holding a steady course without his even touching the rudder. The bilge was taking on water, however, and the motorized pump was not working. He pumped the bilge by hand—750 strokes, 45 minutes—then got seasick and went below to rest.

By evening the winds were howling at 40 knots and Pearson left his bunk only long enough to lower the mainsail. With the dark closing around him and the boat holding a steady course, he planned to stay below all night, going up to check the situation every hour. "Why screw around with something that works?" he wrote.

THAT NIGHT—a "night of terror"—the *Finegold* heaved along, sliding into gaping, squarish troughs with 20-foot walls of water on all sides. Rogue waves thundered down on top of her, pitching her over 45 degrees. Pearson struggled above deck, clipped into a safety line, and lowered the jib. He spotted the Cape Wickham light on King Island. Encouraged, he went below to pump the bilge again. On his next watch, the light was farther away, and in the morning there was no land in sight. He was being blown toward the Furneaux Group.

From the log of the *Finegold:*

"Thursday, Jan. 10, 9:00 A.M.—Still storming. Giant rollers. Rain. Lost my rudder about noon yesterday. No engine, no rudder, no control. Turned on the EPIRB at 5:00 P.M. No response. Only good for 48 hours. Must pump bilge every few hours. Looks very bad as I am in a channel and could go on the rocks. Need help desperately."

As he clung to his bunk, gear clanging around the cabin, he stared out a porthole he had left uncovered. Deep green water rose halfway up the glass each time the boat rolled. He imagined the sickening crunch of rocks against the hull. Would it happen that night? In the next minute? Would Barbara mail the packages? Why hadn't they answered the EPIRB? He was certain of death, yet surprised that he was not terrified of dying. The one disturbing thought he kept returning to was that he had no one to blame but himself. For once in his life, there was no scapegoat for his failure. He was not prepared for that kind of loneliness.

DARKNESS FELL. Pearson was in shock, instinctively pumping the bilge, taking a drink of water, eating a cracker. Suddenly, he heard a drone overhead—a plane. He rummaged through the cabin mess and found his flares. He could not get the hatch open fast enough. He fired two red ones, the international distress signal. The pilot circled. Pearson was waving frantically.

For the next seven hours, several planes spelled each other, keeping track of the *Finegold.* Pearson was out of the bunk only as much as he dared. At about 11:00 p.m. he spotted a glimmer of light out of the porthole. He fired his remaining red flare. The eerie crimson light illuminated a scene out of hell: mountainous black waves, undulating with a vertiginous rhythm. From off in the darkness, a white flare answered his. And then the whole ocean lit up like daylight. A helicopter far overhead dropped an intense white flare, and in the distance Pearson could see his salvation, the *M.S. Iron Prince,* an immense black freighter, moving slowly toward him.

Pearson clipped into his safety line, strung from bow to stern, and continually lit hand flares. He was waist-deep in water at times. When the freighter maneuvered alongside, using its bow thrusters, its floodlights were put on. The first mate bellowed down, "Are you the master?"

"Yes!" Pearson replied, almost eye to eye with the mate. The swells had lifted the *Finegold* level with the freighter's deck one second and dropped her 40 feet lower the next.

"How can we assist you?"

"I have no engine or rudder and am taking on water. Can you tow me?"

"We can try."

The only tow lines were at the stern of the freighter, and she inched forward, eventually putting the *Finegold* beneath the overhang above her stilled propeller. The swells there were just as bad. Pearson reached up at one point and felt cold steel. As his boat plunged, he dove to the deck. On the next swell the mizzenmast and shrouds crashed down around him. The heaving pounded the two vessels together, battening the *Finegold*'s hull.

Finally the *M.S. Iron Prince* inched away, and her crew tossed down a line knotted to a three-inch hawser. Pearson could barely pull the heavy towline across the expanse of water and aboard. Dehydrated and mostly sleepless for the past four days, he collapsed unconscious. When he came to, he managed to tie the hawser to a small stern cleat. Next over the rail of the *M.S. Iron Prince* came a rope ladder, but the swells were too heavy to use it. The crew then tossed him a single line. He stumbled back into the cabin, grabbed his log, a chart of the Bass Strait, and the hand harp. Then he tied the line around his waist and was pulled to safety.

The *Finegold* followed stern-first in the freighter's wake for a short distance and then slipped beneath the blackness. When the crew pulled in the hawser, the cleat was still attached to it.

BECAUSE HE CROSSED the international dateline on the flight home, Warren Pearson was back at the San Francisco airport on the same day he was rescued. "It was as if the *whooooole* thing had never happened," he says in a listless falsetto, sounding like a mad old woman. "It was like I walked out of a theater and was walking across the parking lot to get in my car and go home."

At home, he mulled over the events for weeks. The storm had blown him 120 miles southeast of Kings Island, only halfway to the rocky coastline that had loomed so large in his imagination. If only he had ridden it out. If only he had made it to Kings Island. If only . . .

The expedition had cost him $80,000, $40,000 in the boat and gear and $40,000 in salary he forfeited by taking a year's leave. All he had left to show for his investment was a few mementos: the clothes he'd been wearing the night of the rescue, his log, the hand harp, the crumpled nautical chart, the deck cleat. But it was the loss of the *Finegold* that troubled him most. He felt as if he had abandoned a friend and a guardian. "I had a very deep connection with that boat. It cradled my life and what did I do? I jumped off and let it sink."

Some of his closest friends will not talk about the expedition with him. "A lot of people interpret it as a terrible, devastating thing for me materially," he says. "Others feel I must have paid a tremendous emotional price. Some people are indignant: Who the hell does he think he is that he can do something like that? They had me all figured out and then I did something like this. My mother and family think I am bitterly disappointed." Barbara, however, continues to view the expedition as a vision quest and is touched that he brought back the harp, a symbol of the heart.

Pearson prefers to look at the "other side of the balance sheet as well." He got some publicity for Antarctica—a piece in the local paper that made him out to be a naive chump, a big item in *The San Francisco Chronicle,* this article. "It was also a watershed in terms of my psychological development," he says. "I know I went for it; I did not rot away watching the television set. I followed my heart, took a shot at it, and got a lot back.

"And," he adds, toying with the deck cleat, "you have not heard the last about Warren Pearson and Antarctica."

*December 1985*

*part*

**II**

● ▲ ■

# THE
# HOME
# FRONT

# THE HEART OF THE GAME

## A consideration of hunting

• ▲ ■

### THOMAS MCGUANE

Hunting in your own backyard becomes with time, if you love hunting, less and less expeditionary. When Montana's eager September frosts knocked my garden on its butt, the hoe seemed more like the rifle than it ever had before, the vegetables more like game.

My nine-year-old son and I went scouting before the season and saw some antelope in the high plains foothills of the Absaroka Range, wary, hanging on the skyline; a few bands and no great heads. We crept around, looking into basins, and at dusk met a tired cowboy on a tired horse followed by a tired blue-heeler dog. The plains seemed bigger than anything, bigger than the mountains that seemed to sit in the middle of them, bigger than the ocean. The clouds made huge shadows that traveled on the grass slowly through the day.

Hunting season trickles on forever; if you don't go in on a cow with anybody, there is the dark argument of the deep freeze against headhunting ("You can't eat horns!"). But nevertheless, in my mind, I've laid out the months like playing cards, knowing some decent whitetails could be down in the riverbottom and, fairly reliably, the long windy shots at antelope. The big buck mule deer—the ridgerunners—stay up in the scree and rock walls until the snow drives them out; but they stay high long after the elk have quit and broken down the hay corrals on the ranches and farmsteads which, when you're hunting the rocks from a saddle horse, look pathetic and housebroken with their yellow lights against the coming of winter.

Where I live, the Yellowstone River runs straight north, then takes an eastward turn at Livingston, Montana. This flowing north is supposed

to be remarkable; and the river doesn't do it long. It runs mostly over
sand and stones once it comes out of the rock slots near the Wyoming
line. But all along, there are deviations of one sort or another: canals,
backwaters, sloughs; the red willows grow in the sometime flooded bottom, and at the first elevation, the cottonwoods. I hunt here in the early
fall for the whitetail deer which, in recent years, have moved up these
rivers in numbers never seen before.

WHEN I FIRST start hunting in the fall, I'm not used to getting up so
early. I won't get up that early to fish, not three or four in the morning
just to be out in the middle of nowhere at first light.

The first morning, the sun came up hitting around me in arbitrary
panels as the light came through the jagged openings in the Absaroka
Range. I was moving very slowly in the edge of the trees, the river
invisible a few hundred yards to my right but sending a huge sigh through
the willows. It was cold and the sloughs had crowns of ice, thick enough
to support me. As I crossed one great clear panel, trout raced around
under my feet and a ten-foot bubble advanced slowly before my cautious
steps. Then passing back into the trees, I found an active game trail, cut
cross lots to pick a better stand, sat in a good vantage place under a
cottonwood with the ought-six across my knees. I thought, running my
hands up into my sleeves, this is lovely but I'd rather be up in the hills;
and I fell asleep.

I woke up a couple of hours later, the coffee and early morning drill
having done not one thing for my alertness. I had drooled on my rifle
and it was time for my chores back at the ranch. My chores of late had
consisted primarily of working on screenplays so that the bank didn't
take the ranch. These days the primary ranch skill is making the payment;
it comes before irrigation, feeding out, and calving. Some rancher friends
find this so discouraging they get up and roll a number or have a slash
of tanglefoot before they even think of the glories of the West. This is
the New Rugged.

The next day, I reflected upon my lackadaisical hunting and left really
too early in the morning. I drove around to Mission Creek in the dark
and ended up sitting in the truck up some wash listening to a New
Mexico radio station until my patience gave out and I started out cross-
country in the dark, just able to make out the nose of the Absaroka
Range as it faced across the river to the Crazy Mountains. It seemed

maddeningly up and down slick banks and a couple of times I had game clatter out in front of me in the dark. Then I turned up a long coulee that climbed endlessly south and started in that direction, knowing the plateau on top should hold some antelope. After half an hour or so, I heard the mad laughing of coyotes, throwing their voices all around the inside of the coulee, trying to panic rabbits and making my hair stand on end despite my affection for them. The stars tracked overhead into the first pale light and it was nearly dawn before I came up on the bench. I could hear cattle below me and I moved along an edge of thorn trees to break my outline, then sat down at the point to wait for shooting light.

I could see antelope on the skyline before I had that light; and by the time I did, there was a good big buck angling across from me, looking at everything. I thought I could see well enough, and I got up into a sitting position and into the sling. I had made my moves quietly, but when I looked through the scope the antelope was 200 yards out, using up the country in bounds. I tracked with him, let him bounce up into the reticle and touched off a shot. He was down and still, but I sat watching until I was sure.

Nobody who loves to hunt feels absolutely hunky-dory when the quarry goes down. The remorse spins out almost before anything and the balancing act ends on one declination or another. I decided that unless I become a vegetarian, I'll get my meat by hunting for it. I feel absolutely unabashed by the arguments of other carnivores who get their meat in plastic with blue numbers on it. I've seen slaughterhouses, and anyway, as Sitting Bull said, when the buffalo are gone, we will hunt mice, for we are hunters and we want our freedom.

The antelope had piled up in the sage, dead before he hit the ground. He was an old enough buck that the tips of his pronged horns were angled in toward each other. I turned him downhill to bleed him out. The bullet had mushroomed in the front of the lungs; so the job was already halfway done. With antelope, proper field dressing is critical because they can end up sour if they've been run or haphazardly hog-dressed. And they sour from their own body heat more than external heat.

The sun was up and the big buteo hawks were lifting on the thermals. There was enough breeze that the grass began to have directional grain like the prairie and the rim of the coulee wound up away from me toward the Absaroka. I felt peculiarly solitary, sitting on my heels next to the carcass in the sagebrush and greasewood, my rifle racked open on the ground. I made an incision around the metatarsal glands inside the back legs and carefully removed them and set them well aside; then I cleaned the blade of my hunting knife with handfuls of grass to keep from tainting the meat with those powerful glands. Next I detached the anus and testes from the outer walls and made a shallow puncture below the sternum, spread it with the thumb and forefinger of my left hand and ran the knife upside down clear to the bone bridge between the hind legs. Inside, the diaphragm was like the taut lid of a drum and cut away cleanly so that I could reach clear up to the back of the mouth and detach the windpipe. Once that was done I could draw the whole visceral package out onto the grass and separate out the heart, liver and tongue before propping the carcass open with two whittled-up sage scantlings.

You could tell how cold the morning was, despite the exertion, just by watching the steam roar from the abdominal cavity. I stuck the knife in the ground and sat back against the slope, looking clear across to Convict Grade and the Crazy Mountains. I was blood from the elbows down and the antelope's eyes had skinned over. I thought, this is god-damned serious and you had better always remember that.

THERE WAS A BIG RED enamel pot on the stove; and I ladled antelope chili into two bowls for my little boy and me. He said, "It better not be too hot."

"It isn't."

"What's your news?" he asked.

"Grandpa's dead."

"Which grandpa?" he asked. I told him it was Big Grandpa, my father. He kept on eating. "He died last night."

He said, "I know what I want for Christmas."

"What's that?"

"I want Big Grandpa back."

IT WAS 1950-SOMETHING and I was small, under 12 say, and there were four of us: my father, two of his friends, and me. There was a good belton setter belonging to the one friend, a hearty bird hunter who taught dancing and fist-fought at any provocation. The other man was old and sick and had a green fatal look in his face. My father took me aside and said, "Jack and I are going to the head of this field"—and he pointed up a mile and a half of stalks to where it ended in the flat woods—"and we're going to take the dog and get what he can point. These are running birds. So you and Bill just block the field and you'll have some shooting."

"I'd like to hunt with the dog." I had a 20-gauge Winchester my grandfather had given me, which got hocked and lost years later when another of my family got into the bottle; and I could hit with it and wanted to hunt over the setter. With respect to blocking the field, I could smell a rat.

"You stay with Bill," said my father, "and try to cheer him up."

"What's the matter with Bill?"

"He's had one heart attack after another and he's going to die."

"When?"

"Pretty damn soon."

I blocked the field with Bill. My first thought was, I hope he doesn't die before they drive those birds onto us; but if he does, I'll have all the shooting.

There was a crazy cold autumn light on everything, magnified by the yellow silage all over the field. The dog found birds right away and they were shooting. Bill said he was sorry but he didn't feel so good. He had his hunting license safety-pinned to the back of his coat and fiddled with a handful of 12-gauge shells. "I've shot a shitpile of game," said Bill, "but I don't feel so good anymore." He took a knife out of his coat pocket. "I got this in the Marines," he said, "and I carried it for four years in the Pacific. The handle's drilled out and weighted so you can throw it. I want you to have it." I took it and thanked him, looking into his green face, and wondered why he had given it to me. "That's for blocking this field with me," he said. "Your dad and that dance teacher are going to shoot them all. When you're not feeling so good, they put you at the end of the field to block when there isn't shit-all going to fly by you. They'll get them all. They and the dog will."

We had an indestructible tree in the yard we had chopped on, nailed steps to, and initialed; and when I pitched that throwing knife at it, the knife broke in two. I picked it up and thought, *this thing is jinxed*. So I took it out into the crab-apple woods and put it in the can I had buried along with a Roosevelt dime and an atomic-bomb ring I had sent away for. This was a small collection of things I buried over a period of years. I was sending them to God. All He had to do was open the can, but they were never collected. In any case, I have long known that if I could understand why I wanted to send a broken knife I believed to be jinxed to God, that I would be a long way toward what they call a personal philosophy as opposed to these hand-to-mouth metaphysics of who said what to who in some cornfield 25 years ago.

WE WERE IN THE bar at Chico Hot Springs near my home in Montana: me—a lout poet who had spent the day floating under the diving board while adolescent girls leapt overhead; my brother John had glued himself to the pipe which poured warm water into the pool and announced over and over in a loud voice that every drop of water had been filtered through his bathing suit.

Now, covered with wrinkles, we were in the bar, talking to Alvin Close, an old government hunter. After half a century of predator control he called it "useless and half-assed."

Alvin Close killed the last major stock-killing wolf in Montana. He hunted the wolf so long he raised a litter of dogs to do it with. He hunted the wolf futilely with a pack that had fought the wolf a dozen times until one day he gave up and let the dogs run the wolf out the back of a shallow canyon. He heard them yip their way into silence while he leaned up against a tree; and presently the wolf came tiptoeing down the front of the canyon into Alvin's lap. The wolf simply stopped because the game was up. Alvin raised the Winchester and shot it.

"How did you feel about that?" I asked.

"How do you think I felt?"

"I don't know."

"I felt like hell."

Alvin's evening was ruined and he went home. He was 76 years old and carried himself like an old-time Army officer, setting his glass on the bar behind him without looking.

YOU STARE THROUGH the plastic at the red smear of meat in the super-market. What's this it says here? *Mighty Good? Tastee? Quality, Premium,* and *Government Inspected?* Soon enough, the blood is on your hands. It's inescapable.

IT IS NEW YORK CITY and the beef freaks are foregathering at Bruno's Pen and Pencil. In the kitchen the slabs quiver. In the dining room deals sear the air. Princess Lee Radziwill could be anywhere, fangs aloft to hit the meat that Bruno's Pen and Pencil's butcher's slaughterhouse killed for the Princess. The cow's head and lightless eyes twirl in the rendering vat as linen soars to the Princess's dripping lips.

Aldo Leopold was a hunter who I am sure abjured freeze-dried vegetables and extrusion burgers. His conscience was clean because his hunting was part of a larger husbandry in which the life of the country was enhanced by his own work. He knew that game populations are not bothered by hunting until they are already too precarious and that precarious game populations should not be hunted. Grizzlies should not be hunted, for instance. The enemy of game is clean farming and sinful chemicals; as well as the useless alteration of watersheds by promoter cretins and the insidious dizzards of land development whose lobbyists teach us the venality of all governments.

A world in which a sacramental portion of food can be taken in an old way—hunting, fishing, farming, and gathering—has as much to do with societal sanity as a day's work for a day's pay.

FOR A LONG TIME, there was no tracking snow. I hunted on horseback for a couple of days in a complicated earthquake fault in the Gallatins. The fault made a maze of narrow canyons with flat floors. The sagebrush grew on woody trunks higher than my head and left sandy paths and game trails where the horse and I could travel.

There were Hungarian partridge that roared out in front of my horse, putting his head suddenly in my lap. And hawks tobogganed on the low air currents, astonished to find me there. One finger canyon ended in a vertical rock wall from which issued a spring of the kind elsewhere associated with the Virgin Mary, hung with *ex-votos* and the orthopedic supplications of satisfied miracle customers. Here, instead, were nine identical piles of bear shit, neatly adorned with undigested berries.

One canyon planed up and topped out on an endless grassy rise. There were deer there, does and a young buck. A thousand yards away and staring at me with semaphore ears.

They assembled at a stiff trot from the haphazard array of feeding and strung out in a precise line against the far hill in a dog trot. When I removed my hat, they went into their pogo-stick gait and that was that.

"What did a deer ever do to you?"

"Nothing."

"I'm serious. What do you have to go and kill them for?"

"I can't explain it talking like this."

"Why should they die for you? Would you die for deer?"

"If it came to that."

MY BOY AND I went up the North Fork to look for grouse. We had my old pointer Molly, and Thomas's .22 pump. We flushed a number of birds climbing through the wild roses; but they roared away at knee level, leaving me little opportunity for my over-and-under, much less an opening for Thomas to ground-sluice one with his .22. We started out at the meteor hole above the last ranch and went all the way to the national forest. Thomas had his cap on the bridge of his nose and wobbled through the trees until we hit cross fences. We went out into the last open pasture before he got winded. So, we sat down and looked across the valley at the Gallatin Range, furiously white and serrated, making a bleak edge of the world. We sat in the sun and watched the chickadees make their way through the russet brush.

"Are you having a good time?"

"Sure," he said and curled a small hand around the octagonal barrel of the Winchester.

"A guy in a New York paper said I was destroying you with my life-style."

"What's a life-style?"

"It's a word they have. It means, how you go around acting."

He said, "Oh."

"The same guy said the movies gave us $400,000."

My son looked at me sharply. "What did you do with it?"

"I never got it."

"Who is this guy?"

"Name of the *Village Voice*."

"Is he a liar, liar with his pants on fire?"

"He's a yellow journalist."

"What's that?"

"Filth."

"What happened to all that money?"

"I don't know. Somebody forgot to pass it on. Then the journalist blamed it on me."

"That Marlon Brando got it," Thomas said.

"I don't think so. All he wanted was to be an Indian. We needed more for him to be a cowboy, but he wanted to be an Indian."

"He had the suit."

"I think that was our problem. I think he already had the suit."

"Can he hunt?" asked my son.

"I don't think so, Tom."

THE REAR QUARTERS of the antelope came from the smoker so dense and finely grained it should have been sliced as prosciutto. My Canadian in-laws brought edgy, crumbling Cheddar from British Columbia and everybody kept an eye on the food and tried to pace themselves. The snow whirled in the windowlight and puffed the smoke down the chimney around the cedar flames. I had a stretch of enumerating things: my family, hayfields, saddle horses, friends, thirty-ought-six, French and Russian novels. I had a baby girl, colts coming, and a new roof on the barn. I finished a big corral made of railroad ties and two-by-sixes. I was within 18 months of my father's death, my sister's death, the collapse of my marriage, the recutting of a film I'd made by ham-fisted producers, and the turning of a compact Western I'd written into utter rat shit by the puffy androids of *avanti* cinema. Finally, the fabrications of these birdbrains were being ascribed to me by such luminaries as John Simon, masochistic *New York*'s house Nazi, and Rex Reed, the Prince of Mince. Still, the washouts were repairing; and when a few things had been set aside, not excluding drugs and paranoia, a few features were left standing, not excluding lovers, children, friends, and saddle horses. In time, it would be clear as a bell. I did want venison again in the winter and couldn't help but feel some old ridge-runner had my number on him.

I didn't want to read and I didn't want to write or acknowledge the phone with its tendrils into the zombie enclaves. I didn't want the New Rugged; I wanted the Old Rugged and a pot to piss in. Otherwise, it's deteriorata with mice undermining the wiring in my frame house, sparks jumping in the insulation, the dog turning queer, and a horned owl staring at the baby through the nursery window.

IT WAS PITCH BLACK in the bedroom and the windows radiated cold across the blankets. The top of my head felt this side of frost and the stars hung like ice crystals over the chimney. I scrambled out of bed and slipped into my long johns, put on a heavy shirt and my wool logger pants with the police suspenders. I carried the boots down to the kitchen so as not to wake the house and zapped the percolator on. I put some cheese and chocolate in my coat, and when the coffee was done I filled a chili bowl and quaffed it against the winter.

When I hit the front steps I heard the hard squeaking of new snow under my boots and the wind moved against my face like a machine for refinishing hardwood floors. I backed the truck up to the horse trailer, the lights wheeling against the ghostly trunks of the bare cottonwoods. I connected the trailer and pulled it forward to a flat spot for loading the horse.

I had figured that when I got to the corral, I could tell one horse from another by starlight; but the horses were in the shadow of the barn and I went in feeling my way among their shapes trying to find my hunting horse Rocky, and trying to get the front end of the big sorrel who kicks when surprised. Suddenly Rocky was looking in my face and I reached around his neck with the halter. A 1,300-pound bay quarter horse, his withers angled up like a fighting bull, he wondered where we were going but ambled after me on a slack lead rope as we headed out of the darkened corral.

I have an old trailer made by a Texas horse vet years ago. It has none of the amenities of newer trailers. I wish it had a dome light for loading in the dark; but it doesn't. You ought to check and see if the cat's sleeping in it before you load; and I didn't do that either. Instead, I climbed inside of the trailer and the horse followed me. I tied the horse down to a D-ring and started back out, when he blew up. The two of us were confined in the small space and he was ripping and bucking between the walls with such noise and violence that I had a brief disassociated moment of suspension from fear. I jumped up on the manger with my arms around my head while the horse shattered the inside of the trailer and rocked it furiously on its axles. Then he blew the steel rings out of the halter and fell over backward in the snow. The cat darted out and was gone. I slipped down off the manger and looked for the horse; he had gotten up and was sidling down past the granary in the star shadows.

I put two blankets on him, saddled him, played with his feet and calmed him. I loaded him without incident and headed out.

I went through the aspen line at daybreak, still climbing. The horse ascended steadily toward a high basin creaking the saddle metronomically. It was getting colder as the sun came up and the rifle scabbard held my left leg far enough from the horse that I was chilling on that side.

We touched the bottom of the basin and I could see the rock wall defined by a black stripe of evergreens on one side and the remains of an avalanche on the other. I thought how utterly desolate this country can look in winter and how one could hardly think of human travel in it at all, not white horsemen nor Indians dragging travois, just aerial raptors with their rending talons and heads like cameras slicing across the geometry of winter.

Then we stepped into a deep hole and the horse went to his chest in the powder, splashing the snow out before him as he floundered toward the other side. I got my feet out of the stirrups in case we went over. Then we were on wind-scoured rock and I hunted some lee for the two of us. I thought of my son's words after our last cold ride: "Dad, you know in 4-H? Well, I want to switch from Horsemanship to Aviation."

The spot was like this: a crest of snow crowned in a sculpted edge high enough to protect us. There was a tough little juniper to picket the horse to, and a good place to sit out of the cold and noise. Over my head, a long, curling plume of snow poured out, unchanging in shape against the pale blue sky. I ate some of the cheese and rewrapped it. I got the rifle down from the scabbard, loosened the cinch, and undid the flank cinch. I put the stirrup over the horn to remind me my saddle was loose, loaded two cartridges into the blind magazine and slipped one in the chamber. Then I started toward the rock wall, staring at the patterned discolorations: old seeps, lichen, cracks, and the madhouse calligraphy of immemorial weather.

There were a lot of tracks where the snow had crusted out of the wind; all deer except for one well-used bobcat trail winding along the edges of a long rocky slot. I moved as carefully as I could, stretching my eyes as far out in front of my detectable movement as I could. I tried to work into the wind but it turned erratically in the basin as the temperature of the new day changed.

The buck was studying me as soon as I came out on the open slope; he was a long way away and I stopped motionless to wait for him to feed again. He stared straight at me from 500 yards. I waited until I could no longer feel my feet nor finally my legs. It was nearly an hour before he suddenly ducked his head and began to feed. Every time he fed I moved a few feet, but he was working away from me and I wasn't getting anywhere. Over the next half-hour he made his way to a little rim and, in the half-hour after that, moved the 20 feet that dropped him over the rim.

I went as fast as I could move quietly. I now had the rim to cover me and the buck should be less than a hundred yards from me when I looked over. It was all browse for a half mile, wild roses, buck brush and young quakies where there was any runoff.

When I reached the rim, I took off my hat and set it in the snow with my gloves inside. I wanted to be looking in the right direction when I cleared the rim, rise a half step and be looking straight at the buck, not scanning for the buck with him running 60, a degree or two out of my periphery. And I didn't want to gum it up with thinking or trajectory guessing. People are always trajectory guessing their way into gut shots and clean misses. So, before I took the last step, all there was to do was lower the rim with my feet, lower the buck into my vision, and isolate the path of the bullet.

As I took that step, I knew he was running. He wasn't in the browse at all, but angling into invisibility at the rock wall, racing straight into the elevation, bounding toward zero gravity, taking his longest arc into the bullet and the finality and terror of all you have made of the world, the finality you know that you share even with the Princess and your babies with their inherited and ambiguous dentition, the finality that, any minute now, you will meet as well.

He slid a hundred yards in a plume of snow. I dressed him and skidded him by one antler to the horse. I made a slit behind the last ribs, pulled him over the saddle and put the horn through the slit, lashed the feet to the cinch Ds and led the horse downhill. The horse had bells of clear ice around his hooves and, when he slipped, I chipped them out from under his feet with the point of a bullet.

I hung the buck in the open woodshed with a lariat over a rafter. He turned slowly against the cooling air. I could see the intermittent blue light of the television against the bedroom ceiling from where I stood. I stopped the twirling of the buck, my hands deep in the sage-scented fur, and thought: This is either the beginning or the end of everything.

*September 1977*

# Swamp Odyssey

## A journey in black water and time

● ▲ ■

### DAVID QUAMMEN

**M**y 18th high school reunion was held in the Okefenokee Swamp, 700 miles from the scene of the crime. One advantage of this arrangement was that only two of us showed up. There was the Red Ace and myself. He flew into Jacksonville on a sardine-class ticket aboard People Express and spent a miserable night on a bench at the airport, worst sleep he'd had since May of 1966 when we pulled a late one together cramming Virgil for a senior exam and he crashed until morning in my bedroom chair. This was back before the invention of software, the pocket calculator, possibly also fire. People still memorized Latin verbs. The Red Ace and I, however, must have been the only two high school seniors of our generation so moronically dutiful as to lose a night's sleep over the *Aeneid* within ten days of graduation itself. More sensible souls were driving Chevys to the levee. All things considered, it was a miracle of Jesus that neither Red nor I ended up a priest or a lawyer. He went into professional tennis and I came out of grad school as a bartender and a fishing guide. Eighteen years later we rendezvoused at the Tahiti Motel in Folkston, Georgia, just outside the east entrance of the Okefenokee. Folkston, for you *Pogo* fans, is not far from Fort Mudge.

I had ridden out from Savannah with an old boy named John Crawford, a.k.a. Crawfish, a wizard swamp guide who by happy coincidence of compatibility was just six days younger than the Red Ace and had therefore gone to high school together with us separately—in a different place at the same time, if you see what I mean. We're talking about the infamous midsixties, exactly those years stretching from "Louie, Louie" to the Gulf of Tonkin to the assassination of Malcolm X. Unmatchable for sheer dizziness and an overabundance of nasty, loud sounds. I had suggested the Okefenokee Swamp with a mind to peace and quiet. Also, I suspected it might be a wonderful place to visit.

This cheerful predisposition was based mainly on optimism and ignorance. Turned out I was right, but for all the wrong reasons.

I had imagined that five days of slogging across the Okefenokee Swamp would offer such heights of discomfort and travail that the experience would be exhilarating for its pure intensity. Tangled vegetation, oppressive heat, no solid ground for miles, fetid water, biting insects, 10,000 alligators, and the continent's foremost selection of poisonous snakes—that sort of thing. I had put it to Red like one of those old recruiting ads for the Peace Corps: "Bad pay and long hours, but at least you'll be hungry and in danger." The experts said you should do your traveling in this swamp, if you had to do any, between February and April; that is, before the water dropped, the heat came up, and the mosquitoes appeared in sky-darkening multitudes. So of course I had us there at the end of May. Crawfish, who himself harbors a helpless and unstinting love for the Okefenokee, had told me by phone, "You know, this trip is liable to be hardship duty."

Our last stop in civilization was at a tourist concession on the very fringe of the swamp, a store and boat dock run by a third-generation swamper named Harry Johnson, from whom the Red Ace made last-minute purchases (our eighth or ninth bottle of insect repellent) while Crawfish saw to food and I filled a five-gallon carboy with drinking water. At least I had been told we would drink it. But the water that came out of Harry Johnson's side tap was black, blacker than the coffee at the Folkston café. Johnson's dock sat on a blackwater cove at the end of a blackwater canal leading away into the depths of the swamp, and the faucet was evidently drawing on that selfsame blackness. Also, the stuff smelled like a shoe factory.

"Are we going to drink this?" I asked Crawfish, sloshing a bit out so he could see. Crawfish did not seem concerned.

"Isn't that a bit darker than usual?" he said to Harry Johnson.

Harry Johnson smiled benignly. "Got a little sulfur in there. Do you good. Keep the 'skeeters off you."

THE OKEFENOKEE SWAMP is a great shallow saucer full of water, peat, and vegetation, covering 400,000 acres near the eastern end of the border between Georgia and Florida. Thanks to a foresightful purchase by the U.S. government back in 1937, most of it is protected as the Okefenokee National Wildlife Refuge. It is closer to wilderness condition today than it was during the early decades of this century, when humans lived in it, hunting and fishing and timbering. Motorized travel is now restricted to the fringes of the swamp, and even canoe travel is controlled by the U.S. Fish and Wildlife Service, which grants a limited number of permits each year for the trails that lead to a limited number of campsites.

The Okefenokee is a relatively young ecological system, the wild vegetal growth and the buildup of peat (dead and decaying plant material) having begun about 7,000 years ago. The swamp holds a large volume of water that is gently in motion. Prevented from percolating downward by impermeable clays underneath and slowed by the spongelike peat and the network of living vegetation, the swamp water nonetheless flows gradually down an incline that varies by only ten feet of vertical drop from the northeastern edge of the swamp to the southwestern edge. It is drained away by two separate rivers headed toward two separate seas: the St. Marys River, emptying from the swamp's southeastern corner into the Atlantic; and the Suwannee River, meandering from the western border of the swamp off to the Gulf of Mexico. Within the swamp, the divide between St. Marys flow and Suwannee flow is by no means clear-cut, though a much larger share of the total finds its way into the Suwannee. The current of the Okefenokee itself moves in broad, shallow sheets more than in narrow channels, especially during time of high water, passing over and under and through the vast, filtering mass of vegetation and peat. For a number of complicated reasons related to ground-water seepage and the configurations of islands and troughs, as well as to the general incline, this current proceeds in a roughly circular pattern: a great mandala of dark water, moving around counterclockwise.

The submerged vegetation and peat strain out organic impurities, while also turning the water black with tannic acid. It's the same process that gives color to certain flatland jungle streams, most notably the Rio Negro. Plant life is burgeoning and dying within the drainage much faster than it can decay, much faster than the drowsy current can carry its products of decomposition away.

The result is an acidic blackwater tea, ideal medium for culturing cypress trees, carnivorous plants, alligators. On a bright day that blackwater tea casts back reflections of a complete swamp world seen upside down, as on a surface of polished and oiled ebony. And it's as potable, I learned eventually, as it is beautiful.

WE SET OFF from a point called Kingfisher Landing, the Red Ace and I paddling one canoe, Crawfish standing in the stern of the other, easing his boat along with what seemed to be the effortless strokes of a 12-foot bamboo pole. For an hour or three we moved down long, tunnellike corridors through thick brush, riding the current in a channel that was often no deeper than a bathtub and no wider than a sidewalk. In some places the brush arched overhead into a darkening canopy. In others it closed so tightly ahead that we had to spread branches by hand as we went through. Always the water beneath us was that lovely, inscrutable black. Crawfish led one detour to what he said was a typical gator hole—a small, muddy pond not far off our channel that had been scooped out of the peat by force of reptilian will. It was deeper than we could measure, more turbid than the channel, but apparently unoccupied. Crawfish probed his pole down into the center and made some strange, muted yelping sounds into the end, like a drunken jazzman struggling with a clogged trumpet.

"That's it. Our guide has flipped. He thinks he's a sea lion," said the Red Ace. "We're doomed."

"Sometimes that brings them up," said Crawfish.

"Do we want them up?"

The first of the rains began, which seemed inconvenient only until we stopped trying to stay dry and surrendered ourselves to the cooling effect. A drenching in rainwater seemed preferable to a drenching in sweat, after all, and the temperature had plummeted right into the 80s. Then the sun returned, bringing with it the deerflies. Slim chartreuse vines groped outward like green snakes from the overhanging brush, slender stalks reaching for sunlight, for support, for the brush on the opposite side of the channel, for a passing canoeist, striving to get hold and tighten down, to knit closed on daylight and motion. The vines were called smilax, Crawfish said. It was his swamp, and he knew the names of everything. He said the buds and the terminal leaves of the vines were sweet and tasty.

"You can eat them."

"*You* can eat them," said the Red Ace.

My hands had started to swell from the deerfly bites. A curious new experience for me, who could not even spell anaphylactic shock. I remembered the tale Crawfish had told about a city dude he was once required to evacuate out of the Okefenokee by moonlight. This fellow had coated his whole body with layer upon layer of the fiercest insect repellent; then, when the afternoon heat got serious, started dunking his terry-cloth hat and letting the cool runnels trickle down his face. Soon he had one eye full of *N-diethyl-meta-toluamide,* but the doctors just managed to save it. A little parable, Crawfish seemed to imply, about where insect repellent would get you.

We made camp an hour before dark at Maul Hammock Lake, a modest patch of open water clotted over only partly by waterlilies and another big-leafed floating plant that Crawfish called spatterdock. Our appointed campsite was the Maul Hammock platform, a bare structure of planks and pilings just big enough for three tents and an Optimus stove and a billion mosquitoes. It looked like a little lakeside dock, the kind you would dive from in summer if you were a kid—except here in the Okefenokee there was no real lake to dive into, unless you craved to pack your nostrils and ears full of peat, nor any dry land onto which you could step off. The platform, at day's end, was it. Stride out into that tangle of shrubbery that passed for the landward side and you would sink to your waist. Lie down in a sleeping bag on some comfortable patch of sphagnum moss and you were liable to wake up drowned.

"Who would like wine?" said Crawfish.

"Yes, yes, yes!"

It was a pert but amusing Chablis in a large plastic jug bearing a label that read ANTIVENIN.

That night I thought and dreamed intermittently about missing digits. Thanks to the mysterious toxic deerflies of the Okefenokee, my hand had continued swelling and I had waited too long to transfer my wedding ring; now the ring was bound on at the base of a finger that looked bloated and pale as a boiled bratwurst. I did not want to see this particular ring, which means a lot to me, taken off with a Swiss Army hacksaw. But I had also begun wondering, more than idly, which would give first—the gold band or the blood flow to that finger. It put me in mind of a story Crawfish had told about the time he was snakebit and decided against seeing a doctor.

Crawfish, you must first understand, is one of those singular folk born with an incurable affinity toward reptiles. He is a self-taught herpetologist of professional rigor and a passionate admirer of the animals he knows. Every lizard, to him, is a creature of arresting beauty. Every alligator is like an old friend. Every snake is a poem. The particular poem in question here was a copperhead.

He found it one day on the long woodland drive that led to his house. Captured it easily and, holding the snake in his left hand, resumed driving with his right. He had handled thousands of poisonous snakes over the years, including a pygmy rattler that lived in his bedroom while he was a kid. But this time, according to Crawfish, he got careless. Climbing out of the vehicle, he relaxed his grip slightly and the snake jerked back, nailing one fang into Crawfish's middle finger. "It was like a hot poker jammed in there," he told me. "Worst pain I've ever felt."

He turned down the horse-serum antivenin because a human body sometimes reacts drastically to that stuff: A friend of his in the same situation had once nearly died from it. He didn't even phone a doctor. "I like to let my body try and heal itself," Crawfish told me in the most unassuming and matter-of-fact manner; he would have dismissed the whole subject if I hadn't prodded him for details. "Heal itself *if possible,*" he added. "Within reason." On this occasion his arm swelled up to the shoulder and stayed swelled for three weeks. Evidently he judged that to be within reason. His finger puffed out bigger than he had imagined a finger could puff. Then it turned black. "I thought it would probably just fall off." But it didn't. After three months the finger was back to normal, except for the lingering numbness near the tip.

"What happened to the snake?" I asked.

"You mean did he get sick?"

"I mean what did you do to the sucker?"

"Oh, we kept him around as a pet," said Crawfish. "Just a while. Then let him go."

So this was not a man you would wake from sound sleep with squeaky talk of evacuating your fat little finger. By midafternoon the next day, my ring could be quietly removed.

WE PADDLED for several hours through an open area called Sapling Prairie, near the northernmost edge of the swamp. With clear lines of sight for miles across and little chance that a predator can come up by surprise, Sapling Prairie is one of the favorite habitats of the swamp's biggest birds: three species of heron, several kinds of egret, several ibis, and a good population of sandhill cranes, whose loud, ratchety calls sounded at 300 yards like the complaint of a rusty barn hinge broadcast by loudspeaker.

When they say "prairie" in the Okefenokee what they mean is a large, shallow, marshy pond, a zone bare of trees and bushes but covered almost entirely by grasses and other small foliage such as spatterdock, water lilies, floating hearts, a couple of species of orchid, the carnivorous sundews and bladderworts. In the prairies, water stands two or three feet deep over a substrate of peat, the current is nearly imperceptible, and the only pathways are those kept open by canoeists and alligators.

Large rafts of peat occasionally rise up from the prairie bottom, lifted by the buoyant force of methane gas, a byproduct of anaerobic bacteria at work on the decomposition of the submerged plant muck. Sundews especially seem to favor these risen rafts, colonizing them early and supplementing the marginal diet with insects caught in their own sticky, fistlike leaves. After the sundews, other small plants and even pine saplings get aboard, stitching out a network of roots, until the raft may become a soft, anchored island.

In the distance, across Sapling Prairie, giving a skyline to the flats, are another sort of islandlike feature called cypress domes. Cypress is a water-loving hardwood with seeds that require long submersion (as well as a dry interval) before they will germinate, so the clusters of cypress originate without benefit of a raft, sometimes growing right up out of the peat through a layer of standing water. One tree takes hold, dropping seeds, offering some stability of conditions for other recruits, and a colony of cypress expands outward over the marsh, dome-shaped against the sky because the oldest and largest trees are at the center. Eventually, such a stand will become carpeted at the base with a tussocky layer of mosses and peat and brush—almost but not quite like solid ground. The cypress may be joined by black gum trees and maple and several species of bay. Local slang refers to these patches of soggy forest as "houses," possibly because they provide habitat for a big share of the swamp's mammalian wildlife. But the Okefenokee, with its meager supply of real solid ground, is not nearly so hospitable to mammals as it is to birds and reptiles and amphibians. Most of the mammalian species are small: cotton mouse, gray squirrel, marsh rabbit, raccoon, flying squirrel, evening bat, big-eared bat, seminole bat.

Swimming and flying are the optimal modes of travel. Climbing is also possible. Walking is difficult. It's hard to imagine how even a small deer could support its 70 pounds over those tiny hoofs on a platform of floating peat. When a creature so large as a human strides through this terrain, the ground bounces and the tall trees shudder. The name Okefenokee itself comes from old Indian words—*ecunnau finocau*—that meant "the trembling earth."

"WATCH OUT for cottonmouths above in the bushes," said Crawfish.

"You got it, buddy," said the Red Ace.

"And be careful when you step over fallen logs."

We were bushwhacking through the understory of a cypress dome, sunk to our knees in a lush patch of yellow-green sphagnum, clutching at saplings with each step to avoid sinking farther. In the softest places we had to knee-walk, using our shins like snowshoes. The water was warm, the sensation was surprisingly pleasant. Hiking this way, we could cover a mile in about two days. Crawfish was barefoot.

Lichens in four colors were wrapped like gaudy decals on the trunks of loblolly bay trees. There were some amazing shades and configurations of shelf fungi. In the center of the thicket we paused to admire one especially majestic cypress. A hundred feet tall, its canopy was hung with long beards of Spanish moss; very possibly it had been the patriarch of this whole dome. Then we slogged on in a wide loop back toward the boats. Suddenly Crawfish reversed course, backing hastily out from under the limb of a bush.

He was clutching the side of his face and wheezing in pain. By the time I got near him, though, he already seemed calm again. His left eye was beginning to swell shut.

"It's okay. Only a wasp. Yow. Stings pretty good, but what a relief," he said "I thought I'd been tagged by a snake."

"What's the first aid for having a cottonmouth bite into your eyeball?"

"I can't imagine." He looked at me cheerfully with a good eye and one gone slimy and red. "Just don't put a tourniquet on my neck."

His body would heal itself. Once after a trip in the Ogeechee River drainage, Crawfish had told me, he pulled 52 ticks off his body, every one of which had already gotten itself plugged in. Around that time, he suspected, he must certainly have had a case of tick fever. All the symptoms were there. But his body had healed itself.

·  ·  ·

NO MORE RAIN, no more deerflies, no more oppressive heat and humidity: just mild sunshine and the gradual awareness that this swamp journey of ours was somehow being smiled upon.

The scenery had gotten even more exotically gorgeous after Sapling Prairie, when we turned south toward the very heart of the Okefenokee on a channel that led in and out among cypress domes. The cypress themselves seemed to thrive in this area; they were lofty and stark, exaggeratedly fat where they came out of the black water but tapering quickly down into a long roof-beam trunk, Spanish moss dangling all over the high branches. The smilax vines continued to reach out along narrow runs, but now Red and I were reaching back, letting the navigation lapse while we snapped off those sweet little tips, popping them down like they were huckleberries. There was a noticeable current again, upon which we moved easily. Best of all, for me, was having the Red Ace there in the front of the boat, intermittently rummaging down into his bucket of cameras and zoom lenses and fancy filters, coming back up with some combination of that hardware in front of his face while he tracked the latest alligator on a leisurely swim along the channel before us, the latest heron on a laborious takeoff and slow, graceful walk across the sky. I was glad to have Red here in the swamp because it had been too little and too long. I had barely seen him since 1972.

Certain people can make the most pleasant enterprise seem doleful; others can turn any grim misadventure at least into pretty good slapstick. The Red Ace is of the latter group: I had laughed through some of my life's dreariest moments in his company. I could describe the time he split my scalp open with one crack of an exploding all-day sucker, an event that occurred onstage during a high school melodrama in 1965. I bled on my Buster Brown suit while we went ahead and sang "Never Hit Your Grandma With a Shovel." I could tell about the West Side of Chicago in 1968 and a neighborhood gang that was intent on frightening off a commune of do-gooder white boys. I could recount the one about The Man in the Towel, late at night in the labyrinthine corridors of the Penn Station YMCA, 1969, with the Red Ace and me literally barricaded up in a $5 room. And there were the few weeks he slept on the floor of my garret in England, during the winter of 1971, while he tried to decide whether to fly home and propose marriage and I groped for a plausible excuse to drop out of graduate school. But never mind all that. Just take my word. Space doesn't allow doing justice to those episodes, and anyway this is a story about—at least mainly about—the Okefenokee Swamp.

During the past dozen years we had seen little of each other. It was a matter of history and geography. Time and change. The movement of waters along an imperceptible gradient, dividing to follow different routes to different seas. Then again, it wasn't at all so gentle as that implies. Something ended abruptly in 1972.

What was it that ended? Not the friendship. Not just our youth or his bachelorhood. Not just my romance with academia. It was the sixties themselves, according to my theory, that ended in 1972.

Now I know some pundits argue that the sixties ended at Altamont, in December of 1969, when a Mick Jagger song finally resulted in murder and the band played on. Others would claim that the true end came in April of 1975, at the moment the last U.S. helicopter lifted off the roof of a building that had been the American embassy in a place now named Ho Chi Minh City. I assert otherwise. For me the definite and unmistakable end of the sixties—for whatever they had been worth, and God only knows—came on that evening in November of 1972 when the network computers announced, just minutes after the first polls were closed, that Richard Nixon had squashed an earnest, unfortunate man named George McGovern, on whose behalf I had gone AWOL from all aspects of my own life. And of course I was just one of many.

Me, I slept that night on a pile of leaflets in the back room of a McGovern storefront in suburban Chicago. I used my seersucker politico jacket for a pillow, next morning dropping that into a trash barrel. My reaction within ten days was to depart the civilized U.S., heading back to England and then to Africa and then eventually, still farther, to Montana.

Yes I was young, and my political metabolism was hysterical. I was angry and worried and saddened—everything but surprised. But also I count myself as having been lucky: The abrupt end of the sixties may have been one of the best things that ever happened to me, because Montana certainly was.

Neither the Red Ace nor I got back to southern Ohio for that fifth or tenth or (if there are such things) 15th high school reunion. I heard he was married and then later not and teaching tennis and then not. He was back East in a town he himself had always celebrated for its grim ugliness. He was steady, but there were no giveaways of good fortune. He endured solitarily through a run of bad weather—of the personal variety—that went on just too damn long. It seemed to me like unfairness. I invited him, in a tone that verged on browbeating, to come out and fill his lungs with Montana air. But that never managed to happen. I suggested he move out permanently (although adding to the number of Montana residents, even by one, is a responsibility I don't take lightly). Moving wasn't on. Still he needed—and *deserved,* it seemed to me—to fill his lungs with a new sort of air. Any sort. Shuffle the deck, turn the kaleidoscope, get some fresh alignments and juxtapositions. This was all unsolicited diagnosis by me, the Dutch uncle. A new sort of air.

Finally I said: *Meet me in south Georgia two months from today, and we'll go out and get lost in the Okefenokee Swamp.*

The Red Ace said: *How could I possibly refuse?*

WHICH BRINGS me to another story that Crawfish told in the privacy of the swamp. He didn't push these stories forward, understand, as though he enjoyed talking about himself. On the contrary. It was simply a matter of memory doors opening and anecdotes emerging as a certain swamp-bound but genuine rapport grew up among the three of us. And Crawfish, I learned, was a man of multiple doors, with a luminous little memory behind each.

This one was about being electrocuted. It happened when he was 14. (A hard year, the same year he shot an arrow through his own wrist with a device called a Hawaiian sling. But that's a still different story, and not one that illustrates the human body's capacity for self-healing.) The doctors in this case of electrocution honestly thought he had killed himself, at least temporarily. They suspected that his heart was not beating during the time he sailed through the air.

He was in the upper branches of a tree, doing merely the sort of foolhardy and routinely life-threatening things that 14-year-old boys used to do in trees. Leaning too far, he reached back for support and grabbed hold of a wire. The wire was carrying 10,000 volts. The tree was wet. Zap: legally dead, through that long, dreamy moment while his body fell 45 feet to the ground. "I had the sensation of floating," said Crawfish. "I saw myself floating there, my body in the air. Dead."

But he was a lucky young Crawfish, missing the picket fence by a full three feet and hitting the ground hard. That impact on landing—so the doctors hypothesized—must have started his heart beating again.

The moral, I suppose, is that if the tree had been smaller his death

might have been more permanent. The moral is that you never know
what it might be, causing your lungs to fill with new air. It might be
Richard Nixon. It might be the Okefenokee Swamp.

As LATE AFTERNOON was turning to early evening, we came into an area
called Big Water, which is a lake by the Okefenokee system of figuring,
though in some ways seems more like a river, yet, in real justice, though,
Big Water should not and cannot be reduced to either of those categories.
It is a thing of the swamp world, and you would find its equivalent
nowhere else. It was the loveliest spot Red and I had seen or would see
in the Okefenokee, and in its own style probably one of the most magical
wild places on the continent. It was also high on Crawfish's private list
of Okefenokee secrets, and though he presented it to us with quiet pride,
noncommittally, later we knew that he had been gratified by our appreciation. Here in Big Water was where the alligators came out to greet
us.

What the maps call Big Water Lake is really a liquid canyon through
tall cypress, a long blade of open water running on for three miles but
never more than about 40 yards wide. On each side, beneath the cypress,
are little coves of still water carpeted over with spatterdock. The current
moves north to south, steady enough to carry a canoe but so smooth
that the water never forfeits its texture of polished ebony. With the light
angled low, we could see from 30 yards back the tiny wakes of whirligig
beetles, as they proceeded before us along the surface. In the course of
a couple of miles, paddling quietly, we also saw the wakes of a dozen
alligators, wakes that were larger but not much larger than those of the
beetles: nothing but nostrils and eyes protruding to cut the water, tail
working powerfully but invisibly. Most of these alligators slid away as we
approached, moving off downstream and then, if we gained on them,
diving; they could easily stay down, if they had to, for half an hour. But
some were more curious.

In one of the spatterdock coves we stopped to explore the possibility
of a fish dinner. Crawfish unwound the line from his cane pole and
flopped out a hook baited with salami—the higher technology of angling
has not yet come to the Okefenokee, nor is there any reason why it
should. In a minute Crawfish's bobber was bobbing tentatively. I held
our canoe below Crawfish's in the tail of the eddy, giving him room,
while the Red Ace's camera went clickety clickety. We found ourselves

whispering. Last shards of sunlight breaking through the cypress, and we both felt the same tranquillity and pagan reverence as if we had been sitting the afternoon away in the cathedral at Chartres. We watched Crawfish working his hook and line—and in that we weren't alone. A large alligator came out of the spatterdock, sliding up quietly near Crawfish's canoe to see how the fisherman was faring.

Crawfish twitched the cane, then lifted a small sunfish up and into his boat. We whooped encouragingly, Crawfish said nothing, and the alligator came a couple of yards closer.

Only its eyeballs and snout were visible, but the spacing between those suggested an animal about seven feet long. It was holding position, patient and very attentive, less than ten feet off Crawfish's starboard bow. He could have tweaked it on the nose with his fishing pole. Instead he just ignored it. Caught another sunfish. The alligator moved still closer. I had thought at first, unavoidably, about Captain Hook and the croc-with-the-clock, but this alligator, it became clear, did not represent the slightest menace. It had more the demeanor of a shameless mutt at the back door of a butcher shop.

"He's waiting for a handout," Crawfish said across the quiet water. "Been around too many fishermen at this spot."

Crawfish offered the gator no handout. We understood why. That would have only reinforced its false and dangerous misapprehension of the nature of the human species. Still, it took a person of will as well as principle to say no to such a beautiful animal.

ANOTHER STORY, this one of will and principle.

Back in 1968, about the same time Red and I were being terrorized by that gang in Chicago, Crawfish was enrolled at Armstrong College in Savannah; he was also working part-time as a herpetologist for the Savannah Science Museum. Herpetology being his real true love, he gradually began to spend more time at the museum than at Armstrong. When this fact became known to the members of a certain civic body, John Crawford received a draft notice. The year 1968 was of course a very lousy time to be drafted. Furthermore, Crawfish was opposed on grounds of conscience to the war in Vietnam. So he enlisted in the Navy, thinking this might be a partial solution. He was trained, then assigned as an electrician's mate to a submarine support ship based in Bremerton, Washington. Pulled duty down through Panama, at the Guantanamo base on Cuba, and at a submarine base in Key West. His ship was still there in Key West when word of a large antiwar demonstration to be held outside the gates of the sub base filtered through the ranks. If he had leave that day, Crawfish thought, he would like to participate. He was in no position, at that point in his life, to foresee which way the waters would flow.

The Navy brass at Key West were concerned that there might be trouble from those demonstrators. So they planned to assign a few men to stand guard with rifles, just in case things got out of hand. A finger was pointed while a voice said, "You, you, you, and Crawford." It brought to Crawfish the clarification that until then had been muddled and delayed. He thought, "I can't do that. I might be asked to shoot my own friends." And not just friends, but people with whom he was in political and moral agreement. So he filed for status as a conscientious objector.

It was the wrong time to do that. Convincing the U.S. armed forces that you are a legitimate conscientious objector after you have already *enlisted* in the Navy—and with a Catholic upbringing, which is supposed to make you well fit religiously for war—is only a little more difficult than driving an alligator through the eye of a needle. While his application was pending, Crawfish took abuse from the noncom officers. He was given the nickname Rabbit. He was razzed late at night by patriots stumbling in drunk. A large and solid fellow, Crawfish explained to them in his mild way that, though opposed to war, he had no objection whatever to fistfights. They backed off. And he argued his way successfully to the CO discharge.

Escaping the Navy at that juncture led him to a very different sort of life in the Florida Keys—a little commercial fishing, lots of diving, wildlife photography, lobster research, and eventually some freelance biological consulting. That experience led back to Savannah, where in 1973 he and two friends started an enterprise called Wilderness Southeast, a nonprofit institution providing outfitted and guided wilderness trips with a strong emphasis on ecological education. Crawfish never suspected, earlier on, that he would ever earn a living from what he loved best: mucking around in places like the Okefenokee Swamp, one eye peeled for reptiles. But 11 years later the business was flourishing.

After the Red Ace agreed to come on a swamp odyssey, it was Wilderness Southeast that I called. "The Okefenokee," I said. "Have you got a good guide? Somebody who could show me the reptile life?"

They said, "Do we ever."

·   ·   ·

THERE WAS more. There was much more swamp and many more stories and quite a few other arrestingly beautiful reptiles. We drank all the antivenin. The Red Ace and I did a reprise of "Never Hit Your Grandma With a Shovel," first performance in 18 years, and Crawfish, having sat through it, was made an honorary member of our high school class. Late at night, as we lay on a platform near Big Water, we heard the unforgettable bellow of a very large alligator, throaty and low and prolonged. It was a deep bass rumbling, so deep that we felt it through the planks of the platform almost as much as we heard it, and at first Red and I took it for the sound of a big outboard motor held at very low idle, in the distance at least a mile off. Then it was answered by another outboard, much nearer us. This wasn't anyone's low idle. It was a living sound, a sound with the same magisterial quality as a lion's roar heard after dark on the East African savanna. And for the Okefenokee, it was the precise equivalent: king of beasts.

After five days we had completed our loop and were headed out. Somewhere in one of the prairies south of Big Water we had turned against the current and begun paddling back upstream, toward the divide between those waters destined for the Gulf of Mexico and those waters destined for the Atlantic—but it was impossible for us to know just where that divide stood. We never saw it. From where we sat, so close, this was a single mandala of black water, moving around counterclockwise. That's always the way it is at the time.

Finally, reluctantly, we swung the canoes out through a gap between bushes and onto a wide thoroughfare called the Suwannee Canal—which was, being man-made, the least attractive stretch we had seen in the swamp. The Suwannee Canal would carry us straight back to the black-water cove at Harry Johnson's gift shop and boat landing.

The canal was too deep for Crawfish to pole against the bottom, so he was reduced at last to using a paddle. Paddling his canoe up beside ours, he told a last story:

In October of 1889 the Georgia legislature passed a bill that decreed that the Okefenokee Swamp be sold to the highest bidder. It went for 26 and a half cents an acre. The buyers were a consortium of businessmen calling themselves the Suwannee Canal Company. Their plan was to cut a canal from the east edge of the swamp to the St. Marys River, a monumental engineering feat that was supposed to result in draining the Okefenokee like a squeezed sponge. The waters would rush to the Atlantic, leaving behind thousands of acres and millions of dollars worth of timber and fertile land. The digging began in 1891 and continued for four years. The main canal was cut 32 feet deep and 11 miles long, including the stretch along which we three were presently paddling.

Then in 1897 the work ceased. The project was abandoned, never to be revived. In those days some few things were still beyond the technological will of humankind. At roughly the point in the effort when water was expected to begin surging toward the St. Marys, toward the Atlantic, widening out its own channel with the inexorable force of its call to the sea, the opposite happened. The waters began flowing back into the swamp.

*January 1985*

# FUEL-INJECTED NEOLITHIC
## A passage through Navaho Nation
● ▲ ■

### ROB SCHULTHEIS

It is not our America, not at all: this obdurate, secretive country the Navahos call Dinetah—"the land of Dineh—the people." It is $50-an-acre grazing land, imbued with unseen forces. A small rounded butte outside of Rough Rock, Arizona, is said to be an axis of energy; if you climb it, the Navahos say, you will go blind within a year. A muddy little seep in a cliff is a clan shrine, a place of veneration. The rain gods live in Pollen Mountain.

Imagine a place out of time: a piece of ancient Central Asia set down in the Southwest, with all its warriors and shamans, princesses, beggars and bards dressed more like cowboys than Indians.

"A long time ago, there weren't any pickup trucks," begins a tribal government pamphlet explaining tribal history for Navaho voters. Indeed—not so long ago, either. Back in the 1930s and '40s, almost all Navahos traveled by horseback, or in horsedrawn wagons. Today, of course, pickup trucks are an inseparable part of Navaho life: as "Navaho" as the farming and weaving the Navahos learned from the Pueblos, the sheep and horses they stole from the Spanish, the cattle and guns they got from Anglo America. Navaho culture is rather like a concretion; layer after layer of foreign deposition has built up until the range of Navaho cultural styles becomes gaudy, mind boggling.

There are Navahos who get around on horseback, and Navahos who drive supercharged vans, or hot rod around Lake Powell in speedboats, drinking beer and listening to Waylon Jennings. There are Navaho fundamentalist preachers who rant and rave in the best Pentecostal tradition; Navaho Mormons, Baptists (Peter MacDonald, the slick, sophisticated

tribal chairman, is a Baptist); Navaho Catholics, Methodists, Presbyterians
. . . and many, many practitioners of the Native American (peyote) Church
and the far more ancient traditional Navaho religion. One elderly lady in
the Four Corners area, polled for religious preference by an anthropologist,
checked every *possible* religious preference on the list: Catholic, Pentecostal,
Traditional, Native American Church, etc., etc.—even Unknown. The
perfect Navaho response: add, and add, and add to the rich weave of life
. . . beauty, a *sense* of rightness, is all that matters.

It is no accident that the Navahos' central deity is Changing Woman,
a kind of spiritual personification of resilience, adaptation.

SOMETIMES IT RAINS. Hard, black cloudbursts, or the soft, hanging mists
the Navahos call "female rain." But usually it does not. The Dinetah is
mostly bedrock, dunes, and rockstudded hardpan, supporting a range of
piñon, juniper, sagebrush, and crisp, skinny grass on four or five inches
of rain a year. The Navahos seem to conjure life out of it, like alchemists,
pulling a golden egg out of an empty crucible.

Like this typical Navaho farm, far off in the northern part of the
reservation, in the sere, arroyo-feathered depths of Nakai Canyon. Bad
summer, little rain, only a trickle of old water threading down the canyon
floor. Good country for dust devils, or ghosts; bad country for human
beings. The tough sagebrush grow 30 or 40 feet apart, divvying up the
sparse ground water. But down where the canyon crooks back sharply,
there is a dark patch of alluvial soil, caught and held there. Just above
it, someone has built a wall of cobblestones, and trapped a half moon of
water in a shadow of the cliff wall.

Water: Here hydrology is the purest form of religion, and all water is
holy water. Where water meets soil people have planted six rows of
peach trees and a patch of drab green corn. There is an old-style mud
hogan and a forked-stick sweat lodge off under a great cottonwood tree;
a sheep pen, built out of logs and brush, against the cliff; the gutted ruin
of an old pickup truck.

A skein of tire tracks winds upcanyon, toward a distant spring, or a
sheep camp. The damp sand is stamped shiny by the tracks of hundreds
of sheep and goats. A hobbled horse grazes in a clump of sagebrush.

The Salt family lives here; more of the Salt clan live up the canyon,
and up on the mesa top, back toward Shonto and Low Mountain. It's an
hour on the bus to the school at Navaho Mountain every morning, three

hours to the nearest paved road. The only real ties to the Anglo world are trade: mutton and wool and blankets exchanged for gas, canned food, flour, coffee, salt, and sugar. A living piece of neolithic America.

Fully two thirds of the 150,000 reservation Navahos still live this way: running cattle, sheep, and horses; raising a little corn; going away to Los Angeles, Denver, or Chicago to work; coming home again.

AN ENTERPRISING anthropologist did a study, a few years back, of how traditional Navahos spend their time. He found that they spend most of it just sitting around together—being. Not planning, or working, or talking; practicing, if you will, some kind of physical telepathy. Much is left unsaid, undone; there is a quiet eye of calm at the Navaho center, it seems. Life is full of slow, matter-of-fact magic: The world is made right by a whispered scrap of chant. There are songs for rain, or love; songs to drive away bad dreams, or witch dogs, or snake bites, or those damned Anglos. The earth speaks to those who know it.

"When I ride across the desert herding my sheep," one old Navaho told me, "everything around me seems alive. I can talk to the trees, the sagebrush, the grasses—even the earth and stones. There are birds in the sky, and rain clouds over the mountains. Everything is all right, beautiful."

IT IS THE SECOND DAY of the annual Many Farms Rodeo in Arizona, and Navahos have come from all over the reservation—from Cornfields and Empty Houses, Cow Springs and Two Grey Hills, White Fir Trees and Edge-of-the-Meadow, Spider Rock and Wildcat. Families, clans: an alluvium of names: Laughter, Bruisehead, Yellowhair, Greyeyes, Coyote, Redhouse, Roanhorse, Manygoats, Peaches, Salt, Silversmith, Warrior, Skeet, Atcitty, Yazzie, Benally, Begay, Tsosie and Tso, Gorman, Nelson, Billie, Lee. Nakai, for instance, means Mexican: a clan who intermarried with the early Spanish. Ganado Mucho, Many Cattle: a proud old name, denoting success in cattle-stealing from the Spanish and Anglo invaders. Tsosie means skinny, or thin: some long-ago famine, drought? What stories are wrapped up in that wonderful name, Mrs. Many Grey Billy Goats' Son Number Two?

It is a hot, bleached blue day. A vulture saws circles in the arid sky. To the east, the mountains are heaped with incandescent cumulus clouds that promise rain, but won't deliver. The barbed-wire-fenced arena, with its crude wooden judges' booth, is ringed with pickup trucks, jammed with spectators. A tape deck is playing a number by XIT, the Albuquerque Indian power-rock trio whose motto is "Gonna rock and roll ya till your skin turns red." Another truck blares "Hotel California"; another, "Shake Your Booty." A customized van with a gaudy desert mural air-brushed on the side cruises by, full of young Navaho longhairs. A pickup full of Indian cowboys follows, bumperstickers on the back: "Gods, Guts and Guns: They Made America Great—Let's Keep 'Em" and "Navahos Make Better Lovers."

A lovely epicanthic cowgirl rides by on the tailgate of a pickup truck, smoking a joint. A tribal police cruiser glides by, poker-faced cop at the wheel, black mirror sunglasses, a perfect imitation of a television S.W.A.T. man. Then a whole family, in another pickup: husband in straw cowboy hat; his thin, fierce wife beside him in the cab, holding a baby whose face almost glows; in the back, grandmother and grandfather, old and peaceful; and two little girls and a little boy, pointing their fingers and yelling, "Bang! Bang!"

The announcer calls the rodeo events in both Navaho and classic deadpan redneckese. A bull, a big one, explodes out of the chute, with a sinewy Navaho kid hooked into the cinch rope. He rides, amazingly, like a champ: glued to the rampaging animal, slewing along, the two of them melded together like a Minotaur. His hawk-feathered felt Stetson sails away, tumbling across the sky to land in the dust. And then the time horn sounds, and he slides off and scampers away.

I talk to one of the dust-covered bull riders in the crowd, a kid from Grey Mountain: "I got thrown, man. I got a bad draw." He pushes his cowboy hat back with one hand. "Hey, if you're ever down in Chinle and want any dope, just look for me. I got about two acres growing, up a draw in the Lukachukai Mountains. *Good* stuff. One *little* smoke," he pinches his fingers together, "and you're . . ." He gestures wildly to the sky, and laughs. Susie Coyote skids by on a Honda trail bike, her baby sister on the back.

THE PEABODY COAL COMPANY'S Black Mesa operation, on Navaho-Hopi lands, is one of the largest coal-mining complexes in the world: 11 million tons last year, 64,000 acres of coal-rich land.

The coal is gouged out of the harsh earth of Black Mesa, broken up, rolled down into the valley on a conveyor belt, and then hauled 70 miles on an automated train to the Page Power Plant. From there, hydroelectric lines take the coal-fired energy to southern California.

The Black Mesa mines and all the other energy operations on Navaho land—coal, oil, uranium—should have made the tribe wealthy. Instead, Navaho per-capita income is about a third of the U.S. average, and their unemployment rate stands around 40 percent (not including, of course, subsistence herding and farming).

The Peabody Coal operation, with 845 workers, boasts an 80 percent Navaho employment rate, with the lowest-paying jobs—unskilled laborers—beginning at eight dollars an hour. It sounds good; but the dark side of the Peabody Coal Company record is in the pure math of profit. Coal from leased Navaho lands at Black Mesa currently sells for about $19 a ton; the tribe gets approximately 25 cents royalty per ton, about one and one half percent.

Still, an estimated 20 percent of all America's strip-minable coal fields are owned by the Navaho Nation, and much of it has yet to be exploited. Navahos who favor energy-resource development envision more favorable leasing arrangements. Men like Tribal Chairman Peter MacDonald say that the rapid exploitation of reservation resources is the quick road to Navaho progress: the growth of a Navaho middle class and the strengthening of tribal autonomy through more capital influx. Others say the tribe should go slow in leasing its mineral wealth: "After all," says one savvy Shiprock Navaho, "energy is just going to go up and up—our uranium, our coal, our oil, everything. We should just sit back and wait for the white man to come to us. Then we can get anything we want: jobs, management training, environmental controls—the works. There's no hurry; we've been here a long, long time."

However, there are other, more spiritually minded Navahos, for whom the whole Anglo attitude of economic exploitation of land is just a nightmare, a bad dream dreamed up by the *belagonas,* the greed-crazed whites who think earth and sky, rain and corn and herds are only dead integers in a dead equation.

There is manifest truth in this view, and yet the traditionalists themselves have had an impact on the land they love, and they have changed it. Navaho sheepherding, for instance, is tough on marginal desert rangeland: Sheep chew the range right down through the roots—cynical Westerners call them "meadow maggots." The Navahos, emotionally, spiritually attached to their flocks, view stock reduction and range management with suspicion; the more sheep, the better. The result is something like "strip grazing," the animal-husbandry version of strip mining. Take Marsh Pass and Laguna Canyon, for instance, in the northern reservation: a century ago, when Kit Carson and the Anglo invaders came through, the places lived up to their names. They were lush, lovely oases where Canada geese migrated through in vast numbers. Today, because of overgrazing, they are little better than dust bowls: scrub range slashed apart by arroyos and flash-flood gullies.

But it is mining and drilling—the cold, calculated pillaging of the land for profit—that sickens Navaho traditionalists. They see in it the killing of the Navaho land, and the death of the people themselves—a kind of self-genocide for a handful of dollars.

A YOUNG NAVAHO from around Hummingbird, in the backcountry between Burnt Corn Creek and Beautiful Valley, went away to college in Tucson. He continued on to art school in Santa Fe, bought a Honda Civic, rented a house in the suburban hills and got engaged to a Dakota girl from Pine Ridge.

He went home one summer to help his grandmother string fence across a hundred acres of poor horse pasture along the Piñon Road. His grandmother had bought a string of bony, half-wild ponies. No one could figure out what she wanted to do with them, but the whole family went to work, chain-sawing fence posts out of deadwood, scraping post holes in the stony ground, stringing barbed wire . . . hard work, just to fence in a ragged bunch of range horses. But grandmother said she liked to watch her horses run, white and paint and roan, across the desert in the evening. "It is beautiful," she said. And so they built the fence.

One morning the young man had nothing to do; everyone else had gone up to the rodeo at Lukachukai, where a couple of his cousins, the Starlight brothers, were entered in the team-roping competition. So he wandered into the hills, up a winding, sandstone canyon he vaguely remembered from childhood.

An ancient man came walking down the canyon toward him, leaning every step on a twisted staff, clad in a blanket and deerskin moccasins, a blue headband round his long, ice-white hair. His face was furrowed, seamed like carved stone; eyes milky, luminous. He stopped, facing the young man, and spoke in rough, archaic Navaho. The young man had to listen hard to understand.

"Four years ago I had a dream. I was walking down this canyon alone.

It was morning, a morning like today. I saw a young man coming up the canyon toward me. We walked up to each other. I had never seen him before; but, looking into his face, I saw that this was the man I was supposed to teach, to tell my secrets to, the man I had been waiting for all this long, long time . . .

"Since that night I have walked down this canyon every morning, waiting to meet the man in the dream. Now, today, I have."

The young man walked back up the canyon with the old man, and neither of them were ever seen again . . . so they say. They are now mountain lions, and they hunt up in the lost stone mazeways where no one goes . . . so they say.

THE FIRST TIME I came to Gallup, crossing the tiny, dirty park next to the bus station, I saw a Navaho man lying face up on the ground. His eyes were open, staring blankly. I bent down and felt his forearm. The flesh was cold as marble: dead. Alcohol poisoning, probably; the climax of a slow, torturous suicide as deliberate as a bullet in the brain, or a neck laid across the railroad tracks . . .

Saturday night in Gallup, New Mexico, looks like an alcoholic Stalingrad. This is where the buzzards of acculturation, oppression, despair come home to roost. The sidewalks, gutters, and vacant lots glitter with empty bottles and broken glass. In front of Eddie's, perhaps the roughest bar in town, a group of young Navaho toughs pass around a half-gallon of Ripple. Farther down the street, a man is methodically beating on his wife; but, much to the amusement of several men staggering around him heckling and laughing, he is too drunk to land a solid blow.

There are bodies curled up on the sidewalk, long gone out of this world. A wild man, with a dirty red headband and a big ragged cut on his head, staggers up to us and demands a dollar "to get back to Chinle." Lewis, my Navaho friend, tells him to go to hell. "He just wants to buy more wine," Lewis tells me.

There are interstate truckers, terrified tourists, drugstore cowboys, and Mexican lowriders mixed in with the jostling sidewalk crowds. But mostly there are Indians, Navahos—that great American cliché, the drunken Indian—drawn to bars like Eddie's, the Club Mexico, the American, and the Hogan to inhale Thunderbird, Ripple, Mad Dog, schnapps, Kachina Peach Brandy, the sweet, chugging stuff that takes you straight to oblivion, or the hospital, or jail.

The Hogan is really jumping tonight. The Viciosos, the bloods, the breeds, the troops are drinking themselves into absolute, volatile dementia. Freddy Fender blasts from the juke box: "Wasted Days and Wasted Nights," that classic of barroom nihilism. Some fierce, high-money pool games are going on. And maybe 75 or 100 Indians, and a few Chicano outlaws, are pouring the booze down like water.

People turn to stare or glower as Lewis and I come in. Lewis is all right—a Navaho, a proper Navaho in cowboy get-up, tough looking, with a big confident grin. But me—an Anglo, a belagona—that's something different. In one of the hard-core Navaho bars, like Eddie's or the Turquoise outside of Farmington, the fists and bottles would start flying within five minutes. But Lewis is a regular here, a popular guy, kind of a Navaho Henry Winkler. He waves, shouts a few "yataheys" to his friends, tells one grim-faced heavy that I'm "all right, a friend," and everything calms down.

We find an empty booth and Lewis starts drinking tumblers of Thunderbird; I order shots of tequila with cans of Tecate. We drink hard and fast; at an Indian bar you drink to get *drunk*. Anthropologists have called Indian drinking a "culture of excitement"—a constant round of Dionysiac, damn-tomorrow reveling. But there is a gray undertone of despair beneath all the noisy carousal. A Navaho whose income is $2,500 a year, whose kids have kwashiorkor and who owes his next three years of mutton and wool to the local trading post is not too likely to think of the consequences when the fighting comes down, not when he's living a life of reckless, native existential despair.

A wiry young guy in a tan Levi's suit, hunched quietly over his Coors, keeps getting pushed by a heavyset drunk in a hard hat and work clothes: "Hey, buddy, buy me a drink." "Hey man, you an *asshole,* you know?" Finally, he shoves the guy's arm, spilling his beer. All talk stops at the bar—it is showdown time. The little guy turns slowly and says, smiling, "Hey, man, if you're feeling *froggy,* why don't you just *jump?*" The big hardhat draws back and swings on him, a roundhouse punch from way out in left field. But before it is halfway there, the little Navaho kicks the man's bar stool out from under him and then gives him the boot in the jaw—not hard, but hard enough. The big man gets up, rubbing his jaw, and heads unsteadily for the door. "There's an Airborne saying," the little guy says, "pick your enemy before he knows you're his enemy, and everything on the face comes out, or off. This guy got off *easy*."

A glass breaks. Drinkers topple over onto the bar, unconscious. Someone at the next booth begins to chant, a sacred song, high, keening—Beautyway song, of rainbows and bluebirds—totally incongruous in this terminal barroom.

At closing time the bars empty out into the chill night. The sidewalks look like Kabul or Calcutta: sleepers covered with old newspapers, people slumped against buildings like corpses, a knot of men clustered around a trash fire in a vacant lot. An angelic young girl—14? 15?—offers herself for the price of a bottle of Tokay.

"What would happen," Wilbert Tsosie, a young Navaho activist and legal aide, once asked me rhetorically, "if one of your drugstores had people lying around outside because they took overdoses of the medicines sold inside? How long would that drugstore stay in business? Give the sick, disgusting alcohol back to the honkies. Let them kill themselves with it."

But selling booze to Indians is big, big business in the honky-tonk towns around the edge of the Navaho Nation. State liquor laws seem to fade away when it comes to Native Americans. Bars regularly serve Indian minors, and blatantly intoxicated customers, who may have to drive home a hundred miles, are sold drink after drink. And a raving delirium tremeniac is served a double shot of rye without a question.

THE NAVAHOS say they emerged from the underworld through an ice cave in the Rockies, and then walked south to their desert homeland between the sacred mountains and the Colorado and San Juan rivers—"a long, long time ago." That is one starting point. The other is in the early 1860s, when Kit Carson and the U.S. Army slaughtered the Navahos' herds, burned their hogans, peach orchards, and cornfields, and exiled the tribe to a barren concentration camp at Bosque Redondo in eastern New Mexico. By the time they were returned to a tiny reservation in their homeland, a third of the tribe had died of starvation and exposure or had been sold into slavery to Spanish and Anglo ranchers. "Bosque Redondo" is still a bitter metaphor for genocide among Navahos; and young tribal radicals like to equate Anglo America's Indian policy with Nazism—not such a farfetched analogy when one considers that, according to historian John Toland, Hitler got his idea for the concentration camp from America's reservation system. Young Indian radicals like to quote Toland, who wrote that Hitler "often praised to his inner circle the efficiency of America's extermination—by starvation and unequal combat—of the red savages who could not be tamed by captivity."

When the Treaty of 1868 was signed there were only 7,000 Navahos left. Since then that gutted tribe has grown into a nation of 150,000.

POLITICAL POWER does not grow out of the barrel of a gun; it grows out of the land, like corn, like sagebrush, like the dream flowers of jimsonweed.

Listen to the Baptist, Republican Navaho Tribal Chairman Peter MacDonald speaking before a gathering of the National Tribal Chairmen's Association in May 1977:

> The Navaho Nation, all Indian nations have arrived at a fateful point in history. Our energy resources and other critical resources—water rights, fishing rights, timber—face extinction from powerful interests that have organized on a state and now a national level to battle us in the courts and legislatures. The land controversy in Maine, the fishing controversy in the Northwest and the water-rights controversy in the Southwest have aroused enormously powerful economic interests against the Indian— interests which are now set to wage the final Indian wars, to complete the job of winning the West by expropriating what little remains to us. Our energy reserves and our treaty rights are the only assets we have except for our land, our culture and our people. We are either at the point of a new beginning or we have reached the beginning of the end —the last mile of the Long Walk, the end of the Trail of Tears.

Navaho tribal leaders as high up as MacDonald and Arizona state representative Daniel Peaches have talked of Navaholand as the 51st state—even a commonwealth, like Puerto Rico or American Samoa. And some Navaho radicals even fantasize a *literal* Navaho Nation. After all, they say, should not Dinetah, with its unique people and its traditional land base, which the U.S. Civil Rights Commission has called "an American colony," become a reality—a nation, legally as well as in fact? Last year I sat in an Albuquerque motel with several Navaho college students. They were eating peyote and talking about the Land and the People.

Peyote—big, dry buttons as bitter as boiled-down earth. The talk went on, and the dreams coalesced into words, plans: an *Athabascan* empire, crystallized around the Athabascan-speaking tribes that range from the Arctic Circle in Alaska and Canada south to the desert tribes of Navaholand and Apacheria. It makes sense, particularly in that predawn motel room,

where they choked down the holy cactus: a *natural* nation, a loose con-
federation of all those tribes scattered down the length of western North
America, down the spine of the Rockies, from Great Slave Lake in Canada
to the Mogollon Rim; a country made from blood, custom, tongue, and
formed by the curve and angle of land—mountain, desert, forest, river,
ice.

ONE SPRING AFTERNOON I rode north out of Flagstaff with an old Navaho
in a brand new, supercharged turquoise pickup truck. He wore a purple
satin cowboy shirt; double-knit Western slacks; Tony Lama cowboy boots;
a heavy, beaver-felt, ten-gallon hat; a string tie with a silver thunderbird
at his throat; and a digital timepiece with a fire-coral-studded silver
watchband. There was an eagle plume hanging from the rearview mirror.

He must be a *naat'aani,* a clan leader, I thought, or perhaps a Singer
or a Native American Church Roadman: a fine-looking man, a person of
substance, of power.

"Where you goin'?"

"Colorado. North of Cortez."

"I'm goin' to Tuba City."

We accelerated out of Flagstaff, faster and faster, the tape player
blasting out an Indian chant: settling to a rock-steady 100 miles an hour
down that bumpy road northeast into Navaho country. There was a lot
of traffic on the road—the Friday tourist rush, and caravans of Indians
coming into Flagstaff to shop, or drink. But the old man never slowed
down.

We passed Magic Mountain and then Grey Mountain, that honky-tonk
reservation border town; and crossed the corroded red desert that descends to the Little Colorado River, to the west. The old Navaho pulled
out the Cobra CB microphone from under the dashboard and talked away
to somebody in the intricate, slurred Navaho tongue—wool and mutton
futures? an epidemic of *chinde,* ghosts, out by Chilchinbito? the Peabody
Coal leases on Black Mesa? On we went, at 100 mph, steady and sure
as fate.

Finally, close to Tuba City, we hit a jammed-up herd of tourist traffic,
snailing up a long, winding hill behind a Winnebago. There were a lot
of cars in front of us—a dozen, maybe—and a blind curve ahead. The
old man pulled out around them without a pause, and jammed it on.

We were about two-thirds of the way past the pack when another

Indian in a pickup truck, also speeding, rounded the curve above us. He leaned on his horn; the old grandfather leaned on his. Neither touched the brake pedal. We headed toward each other like a couple of jousting bighorns, or robots playing chicken.

There was no conceivable way we could get by. There was the Winnebago on our right, blocking the right lane; and an arroyo to the left, which would have been like bailing out straight into the grave. It was time for one of those cartoon cars that squeeze through tight places like toothpaste. But the wizard, deadpan as ever, kept the pedal to the floor, as if there was nobody else on the road. I instinctively cringed, and jammed my left foot down on an imaginary brake pedal. At the last possible instant the old man simply *pulled over* into the righthand lane, veering into the Winnebago, broadside, driving it off the road, over the shoulder and into the desert. I looked back and there was the colossal recreational vehicle, costing more than the yearly incomes of ten Navaho sheepherding families, jouncing across the dunes, tearing through a barbed-wire fence.

When I looked over at the old Navaho, he was grinning at me out of the corner of his face; and then he laughed, and suddenly we were both laughing together, at the mad perfection of it all.

*June 1978*

# THE IMPORTANCE OF DUNES

*Enduring lessons from the shores of Lake Michigan*

● ▲ ■

ANNICK SMITH

Sumor: The Old English word tastes sweet, like peaches. One definition says, "Any period regarded as a time of fruition, fulfillment, happiness, or beauty." This pure and easy concept of summer is beguiling, but fraudulent as nostalgia. I remind myself that summer's peach must have at its heart a pit, a seed, the hint of bitterness.

All the summers of my childhood, I lived on the beaches of Lake Michigan. My second-story bedroom faced west, toward the lake. I slept with the sounds of waves lapping or waves crashing, waves roaring in the gusts and thunder of an electrical storm. There were gulls diving and thin-legged sandpipers on the beach where I stood. When sky drops into lake and waves pull at toes, any summer child knows she is on the edge—a small person in a great blue world.

The creatures that lived in the sand were also small and sometimes stinging: sand fleas, burrowing wasps, red ants, beetles, a swarm of lady-bugs on my baby sister's bottom. I tried to catch minnows in the shallows where a warm, ginger-colored stream ran into the lake; my little sisters and I trapped tadpoles in mason jars so that we could watch their astounding tails turn into feet. Alewives washed up on the beach some years, so many and so rank that we would rake them into a pile a foot high, dig a deep hole, and bury them to keep our beach from smelling of fishy death. We tried to catch gold monarch butterflies in nets, but I hated the powdery feel of their black-veined wings and the clumsiness of my fingers.

Once I witnessed the killing of a snake. My father's cousin, Paul, on furlough from World War II, had come to visit. He was slim, dark, romantic—the only soldier I knew. I was riding his back, playing horsey on the beach, when a curious movement where nothing should have moved froze him. A gray, sandy twist of driftwood had come alive at our feet.

"Rattlesnake!" Paul screamed, and dumped me in the sand. He grabbed a stick and clubbed the snake to death. I was more scared of him than I was of the snake.

After the war Paul gave me his Purple Heart, but he had been wounded beyond any healing. He would ditch his European, educated ways and become a busboy in greasy spoons from Kansas City to Baton Rouge. He would descend into catatonia until science invented antipsychotic drugs. Then he would grow fat, live in a halfway house in Chicago, and peep into windows at women; and then he would choke to death on a five-inch bite of steak.

THE BEACHES where I discovered venom are on the southeastern shores of Lake Michigan, just past the refineries and steel mills of Gary, Indiana, some 80 miles east of Chicago. My family spent summers in the town of Lakeside, Michigan, until I was seven, then bought a house in a beach community called Tower Hill Shorelands near Michigan's Warren Dunes State Park. Fifty years later, when I go to visit my parents, I sleep in my old bedroom on the second floor, where the waves still sing through the open French windows.

In Lakeside I learned to be ashamed of my body. My parents were foreigners, born and raised in Hungary, who came to America from Paris after I was born. French children played naked on the beach; so did I. My parents were photographers. They liked to take pictures of me at the edge of waves—my plump legs, my little bucket. One hot July afternoon, when I was two, a policeman accosted my father.

"You better get that kid off our beach."

My father was perplexed.

"You're lucky I'm not pulling you in."

"But this is America!"

"You bet it's America. This is a Christian community."

The nuns in the convent adjoining the public beach had complained of my indecent exposure. I was rushed into panties, never again to feel unconscious of my body in public until I was grown and a mother and bathing in hot pools on the Middle Fork of the Salmon River, deep in the Idaho wilderness. Here is one value of wild places: You are not important there. You are a leaf, a common weed. Insects speak your language.

The beach is a desert, and that must be why, when I finally spent some months in the Sonoran desert, I felt drawn to it, fulfilled, happy in the spare, thorny blossoming of life. The Yaqui have a name for their desert: The Enchanted World of Flowers. Life begins on a beach. Unlikely plants poke out of pure sand: firstborn is marram grass, a sharp-edged green pioneer waving to its followers—sea rocket, bugseed, winged pigweed, cocklebur.

Creatures who first found life on a beach have left us legacies. We often walked among green and rust-colored pebbles, backs stooped and aching, looking for fossils called Indian stones. These petrified animals, tiny rings with star-shaped holes, we strung on threads for necklaces. They were our jewels. My mother, who knew nothing of geology, told me the fossils were a million years old. I could barely comprehend one year. The Indian stones around my neck signified time.

On clear August nights we would lie on blankets, counting shooting stars. In Chicago, where my family lived in an apartment through the long winter, you could not see stars in the sky, which was filled with the orange reflected light of the city. So the beach became our planetarium. We learned the names of constellations. This was space.

You can fall in love with space and sky. A girl from Chicago can go west and find mountains. These days I live surrounded by grass on a Montana meadow. There is no water in sight, and yet the wind blows. The grass undulates in sunshine. A hummingbird, iridescent, green-throated, plunges the needle of his tongue into a common red petunia.

FOREDUNE. THE WORD is a seduction. Prevailing winds blow sand inland until the particles hit a tuft of little bluestem, a driftwood log. The sand piles up against the windward side of the object and, having lost its momentum, rolls gently down the sheltered side, forming a mini-dune. In this sheltered space, sand cress, bearberry, wild rye, hoary puccoon, even prickly pear cactus take hold. More sand accumulates, enriched by decaying vegetation and held secure by a tangle of surface roots. Insects find sustenance, rodents burrow, songbirds fly from the oak forests to feast on seeds and berries. They are building a foredune.

The cliff at the edge of our beach is formed by the waves of winter storms slicing into the foredunes. Severe winters cut the dunes back, leaving a wide, flat beach. Other years the water level rises and the beach is reduced. The miniature mountains and cliffs rising from the beach to the more permanent tree-anchored dunes are my memory's password for play. When my sisters and I were bored with swimming and sand castles, we would leap from our cliff's tiered ledges. I was Wonder Woman with a beach-blanket cape.

Above the cliff, our no-man's-land of foredunes swelled to a wooded ridge. On top, where the sand turns smoky gray in the process of becoming dirt, our white frame house sits among oak and sassafras trees, its broad, screened-in porch looking west over the lake to the setting sun. On windy days, when it was too cold to swim, we would descend the steep, splintery stairs from the house, cross a wooden ramp over the gully that separates foredunes from permanent dunes, and thread through thick, white-powdered poison ivy to the clearing where our cottonwood tree stood.

We nested there and played house under the airy roof, collecting sand cherries and acorns for food, seed pods for money. I did not know then that cottonwoods are the only trees that survive on foredunes. Such trees grow fast, come to maturity, and begin to die within the span of a human life. Ours was old in cottonwood time.

Sometimes we carried a lunch of peanut-butter-and-jelly sandwiches, plums, chocolate-chip cookies, Kool-Aid in a thermos. Sometimes we brought dolls, a deck of Old Maid, our doctor's kit. We spread our blanket. We climbed the silver-limbed tree. The sun dove toward a purple horizon.

*Clang, clang,* our grandmother beat on the horseshoe dinner-bell. "Annick, Kaati, Carole—where are you?" She would call herself hoarse, with her Hungarian accent, but we would not answer. We were too busy playing doctor. Who can forget the probings of child-doctor hands, the unbearable tickle and tingle of a stethoscope on bare skin? Most girls play doctor with boys, and eventually we did, too, but awakening to sexuality in such female-child intimacy will for me always be connected to foredunes, treetops, the green filtered light, the rumble of white-capped waves. It is the domain of sisters.

WHILE SUMMERING at Lakeside the year I turned seven, I was infected with polio, transmitted, perhaps, by the waters of Lake Michigan or by other children on the swarming beach. At first it seemed another cold with sore throat, fever, exhaustion. "Just flu," said our country doctor, fishing in his black bag of pink, purple, blue, and yellow placebos. When I didn't get better, my mother took me home to Chicago. And then, in the middle of the night, I was bundled into blankets and rushed to the hospital, where another doctor put me through the pain of a spinal tap.

I was lucky; I did not become paralyzed. This was at the apex of a great epidemic, before Jonas Salk discovered a vaccine. The children's polio ward was jammed with girls and boys, even babies, all of us together in a ballroom-size infirmary. But even in my fright, I felt blessed. The ten-year-old boy in the next bed was in an iron lung.

"Does it hurt?" I asked him.

"Not much."

"Are you scared?"

"Yes."

There was wailing and nighttime moaning, swift nurses with white caps, and strong, whitejacketed orderlies who pushed wheelchairs and lifted the paralyzed children into their beds. I mostly watched and kept quiet and felt ashamed because I could move all my limbs. I played with the beautiful doll my parents had bought for me, and I read books, and for the first time I felt truly alone. Myself.

It was the end of summer. I would come back to the beach more wary and yet more reckless. I would swim beyond the sandbar where the lake was cold and black at its bottom. My frantic mother would call me back, but I would keep swimming toward the horizon along the glittering path of the afternoon sun until my breath gave out. I had begun to learn no one is invulnerable; take chances; you can be alone and not bored.

BLOWOUTS ARE sand craters scooped out of the dunes by swirling winds. They are maybe 50 feet deep, flat and round at the bottom, fringed with jack and white pine on top, dotted with clumps of blue-leaved willow, starry false Solomon's-seal, the ever-present marram grass. You might come to a blowout with a serious novel. You might bring a sketch pad or try to write a poem. I would lie on my back and study the drifting clouds. This was a place for dreaming, the inverse of mountains.

My father, Stephen Deutch, was famous for his photographs of nudes. Occasionally he would bring a model to the dunes. We were not allowed to observe, but Kathy and I would sneak after the two of them, the model in shorts, my father's neck strung with his Rolleiflex and lenses.

They went in the morning, when the light slanted and shadows were possible.

Creeping like the Potawatomi who once walked a trail along the shore, we tracked them to the blowout. The model would shed her bra and underpants. We held our breath. We had smelled the woman's perfume.

My father would direct the naked woman to the configuration of sand he wanted as background. He was also a sculptor, and he tried to capture an illusion of three dimensions—a shaded thigh, breasts curving against the waves of sand. Voices drifted up to us, sometimes laughter. They never touched. Maybe my father knew we were watching. He was sexy—dark and handsome. We knew he loved women. We were in love with him, too. The blowout was a wild place where anything could happen.

It must have been tough for my mother—three daughters, longlimbed models, all this adoration of her husband. No wonder she sometimes nagged and slammed doors and broke down in hysterical weeping. No wonder she took to walking the beach alone. I see her in my mind's eye heading away from us—a small, large-breasted woman with good legs and a floppy hat.

I always thought of myself as my father's surrogate son, and he was my main hero. I would not learn to sew like my mother. I did not cook or bake my grandmother's fine Hungarian recipes. I cut my long black hair short, wore jeans, and preferred the company of men. And then, at 11 and a half, I was besieged by hormones. I had not been paralyzed by polio, but as my body betrayed me into womanhood, I was paralyzed with self-consciousness. Awkward, slumped at the shoulders, withdrawn, I flinched from my father's embraces, not daring to shout the danger I felt.

On the beach, in front of my parents and their friends, I took to shameless wrestling with a boy who lived down the road. I would drift far into the lake with him, legs and arms entwined in a black inner-tube, exchanging wet kisses. I wonder what I was trying to prove. That I was free of my father? A girl like the rest? Wild?

Freedom from self-awareness came only when I was alone in the sand and grass, or reading, preferably both. That's why I loved the blowout —even the idea of the blowout—where you could think, feel, and see with no one watching but the insects and crows. I was lucky to have found this haven, this addiction, so early and so close at hand. I would grow to be a walker, like my mother, seeking solace in nature as others seek religion or booze or drugs.

"PROSPECT AND REFUGE" is a theory that attempts to define cultures, and perhaps individuals, by patterns of habitation. The roots of these patterns can be traced back to hunters and gatherers and to the animals that were their models and their meat. Those who lived in the high open sought a dwelling place of prospect and predation where they could spot herds of ungulates or invading tribes. Jungle peoples lived at the fecund bottom of life, looking up to monkeys in the trees, snakes curling like vines, the bright plumage of toucans. But the places of greatest possibility and complexity are the edges of mountains and woods, looking down or out to a wider space. That is where our beach house sits, at the edge of an oak savanna overlooking the lake. A hardwood forest rises behind.

From childhood on I have known artists and have aspired to be one, and in my experience artists (and Indians) will choose prospect over refuge any day, unless they can have both. Carl Sandburg once lived just down our sandy road in Tower Hill. Later he moved a few miles away to a farm in Harbert, Michigan, where his wife raised goats. My father took us to visit. Sandburg was not home. What I remember are the goats. Gregarious, bearded creatures, they ambled on the sod-roofed house; one jumped onto the hood of our Buick.

The dunes have been a retreat for Chicago artists and intellectuals since the early 1900s, and literary warriors were our neighbors and visitors. Norman Maclean would ride the Yellow Peril (the electric train that ran from Chicago to South Bend, Indiana) to Michigan City, Indiana, to visit his mentor, the historian Ferdinand Schevill. Nelson Algren, my father's best friend, came to drink whiskey on our porch, and we listened to his stories as the sun slid into the lake. The Greek-American writer Harry Petrakis, another friend, still lives near New Buffalo, Michigan. Ben Burns who edited the *Chicago Defender* newspaper and *Ebony* magazine inhabits Sandburg's old studio and is close as an uncle. When Sandburg moved away to North Carolina at age 67, he said, "It's only my ghost that's leaving the Middle West."

THE DUNES are full of ghosts. The oldest are prehistoric mammoths, mastodons, giant beavers. Retreating glaciers carved the Great Lakes, and our geologically young dunes blow up against moraines, drifts, and outwash plains. Under the sand are the limestone beds of a Paleozoic sea, piled up over millions of years before the coming of vertebrate life. Sand upon sand upon sand is a way I like to think about history.

In ancient times, 100 B.C. to A.D. 700, Hopewell Indians established villages and gardens in what is now New Buffalo, Michigan. They dug pits to store corn, wild rice, and beans a few miles inland, near the town of Three Oaks. We also went to Three Oaks for our food—sweet corn and ripe tomatoes and bushels of golden delicious apples sold at roadside stands.

A forest band of Potawatomi had lived near St. Joseph, Michigan, where my Old Country grandmothers would go to "take the waters," easing their rheumatic limbs into the mineral baths of a Victorian spa. In 1838 the Potawatomi, casualties of white man's sickness and white man's wars, were packed off to a reservation in Oklahoma. One recalcitrant band moved to Cass County, Michigan, where a small group of survivors still lives. I identify with survivors; most of my relatives died in Auschwitz.

Much of the thronging wildlife that lived by the lake did not survive. Bison were hunted out by Indians and whites by 1750. Even before white settlement began in the early 1800s, elk and most of the beaver had been killed. Timber wolves were gone a few years before the last wild turkey graced a pioneer's table. Before long there were no more black bears, panthers, lynx, otters, or wolverines. Wild ducks and geese used to fly over the lake in great Vs when I was a child. Now there are only a few small flocks. Huge sturgeon once swam up local streams in the spring spawning run. Farmers netted suckers by the wagonload to be fed to hogs. In New Buffalo, 5,000 whitefish were caught in one day.

I can only imagine the legendary forests that spread to the east— Galien beeches, maples, and the famous "oak openings" that James Fenimore Cooper wrote about, though it is possible to glimpse the aboriginal woods in the nature sanctuary of Warren Woods, near Lakeside. We would take Sunday visitors to walk among the giant trees, hushed and filled with sunlight at their tops, cool in midsummer along the green-shaded paths. Those walks were as close as I had come to what church is supposed to be.

The forest behind our house at Tower Hill is a spiritual retreat, under covenant never to be developed. I never knew the deep woods of Michigan, but ours were filled with pussytoes, aster, and bastard toadflax. With my mother and sisters, I gathered wild geraniums in June, blue and yellow violets and columbines in May, and the delicate, white, orchid-centered trilliums that light the woods in the aftermath of an early-spring snow.

The forest was filled with a dank perfume from layers of rotting leaves, hushed except for the raucous bluejays that hunted the eggs of the red, crested cardinal. These are my family's sacred woods. The only people who live on the other side of our road are a handful of ministers. We understand each other. We pray in our ways to the god of the deep woods.

THE MOVING DUNES in the state park just down the beach from our house change shape from season to season. My sisters and I have come to maturity transformed and transforming like dunes that won't stay put. We, who still think of ourselves as children, have children old enough to be mothers and fathers. Very little remains the same, except Old Baldy, the highest dune, which we climbed as if it were Mount Everest.

It would be an expedition, with rucksacks full of snacks and towels. We'd parade past the church camp to the public beach where bathers of all shapes, ages, and nationalities camped under red-striped umbrellas. Old Baldy loomed above the stove-hot cement of the parking lot, its steep flank hollowed like the trough of a wave. We'd race to the top, drop our loads, and tumble down. We'd land, laughing, our mouths filled with sand.

The sloping backside of our mountain was thick with pine trees, poplars, and poison ivy. We swung on vines—"me Tarzan, you Jane"—and the little kids were chimps. Years later I read an interview with Johnny Weissmuller. His advice is now tacked to the wall above my word processor: "The main thing is not to let go of the vine."

Behind Old Baldy the dunes spread like the Sahara. In moonlight, when I was 17 and in love with a fair-haired Minnesota boy named David Smith, the great dune was our necking tryst. Once, rolling and panting at the edge of the woods, I forgot about the poison ivy. The next week in school, the gym teacher would not let me into the swimming pool with my crusty, oozing sores. I learned that love is full of perils. Later, lying on the sand, Dave said: "I love your mind, your soul, your body." What else could a girl ask?

I made my escape from the Midwest at 19, when I married David Smith. My trajectory from that time to now has been westward, toward the last wild places, toward those who would share with me the ecstatic pull of landscape and sky. We settled on a homestead in western Montana surrounded by meadows. Bear and elk roam in my woods, and coyotes howl from the deep grass. Desire for wildness is what I took from the beach, the foredunes, the blowout.

THINK OF A FUNNEL. The Michigan dunes have been a gathering place for four generations blown in from Hungary and France and Montana, from Chicago, Boston, San Francisco. Dave and I had four babies who would learn to walk with us on sand. My sisters also married and had their babies. For more than 20 years the eight cousins spent every summer together.

Our family album is filled with elongating limbs and silvering hair—playing, like these memories, against the blues and browns of lake and sand. Some faces are gone: Dave Smith, dead in 1974; Kathy's husband, Chris, dead in 1976; Nelson Algren, dead in 1981. My parents are in their eighties. I shudder to think who will be the next ghost.

The dunes are changing with us: more summer homes, retaining walls to keep the beach from eroding, our blowout now filled by a Caterpillar bulldozer. Accustomed to Montana mountains, I see Old Baldy small as an anthill. Four miles down the beach at Bridgman (where the Wobblies once hid out), we stare at the ominous cones of a nuclear power plant. Lake water cools its generators.

Winter and summer, my parents spend most of their time at the dunes. He sculpts nudes from hardwood; she cooks, sews, walks the beach as always. Mother is in love with generation. She yearns for a great-grandchild before she dies. We know winter is coming, the wildest season. Waves will freeze in mid-motion. Snow will make lace of the woods. Spindrift will meld with sand. Winter will be heavy and elusive as mercury.

Not long ago, my sister Kathy and I came to the dunes in winter. We walked the beach with Mother. She is small as a child these days, yet strong on her still good-looking legs. She ran ahead of us in a stinging wind. We were walking the frozen foam when we saw her tumble headlong into a patch of deep slush. We pulled her out, wet to the waist and laughing. We held her and dried her—our daughter.

I have come back to the edge where water and sand create unlikely life. There are snakes in the marram grass, and monarch butterflies so fragile we don't dare catch them, and Indian stones from Paleozoic seas. The dunes are moving; the dance is monotonous, shifting . . . one-step, one-step, one-step. It is my heart. I am summer's gray-haired child in love with this blue world.

*July 1991*

# THIS DOG IS LEGEND

*Say what you like about Gator.*
*It's probably true.*

● ▲ ■

RANDY WAYNE WHITE

**O**nce, visiting the Key West docks, I struck up a conversation with a shrimper, a true Conch, which is to say he talked through his nose and wore white rubber boots. When I told him where I was from—a coastal town more than 400 miles away—he said, "Hey now, you ever heared about that dog what they got up there?"

Dog?

"Yeah, that there dog. Dog can swim underwater and bring up cement blocks—whole ones—from 15 feet a water, then swim them back to shore. Big brown curly lab. And understands *words*. Say this dog can swim-down fish; catch them, too. Catches snook, reds, even a shark once. A friend of mine was talking it around the docks. An ol' boy he knew, knew somebody what'd seen it. Man, I'd love to have one a his pups."

The shrimper thought I might know something about the stories, being from the town where this dog was said to live, and that led us into a discussion of other dogs, dogs that neither of us had really encountered but had heard much about. The shrimper told me the story of the grouper-boat cocker that twice saved all hands, once by leading them to a fire in the dunnage box, another time by waking them when the anchor broke during a storm. Then he told me about the shrimp-boat golden retriever that dived overboard and drowned itself on the first trip after its owner drowned. The golden, it was said, had a 200-word vocabulary and knew the days of the week. It was a great loss, felt by all.

I had already heard both of these stories, and the shrimper had probably heard my stories about the feral hog that killed 27 catch dogs but was finally brought down by a collie-rottweiler mix and about the pit bull from La Belle that would sink its teeth into a moving truck tire and flop around and around until the truck stopped.

All regions have their legendary dogs, and it has been my experience that outdoor people collect those stories, knowingly or not, perhaps because dogs, unlike people, are still safe harbors for exaggeration. We can tell the wildest tales about animals we have never met, absolutely fearless in the certainty that our wonder and our admiration will never be dashed by a "60 Minutes" exposé or Senate subcommittee hearings. That people are human is a reality beyond escape; that dogs are not makes them, perhaps, the last stronghold of legend.

The shrimper had wanted to know about the dog in my town—the dog that could retrieve cement blocks and out-swim fish, that understood words. But instead of telling the truth, I told him what he wanted to hear, because, although I had not propagated the legend, I was necessarily, through association and loyalty, one of its protectors. And I did know the truth. The dog he was describing was once my dog.

I CALLED HIM Gator because that's the animal he most resembled while in the water and because, like the reptile, he possessed certain quirks of character not normally ascribed to creatures allowed outside a zoo, let alone welcomed into a house. He was not a lab, though I still occasionally hear him called that. He was a Chesapeake Bay retriever, seven months old when I got him from an Everglades hunting guide and already the subject of dark rumors, though I did not know it at the time. A northern client had given him to the guide as a present, but the guide, who favored tall pointers and catch dogs, didn't know what to do with him. He was kept in a run with the guide's pit bulls until the Chesapeake—then called Wolf because of his yellow eyes—opened the carotid artery on a prize bitch. The guide decided to try and sell the dog, and if that didn't work, he'd shoot him and burn the damn papers. All of this I heard later.

Coincidentally, I had recently ended an 11-year association with a nice setter and was looking for a new breed to try. Most people who like dogs have some vague mental list of breeds they admire, and at that time I was leaning toward a Border collie, a flat-coated retriever, or a nice mixed-breed from the humane society. See, the difficulty in choosing a good dog now is that some of the great breeds have suffered at the hands of pet-store puppy factories and certain low-life bench-show fanatics who have bred only for confirmation or cash flow, and I did not want one of their mindless, hyperactive progeny. It was then that I happened to read an article about a Chesapeake that had leapt into a flooded creek and pulled out a drowning child. I liked that. I had one very young son and another on the way, and I lived on a creek. I began to research the breed—just as anyone contemplating dog ownership should. There were relatively few registered Chesapeakes in the country (little chance of overbreeding), and only the most generous of souls would describe them as pretty (of no interest to the puppy factories). Everything I read, I liked, so after I had the dog x-rayed for hip dysplasia, and after I listened patiently while the guide insisted the dog had championship bloodlines (I've yet to see a registered dog that didn't), Gator ended up in my home.

Every dog I have ever owned learned the basic obedience commands —to sit, to stay, to heel, and to come without hesitation—within about four weeks of short, daily training sessions. Gator took twice that long, but once he learned something, it was as if it had been etched in stone —an appropriate metaphor, considering his intellect. The dog was no Einstein, but the orders he did learn, he carried out like a marine. What I didn't have to teach him was how to get things out of the water. Water was to Gator what air is to birds. On land, he might lose himself in the mangroves (more than once) or run into walls (often), but water transformed him into a fluid being, a graceful creature on a mission from God. The mission was simple: There were things in the creek—many things —that needed to be brought out. Our backyard became a littered mess of barnacled branches, shells, and other flotsam, even though each exit from the creek required that Gator latch his paws over the lip of a stone wall and haul himself over, much like doing a pull-up. Since the dog did this hundreds of times a day, month after month, his chest and forelegs quite naturally became huge. And as the dog grew, so did the size of the things he retrieved. Tree branches became whole tree limbs. Shells became rocks—big rocks—for the dog learned early on that if the creek's surface was sometimes bare, the creek's bottom always held treasure. On a flood tide, the water was seven feet deep and murky, but it made no difference. He would dive down and hunt and hunt until I thought surely a real gator had taken him, only to reappear 20 yards away, a rock or a limb in his mouth. One morning I was sitting on the stoop reading, when I noticed a neighbor's Boston Whaler vectoring pilotless toward our property. I thought this odd, until I realized my dog was towing it home. He had chewed the lines free, and an emergency survey of other mooring lines in the area provided strong evidence that, had I accepted the Whaler, a 30-foot Chris-Craft would have soon followed.

During that era of boat thievery, four more things occurred that enhanced Gator's already growing reputation in the region: He dove underwater and retrieved his first cement block, he caught his first fish, he got an ear infection, and he jumped through a second-story window to attack a pit bull. Swimming the block ashore didn't surprise me, though the stranger who came asking to see the dog and then threw the block seemed genuinely shocked. Catching the fish did surprise me, because I had watched Gator sit on the dock studying waking fish, only to dive and miss them year after year. Finally, though, he did manage to stun one and swim it down, and he brought it to me, his tail wagging mildly (a mad display of emotion for that dog): a ten-pound jack crevalle that swam strongly away when I released it. The ear infection was a more subtle touch. It required an operation that left the dog's head listing slightly to the left, and people who came to see him would say, "See there? He knows we're talking about him, and he's trying to understand," for the tilt did lend an air of rakish interest to an otherwise blank expression.

Added to all of this were Gator's all-too-frequent displays of his own dark nature. Spending his earliest months in a run with pit bulls had left him with a jaundiced view of dogs in general and pit bulls in particular. I could take him jogging on free heel, and he would never look at another dog. But if one strayed onto the property, bad things happened. We were moving into a new stilt-house when a big pit bull came trotting into the yard, giving great ceremony to his decisions about where to pee. I had been warned about this dog; he had free rein in the neighborhood terrorizing pets and children, and the owners would do nothing. Gator was on the upstairs porch, watching with me through the screened window —and then, suddenly, he was no longer there. It took me a long, dull moment to understand what had happened, looking through the broken screen as Gator, making an odd chirping sound because the wind had been knocked out of him, attacked the pit bull.

I consider what he did that day less an act of bravery than just one more demonstration that certain basic concepts—the effects of gravity, for instance—were utterly beyond him. I don't doubt for a moment that he would have dived into a flooded creek to pull out a drowning child.

But he would have gone in just as quickly to rescue a log or a Volkswagen. We love to attribute to animals those noble qualities that we lack but often long for.

TELEVISION STATIONS sometimes called to see if I would allow them to do a piece on Gator (always refused), just as the friends of friends sometimes stopped to watch the dog who swam underwater, and more than once I have heard a stranger describe my own dog to me with details as wondrous as they were exaggerated. But Gator was just a dog, a good dog who minded well, and he was mine. Where I went, he followed. He was good with the boys, didn't yap, didn't hump, didn't eat the furniture, didn't jump up on strangers unless he meant to bite them, only stole one boat unless you count canoes, and wouldn't have gone for the cavalry if I had waited a year. He wasn't an overly affectionate dog, either; he liked to have his ears scratched, but I can only remember one time in our nine years that he actually licked me. I had given up hunting because I simply took no joy anymore in killing for sport, but I had made that decision without giving any thought to the animal I had trained exactly for that purpose. I had, I realized too late, defected, in a small way, to the ranks of bad breeders and bench-show fanatics by robbing another working dog of its heritage.

So I decided to give it one more try. I loaded Gator and shotgun into the boat and ran the tidal creek into a saw-grass marsh where I knew there were brackish ponds that held scaup and mallards. It was a fine day for ducks: February gray and windy, with sea fog over the bay. Gator felt good: He kept his ears perked like a puppy, and his yellow eyes glowed, and I wondered, How can he know? It had been years since we had hunted, but now, as then, he understood that this was not playtime; cement blocks and sunken logs were meaningless; this was what he was born for, this was work. I positioned him at the water's edge, close enough that my left hand could reach his ears, and we waited. I missed two easy shots before I finally took a single, a mallard drake, and Gator vibrated beneath my hand, listening for the release—*Bird!*—before sliding into the water, throwing a wake in the dark chop as he found the mallard and pivoted as if equipped with a keel. I watched him swimming toward me, that big, brown, tilted head, and those eyes. He should have brought the bird to my feet and then sat, but he didn't; he couldn't. His hips were ruined by disease, and he licked my hand as I scooped him up, telling me it hurt when I held him that way, but there was only one alternative, and that would soon come.

I carried him back to the boat, and drove him toward his rendezvous with 9 cc of pentobarbital and the grave I had already dug for him.

*July 1989*

# ADIRONDACK REPRISE

*Can people make a living where nature makes a living too? The Northeast's last great wilderness came back from the dead with an answer. Is anybody listening?*

● ▲ ■

BILL MCKIBBEN

When the Sierra Club was fighting many years ago to save the Grand Canyon from a hydroelectric dam, it ran a big ad comparing the project to flooding the Sistine Chapel. This is not that kind of story, not at all. There are dozens of spots in the Adirondack Mountains that can make you catch your breath in Alaskan-Sierran-Coloradan awe. But that's not the real point.

A hundred yards out my back door in the rolling southern hills of the Adirondacks, the woods take over, and they go on for miles. It's wilderness—there's nothing there. Small hills, and beaver ponds, and dense spruce forest with burned-over patches filling in with berries and maples. No waterfall grand enough to build a trail to, no spire of rock requiring rope and nerve, no gorge demanding reflection on your insignificance. Just the woods, and the life in them. Nothing special, and therefore the most special place I can imagine.

On a road map of the United States, most of the East looks like a tangled wiring diagram, twisting strands of red and black and blue, the pasta of progress and settlement. The spaces between these major roads are small, a few miles at best, and most of them are filled with yet more roads, the Ovals and Courts and Lanes where people by their millions actually live.

But there are a few green splotches left. Just a few: Florida's Everglades, and the North Woods of Maine, and especially Adirondack Park, six million acres in the north of New York State. Six million acres is a western number. In fact, six million acres is Yellowstone and Yosemite and Grand Canyon and Glacier national parks added together, with room left over.

It's better than that, though. There are a few roads here, and a few people, just over 100,000. More than half the land is privately owned, subject to some of the strongest rural zoning in the world. Most of it is timber land, managed pretty responsibly. A few farms linger around the edges, and of course there are some tourist centers. So the Adirondacks are a "park" unlike any other in America: They're a laboratory for figuring out how people might actually live with the world around them, which seems to be the great question we face as a species. Can people make a living where nature makes a living too? Not easily; the Adirondacks comprise the poorest counties in New York, poorer than the Bronx. But it's not impossible, either, and we're still learning. The Adirondacks haven't been malled, and they haven't been roped off. They're a real place.

History makes the story better still. A hundred years ago you'd have been lucky to find a tree to climb, and if you had you'd have looked out on desolation. Almost every acre in the Adirondacks was logged to the ground. The moose was wiped out, and the lynx, and the wolf, and nearly everything else. So all that's here now has come back. This is what the world can do, left to its own devices. Given enough rain and enough rules, the woods can recover. The Adirondacks are a second-chance wilderness, and the sweeter for it.

America has done a pretty good job of saving its Sistine Chapels, so it's no real surprise that the High Peaks of the Adirondacks are wild. But well over five million of those six million acres are foothills and swamp and lake and ridge and forest, endless forest, like the land out my back door. Get up on a 3,000-foot mountain in the middle of it all and climb a tree; all you'll see, to the horizon, is a sea of 3,000-foot round-topped mountains, stretching out forever. Here as nowhere else, the advice of biologists and ecologists has been heeded. An ecosystem, a bioregion, has been preserved. It's what the world looked like.

But . . . Earlier this year, Henry J. Lassiter, a Georgia land speculator, announced a "liquidation sale" on his 87,489 acres of Adirondack property, including "a minimum of . . . 40 miles of river frontage, three miles of lake frontage, 225 acres of ponds, and several majestic waterfalls." Other big landowners stand poised to sell their land for vacation-home development, while the state government, after decades of acquiring new parcels in the Adirondacks, refuses to set aside money for more. Meanwhile, many longtime residents are bridling at proposed new restrictions that would save much of the wilderness. The coming decade may change the Adirondacks from a wilderness with small pockets of development to a resort range larded with parks.

For a hundred years the Adirondacks have been an anomaly. Long before the rest of the nation thought about "land-use management," these ancient hills were becoming a preserve. But now—just when more of America is catching on, just when science is confirming the wisdom of those who protected Adirondack Park—the momentum seems to be running out here in northern New York.

BEFORE THE STORY of the Adirondacks can really be told, though, there's one point that needs settling: Is it really wilderness? C'mon—in New York State? Those of us in the East suffer from an inferiority complex bred by long years of looking at the calendars produced by certain environmental organizations. Sometimes, in a boring month like November, they'll include a token photo from the crowded megalopolis—a shorebird wading off Mount Desert Island or a Vermont barn against a steely sunset. Always, though, we worry that it doesn't really belong, that there must be a thousand grander places in Montana or Idaho or British Columbia. When I tell people that I live in the Adirondacks, they usually ask what state that's in. Certainly not New York; New York is pavement giving way to suburb, center of the greatest urban conglomeration in the world.

And yet 60 percent of the state's population crowds into less than 5 percent of its territory, the northern suburbs and the city itself and Long Island. To the west, stretching out above Pennsylvania, the farming heart of the Empire State runs from Albany to Niagara Falls. And to the north there's the valley of the Hudson; above Albany it narrows and heads for the mountains, where the river has its source in a small lake on the shoulder of Mount Marcy, tallest peak in the state.

But with "tallest peak in the state" we're in trouble again, for Mount Marcy stands only 5,344 feet high. Rationally, this should be plenty, but peak envy is rarely rational. A recent issue of *Outside*, for instance, advised visitors to the Adirondacks that "no trip is complete without at least one hike up the surrounding big hills, called mountains in these parts."

Taunted, we fall back on a dozen lines of defense. For one thing, it used to be higher: A billion years ago, geologists say, the Adirondacks may have been 20,000 feet high. And the 5,344 feet that remain are true feet; Lake Champlain, 40 miles distant, is less than 100 feet above sea level, and from there the mountains rise in Swiss grandeur. And by God it's rugged—people die up there almost every year. I have actually heard locals pointing to the annual fatalities with a certain pride; I've done it myself. Rugged! And remote! Last fall a hunter killed a big old bear in one corner of the park. When the state biologists examined its teeth, they decided it was nearly 43 years old, a record. That bear had been up here avoiding people since the Truman administration. Remote, by Jesus.

But forget the edgy defensiveness of a chip-on-his-shoulder resident. History makes the same point. Arrowheads are scarce in the Adirondacks because few Indians stayed here for long. They passed through in search of game, but it was too cold and harsh and poor for permanent settlement. (Adirondack, according to legend, is Iroquois for "bark eater," a derisive name for the poor Indians who did try to live here and were reduced to consuming that delicacy.) In the 1700s, farmers began to work the rich land along the shores of Lake Champlain, and areas along the southern fringes had been under cultivation even earlier. But the interior was unexplored. It was not until 1837 that a white man climbed Mount Marcy—30 years after Lewis and Clark had pushed across the continent.

And even now it can be a hard place. Farming didn't last, except along the edges. A 90-day growing season is bad enough, but when the first 30 days are rendered miserable by clouds of blackflies it's time to give up and head back south. And the winters! Many days Newcomb and Saranac Lake vie with International Falls, Minnesota, and Gunnison, Colorado, for notoriety as the coldest spot in the nation. Some years the Tug Hill Plateau, just over the western edge of the park, gets more snow than any other place on earth—it averages 300 inches. Take that, Idaho!

After a while, in fact, our insecurity vanishes. Christopher Shaw, former editor of *Adirondack Life* magazine, guided rafters through the Hudson Gorge during his early years in the park. "It's 16 miles of continuous Class III and IV whitewater," he says. "Big wild trout, waterfalls plunging in, 3,000-foot peaks on either side. All the time I'd have people from New Mexico, from Wyoming, from Colorado, and they'd tell me, 'I had no idea you had anything like that out here.'" The canoeing routes rival those in Ontario's Algonquin and Quetico provincial parks and Minnesota's Boundary Waters. Adirondack Park has 1,345 named lakes and an awful lot more that don't make the maps, many of them arranged in long chains perfect for paddling. And huge stretches of the Adirondacks are all but untraveled. Bob Marshall, who founded the Wilderness Society, got his start climbing here and returned most years to hike some more. His basic yardstick for American wilderness—a tract big enough to hike in for two weeks without crossing your own tracks—came from his experiences in the Cranberry Lake–Five Ponds area. For a compact combination of navigable waterways, expansive forests, and open mountains, the Adirondacks are unrivaled.

They're worth saving.

AND, CURIOUSLY, virtually alone among all the landscapes of the East, the Adirondacks have been saved. So far. In the middle of the nineteenth century, not long after the first ascent of Mount Marcy, loggers moved into the area with a vengeance. Previously, the great prize had been the biggest, straightest white pines, perfect for ship masts. But when it turned out that spruce was ideal for saw logs and then for making paper, the great massacre was underway. Working with horse teams, crosscut saws, and the free transportation offered by the Hudson and other rivers, men cleared the forests at a pace that would make a Brazilian blush. Subsidiary industries flourished—tons of hemlock bark gave birth to tanning plants, for instance. In the space of a few decades the Adirondacks were utterly transformed. There is little old-growth forest left, and in fact hardwoods, which pushed their way onto the logged-over lands, now dominate the forest, while white pine covers maybe 20 percent of the park.

But loggers were only the half of it. At about the same time, another human economic force—tourism—was also accelerating nearly out of control. Rev. W. H. H. "Adirondack" Murray visited the mountains throughout the 1860s and published his classic *Adventures in the Wilderness; or Camp-Life in the Adirondacks* in 1869. Murray was a Boston reverend with the common touch; in the north woods, he wrote, "sleep woos you as the shadows deepen along the lake, and retains you in its gentle embrace until frightened away by the guide's merry call to breakfast." Until Walt Disney came along, perhaps no single American ever altered so many vacation plans.

In the space of a single year after Murray's book was published, the few hundred annual visitors to the mountains turned into tens of thousands. Mostly swells, they were the folks who had read Emerson and Thoreau and were making one of the first American pilgrimages back to the land. And they were enchanted by the local mountain guides, who were shrewd enough to understand their new clients and kept saying quaint things for their amusement. ("Soap is a thing I hain't no kinder use for," declared Orson "Old Mountain" Phelps, to the delight of the party that had engaged his services.) Though the visitors were intent on communing with nature, they were often relucant to leave the conveniences of their Fifth Avenue or Beacon Hill homes. Soon the conveniences followed: By the middle of the 1870s more than 200 hotels had opened. They included the grand Prospect House at Blue Mountain Lake, the first hotel in the world with electric lights (installed by Thomas Alva Edison his own self), not to mention an elevator and a bowling alley.

Even more spectacular were the great private "camps" built by the wealthiest industrialists and railroad tycoons and stock manipulators. Fireplaces big enough to hold three fires; corridor upon corridor of guest rooms for weekend visitors; boat houses for private steamers. A few of these palaces remain, and in them you can sense that having money used to really mean something. Robin Leach wouldn't know where to start.

But the architecture was consciously rustic, a reflection of the "simple" harmonies these people were trying to rediscover in the woods. Their style has survived as the great arcadian vernacular. L. L. Bean furniture, the Ralph Lauren outdoors collection, the distinctive signs and buildings of the national parks, all are direct descendants of the great Adirondack camps. Much of our sense of what it means to "go to the woods" came from these few decades.

This sentimental affection of the powerful, which faded as the twentieth century wore on and Florida was cleared of mosquitoes, was one key reason the Adirondacks were set aside. But not the only reason. Then as now people were trying to tie the environment to the economy. George Perkins Marsh, in many ways the first American ecologist, wrote a book in 1864 called *Man and Nature,* the *Silent Spring* of its time. Marsh argued that the deforestation occurring at a rapid pace across the continent and around the world would have a disastrous impact on everything from local climates to soil erosion. "The face of the earth is no longer a sponge but a dust heap," he wrote, words that worried the powerful merchants of the Empire State who depended so heavily on a navigable Hudson River and Erie Canal.

And so the state legislature went to work, beginning the long and contentious process of defining the nature of this exceptional place and determining how to protect it. A line was drawn—the Blue Line—and the government began acquiring land inside it. At first the thinking was to take it all someday, but that goal faded, and the state still owns less than half the land within the park boundaries. Almost all the land it does hold, however, was enshrined in the state's constitution as "forever wild," not an acre to be logged.

For decades in the twentieth century, that was protection enough. The grand hotels declined, and though automobile tourism slowly grew it didn't alter the character of the region. Always the Adirondacks were just a little too far out of reach—a five-hour drive from New York, a five-hour drive from Boston. (Much closer to Montreal, actually, but that was across a border.) Most of the private land stayed in the hands of the great paper companies—International Paper, Finch Pruyn, and so on. Most of the rest belonged to a few baronial families like the Whitneys or to "clubs" of rich New Yorkers or Philadelphians who maintained large hunting domains. The year-round residents worked out a living with small-scale farming and small-scale logging and small-scale guiding—it was a small-scale living, to be sure. The Adirondacks seemed to be sliding back into the timelessness they had always enjoyed save for those few hectic decades in the late 1800s.

IT WAS NOT until the late 1960s that the real threats began to surface. A few proposals for large-scale resort communities in the backcountry reminded people that the park's private land was protected only by isolation, not by law—and that in an ever richer, ever more mobile East, that isolation was not guaranteed. Enough of the old-time power survived to save the mountains once again, though only halfway. Nelson Rockefeller, the last patrician governor of New York, appointed a committee headed by Harold K. Hochschild, a mining magnate whose 6,000-acre Eagle Nest was one of the greatest remaining camps. The committee recommended tough new zoning on private land (in many places you're allowed one building per 42.7 acres). And it called for the creation of the Adirondack Park Agency to approve and monitor new projects. The APA set up several categories of state land, the two most important being Wild Forest, where you can take your mountain bike or snowmobile, and Wilderness, where you can't.

These were not popular steps. Residents attacked the APA as socialism and the zoning as outside interference, which of course it was. Rockefeller took a lot of political heat to get those measures passed. As it turned out, however, the new laws didn't go far enough. To win their passage, backers had made a couple of great concessions: Some backcountry building could continue, and private lakeshore development was not heavily regulated. Private lakeshore, of which there is still quite a bit, may be for the Adirondacks today what spruce was a century ago, its great resouce and its great undoing.

In the 1980s, vacation homes sprouted on half the hillsides in Vermont, the Hamptons filled to bursting, Maine's rocky coast yielded a bumper crop of condominiums. And five-hour drive or no, the Adirondacks seemed suddenly within reach. The remaining backcountry became more valuable for its development potential than for its timber. Patten Corporation, a cheesy subdivider, began buying up big parcels and cutting them into "wilderness" lots. And then Diamond International, one of the big paper companies, decided to sell its holdings.

The Diamond sale was prime land, connecting many of the state's wilderness holdings—just the sort of undeveloped land that would have to be preserved if the Adirondacks were to remain the last great wilderness in the East and not become an enormous resort area dotted by parkland, the Poconos North. But when Diamond, seeking money to pay interest on a leveraged buyout in classic Reaganomics fashion, needed to unload land, the state couldn't get its act together. The Department of Environmental Conservation, slowed by its massive bureaucracy, looked on as Lassiter bought the parcels. Uproar followed, and the kindly Lassiter sold some of his new property back to the state—for half again as much as it would have paid had it bought it in the first place. The furor convinced Governor Mario Cuomo to appoint a commission on the park's future, just as Rockefeller had done 20 years before. And here, more or less, is where all hell breaks loose.

CUOMO'S COMMISSION on the Adirondacks in the Twenty-First Century, chaired by Audubon Society president Peter Berle and directed by veteran Adirondack conservationist George Davis, met for more than a year and drew up a list of 245 recommendations for the future of the park. They ranged from the minuscule ("the use of a distinctive Park highway sign color combination and self-oxidizing guiderails should be continued and institutionalized") to the majestic ("restoration of all native Adirondack species should be undertaken where biological investigations show a reasonable chance of success"). They called for strategic land acquisition in order to create the Bob Marshall Wilderness (at 400,000 acres, a tract large enough to perhaps reintroduce the wolf someday), the Boreal Wilderness (which would have protected the largest stretches of taiga south of Canada), and several other magnificent areas. Taken as a whole, the commission's report was almost certainly the single most far-reaching, forward-thinking environmental document ever prepared by an American governmental body.

And it set off the greatest Adirondack firestorm since 1903. Back then, real flames feeding on the slash of hastily harvested timber destroyed 600,000 acres in 60 days; this time the smoke and heat were confined to speeches and open letters, but they caused what will probably be longer-lasting damage to the fragile peace that had existed in these mountains for a century. Even before the report was made public, copies were leaked and protests began. Thousands of cars drove the main highway south to Albany in a slow-speed motorcade that tied up traffic for hours. Fairness Coalitions and Solidarity Alliances blossomed like trillium in the April sun, outdoing one another in their passionate attacks on the commission's call for tighter regulations and more land acquisitions. Bumper stickers appeared everywhere: ADIRONDACKERS—AN ENDANGERED SPECIES. No one escaped the heat; when the hardworking head of the regional library system innocuously asked the commission to make some mention of libraries in its report, local zealots branded him a traitor and demanded that he be fired. More than a year later, the conflict continues. In July of this year, several APA employees making a wetland inspection in a state truck were ambushed by at least two as yet unidentified gunmen. No one was badly hurt, but not for lack of trying—bullets hit the cab and wheels of the truck.

Part of the problem was cultural. The commission was made up largely of the same kind of patricians who had protected the park so ably in the past: the people whose tie to the mountains was through summer homes and fond memories of climbing Haystack, not skidding logs or collecting unemployment, the sort of people who have protected wilderness across America. As a result, the report was studded with dumb calls for removing junked automobiles from people's lawns or telling them what color they should paint the roofs of their houses so they wouldn't interfere with the view from above treeline. Twenty years ago, when Harold K. Hoch-schild issued his report for Governor Rockefeller, this sort of baronial highmindedness was not quite out of fashion. (Hochschild himself still employed much of the town of Blue Mountain Lake and enjoyed its devoted affection.) In the two decades since, though, democracy has clearly arrived in these mountains.

Style was only part of it, though. The anger came from real clashes of economic interest. It was fanned by developers and real estate salesmen who saw their dream of tens of thousands of vacation homes threatened. And they were able to rile folks up because, more and more, folks were finding their livelihoods in building those second homes for aging boomers from the big cities. Though the commission's report talked of jobs in "forest products, including small-scale wood products manufacturing, recreation, and tourism," the reality was that more and more people put up houses. It's a lot cheaper to get into than logging (no need for an $80,000 skidder) and a lot less dangerous; though the work fluctuates, it's not as bad as the wavering price of timber. And it not only pays better than most of the "recreation" and "tourism" jobs, it's also inde-pendent in a way that appeals to Adirondackers. The only problem with building second homes for a living is that it gradually wipes out the wil-derness.

In any event, most of the major conservation groups had decided that it was not vitally important to win the hearts of Adirondackers, who after all make up less than one percent of New York residents. The legislature needed to be persuaded, and environmentalists counted, as they had for a hundred years, on a groundswell of downstate support to carry the day. The governor had backed away from his commission after the Adirondackers' outcry, but he was still behind a large Environmental Bond Act on the November 1990 ballot. Second only to California's Big Green initiative in size, it would have set aside nearly a billion dollars for public land acquisition, much of it earmarked for the Adirondacks. And surely it would pass! Hadn't a million people—ten times the population of the Adirondacks—gathered in Central Park just six months before to listen to the music and commit themselves to saving the planet?

The Environmental Bond Act went down to defeat, of course, like most other environmental initiatives across the country. With it went the funds necessary to purchase land in the Adirondacks. Deals that had been years in the making are now falling through—the state may soon lose a 15,000-acre chunk along the Raquette River, for instance. It can't make a bid on the Lassiter land or even dream about the proposed Bob Marshall Wilderness.

But something even more important went down with the bond act. "Many politicians lost their fear of having a lackluster environmental record," says Neil Woodworth, the Albany lobbyist for the Adirondack Mountain Club. As a result, New York politics have returned to their tawdry usual. This year, in the middle of a state budget crisis so severe that the papers were filled with stories of drug treatment centers shutting down and AIDS patients losing services, Governor Cuomo, having vetoed even the $280,000 needed to continue the state's lynx-restoration program, insisted on spending $10 million in the Adirondacks—to improve and expand a state-owned ski resort that is driving precisely the kind of development his commission warned against. Once the legislature had gone home, he finally called for some tightened regulations on lakeshore development and other modest protections. But it remains to be seen if they'll pass the legislature; the potent real estate and construction lobbies are banding together to call for a "moderate" and "balanced" approach to the future of the park.

Environmentalists talk of returning to the grass roots—the people of downstate New York who shrugged off the bond act and who have failed to make their legislators fear a backlash. They hope for a renewal of the grand coalition that protected the Adirondacks in the past. Education is certainly needed; most folks in Westchester or on the Island know far more about the forests of Brazil. But new approaches may be just as necessary. Christopher Shaw, for one, talks of the need to end "the battle of emotional buzzwords" that have defined the debate for the past two decades—"priceless wilderness" on one side and "property rights" on the other. The best way to think about this place, he maintains, may be less as a vacation park than as a "biosphere preserve," where the people who live there protect a vital ecological outpost.

And in fact the most hopeful developments may be inside the park itself, among the sort of people often written off by the conservation movement. A new group, the Residents' Committee to Protect the Adirondacks, lacks the membership or the financial backing of the various "anti" outfits. But it has been growing steadily for nearly a year, reminding many Adirondackers that though they may hate "outside interference" and "big government," they don't want to live in Killington or North

Conway or Aspen or Sedona—reminding them that if being an Adirondacker means anything, it means loving and protecting the mountains.

Recently the Residents' Committee published a small pamphlet, "Adirondack Voices," which was inserted in most of the park's newspapers. On the front page, Richard Stewart, an eighth-generation Adirondacker, wrote of the pressures that led his neighbors to protest the commission's recommendations. "My ancestors resided in these mountains long before there was an Adirondack Park," he wrote, and when the proposed regulations on land use first appeared, he'd been angry: "I'd be damned if any government agency was going to tell me what I could do or couldn't do with my land." He understood, too, why people wanted unrestrained development. "The smell of wealth is a great intimidator, especially in the areas that suffer from a depressed economy. The poor become easy prey for the greedy," he wrote. "I know that these feelings exist, because I know what it's like to have my feet stick through my only pair of shoes." But easy-money jobs raise the cost of living; broader tax bases come with demands for greater services. Before long, the Adirondacker really is an endangered species. "To protect our land also protects our homes, protects our way of life, protects ourselves," Stewart wrote. "Through the years I've had to change my positions on things and have accepted these new rules as necessary to save the things about our way of life in these mountains that I cherish." Which is maturity defined.

This new maturity will spread, I think. But it may not be till after the developers have left their trail of strip malls and dockominiums and exclusive resort communities.

I WAS UP AT LAKE PLACID today to see a friend. Lake Placid, the vacation heart of the Adirondacks, nestles in among the High Peaks. It bustles, and not just with the serious athletes out roller skiing on the county roads or biking up the steepest slopes or summer-leaping off the plastic-covered ski-jumps. Tourists come and go down the main street, pausing to read the listings in the windows of the real estate offices. Antiques and souvenirs sell for high prices, fast food for low prices, and everyone is happy. It's a happy town, and in winter, when the lake freezes and the skaters show up against the gray 4 P.M. sunset, it's a beautiful town, too.

Still, I'm always happy to leave, to head out the two-lane road toward Saranac and Tupper and swing south toward Long Lake around the edge of the tall mountains. Most of the way the road is lined with trees—no sweeping vistas, just the steady screen of trees. East toward Newcomb and Minerva, down the one road through the center of the park, a road on which you meet another car every ten or 15 minutes. The woods are so dim. And then home, in the endless southern foothills.

Out the back door tonight nothing is happening. Nothing except the owl hooting and the bear grunting and the coyote howling. You could hike out there and find a couple of pretty good spots to watch the sunrise. But no epiphanies, no views to strip the soul bare. Just hills upon hills, forest leading on to forest. Just the real world. Worth saving.

*November 1991*

# OUTFOXING THE RADISH PATROL

*What could a 31-year-old learn from Boy Scout camp?*

● ▲ ■

### PETER NELSON

**S**even Camps, northern Minnesota. The senior staff of Boy Scout Troop 110 is seated at a picnic table, eating sloppy joes, crackers, salad, and chocolate pudding with bananas in it, and drinking something orange, which alternates with something purple from meal to meal. Needles drop into the food from pine trees overhead.

The scoutmaster is Gary Holstad, a Minneapolis grade-school teacher. He's bearded now, but 20 years ago, when I was a scout, he sported bow ties and a flattop haircut. I last saw him ten years ago, when my old patrol, the Foxes, had a reunion—he brought super-8 movies he'd taken (which I'd forgotten) in which we made he-man muscles and mugged every time the camera was on us. He remembers me, and says he's glad to have me back, if only as an observer.

Frank Caldwell, his assistant scoutmaster (also bearded), is a psychiatric social worker from Minneapolis who treats disturbed children in Hennepin County and serves as the troop medic. He helps out in part because he believes in community service and in part to observe, at length, "normal" kids. Doug Palmer, a junior-high-school teacher and an old scouting hand back in my time, is in charge of the food. A third teacher, three counselors in their twenties, and a few volunteer dads round out the leadership.

The talk is of porcupines. Porcupines love the taste of the glue in the laminated plywood, of which much of 7 Camps is made. They're devouring the camp, nibble by nibble. Talk is also of the kids, all the Matts and Marks and Jasons and Jesses, how this one is bigger than the boys his age, how that one hasn't signed up for enough skill awards, another too many, how an older scout who has been assigned to be the patrol leader for a group of younger scouts seems to be spending too much time with his own friends.

I ask how the boys have changed in 20 years.

"Well, for one thing," says Doug Palmer, "did you see how fast that bowl of lettuce went? It used to be we wouldn't go through that much lettuce in a week; they just wouldn't eat it. You also can't get them to eat canned vegetables anymore—they have to be fresh. They don't use salt either, hardly at all." Troop 110 eats well: pork chops, barbecued chicken, homemade soups, and bread baked on the spot. How Palmer orders the food has changed, too—now he uses a computer to minimize shortages and waste.

"Don't forget government surplus," a counselor says. "Under Jimmy Carter we got all the peanuts we could eat."

"What is it under Reagan?" I ask.

"Prunes," another says, "whatever that means."

I ask if scouts still get homesick.

"Give the kids peanut butter sandwiches three days in a row," says Palmer, "a lot of free time with nothing to do, and then let it rain for a day or two, and they start getting homesick in droves. We used to keep bunnies, and whenever a kid got homesick, we'd let him take care of a bunny for a few days, and he'd get over it."

Holstad's troop is sponsored by Mount Olivet, one of the largest Lutheran churches in America, and it's always been a success. Supplemented by money raised from peddling Christmas wreaths, Troop 110 has camped well—trips to Norway and Hawaii, even. But success is relative.

"A few years ago," Holstad tells me, "we had more than a hundred boys here. Now we have trouble getting anybody to come with us on weekend trips. It's like pulling teeth." There are only 41 at 7 Camps this year. In my day, there were about 70.

The camp's philosophy, engraved in wood and mounted near the activities area, is an Indian prayer advocating a respect for Nature, humility in the presence of its magnificence, and so on. Legend has it that just north of 7 Camps, on the Leech Lake Reservation, real-life Indians strip their government housing from the inside out to use the wood for heating fuel in winter, and your average 16-year-old from Minneapolis knows that an Indian is the guy you look for on Franklin Avenue to buy you the hard stuff from a liquor store. And if neither image holds true— noble savage or wino—still, it's a swell prayer.

Scouting's approach to sexuality is no more in touch. One kid tells me the only way to improve scouting would be to make it coed, *but only let in good-looking* girls. There's nothing a scout is more eager to learn about than girls, and no situation more conducive to getting the story than camp, where men and boys work together, respect each other, and have all the time in the world to talk. The best scouting can do in any formal way, however, is to supply a pamphlet on family living, and it reads as if it hasn't been updated since the late fifties, like most official Boy Scout pamphlets.

The Emergency Preparedness pamphlet, for example, under "Nuclear Emergency," tells you what to do in case of attack—how to make a shelter using bricks and boards and six inches of sand or 12 inches of magazines (*Boy's Life?*) and wait there until "local officials" come to save you. . . . And by the way, you aren't supposed to look at the flash.

"Oh sure," one kid says. "How can you know not to look at it until you've already seen it?"

"I'd just get a chair," another scout says, "and take it out on the lawn and just watch it, 'cause when it happens, there's nothing you can do."

"I'd find a girl and quick have sex with her," adds a tenth grader.

A seventh grader has his own plan. "I'd go down to the 7-Eleven for one last Big Gulp."

They look at him funny. The next time the subject comes up, he'll say he wants to have sex, too.

HOLSTAD ASKS ME if I'd mind supervising a work project, an old wooden boat that needs cleaning, painting, and naming. I'm supposed to say things like "more elbow grease, lads" or "no, not half of the boat—*all* of the boat."

I'm in charge of the Radish Patrol. (No law says you can't name a patrol The Radishes.) It consists of only two scouts, Danny and Nick, eighth graders and faithful friends. As we scrub the boat with Brillo pads, I'm tempted to make up some story about how the Fox Patrol became Green Berets in 'Nam. It turns out I don't have to—*they* ask *me* how things have changed in 20 years.

"Well, for one thing," I say, "we didn't have a rifle range."

"Why not?"

"Knowing the Fox Patrol," I say, pausing for effect, "it would have been a bloodbath." This piques their curiosity. I tell them how Jim Beetsch and Kevin Boyd and I used to shoot people coming across the Minnehaha

Creek bridge with BB guns, how at a shooting gallery at the state fair, Beetsch ignored the targets and went for the lightbulbs. He also liked to stab his knife through your tent, while you were inside it, but again, it was just a joke. No one got hurt. I tell them how there used to be a 25-cent fine for every square inch of birch tree damaged by a scout, so we stripped one in our campsite down to the pulp, purely by accident, you understand, and then fooled Holstad by wrapping the birch in a six-foot section of pine bark we pulled off a fallen tree, whistling inconspicuously, and leaning against it to hide the seams during inspection. Nick and Danny seemed impressed. I ask if any monkey business like that still goes on, but they can't think of anything, beyond guys sneaking off to have cigarettes.

In the mess area 13-year-old Neil and I are having a great conversation about dogs: favorite breeds, their personality characteristics. He knows more than I do, and I live with three dogs. His family doesn't have a dog. They recently had to put their golden retriever to sleep.

Just when I'm thinking that sometimes it's more fun to talk pets with a kid than it is to talk politics with an adult, Nick the Radish comes up to us and asks Neil if I've been made a member of the Ooga-Booga Club yet. Neil says no. Nick asks me if I want to be a member. I say sure. What trick could a Radish possibly put over on a Fox, especially when the Fox has an 18-year advantage?

I'm sorry, but as a new member of the Ooga-Booga Club, I'm not allowed to say what the trick is.

EVERY SCOUT I ASK says the highlight of camp is the Order of the Arrow ceremony, when the troop votes on who it wants to honor as fun campers. The troop assembles after dark that evening and is sworn to silence until dawn. At the head of a path, Frank Caldwell cries out like a coyote. After a pause another coyote answers from far away. (One year everyone thought the answering coyote sounded remarkably authentic—then learned it was a *real* coyote in a nearby clearing.) A big blond Indian (it's Blake, the senior patrol-leader, but pretend it isn't) comes up the path, dressed in loincloth and moccasins, carrying a torch. He beckons. The troop follows in single file, down a trail marked by burning toilet paper in coffee cans, until we reach an amphitheater-like glade.

There are logs to sit on and an unlit fire in the center of the clearing with five arrows stuck in the ground before it, one for each inductee.

Three blond kids in loincloths hold torches. The Story Teller is in the center ring, decked out in full-fringed, beaded and feathered Indian evening wear. His real name is Scott Slocum; I used to camp with his older brothers, and he used to pal around with my younger brother. Scott does this every year at 7 Camps. His story, in short, is the legend of Red Arrow, an Indian boy of 12 summers who kills a bear with his bare hands, but the Story Teller spins it out so it takes almost an hour to tell, including sound effects.

"Every year," he concludes, "his tribe had a bonfire to honor Red Arrow. So, too, every year, we have a bonfire to honor those among us whom we deem worthy."

Then comes the selection. The nominees have goose-size butterflies in their stomachs. Scott goes down the rows of boys, staring into their firelit faces, partly to build tension and partly to find the right boys. Suddenly he stops, screams, bodily picks up one camper, then another, and another—five in all—and sets them before the troop. Each receives one of the coveted arrows.

Later, Slocum the Story Teller (now back in his street clothes) tries to gather a crowd of adults to go to Yodelin' Swede's, a nearby tavern. Only I'm thirsty. Over a pitcher of Grain Belt, we talk about what great times we had when we were kids. Scott, who is a schoolteacher, has seen a lot of kids, and we both agree: Kids these days expect their lives to be edited like rock video, with no shots lasting more than three seconds, no songs more than three minutes. They like the Order of the Arrow ceremony because it approaches high drama—but how is a kid supposed to appreciate something as slow moving and unchanging as a moonlit northern lake at midnight, a lake so still you can take a stick and trace the constellations on its surface?

Has MTV sounded Nature's death knell? Could it?

No. At a still northern lake at midnight, a kid has to respond with awe and feel reverence, because Nature has always inspired awe and taught reverence. But you have to get the kid there first. Gary Holstad has been getting them there for more than 20 years.

We're down at the lake. I'm fishing off the dock, and Holstad's taking a bath. He usually comes down to bathe after supper, when the sun is low in the sky and the water is calm, and it's so scoutlessly quiet you can actually hear the loons oodle-oodling all the way from the opposite shore, the beavers slapping the water with their tails.

"Sometimes I just can't take the kids," he says. "If it wasn't for Frank and Palmer and my 20-year-olds and the rest, I don't know if I'd still be doing it."

One counselor told me he and the other staff members were staying with the troop in large part out of loyalty to Holstad. In my day he did everything, from driving the bus to blowing our noses. Now he delegates, but he still teaches kids how to identify all the plants in a ten-foot-square area, how to read a landscape, how to watch the weather.

What scouting teaches in general, and Holstad teaches in particular, is this: common sense, how not to be stupid in the woods; that it's crucial, in *any* situation, to know what things are and how they work; what you're capable of on your own; how to work with others; and how to set a goal and take intelligent steps toward it. Basic problem solving. It's low-tech, but not irrelevant. I'd paraphrase the true lesson of scouting thusly: You have a choice in this world, so if you're ignorant, selfish, and lazy, you suck.

By example, Gary Holstad has always taught scouts how to be serious about the world, how to pass it on, how to be limitlessly generous, how to put your beliefs into practice, and how to stay cheerful when you've camped in a quagmire through 13 days of rain, while mosquitoes big enough to drain the blood from cows in just seconds swarm about in attack formation.

"Dawn in the swamp!" Holstad shouts out. "I used to yell that every morning back then." I remember. "Boy that was rotten, wasn't it?" he continues. "We were so excited about getting an independent campsite, I think we took the first one we found. Of course the rain didn't help."

I take a brand-new daredevil out of my tackle box, tie it to my line, cast once, and watch the lure fly out into the lake, parting from the line at the top of my cast.

"You should have taught us fishermen's knots," I say.

NOT LONG AFTER my visit, Gary Holstad died of a heart attack. He woke up in the morning, felt bad, called an ambulance, and arrested shortly after reaching the hospital. He was only 47, never smoked or drank, had all the usual bets covered. The act of calling your own ambulance, and then dying in it, presents an image of loneliness I've sometimes associated with Holstad, a sort of quintessential Norwegian bachelor farmer, married, as one of his assistants put it, to his scout troop, to teaching. He never said anything about loneliness, but he wouldn't have.

So I took a long walk in the New England woods to honor Gary Holstad, because I couldn't make the funeral. I remembered how he'd taken me and the other Foxes into the woods and showed us the kind of pinecones that only open after forest fires, death making way for new life. How he'd caught me throwing my knife at a frog and rapped me so hard on the skull with his knuckles that my teeth rang like tuning forks. How he took us out on a moonlit lake smooth as glass, showed us the constellations, told us their names and the stories behind them, and taught us by implication that if there were pictures in the sky, then maybe there was an order and logic to existence.

After breakfast my last day at 7 Camps they were breaking camp. The scouts would bus back to Minneapolis to meet their folks at the church parking lot, go home, pet their dogs and cats, drink pop, and play loud music. I was on the way home myself. I looked for Holstad. He was in the activities area.

"It's been good seeing you again," he said. I told him likewise.

"You know," he said, "you guys were the wildest patrol I've ever had, but out of everybody who's passed through here, you're the only ones who've kept in touch."

It's funny, too, because the Fox Patrol never made it very far in scouting. From what I've heard, we all turned out OK: cops, lawyers, ski bums, glass blowers, a minister. Personally, I never made it past Second Class. I had everything I needed for First Class, but when the troop dads at the board of review asked me what my plans were, I decided a scout should be honest: I said I planned on quitting, and they didn't give it to me.

On the other hand, a good scout knows what to do with a hatchet, including how to bury one. I still believe in all the scouting virtues. I'm not real obedient, but I'm as clean as the next guy. I revere some things. I definitely revere some things.

*May 1986*

# Overthrust Dreams

### Evanston, Wyoming: Another boomtown, another bonanza, and an American conflict that won't go away

● ▲ ■

## WILLIAM KITTREDGE

See them coming, headlights out of the dusk over the Wyoming desert north of Evanston. These are the roughnecks, oil-field hands, our latter-day warriors in this combat zone of American energy solutions. They are coming off shift and burning with real money and fine innocent hubris. Later tonight in the barrooms they will grin and look you in the eye and call themselves cannon fodder. But you know, goddamnit, that they don't mean it. They are boomers, and they are spinning through the urgent main adventure of their manhood, and they love these days without shame.

The broken-fingered youngsters here are the princes of our latest disorder. And this is Christmastime, our most hopeful season. They stomp the streets of Evanston in their moon boots, felt-lined Sorels like the ones you can buy from the L. L. Bean catalog, their uniform a pair of damp coveralls sheened and splattered with drilling mud. They tip their yellow hard hats to the ladies while they figure some way to feed themselves in a town without franchise foods, and they get revved up for another night of shooting pool in some joint like the Pink Pony, or for courting the Mormon girls who flock up the 60 miles from Ogden to the Whirl Inn Disco Bar. Roughnecks. They like the name.

ME AND THE HONORABLE SCHOOLBOY, my friend and guide in this land, were picking up some fried chicken breasts from the deli in the Evanston IGA store. We were going to carry our food a couple of blocks to the laundromat and eat there in the bright warmth amid odors of detergent and bleach, sharing space with the young oil-patch wives and their knots of beggar children. A clean, well-lighted place, a haven. *Got those all-night laundromat blues, washed everything but my shoes.* Christmastime in Evanston.

Out on the main drag, 90 percent of the vehicles were 1980-model 4 × 4s, tape decks squalling some symbolic version of "Sympathy for the Devil," most of them burning diesel pumped from tanks alongside the great Caterpillar and White engines that power the drilling rigs. In a stricter, less dynamic world, that would be called theft. Here in the heartland of our heedlessness it is called small potatoes. *Forget it Jake, it's Chinatown.*

AMERICAN DREAMS are woven, like strands in a rope, from two notions: radical freedom and pastoral communalism. These cold boom-town distances in the West have always been traveled and inhabited by those who want both in an improbably happy package containing money and something else, something more complex, something that stays secret, sensed rather than known, always there to be yearned toward.

My own great-grandfather left Michigan in 1849 to travel down the Mississippi and across to Panama, where he hiked west through the jungles on the route Balboa had blazed, and caught a ship north to California and the gold camps. After a long and bootless career of chasing mineral trace in the mountain streams, first in the central Sierra and then up around the foothills of Mount Shasta, he gave it up and turned to ranching and school teaching, one place after another around the northwest until in 1897 he died white-trash poor in the sagebrush backlands near Silver Lake, Oregon, leaving a family determined to shake his suicidal despair.

It wasn't just gold that he never found—such instant boomer riches were to have been only the beginning. The ultimate reward for his searching was to have been the green and easy dreamland fields of some home place, the grape arbor beside the white house he would own clear and outright, where he could rest out his last serene years while the hordes of grandchildren played down across the lawns by the sod-banked pond where the tame ducks swam and fed and squawked in their happy, idiot way. The pastoral heaven on this earth—some particular secret and heart's-desire version of it—has time and again proved to be the bottom line in American dreams.

An old sweet story. Our central privilege as Americans has always been our luck—the spectacular heritage of the great good places in which we live. Since the days of the Puritans, we have been defoliating that heritage, mining it in one sense or another, as if it were inexhaustible. As if there were no tomorrow.

*That which is not useful is vicious*—Cotton Mather. For most of 350 years, Americans have acted as if he were right, not insane, as if the spaces amid which we reside, outside Evanston or anywhere else, were as alien as the moon.

And we still do, which accounts for the voices in Evanston. "Well, shit," you hear them say. "It's just the goddamned desert. They really aren't hurting nothing."

The local folks do know what they are losing, but they seem unwilling to recognize how very expendable the homeland of their childhoods has become, how truly it is being sacrificed. Even when home is some sagebrush Wyoming foreverland.

However big the rewards of petroleum may figure in imaginations around Evanston—airline tickets to romantic places and new hay balers for the ranchers, easy sex and pure, clean drugs and booze and the dancing beguilements of rock-and-roll for the roughnecks—they are not the final prizes, either. Maybe, just this once—the reasoning goes—we can drill and grade this little bit more of desert to death, and then we will quit. Then we will be home, to live out our lives in harmony with the dictates of our secret hearts, at peace with the blossoming earth.

THE YOUNG ROUGHNECK, a crony of The Honorable Schoolboy, was talking about Christmas. About tree decorating and the strings of popcorn they used to drape on the boughs back when he was a hired-hand poorboy in the wholesome dairy country of Wisconsin. Before he got wise and went chasing over to Madison for the strobelight concerts and rebellion in the parking lots, the small-time dope peddling and a couple or so counts of car theft before he was voting age.

But all that was behind him now. The Young Roughneck was talking household gifts, like maybe a little battery-powered coffee-bean grinder of modernistic NASA-inspired design. On the shopping-center hippie fringes of Salt Lake City he had discovered the pleasures of fresh-ground Viennese Blend. So no more Instant Folgers for this roughneck child. Not after Xmas.

"Just going to buy me that little whirring son of a bitch," he said. "Cash money." He looked across the breakfast table and grinned. A roll of folding money like the one he dug out of his pocket equals a start toward shareholding in America. No more teacher's dirty looks.

Outdoors, the morning was bright clean bluebird, four inches of glittering old snow and zero degrees. We were 30 or so miles north of Evanston, in the gut of the drilling country, where The Young Roughneck and The Honorable Schoolboy and some others had spent the previous summer camped on BLM land while they worked the towers—squatters alongside a spring some rancher dug out and piped into troughs for his livestock in the old days, before Amoco and Chevron started deep drilling in a serious way.

Shaking the chill and some hungover nerves, we were sipping coffee laced with Crown Royal and sitting jammed into the jacked-up pickup camper where The Young Roughneck resided full-time with his wife, The Cornflower Bride, a pretty girl of 19 with a blue cornflower tattooed onto her right breast, and their year-old son, The Oilfield Urchin, a bright-eyed winsome lad. The seating was a little cramped, but the hospitality was generous, and we were plenty warm. Could be more desperate.

Down the road a mile or so, in what they called Ragtown, where drifting roughnecks had lived all last summer in tents or less, packing water from the rancher's spring and cooking over open fires when they came off shift, there was still one stalwart living in his automobile, a late-model General Motors product. The exact make was hard to fix, since it was covered over with old blankets and tarps for insulation. The only heat in there was a two-burner Coleman stove. Light up and risk asphyxiation. Or stay tough and freeze a trifle.

The idea being to live close to the work and the time-and-a-half for overtime, which could often amount to 60 hours and a thousand dollars a week for even the mildly skilled.

"Yeap," the Young Roughneck said. "Executive wages."

Well, maybe not quite, but freedom. Last summer one of the boomers from Ragtown took his big-tired diesel Ford pickup down to Ogden and hauled back about three thousand dollars worth of motel furniture from a wholesale outlet, everything but a TV, and set up housekeeping in the sagebrush around a fire ring. He lived there like a crowned king of the imagination until October, when the rains commenced. He sold the stuff and headed back to winter in Texas. Radical freedom, a deer rifle you feel no need to fire, a fly rod from Orvis, and a $600 tape deck and transoceanic radio, everything on rubber, and open roads.

The Young Roughneck and family said they were staying until spring, according to latest plans, and then they were taking a vacation tour of national parks in their pickup camper. For Christmas they were going to go down to Salt Lake City and rent the best motel room in town for two or three days and buy presents and set up a tree. The Oilfield Urchin was going to have himself a traditional time, tearing up bright tissue-paper wrappings. And the first package they would open was going to be the Polaroid camera.

THE BOTTOM LINE out here is beyond all sensible reckoning, too long for a lifetime of finger counting, something reasonable only to the make-believe of computers: One Hundred Billion Dollars.

One hundred times a thousand million dollars. That is how much, in 1980, we in the United States spent importing foreign petroleum. That's a hellacious load of economic thrust, much of it aimed into these boom towns like Casper and Evanston and Gillette and Wamsutter in Wyoming, and in Rangely down in Colorado.

The Ryckman Creek oil field north of Evanston has estimated reserves worth far more than $500 million, at present prices, and in the Whitney Canyon field there is an estimated reserve of natural gas worth more than $800 million. Amoco predicts that the area's total reserves will amount to the energy equivalent of about one-quarter of the reserves in Prudhoe Bay, the Alaskan field now producing almost 10 percent of the nation's oil.

Though reports vary wildly, oil companies have spent at least $250 million in the Evanston area. Only the beginning. This Wyoming cow town—four or five blocks of hardware stores and notions shops, a single theater, a half-dozen bars, neat houses under Chinese elms and lilac blooming in springtime, a string of motels out by the freeway off-ramp, and a population of 4,500 only three years ago—this town has 4,000 transient newcomers already, and another 4,000 expected this year with 60 to 100 new drilling rigs. It's an old western story: the boom-town syndrome.

The litany of ills has always been much the same, whether we're talking about old-time cow towns like Caldwell, Kansas, or contemporary company towns like Colstrip, Montana; lumber towns like Mabel, Oregon, or military communities like Mohave, Arizona. In *Roughing It* Mark Twain talks about the town of Unionville in Nevada, where "We were stark mad with excitement—drunk with happiness—smothered under mountains of prospective wealth."

The beginning has always been characterized by careless haste in the expectation of landing in the chips, quick profit for the skillful and lucky, city planning generally nonexistent or close to it, and residents willing to pay almost any price for whatever it was they wanted, from dentistry in the old days to cocaine in Evanston. The central theme is easy money, followed by large numbers of people, gambling, prostitution, sewage problems, and all the macho you could hope for—all combining to make law enforcement nearly impossible, all undermining respect for what have been called the civilized virtues of home, the arts, regular bathing, and literature.

And then the money runs out, and everybody leaves for somewhere else. Look even at the towns that lasted a long time, like Butte, or even worse, Anaconda, where ARCO shut down the company plant, tossing most of the town's employees into the arms of Unemployment Compensation.

The city fathers of Evanston are aware of all this. A couple of years ago they were shocked into a possible vision of the future by the drug-crazed, cathouse horror show in Rock Springs, 80 miles east on Interstate 80 and already deep in the energy boom-town syndrome, as depicted by Mike Wallace on "60 Minutes." Not here, they said, and they have done a reasonable job of holding the line. That's why there are no fast food franchises in town. Outsiders have an expensive time getting building permits.

But already raw sewage is being dumped into Bear River, which runs through the outskirts of town, and older single-story houses cost nearly a hundred thousand dollars, with damned few on the market. Parking space for a mobile home costs $250 a month, without water and sewage connections, and the waiting list runs as long as your arm. Living in a motel room decorated with plants to make it feel like a home will cost you a thousand a month. The Ramada Inn, when I was there, had no rooms and didn't expect to have any soon. Hundreds, including company men from the oil towers, get their mail general delivery because all the post office boxes have long since been subscribed. The roads are torn up, the schools are jammed, property taxes have gone beyond all reason, bar fights and family shoot-outs and all-around thievery are becoming commonplace—the old community trying to hold on but increasingly engulfed, at the same time growing richer and richer, some say sacrificed.

"They have strung us up," a hardened downtown Evanston businessman told me, "and take or leave it, like it or maybe, they are skinning our hides. Right away they're going to start cutting steaks." At the time he was buying drinks for the house about every 20 minutes, paying for them with one fifty-dollar bill after another.

OUTSIDE THE YOUNG ROUGHNECK'S jacked-up camper, after one final pull straight from the Crown Royal bottle, we watched a seismic survey helicopter lift from a hilltop over north toward the Chase tower, the drilling rig where my friends had worked until the previous week.

During deer season last fall some hunter brought down one of the helicopters. One high-powered rifle shot to the guts, smoke and explosions and a modified crash landing. Late last summer a rancher from down on the hayland flats beside the Bear River drove up in midday and dropped a dead and reeking badger into the tank of fresh spring water all the campers here were using for drinking and cooking. The snowy Uinta Mountains down across the Utah border gleamed in the sunlight, and we were reminded that problem solving tends to run toward direct action in places where the air is so clean.

My friends were not working because they'd got themselves fired for fighting on the rig. They'd been working a morning tower from midnight until eight, and one of the hands showed up drunk with four of his friends and started beating on the motor man. That led quickly to group loyalties and bloodshed. One fellow took a ball-peen hammer to the head, and it will be some time before he remembers his name.

But not to worry. The cops ran those boys out of town, and in this boomer world jobs are never a problem. At least not for long. Just start roaming around from rig to rig after the midnight shift change, and you will find some crew where a man showed up drunk or too stoned to function, or not at all, and they will be coming out of the hole with 10,000 feet of five-inch pipe, getting ready to replace the triple-headed Howard Hughes drilling bit, and right away you will have a job. Down time on these rigs costs about a thousand dollars an hour, so they like to keep them turning.

But The Honorable Schoolboy didn't want a job. Starting in June as a green hand, he'd learned to work every spot on the rig—"from the crown to the ground," as they say—and he'd saved up better than $10,000 by the winter. That was enough for a year in film school at UCLA, with some weeks in the summer for climbing in Yosemite.

The Young Roughneck, who had never finished his third year of high school, did not have those options, and things between them, on this score, were a little tricky. But what the hell, this is a world of come and go, and they both knew that the sons of stockbrokers and physicians don't look to spend the rest of their lives roughnecking on the towers. In winter there is a limit to the utility of romance.

They shook hands and looked away. Catch you later.

"He's got that girl," The Honorable Schoolboy said as we drove away. "Out here that's like a gift. Most of them just got the work, and that's a hard place to find your pride. Out here." Then he smiled at himself for having absorbed too much Hemingway. Men without women, and work, the complex attractiveness of combat zones.

WHEN THEY ASKED ME what I was doing in Evanston I would say anthropologist. Journalists and sociologists have a history of getting beat up around here. It's a new roughneck sport—thumping on the pudgy creeps who come to study them as if they were a hill of ants.

When I told the woman down the bar that I was an anthropologist, she looked as if she didn't believe me.

She was one of a tribe called morning-tower widows; at least that's how I saw her at first glance. Married to men who work the morning tower, these women sleep out the days and drink away the evenings. This one was attractive in a lean and red-headed 37-year-old way, all her visible parts covered with freckles the size and color of pennies, and she was well into a red beer at 9:15 on a Saturday morning, wiping her lips with a napkin after each sip.

"God's truth," I told her. "Anthropology."

"If it gives them something," she said, "why not."

Turned out she was talking tattoos. People bouncing trailer court to trailer court can lose track of every blessed thing but themselves, and they start having multicolored pictures engraved on their skin. "Only thing they got," she said. "Keeps them company at night, while they are praying to themselves."

She was married to a helicopter pilot, and they lived 60 miles down the road in the Utah ski resort town of Park City. "No more of these rat towns," she said, twisting her mouth as if the beer had gone sour. "We drink in them class bars, and we own the condo. So things are just fine. Them hippie girls got themselves to blame. Some gotta win and some gotta lose."

She looked dead into me with her dry, gray, red-head eyes and bought me a drink as she was walking out. So much for the romance of morning drinking, morning-tower widows, and the anthropology of inky self-deception.

THE HONORABLE SCHOOLBOY and I headed to the Chase rig on the hill. Most of the leases around Evanston are held by Amoco and Chevron, but the actual drilling is done under contract by specialty firms such as Brinkerhoff and Chase and Parker. The Schoolboy was hoping to pick up his last paycheck, about $1,500 earned before the fighting broke out.

But right away we saw that the drilling pipe was stuck in the hole, and he got worried. They were fishing, as they call it on the rigs, sending complex tools down the hole, to about 9,500 feet in this case, latching onto the pipe and trying to break it loose from whatever formation it was locked into by a series of complex twistings and jerkings. The basic idea in this kind of operation is to get the pipe up so the drill bit can be replaced. So far they'd had about 30 hours of down time, at the infamous $1,000 an hour, and tempers were most likely running frothy.

These deep holes, down to 15,000 feet in many wells around here, are tough propositions, hard to hold straight as the bits cut through the slanting ledges so far below. The rigs are enormous steel-girder structures towering 120 feet above the desert, and they work in a long, repetitive rhythm—at most two hundred hours through the entire cycle. That's the best you'll ever get from one of those high-rental Hughes drill bits.

Most of the work takes place on what is called "the floor," a wide, enclosed platform some 30 feet off the ground, atop the substructure that houses the huge flower of blow-out protection valves designed to prevent the tremendous hydraulic pressures of the earth from blowing deadly $H_2S$ gas into their faces. In case the valves don't work, there are gas masks. It's like war. In case of gas, the rule is: Kill for a mask, if you must. Repent later.

All the work is dangerous on these small-scale factories in the wilderness. Enormous weight hangs above the floor on cables—the Kelly gear head that turns the drilling, the huge block and tackle used to lift the tons of drilling pipe from the hole while they are changing bits—and cables can break; everything can come down. The wrap of chain used to turn the pipe into its threads can fly loose from the hands of the chain man and take off your head. Or the derrick man, 95 feet above your head, can drop a Coca-Cola can just after he pops the top.

Going out to such work, shift to shift, breeds hardness, and contempt for those who give it up. The Tool Pusher on the Chase rig that morning didn't have much time for The Honorable Schoolboy. Class differences, if you will, matters of vocabulary. And he was pissed to be bothered with the trivialities of a boy seeking a paycheck.

And the paycheck, the $1,500, was not there. The Tool Pusher, an old Texas professional, exasperated by all these long-haired drop-out newcomers, finally recalled that he had sent it back to the drilling company. "Shit," he said, grinning cold at The Honorable Schoolboy. "I got no time to baby-sit your money."

Comes with the territory. The money, which he would no doubt recover in time, didn't bother The Honorable Schoolboy so much as this shitty way of leaving a line of work he had gone at with pride and determination. "That's Evanston," he said, and my mind heard Chinatown.

THE BOEING 707 LIFTED from Salt Lake International into a bright morning. The flats below were covered with the undulations of a luminous ground fog that had burned at our eyes, and off west the snowy mountains of desert Utah and Nevada stood shattering white and intricate against the sheltering endlessness of clean sky, each rock-fall precisely defined by shadow. Bingham Canyon—the world's largest open-pit mine—was also lovely in its unnatural way, down there under the new snowfall, a vast spiral of earth sculpture, like the Tower of Babel turned upside down.

These occasional visions of our landscape are another sort of bottom line. Those of us who live in the West, our better selves mirrored in a great and clean good place, must weigh that image against a long history of rootless boomtown extravagance that is equally our heritage.

The locals try to pretend their lives aren't changing; the boomers swagger through town with burning money in their pockets; and the professionals do their work and try to live somewhere else, maybe down in Park City, among the skiers.

And the sociologists and journalists, the people like me, come to view the rush of vitality and rich-kid chaos as if it were theater, another episode in the Wild West Extravaganza. Out along the frozen-over ranchland meadows along Bear River north of Evanston I rode a creaking hay wagon with a man who had been born in the house where he lived. "The sons a bitches," he said. "I got some of their lease money, and I like it fine

. . . and you think you shouldn't stand in the way, with gas the price it is.

"But goddamn," he said. "That was country I knew, each and every rise and fall of it, and now she is roads and derricks and a lost cause. The only pretty thing about it is those towers out there at night, lighted up like Christmas trees."

*June/July 1981*

# SHIP OF FOOLS

## To railboat Montana is to know a rare and complicated happiness.

——————— ● ▲ ■ ———————

### BILL VAUGHN

It is a belligerent April Sabbath above the 47th parallel, and we are braced against the gunwales of the sloop *Molly B.*, scanning the livid western sky, waiting for all hell to break loose. Finally, of course, it does. It always does in this part of the world. When the squall hits us upside the starboard bow, the boat heaves, the jib snaps, the mainsail swells, the mast shudders, and off we go on the ride of our lives.

By the time I can grab a pair of goggles to keep the rain out of my eyes, we're pushing five knots. At ten knots my wife Kitty ties herself to a cleat. At 15 knots the jib wrenches from its stay and flaps around like bad laundry. At 20 knots the wind suddenly pulses and the boom lashes about, knocking my prized Tokyo Fighters baseball cap off my head and over the stern. I start to lunge for it, but pull back as I discover a more pressing matter 300 yards aft. Bearing down hard on us, loaded to the tippy top with pine chips and logs, retching diesel smoke like some Third World iron works, is a 15-car freight train.

Bummer.

This is clearly the chief danger of sailing on railroad tracks. And for some veteran rail dogs like my cocaptain, an attorney we call Loophole, it is also the chief thrill. I yank on his slicker for attention and shake my arm at the problem. To my profound alarm, he laughs. "I can beat this sucker!" he screeches like a park bench lunatic. I wrestle him for the mainsheet, but insanity has made him stronger, and he keeps control. "Think about it!" he shouts. "In two miles we'll be at the spur and home free. We stop now, we're cream cheese."

I do think about it. We're moving west along the banks of Montana's

Flathead River. The relatively lethargic freight, pulled by a ponderous 1700-series locomotive called a jeep, will stop ahead in Dixon, a Montana hamlet that serves as tribal headquarters for the Flathead Indian Reservation. A crewman will hop out and throw a switch so the train can veer off and deliver its load to a mill in Polson, 30 miles to the north. If this blow holds, it'll push us past the switch and down the main track to safety.

Or I could jump out right now. Does the rule about the captain going down with his ship apply here?

The freight has slowed not one whit. Either the crew hasn't seen us, or they have and want to kill us, or they don't believe what they've seen. And why should they? A 14-foot Creole-blue and Miami-Vice-orange boat with bone-white sails rigged to an 18-foot mast, operated by people who are obviously escaping some unhappy past by sailing on private railroad tracks? *Whoa! Bobby Dick, what the heck didja put in the java?*

"Do it!" I shout at last. But Loophole's already doing it. As he trims the mainsail to capture all the wind we can get, we begin to accelerate. The wheels shriek like fingernails on a blackboard. Our third mate, an advertising designer whose height and scarlet hair have earned her the moniker the Big Red One, is wide-eyed, clutching Teddy, her little white dog, to her bosom.

The wind holds, and in no time at all we've put another hundred yards between us and the headline "Reservation Freight Nixes Nitwits." Soon we are clattering into Dixon toward the switch that means life and not death. Indian kids wave; their parents stare. We holler like chimps, jubilant, as the *Molly B.* soars past the Polson spur and out into the Jocko River Valley below the grassy hills of the National Bison Range. I pull on the brake. Loophole lets the mainsail luff, and we coast to a stop. The silence, as they say, is deafening. Above us, a bison interrupts its grazing for a look, then goes back to work.

IT'S LONG BEEN my belief that Montana's ferocious winds have caused a high rate of mental illness in the state. Day and night, season after season, they swoop down the valleys and explode from the Rocky Mountain Front like swarms of big, evil birds, ripping Ford Broncos and antelope and hapless Production Credit Association comptrollers from the sweet-smelling prairie, lofting them across the northern plains, and letting them fall softly onto Duluth and Lansing.

Well, maybe not, but it is a fact that two of the windiest burgs on earth lie in Montana. It was near one of them, Great Falls, that the *Molly B.* was conceived. One late night on my sister's ranch, I had been forced by lack of diversion to sit and stare. The ranch has no cable TV, no periodicals other than *Farmer-Stockman,* and nothing in the library more compelling than *Smokey the Cow Horse.*

So I sat. I stared. And I heard it: a mournful yowl that rose and fell like the plaint of lost souls. It was a sound I'd been around most of my life, yet one I'd never really noticed until that moment. It was the sound of wind rushing through chicken wire.

I went outside and looked at the coop. The sound was louder. What a waste of energy, I thought; a guy should harness this force. I didn't want to use it for anything productive; there was already far too much of that attitude at large in our Republic. But it did occur to me that you could sail across the state on that wind, from left to right, and then left to right across the next state, all the way to Minneapolis, where they definitely have cable TV.

The notion was all the more appealing because I have always hated the ocean—its depth, its mystery, the beasts within that crave my flesh. I suppose this is because, like most native Montanans, I am an inept, ignorant swimmer. But something about sailing transcends its unfortunate connection with the sea. Especially if you can reduce to almost nil the relentless monkey business of changing sails, trimming sails, tying knots, manning the tiller, and hiking out on one side or the other all day long. And extra-especially if you don't have to do it on water.

The next day it took me five minutes to find five volunteers eager to share the *Molly B.*'s ownership and responsibilities. Montanans are batty —the wind, remember—and will try anything once. We called ourselves the Shellbacks, a nickname bestowed on World War II sailors crossing the equator for the first time (before they crossed, they were just pollywogs). We sketched a crude design, secured welding bids, and set out on the search for a tight little vessel. We gave ourselves one warm-weather season to build the craft and sail it across the state, an arbitrary deadline but a critical one if the scheme was actually going to move from armchair to railbed.

IT IS AUGUST, and the *Molly B.* is dead in her tracks, five miles out of Geraldine in the wheat and cattle country of central Montana. The term "middle of nowhere" was coined here; the topo map looks like it was drawn in an art therapy class for manic-depressives. The Missouri, that great lummox of a river, has left the marks of its confusion everywhere. Concealed serpentine valleys, called sags, wind through the bench lands. Not far away are the Dry Falls 300-foot sandstone cliffs over which the river roared 10,000 years ago, then changed its mind. Running down the buttes and ridges almost to the tracks are natural stone walls called dikes, formed from lava squeezed out of the tortured ground. The region is suffering through the century's worst drought and feels positively primordial. The sky is full of smoke from two mammoth fires that the Forest Service has decided to let burn until the October snows put them out. The sun is a milky red. All the place needs is *Tyrannosaurus rex* ripping the spine from some lower monster.

With permission this time, we're on a 65-mile stretch of track privately owned by Central Montana Rail, Inc., a genial cartel of grain growers and small-town bankers that uses its line to move product to Burlington Northern's main track connecting to Seattle. As usual, the wind doesn't blow at first. But we don't much care: The cooler is packed with vodka and soda. Kitty is slapping at horseflies with a *W* magazine. The Big Red One is off the stern, pushing. Loophole is taking photographs of her. In our small ways, we are content.

Soon enough, a little bully of a breeze elbows in, and we're moving. Exultant, I lean on the airhorn we've been asked to blow at crossings. The racket echoes off the chalky bluffs around us, and fool's hens flee in terror, their feet blurring like a Roadrunner cartoon. It is a complicated happiness that makes us smile, something more than the mere pleasure of forward motion. Our friend Peter, part owner of the *Molly B.,* says it best. "What we do is the highest form of luxury," he likes to boast. "It's grace without cost, freedom without responsibility, travel without the perpetually annoying question, 'Where should we go now?'"

This time, alas, we travel only three miles before the wind dies in the village of Square Butte. The place is mostly a rodeo ground, but 50 feet from the track is a bar. We decide this might be a good time to see what port life is all about.

Bob and Ralph and their wives are already inside. They are retired ranchers who have been gleefully tailing us all afternoon, holding fingers out the window of their pickup to indicate our speed when we were moving at all. "Eight miles in four hours!" Bob would whoop. "Get a horse!"

WIND OR NO WIND, the *Molly B.* is a marvel of simplicity. A $50 rowboat was bolted to a six-ribbed cart of heavy channel steel. Stubby axles were welded to each corner and eight-inch aluminum wheels designed for railroad work carts were mounted on the stubs. The mast, boom, mainsail, and jib were cannibalized from a 1910 New England knockabout called a Whitecap Sailor, and rigged with steel cable shrouds. The brake system consists of a lever that forces pine blocks lined with industrial belts against the rear wheels.

Smitty, the mechanic who installed our brakes, looked the craft over and announced, "This here's a railboat, ain't it!"

"How'd you guess that?" I asked. "It's the only one around."

"I built me a sail-powered snowmobile."

After a polite pause, Loophole ventured, "How's it work?"

"It don't," Smitty said. "Thing went ten feet, fell over, and broke."

I didn't laugh. We had experimented with a braking system that involved throwing a big triple hook over the stern and hoping it caught in the ties. The fact that it never did saved the boat from being ripped in two.

Now, of course, I would like to claim that the railboat is my invention. But I cannot. Some months ago I came across a drawing that showed men clinging to a railboat as it tore across the plains. The accompanying text explained that the Kansas and Pacific Railroad used these vessels in the 1880s to ferry maintenance men to track that needed repair. This has helped me understand Harry Truman's dictum that the only thing new in the world is the history you don't know.

On the *Molly B.*'s maiden voyage, after a pious christening with a bottle of Kessler beer, Montana's finest, we hoisted a homemade square-rigged sail of ripstop nylon attached with D-rings to an aluminum mast. Amazingly, this Spanky-and-Buckwheat contraption survived the first big blow. The second gust snapped the top piece in two. We tried to make a splint with a two-by-four and duct tape, but it was not a pretty sight. We concluded that square sails, because they can't apprehend enough port and starboard wind, are not good for railboating anyway. The triangular fore-and-aft rig of the traditional sloop, on the other hand, has proven to be just what the doctor ordered. When the crew is a little more railworthy, we aim to try out a spinnaker, that tricky, handsome sail that balloons from the bow like a frog's air sac.

Because the *Molly B.* weighs less than 400 pounds, it's easy for the crew to hoist the bow into the four-horse trailer we use for transport. Once the bow is up, the rest of the boat, minus the mast and boom, rolls right in, ready to be secured with rope. Transport by horse trailer is good because railroad police cruising the highways next to the tracks aren't likely to stop people who look like witless shitkickers. We hope.

Eluding the authorities has so far been a minor irritant in our quest for the perfect rail, but it will probably become a real problem. In 1987 there were 45,000 miles of neglected track in the United States; there is much less now. Scrap steel is worth plenty, the railroad business is in flux, and salvagers—the bane of railboaters—are as thick as maggots. There is some truly "dead," or abandoned, track in Montana, but most of our voyages have been on "fallow" track that is used only occasionally and irregularly. Freight moves over these lines "on orders," whenever there's enough to warrant a trip. We have steered clear of Montana's tantalizing main lines, despite the fact that the two big ones span the entire length of the state. The *Molly B.*'s wheels would close the electrical circuit on the rails, alerting a minion at a flashing screen somewhere that dopes were violating the sanctity of the line, and exactly where. Traffic on several miles of track on either side of us would slow, then stop, and irate henchmen would be dispatched to haul us in.

SO MUCH TRACK, so little time. We still have a 70-mile spur from Missoula to Darby to conquer, and then there are some legendary legs out in eastern Montana, such as the Bainville-to-Opheim spur. Yet here it is World Series time and we're only just getting around to completing the Granite County trip that was called a month ago on account of darkness.

It's warm out, but the sky is sending messages about changes to come. We've got a full crew today—another lawyer, the Rocket, and his wife, a student we call Stretch, have joined us. We put in and are immediately whisked away on a good strong wind. A mile down the line, however, we have to brake. Some rancher has built a jackleg fence right over the track. A string of lurid Irish Catholic expletives bursts from Loophole's mouth. Rather than portage, we disassemble a section of fence, roll the *Molly B.* through, and rebuild. Then we're off.

Around the bend we're stopped by a crew of teenage boys working cattle. They're on horses and three-wheelers, and their horses spook as they approach us. "We stopped you 'cause we thought you was hunters, and this land is posted," one of the kids says politely, staring at us as if we had dropped from the sky. "But I see you ain't hunters. Damn, that is the strangest thing I ever did see."

We agree, and they let us go on our way. It has gotten a little cooler, and the sky has darkened. The *Molly B.* suddenly lurches to a grinding stop: The rusted rails here have been bowed by the sun, and the boat has dropped right onto the ties. We get her back on the track and move ahead on a spirited wind. A mile later we pass a hundred head of beef cattle that stare for a moment in their dense, passionless manner, then decide to accompany us. We move down the tracks in the middle of a herd that believes we are the hay wagon. It's fun for a while, but someone notices that four young bulls on the edge of the crowd are put out about something. The wind dies abruptly and the *Molly B.* squeaks to a halt. The cattle stop. The bulls stop. There is some exploratory bellowing and pawing of earth. "We're probably safe as long as we stay in the boat," I announce quietly. "But if they decide to get physical, we'll need a volunteer to decoy them while the rest of us run to the fence." I point to Loophole. "You."

But heroics aren't necessary. It has begun to snow. Big, soundless flakes soon turn us and the cattle white. Forlorn, they turn away from the tracks and amble back to their pasture. Two of the bulls butt heads, lose interest, and wander away.

The season is over, for the cattle and for us. We didn't exactly sail across Montana, but we covered a lot of ground. If we wanted an entry in the *Guinness Book of World Records*, we could probably have it—there are no rivals. But we don't care. We scorn glory. It's enough to know that when the spring sun melts the snow off the railroad tracks of Montana, the Shellbacks will return.

*May 1989*

# Smokey the Cop
● ▲ ■

### EDWARD ABBEY

*No! Topsman to your Tarpeia! This thing, Mister Abby [sic], is nefand.*

— James Joyce, *Finnegan's Wake*

The Smokey we're talking about is not the natty chap in the sharp sombrero, bane of truck drivers, who lurks behind billboards along the interstate. No, the one under discussion here is the fellow in the suit of forest green who hands you the ticket, leaning out of his box office, when you buy your admission to Yosemite, Grand Canyon, Yellowstone, or other of our national parks, the crown jewels of America, as someone once said. No doubt. Guarded, patrolled, looked after, explained (more or less) by the rangers of the National Park Service. Who are sometimes known as tree fuzz, tree pigs, or Smokey Bears; distant kin of that other Smokey Bear (the famous ursine bore) who served as an original symbol for the Forest Service until he died (tertiary syphilis) in the Washington, D.C. zoo.

Perhaps there are still some people who don't know the difference between the National Park Service and the U.S. Forest Service. Let us review the question one more time. The Park Service is an agency of the Department of the Interior, entrusted with the care and management of such federally protected lands as national parks, national monuments, and national recreational areas. The Forest Service is a bureau of the Department of Agriculture and was given charge, by Congress, of our national forests. Park Service lands were established to be preserved and yet kept open for the enjoyment of the people. The forests, on the other hand, were set aside for various uses: watershed protection, wildlife habitat, recreation, livestock grazing, logging, even mining.

No matter. The difference between one service and the other, and between national parks and national forests, is not so great as it once was. Since the second world war, commercial uses of national forests have predominated. And multiple use is really, in the view of many, multiple abuse. With mass motorized recreation becoming a bigger and bigger industry, the national parks as well as the forests have been sub-jected to ever-increasing development: paved roads, motels, hotels, mar-inas, gas stations, stores, banks, hospitals, cloverleaf intersections, parking lots, traffic lights, even jails.

In any case, I myself have worked for both agencies, in both kinds of places, and can testify from ample personal experience that the difference between the Park Service and the Forest Service is more nominal than real; both labor under the domination of the Gross National Product, the National Association of Manufacturers, the corporate pursuit of pecuniary happiness. "The business of America is business," said Calvin C. Coolidge, our last honest president, and he was never more right than now, here, where even sex therapy and spiritual fulfillment have become growth industries.

What has all this whining to do with Smokey the Cop or the out-of-doors, that other world *out there*, outside, beyond the expanding labyrinth of walls that cuts us off from what we long for, more and more, as it recedes into our past? Not much. Very little. But some.

FOR 17 SEASONS, off and on, I worked as a ranger, as a fire lookout, as a garbage collector, as a time server and petit bureaucrat, for the Park Service, occasionally for the Forest Service. Since most of these jobs involved, to some extent, what is called "protection" (law enforcement) as well as "interpretation" (answering questions), I too have played the role, or more exactly played *at* the role, of Smokey the Cop. I wore a uniform and a badge, I carried a .38 (usually in the glove compartment of a government pickup). I sometimes hassled, harried, and harassed people, especially hippies. And shot two dogs and a number of beer cans. In self defense, of course. An odd part to play, you might think, for one who considers himself a libertarian, an anarchist, and a dedicated scofflaw. But perhaps not. I've never known a serious policeman who had much respect for the law; in any well-organized society the police constitute the most lawless element. Policemen are not legalists, they are moralists, stern believers in good and bad, right and wrong, and that distinction, as many a false-arrest victim can testify, is quite an important one. I too am a moralist, not a legalist, and thus fulfill the basic qualification of cophood.

My career as a P.I.G. (Pride, Integrity, Guts) began not with the Park

Service, however, but during my stint with another overgrown governmental bureaucracy affiliated with the Department of Commerce, namely—the U.S. Army. One morning I was coming down off a boat onto the bomb-wrecked docks of Naples, Italy, when this man I'd never seen before tapped me on the shoulder and asked how tall I was. I told him I was six-foot-two on a warm day, but contracted a bit in cold weather. You're a cop now, wiseass, said the man. He was a second lieutenant in the Military Police; I was an acne-haunted, teenage draftee in the infantry. The boat from which I'd just disembarked, traveling tourist class, was a troop ship; and on that particular day every replacement six feet tall or over was being shunted, willing or not, into the MPs. Typical of the Army: keep the big men in the rear, let the little guys do the fighting.

My feelings were hurt at being assigned to the MPs, since my true military ambition was to become a clerk-typist in the tradition of James Jones and Norman Mailer. But of course it did no good to object. Some supply clerk put a black-and-white, Nazi-like armband on my sleeve, a white helmet liner on my head, a nifty red scarf around my neck, and a club and a .45 automatic in my hands. Almost at once I began to feel mean, brutal, arbitrary, righteous. Let's stop coddling criminals, I wrote home to mother that first night in Napoli, Italia; let's put father in jail where he belongs. (My father was the village socialist back in Home, Pennsylvania.)

ALL VERY WELL, the bemused reader begins to complain at this point, very amusing no doubt, but—what has all this nostalgic bullshit to do with the subject purportedly under discussion, i.e., the park ranger as cop? Tree fuzz? Smokey the Pig? We want to hear about Smokey Bear and the Tree Pig!

Very well. About ten years later, armed with my more or less honorable discharge and my five-point veteran's preference, I began a long series of sometime seasonal jobs as a ranger with the National Park Service. My first was in Arches National Park in Utah, then quite a primitive place, where I enforced the law (natural law, that is) by pulling up the survey stakes from a new road the Park Service was attempting to build into *my park*. That didn't do much good; I moved on.

I spent three winters as a ranger in Organ Pipe Cactus National Monument in southwest Arizona, a lovely place swarming with rattlesnakes, Gila monsters, scorpions, wild pigs, and wetback Mexicans. The only useful police work that I did there was citing picnickers for drinking beer from cans—beer should always be properly aerated and drunk from a mug, tankard, or schooner, any fool knows that—and rescuing rattlesnakes discovered in the campground, catching them alive with my wooden Kleenex-picker before some vicious tourist could cause them harm, then dumping them in a garbage can and relocating the snakes by stuffing them down a certain rodent hole about six miles out in the desert. (Herpetologists believe that a snake will not walk more than five miles from anywhere, but I'm not sure about that. I'd say, to be safe, you should always hobble your snake, if possible, and hang a little bell around his—or *her*—neck [a snake's neck is found just forward of the shoulders. The hobble may, if necessary, he fastened above the hips.]) Always the same hole, naturally; I was trying to create a genuine snake pit. But with uncertain success; no matter how many rattlesnakes I packed down that hole I never found a single one emerging to greet me on my next visit. I suppose the rodent ate them all.

At Petrified Forest, the worst position I ever held with our National Park Service, I worked the box office. That is, I sold tickets to tourists entering the park and interrogated those departing. The latter task was carried out in this manner: The tourist, obeying the stop sign, would rein in his car beside my station. Looking him straight in the eye I would say, "Sir, have you or any members of your party removed any petrified wood or other objects from Petrified Forest National Park?" Looking me straight in the eye, the man at the wheel would generally reply, "Oh no, just looking," and his wife, at his side, would nod in solemn agreement. Then one of the little kids in the back seat would say, "But daddy, what about that big log we put in the trunk?" So that's why the rear bumper was scraping the asphalt. Well, I'd radio at once for reinforcements, we'd open the trunk, remove the petrified log (worth about $300 on the curio-dealer black market), club the driver into insensibility while his family stood around screaming and bawling and getting in the way, arrest them all, generally have the husband and wife locked up for five to 15 years, and pack the kids off to an orphanage where they'd probably get better-balanced meals anyway.

But such diversions seldom occurred more than two or three times a day. In general the job was a bore; if it had not been for the financial rewards, I would have quit much sooner. Financial rewards? True, a seasonal park ranger was then paid only about two dollars an hour. But the tickets! Each time I sold some turkey his admission ticket I would remind him to keep that piece of paper in plain view at all times, so as to verify his right to be in the park. (Really. For Petrified Forest, like Grand Canyon or Yosemite, is a *national* park—not a people's park.) And when the tourist was leaving the park I would lean far out my window, extend my hand and say, "May I see your pass, sir?" (We called them passes; sounds better than tickets.) So the poor mark would give me his ticket, I'd look it over, say, "Okay sir, thank you," and he'd drive away, glad to be gone. I would resell the same ticket to the next innocent coming in off the interstate. In that way I'd clean up about $500 to $600 on a good day, sometimes more on weekends when the action was lively. But as I said, the job was a bore; I moved on. (This really happened, once, at Grand Canyon National Park.)

I moved on, to Everglades National Park, down in Florida, where the rednecks and alligators live, thriving on one another. Only an alligator will eat a redneck, and vice versa.

At Everglades they gave me a souped up Plymouth Interceptor with sireen and red and blue gumball lights on top. I was a traffic cop, a highway patrolman. Night shift. I wrote a few warning tickets, out of sheer meanness, but spent much of my time careering down the Pine Island–Flamingo highway, late at night, lights flashing, to see what that Interceptor would do (125 mph). Sometimes I halted traffic on the highway in order to shepherd one of those eight-foot diamond-backs across the pavement.

Another chore was checking doors at the visitor center and chasing skunks, drunks, and alligators out of the rest rooms, which were left unlocked at night. But the grimmest part of the job was lying in wait at night, far out in the sloughs, watching for 'Gator Roberts. You never heard of 'Gator Roberts? He was simply the most famous alligator poacher in the state of Florida, maybe in the whole Southeast; a legendary figure, phantom outlaw, folk hero and a bone in the throat of Everglades park rangers. We hated him. But we had an informant, a waitress who worked at the Redneck Cafe, near Pine Island. She had connections with the poaching business and would tell us, from time to time (for a price), exactly where old 'Gator Roberts was planning to strike next. We'd stake out the place—some stinking, stagnant pond deep in the dismal swamp—and would wait there all night, sweating, scratching chigger bites, cursing, slapping mosquitoes, fondling our guns. He never appeared. Next morning we'd learn that 16 skinned alligator carcasses had been found somewhere off at the other end of the park, 40 miles away, with a note attached: "You Smokies ain't got the brains Gawd give a spoonbill duck. Regards, 'Gator."

ONE WINTER in that low-rent bog was enough. Retiring phase by phase from the law-enforcement business, I returned to Arizona and got myself a job as a fire lookout up in a 60-foot tower on the North Rim of the Grand Canyon. And the last I heard of Smokey the Cop was over the airwaves, through the Park Service radio in my lookout tower. It seemed that some scruffy types from southern California, degenerate immoral hippies, were smoking a controlled substance somewhere in the vicinity of Indian Gardens under the South Rim. Far out in the wilds, as they doubtless imagined, far far from the fuzz, the law and all of those who call themselves "the authorities." So they thought. But they were wrong.

A humble maintenance man, fixing a water line, saw them, smelled the peculiar smell, and radioed park headquarters. Minutes later, a helicopter—a helicopter!—with armed rangers inside was sent down to make the bust. I can see those hippies now, in my mind's eye, sitting naked and cross-legged in their little circle under the shade of a juniper, passing the pipe of peace from hand to hand, each one far out in the cool of inner space, becoming gradually, horribly aware of a giant dark bird with whirling wings hovering above, shrieking at them with the voice of steel and power and outrage—*God is the great black spider in the sky!*—coming down, down, down upon them. . . .

Was it then I finally gave away my Smokey Bear hat? The one with the four dimples in the high crown and that wide flat rigid brim, hard as iron, with which you could chop a man's head off if necessary? (We kept the brim flat by installing the hat under the seat of a toilet bowl each night; the same way your friendly state police do it.) Don't remember. Can't seem to recall things as good as I used to. As the French say, *quel dommage.* But I did give it away, I remember that, to a short boatman with a big head. He promptly ruined it by wearing it headfirst through the Big Drop in Cataract Canyon down there in Utah.

*February 1978*

# THE SAME RIVER TWICE

## Stenothermal waters and the remorseless flow of time

•  ▲  ■

### DAVID QUAMMEN

**I**'ve been reading Heraclitus this week, so naturally my brain is full of river water.

Heraclitus, you'll recall, was the Greek philosopher of the sixth century B.C. who gets credit for having said: "You cannot step twice into the same river." Heraclitus was a loner, according to the sketchy accounts of him, and rather a crank. He lived in the town of Ephesus, near the coast of Asia Minor opposite mainland Greece, not far from a great river that in those days was called the Meander. He never founded a philosophic school, as Plato and Pythagoras did. He didn't want followers. He simply wrote his one book and deposited the scroll in a certain sacred building, the temple of Artemis, where the general public couldn't get hold of it. The book itself was eventually lost, and all that survives of it today are about a hundred fragments, which have come down secondhand in the works of other ancient writers. So his ideas are known only by hearsay. He seems to have said a lot of interesting things, some of them cryptic, some of them downright ornery, but his river comment is the one for which Heraclitus is widely remembered. The full translation is: "You cannot step twice into the same river, for other waters are continually flowing on." To most people it comes across as a nice resonant metaphor, a bit of philosophic poetry. To me it is that and more.

Once, for a stretch of years, I lived in a very small town on the bank of a famous Montana river. It was famous mainly for its trout, for its clear water and its abundance of chemical nutrients, and for the seasonal blizzards of emerging insects that made it one of the most rewarding pieces of habitat in North America, arguably in the world, if you happened to be a trout- or fly-fisherman. I happened to be a fly-fisherman.

One species of insect in particular—one "hatch," to use the slightly misleading term that fishermen apply to these impressive entomological events, when a few billion members of some mayfly or stonefly or caddisfly species all emerge simultaneously into adulthood and take flight over a river—one insect hatch in particular gave this river an unmatched renown. The species was *Pteronarcys californica*, a monstrous but benign stonefly that grew more than two inches long and carried a pinkish-orange underbelly for which it had gotten the common name "salmonfly." These insects, during their three years of development as aquatic larvae, could only survive in a river that was cold, pure, fast-flowing, rich in dissolved oxygen, and covered across its bed with boulders the size of bowling balls, among which the larvae would live and graze. The famous river offered all those conditions extravagantly, and so *P. californica* flourished there, like nowhere else. Trout flourished in turn.

When the clouds of *P. californica* took flight, and mated in air, and then began dropping back onto the water, the fish fed upon them voraciously, recklessly. Wary old brown trout the size of a person's thigh, granddaddy animals that would never otherwise condescend to feed by daylight upon floating insects, came off the bottom for this banquet. Each gulp of *P. californica* was a major nutritional windfall. The trout filled their bellies and their mouths and still continued gorging. Consequently the so-called salmonfly so-called hatch on this river, occurring annually during two weeks in June, triggered by small changes in water temperature, became a wild and garish national festival in the fly-fishing year. Stockbrokers in New York, corporate lawyers in San Francisco, federal judges and star-quality surgeons and foundation presidents—the sort of folk who own antique bamboo fly rods and field jackets of Irish tweed—planned their vacations around this event. They packed their gear and then waited for the telephone signal from a guide in a shop on Main Street of the little town where I lived.

The signal would say: *It's started.* Or, in more detail: *Yeah, the hatch is on. Passed through town yesterday. Bugs everywhere. By now the head end of it must be halfway to Varney Bridge. Get here as soon as you can.* They got there. Cabdrivers and schoolteachers came too. People who couldn't afford to hire a guide and be chauffeured comfortably in a Mackenzie boat, or who didn't want to, arrived with dinghies and johnboats lashed to the roofs of old yellow buses. And if the weather held, and you got yourself to the right stretch of the river at the right time, it could indeed be very damn good fishing.

But that wasn't why I lived in the town. Truth be known, when *P. californica* filled the sky and a flotilla of boats filled the river, I usually headed in the opposite direction. I didn't care for the crowds. It was almost as bad as the Fourth-of-July rodeo, when the town suddenly became clogged with college kids from a nearby city, and Main Street was ankle-deep in beer cans on the morning of the fifth, and I would find people I didn't know sleeping it off in my front yard, under the scraggly elm. The salmonfly hatch was like that, only with stockbrokers and flying hooks. Besides, there were other places and other ways to catch fish. I would take my rod and my waders and disappear to a small spring creek that ran through a stock ranch on the bottomland east of the river.

It was private property. There was no room for guided boats on this little creek, and there was no room for tweed. Instead of tweed there were sheep—usually about 30 head, bleating in half-hearted annoyance but shuffling out of my way as I hiked from the barn out to the water. There was an old swayback horse named Buck, a buckskin; also a younger one, a hot white-stockinged mare that had once been a queen of the barrel-racing circuit and hadn't forgotten her previous station in life. There was a graveyard of rusty car bodies, a string of them, DeSotos and Fords from the Truman years, dumped into the spring creek along one bend to hold the bank in place and save the sheep pasture from turning into an island. Locally this sort of thing is referred to as the "Detroit riprap" mode of soil conservation; after a while, the derelict cars come to seem a harmonious part of the scenery. There was also an old two-story ranch house of stucco, with yellow trim. Inside lived two people, a man and a woman, married then.

Now we have come to the reason I did live in that town. Actually there wasn't one reason but three: the spring creek, the man, and the woman. At the time, for a stretch of years, those were three of the closest friends I'd ever had.

This spring creek was not one of the most eminent Montana spring creeks, not Nelson Spring Creek and not Armstrong, not the sort of place where you could plunk down $25 per rod per day for the privilege of casting your fly over large savvy trout along an exclusive and well-

manicured section of water. On this creek you fished free or not at all.
I fished free, because I knew the two people inside the house and, through
them, the wonderful, surly old rancher who owned the place.

They lived there themselves, those two, in large part because of the
creek. The male half of the partnership was at that time a raving and
insatiable fly-fisherman, like me, for whom the luxury of having this
particular spring creek just a three-minute stroll from his back door was
worth any number of professional and personal sacrifices. He had found
a place he loved dearly, and he wanted to stay. During previous incar-
nations he had been a wire-service reporter in Africa, a bar owner in
Chicago, a magazine editor in New York, a reform-school guard in Idaho,
and a timber-faller in the winter woods of Montana. He had decided to
quit the last before he cut off a leg with his chain saw, or worse; he was
later kind enough to offer me his saw and his expert coaching and then
to dissuade me deftly from making use of either, during the period when
I was so desperate and foolhardy as to consider trying to earn a living
that way. All we both wanted, really, was to write novels and fly-fish for
trout. We fished the spring creek, together and individually, more than
a hundred days each year. We memorized that water. The female half
of the partnership, on the other hand, was a vegetarian by principle who
lived chiefly on grapefruit and considered that anyone who tormented
innocent fish—either for food or, worse, for the sport of catching them
and then gently releasing them, as we did—showed the most inexcusable
symptoms of arrested development and demented adolescent cruelty, but
she tolerated us. All she wanted was to write novels and read Jane Austen
and ride the hot mare. None of us had any money.

None of us was being published. Nothing happened in that town
between October and May. The man and I played chess. We endangered
our lives hilariously cutting and hauling firewood. We skied into the
backcountry carrying tents and cast-iron skillets and bottles of wine, then
argued drunkenly about whether it was proper to litter the woods with
eggshells, if the magpies and crows did it too. We watched Willie Stargell
win a World Series. Sometimes on cold, clear days we put on wool gloves
with no fingertips and went out to fish. Meanwhile the woman sequestered
herself in a rickety backyard shed, with a small wood stove and a cot
and a manual typewriter, surrounded by black widow spiders that she
chose to view as pets. Or the three of us stood in their kitchen, until
the late hours on winter nights, while the woman peeled and ate un-

countable grapefruits and the man and I drank whiskey, and we screamed at each other about literature.

The spring creek ran cool in summer. It ran warm in winter. This is what spring creeks do; this is their special felicity. It steamed and it rippled with fluid life when the main river was frozen over solid. Anchor ice never formed on the rocks of its riffles, killing insect larvae where they lived, and frazil ice never made the water slushy—as occurred on the main river. During spring runoff, this creek didn't flood; therefore the bottom wasn't scoured and disrupted, and the eggs of the rainbow trout, which spawned around that time, weren't swept out of the nests or buried lethally in silt. The creek did go brown with turbidity during runoff, from the discharge of several small tributaries that carried melt-water out of the mountains through an erosional zone, but the color would clear again soon.

Insects continued hatching on this creek through the coldest months of the winter. In October and November, large brown trout came up-stream from the main river and scooped out their spawning nests on a bend that curved around the sheep pasture, just downstream from the car bodies. In August, grasshoppers blundered onto the water from the brushy banks, and fish exploded out of nowhere to take them. Occasionally I or the other fellow would cast a tiny fly and pull in a grayling, that gorgeous and delicate cousin of trout, an Arctic species left behind by the last glaciation, that fared poorly in the warm summer temperatures of sun-heated meltwater rivers. In this creek a grayling could be com-fortable, because most of the water came from deep underground. That water ran cool in summer, relatively, and warm in winter, relatively—relative in each case to the surrounding air temperature, as well as the temperature of the main river. In absolute terms the creek's temperature tended to be stable year-round, holding steady in a hospitable middle range close to the constant temperature of the groundwater from which it was fed. This is what spring creeks, by definition, do. The scientific jargon for such a balanced condition is *stenothermal*: temperatures in a narrow range. The ecological result is a stable habitat and a 12-month growing season. Free from extremes of cold or heat, free from flooding, free from ice and heavy siltation and scouring, the particular spring creek in question seemed always to me a thing of sublime and succoring con-stancy. In that regard it was no different from other spring creeks; but it was the one I knew and cared about.

The stretch of years came to an end. The marriage came to an end. There were reasons, but the reasons were private, and are certainly none of our business here. Books were pulled down off shelves and sorted into two piles. Fine oaken furniture, too heavy to be hauled into uncertain futures, was sold off for the price of a sad song. The white-stockinged mare was sold also, to a family with a couple of young barrel-racers, and the herd of trap-lame and half-feral cats was divided up. The man and the woman left town individually, in separate trucks, at separate times, each headed back toward New York City. I helped load the second truck, the man's, but my voice wasn't functioning well on that occasion. I was afflicted with a charley horse of the throat. It had all been hard to witness, not simply because a marriage had ended but even more so because, in my unsolicited judgment, a great love affair had. This partnership of theirs had been a vivid and imposing thing.

Or maybe it was hard because two love affairs had ended—if you count mine with the pair of them. I should say here that a friendship remains between me and each of them. Friendship with such folk is a lot. But it's not the same.

Now I live in the city from which college students flock off to the Fourth-of-July rodeo in that little town, where they raise hell for a day and litter Main Street with beer cans and then sleep it off under the scraggly elm in what is now someone else's front yard—the compensation being that July Fourth is quieter up here. It is only an hour's drive. Not too long ago I was down there myself.

I parked, as always, in the yard by the burn barrel outside the stucco house. The house was empty; I avoided it. With my waders and my fly rod I walked out to the spring creek. Of course it was all a mistake.

I stepped into the creek and began fishing my way upstream, casting a grasshopper imitation into patches of shade along the overhung banks. There were a few strikes. There was a fish caught and released. But after less than an hour I quit. I climbed out of the water. I left. I had imagined that a spring creek was a thing of sublime and succoring constancy. I was wrong. Heraclitus was right.

*May 1986*

# THE PROPWASH CHRONICLE

## How one freelance hotshot buzzed America and got what he deserved

• ▲ ■

### PHIL GARLINGTON

I woke up one morning realizing that I was a stranger to my own land. I had never taken a look at America. It wasn't that I wanted to *comprehend* everything from sea to shining sea like some sappy Bill Moyers. No, I was interested in a visual inspection of my homeland, accompanied by appropriate calm reflections. I simply wanted to *see* America, not make a three-piece suit out of it.

Of course, I had done all the usual hack traveling that everybody does: the trip to France, Eurail pass in hand, with the optional truck ride across North Africa thrown in, from which I returned thinking, "Thank God *that's* over with," like some sorority girl mentally ticking off her life experiences . . . "Let's see, I've been laid, I've got my B.A., I've been to Europe . . . should I get my ears pierced?"

If I was going to pursue America I'd be damned if I'd repeat the mistake of my younger days, and fall in line with the hordes of other neo-Vespuccis loose in the land; yet another bearded loony careening along Interstate 40 in his Volks, looking forward to the day's high point, a hot shower at a KOA.

Or God, hitchhiking. I was not about to join those glassy-eyed malaria victims sounched at freeway on-ramps, holding up cardboard signs with "East" scrawled in Crayola. Moreover, to "discover America" on the Dog was out of the question. In a word, I despise the bus, don't care much for cars, refuse to thumb . . .

That's why I traded my 1965 Volkswagen (R/H, snrf, runs gd) for 35 hours of flying lessons. This is not to imply that I had ever taken a previous interest in flying. I certainly was never one of those jerks who looks up at the sound of an aircraft engine: "Gosh, guys, a Beechcraft Bonanza."

But it hit me, in my own plane I could *fly* around America; that way I could see everything, yet I wouldn't actually have to rub elbows with every Father-Knows-Best showing his kids the country. That's what I thought.

The plane I bought was a 13-year-old two-place Cessna trainer. It weighed 900 pounds and had a 100-hp engine that looked exactly like the one in my Volkswagen. The radio didn't work, and the instruments had their own eccentricities. Fred Sanford would have known better, but for this bargain I paid $3,000.

Owning an airplane meant I could no longer afford a roof. To be sure, I was getting $300 a month in unemployment, but the plane payment took $200. I had a friend, however, who was working out his own quirky impulses by living in a barn outside the remote mountain town of Igo, population 50, in Northern California. Conditions there were primitive, no running water or indoor plumbing, but I was welcome. There wasn't actually room for me, but I could set up my Army cot under the big tree in his orchard.

It was a warm spring, why not. I was soon living under a tree. For money John cut firewood, and I had the tail end of my unemployment, enough not only to establish the Milton Friedman Beer Fund, but also to buy enough aviation gas to check out the little strips dotting Northern California: Trinity Center, Manton, Shingletown, here and there.

THUS BEGAN MY SOJOURN as an airplane bum, the beginning of two years of bushing. Bushing, by the way, is flying strictly confined to the boondocks, flying off the airways, in the bush, from pea patch to sod field. The radio gathers dust. All navigation is done by trying to match something on the sectional map with something on the ground. The best bushing is through the western states and Canada to Alaska, something I found out when I quit the soft life at the barn to cash in on the North Slope oil boom.

My ideas were vague, but I did know that the Alyeska consortium was building that pipeline from Prudhoe Bay and it seemed to me that with all that oil, and all that money, *some* opportunity would . . . Besides, I'd heard that Fairbanks had become awfully decadent, and the notion of a roaring, drunken, violent frontier boomtown engaged daydreams that had been quiescent since Randolph Scott went into retirement.

I had planned to make the trip alone, but before I left the barn I got into a wrestling match with John's three kids and pinched a nerve in my neck. Cissy, a friend of John's wife, drove me to the hospital. Naturally, I told her about my plan, what an adventure it would be, blah, blah, and pretty soon she decided that *she* wanted to go even though she already had a husband and a two-year-old kid. Until then I think she thought of me as "that bum under John's tree," but this business of an airplane ride to Alaska must have colored me in more romantic tones. Anyway, I talked her into ditching her husband.

At the library I got this FAA pamphlet that said Canadian law required pilots to take along survival gear: fishing hooks, a gun, *snare wire*, if you can believe that. (To me, asking for snare wire at a hardware store would be as embarrassing as it used to be to order Sheiks over the counter.) While I was okay at kayoing deer at 30 yards from the back of a truck, I had no illusions about my skill as a Bumpo. Thus, for *my* survival kit, I took along a dime-store compass, two mosquito nets, and a seven-pound jar of peanut butter.

Cissy and I flew north, entering Canada at Penticton. Then we went winding through innumerable mountain passes to the Peace River and to Northway, Alaska. Accommodations were never a problem. There are hundreds of little boondock airports, each one having an airport manager who is generally glad to see you. Sure, you can pitch your tent right on the field. And the john never has a coin lock. Oftentimes, there's even a shower you can use. Well, it's better than trying to take a bath in the restroom sink at a Shell station.

We took advantage of whatever hospitality was offered. Some Forest Service types let us stay in a trailer one night in Oregon when it was raining like hell. We slept in airport offices, in hangars. Somewhere in British Columbia a guy let us stay at his fishing lodge overlooking a lake. I remember the walls were plastered with snapshots of boring-looking people holding up fish.

THE RIGHT ALTITUDE for a long crosscountry turned out to be about 500 feet above the terrain. There's a feeling of mastery at that height. If I ascended to 5,000 or 6,000, the world became uninhabited, lifeless, strictly scenery.

At 500 feet I could see everything. If eroticized looking is called scoptophilia, then that was it. I was a spy, a voyeur. I flew over towns, looking into people's backyards, watching them poolside or by the barbecue. And they were oblivious, because pedestrians never realize how much the low-flying pilot can see. That's why jails are full of housebreakers and car thieves pondering the efficacy of police aerial surveillance. It's like looking through the crack of a door into a crowded room; they can't see you, your view is perfect. I could see the movie theater with the line in front, and the kids trying to sneak in the side door. I could see the main streets and the back alleys, the car lots, baseball diamonds, the teenagers' favorite hangout, the graveyards, junkyards, all at a glance. It was like that exquisite flash of understanding at midnight.

Flying over the wilderness is different. In Alaska or Canada. By flying off the roads, it's possible to remove yourself from all signs of human life very rapidly. There is nothing out there, not a house, not a telephone pole. And something strange happens when there is no man-made object to put the vastness into perspective. If seeing a town whole is the midnight flash of understanding, then seeing unmitigated wilderness is the confusion of dawn, when one struggles to remember what it was that had seemed so damned brilliant the night before.

WE ARRIVED IN ANCHORAGE without two pennies to rub together and the work situation turned out to be this: At the first smell of oil, all the regular Alaskans dumped their shit jobs and headed for the slope, and the first wave of carpetbaggers took whatever the Alaskans left behind, leaving unskilled latecomers like me to scramble for whatever menial work was left. At the unemployment office I was thus called lucky when told about a job for a "lodge couple" at Bear Mountain Lodge. The man had to tend bar, pump gas, and maintain a 500-watt generator; the woman had to wait tables and clean cabins. Not ideal for a couple of our refinement, but the lodge had an airstrip in the backyard.

Two hours later we bumped down at Bear Mountain and met the proprietress, a decrepit stick of a woman who looked exactly like Gravel Gertie. (Her B.O. Plenty, it turned out, was in the hospital sweating off a case of the D.T.s) In another hour I was embarked on the first of my new duties, the burning of 200 pounds of accumulated garbage.

The lodge was set in the Wrangell Mountains on the road to Slana. I looked at the copper-colored peaks rising in all directions and began to understand what the words "awesome grandeur" really meant. All right, Ansel Adams at his most clinical, a view as clear as a Sierra Club calendar.

Plus, a living river of ice, the Nebesna Glacier, spilled out of the canyon across the road. But such is the perversity of things that right at the base of all this beauty was Gravel Gertie, a speck of humanity at its most peevish. Gertie was so miserly that she wouldn't give me one of her goddamned cookies until she made sure that none of her small group of lodgers would buy it; and when I asked for milk I got a tablespoon of powdered chalk in my water glass.

One night about 3 A.M. she came screaming out to the Airstream trailer where Cissy and I stayed. "I'm being robbed," she cried. "Stop them." Sure enough, a couple of young guys were hammering away at the lock on the gas pump. "No free glass with that fill-up," I thought.

It's quite wrong, you see, to think that everybody in Alaska is a wilderness buff, tromping around on snowshoes in pursuit of a moose. These two punks at the gas pump—like most Alaskans, in fact—had the atrophied leg muscles of the typical energy-dependent urbanite. The punks were tied to their car, and the road; and their idea of living off the land was knocking over a gas station.

I sauntered over to the guys and said: "Listen, either you guys leave right now or I'm going to shoot you both." The amusing thing is that I didn't have a gun, and they could see I didn't have a gun. Yet, just because I said it, just because I looked serious when I said it, they thought that *somehow* it might be true. Amazing. And they left. It's the same principle that sells used cars.

On our day off we decided to fly over to Valdez, the southern terminus of the pipeline, to try to better our lot. Here, I thought, might be a good place to cash in on whatever was going on. No sooner had we gotten through the pass than the weather closed down and we couldn't get out. It was raining; we didn't have our tent or sleeping bag. Happily, a geologist we knew from the lodge picked us up. He and his wife were avid mushroom hunters, which was fun enough, jouncing around on old mining roads looking for buttons. But they were Seventh Day Adventists, and their board suffered accordingly.

As for looks, Valdez is not bad, perched on a gem of an inlet and surrounded by cliffs so sheer and lushly verdant that a comparison with Maui has become trite. Otherwise, it's not much, and as for rowdy nightlife, you might as well be in Norman, Oklahoma. Anyway, by the time we got back to Bear Mountain we'd been replaced. Gertie sniggered and paid us off. Ready? Our combined check for the week came to $87.

We flew to Anchorage and, hearing about a job with a chain saw operation, I promoted myself as an experienced sawyer. My experience was based pretty much on seeing the previews to *The Texas Chainsaw Massacre*, but I figured that once in the boondocks the company would keep any amateur no matter what his ineptitude since the pay was only $5 an hour, Jack-in-the-Box wages by Alaskan standards.

The company wanted to hack a road through the forest near Wasilla to abet its scheme to unload parcels of miasmatic swamp on the unsuspecting. The crew boss, a young guy from Montana, was not fooled by me, but it didn't matter. You should have seen the rest of his men, my colleagues.

We got the dregs on that crew. One young lout from New York insisted on bringing a portable radio to work his first day. By the time this guy showed up I had developed considerable virtuosity with the saw, and when the lout put his radio on a stump and tuned it to an Anchorage hard-rock station, I am proud to say that I dropped a tree on it before the second, "Let me hear you say 'Yeah.' "

Along with this clown, we had a former cow milker from Wisconsin (who spent his lunch hour studying the mysteries of the Rosicrucians, which he'd sent away for) and a guy from Minnesota, whose last job had been with a mosquito abatement experiment. It was his part of the experiment to let the mosquitoes bite him. He was perfect for our crew.

The work was hellish, mostly because of the bugs. Although it was hot and steamy in the woods, we had to wear gloves and netting, not so much because of the mosquitoes as the yellow jackets. Their nests were in every other tree, and in burrows under the ground. Yellow jackets flew up your pantlegs, they bumbled under your netting, and they hit the exposed part of your wrists with uncanny accuracy.

The "bees," as we called them, were the nemesis of Frank Peets, one of life's rolls of toilet paper. Peets was former career Army who'd been shot up so badly in Vietnam that, internally, he'd lost half of everything. Mustered out of the Army, he used his disability money to buy a fishing camp on the north side of Cook Inlet. But he lacked the money to stock it. What to do?

First he entered a snowmobile race for a cash prize. A few miles from the finish he was leading the pack when his Snopac flipped. He banged against a tree and smashed his leg. The jubilant finishers shot past him and he lay in a drift, forgotten, for ten hours. Now, just out of the hospital bed, still hobbling, he was with us as a sawyer.

Peets started the job with a partner, but the partner immediately slashed his leg with the saw, and that was it for him. A few days later, Peets found himself standing on the all-time monster bee nest. The bees, pouring out by the thousands, enveloped him. His chain saw went flying and, staggering, he tumbled over a log and fell, separating a disc. Then the bees really had at him.

I was somewhat sympathetic until it became obvious that he was paralyzed, and that, consequently, we would have to carry his 210-pound carcass a mile and a half over brush. His paralysis, however, was only temporary. He mended in a few weeks, and he and his gimpy partner bought a boatload of supplies for the fishing camp with their combined disability insurance money.

Now I am not making this up. On their way across the inlet on a calm summer's day, a freak storm blew up, sunk the boat, and the luckless duo, sans boat and supplies, had to be rescued by Coast Guard helicopter. Suffering from exposure, they were both hospitalized again. It amazed me that Peets was in no way disheartened by any of this. Despite everything, he thought Alaska was paradise, and extolled it for hours as he limped around. "God's country," he would say, as he beat his frostbitten fingers against a tree.

For $15 a week Cissy and I rented a converted school bus located behind Wasilla's gas station. The mosquito abatement guy from Minnesota and his wife would bring over their infant son to visit us. They'd stay for hours, their entire conversation aimed at the drooler on the floor. Not only that, the guy actually bought a parcel of the swamp we were cutting through after seeing the color brochure the company put out.

Ironically, it was obvious that the guy from Minnesota would hang on and prosper in Alaska, while the romantic Peets, for all his maundering about paradise, would be crushed out like a cigar butt. The guy from Minnesota didn't give a shit about mountains, or breathtaking vistas or good fishing. He was a Snopes; he planned to Stay forever in Wasilla, and in 20 years he would own the gas station, the grocery, and the café. It's always the dreary pluggers who make it in harsh climates.

BY THE END OF AUGUST we finished the road and I had enough money to get us out. By flying nine- and ten-hour stints, we crossed the border into Cut Bank, Montana, three days after leaving Wasilla. I'd scared myself so many times in the mountain passes I'd decided to go back on the east side of the Rockies.

But at Cut Bank I had another thought; I would visit my cousin in Missoula, even though this involved crossing the Rockies at one of its higher points. Laboriously, I coaxed the plane up to its service ceiling, 10,000 feet. A 30-knot headwind had been forecast, but at altitude it seemed much stronger. As the granite peaks loomed closer I got the feeling that this wasn't going to work out for me.

Half a mile past the little town of East Glacier Park the trap door opened, and whatever magic that holds up planes ceased to work. A strong westerly wind rushing over the mountains had created a tremendous downdraft on the lee side. Our sickening plunge earthward reminded me of soaring, only inversely. When a glider hits a thermal generating a lot of lift, whu-mmp, you go up like Hertz was taking you out of the driver's seat. Our plight was just the reverse. The wings were quivering and it was all I could do to get the plane turned around. Fuck Missoula, I quickly decided; we'd just cruise around on the east of the Rockies, forever maybe.

So we drifted back, through Wyoming and into the Dakotas. In the Black Hills, we flew past Mount Rushmore to inspect the presidents at eye level. I had Cissy snap a picture of me with the monument in the background, to be entitled "Five Great Men," which I thought I might use as a Christmas card some day. But I didn't like the result: In the picture it looks like Washington is staring into a cage at a chipmunk.

This, I felt, must be an omen of sorts and I reconsidered my plan to tour Mexico. I decided that crossing the border without *mordida* money would be next to insanity. Instead, four weeks later, we were in San Francisco and down to bare metal again.

I was sitting in a newspaper bar when I heard that the *National Enquirer*, king of the check-stand tabloids, had a guy recruiting reporters that very minute at the Clift Hotel. With my last three bucks I cabbed to the Clift, walked in unannounced on the *Enquirer*'s diminutive Mr. Munchkin, and demanded an interview, figuring with the *Enquirer* it wouldn't pay to be too polite.

Munchkin asked me if I could stand to be in Paris one day and Mexico City the next. I said I thought I could tolerate it. He asked if I could walk right up to somebody like Ted Kennedy for an interview. I said, if I had to, I'd kick Teddy in the shins to get his attention.

Thus, Cissy and I flew to *National Enquirer* headquarters in Lantana, Florida, arriving literally penniless. For more than a year I'd been living in trailers, under trees, on airstrips, seldom two nights in the same place. When I reported for work, my wardrobe fit easily into a modest-size duffle bag, with plenty of room left for a watermelon. But in a couple of days I had a brand-new Hertz gas guzzler, a wad of cash, spiffy clothes, and the promise of a stack of credit cards to come, everything from a lowly American Express to an exotic RCA Global Communications card that insured press telex service by satellite from anywhere.

"Obviously, Faustus," I said to myself as I admired my new floral shirt in the hotel mirror, "there's a price on all this." But that came later. In the meantime, I would enjoy my new surroundings.

A MERCENARY ATTITUDE prevails at the *Enquirer*, "Home of the Whoppers," as I called it. There's lots of money and lots of travel, and everybody tries to grab as much for himself as possible. Of course, as Bruce, my editor, said, you have to keep your socks up. The *Enquirer* swallowed reporters by the handful on Monday and had diarrhea on Friday. Thus, good money, unstable personalities, and an uncertain future led inevitably to a pronounced carpe diem outlook.

Most of the editors and reporters are Brits, guys from England, Scotland, South Africa, Australia. The Brits, by and large, are rowdy, good-natured, hard-drinking, soccer-playing Monty Python fans who love to go out en masse to the local honky-tonks to fight the rednecks. As a result, *Enquirer* staffers are banned from a couple of Lantana dives. In all, the office atmosphere was something like the petty officers' mess aboard H.M.S. *Invincible*.

The most fun I had in all this was arranging the logistics for a visit from outer space. The *Enquirer* had determined that a small town near Austin, Texas, on the Pedernales River had reported more saucer sightings than any other place in America. So they wanted to dress up a couple of guys as space creatures, have them walk into town, and see what would happen.

To play the extraterrestrials, I hired a couple of muscular midgets through the stuntmen's local in Hollywood. Midgets because I thought small space visitors would be less intimidating to the gun-toting Texas redneck; and muscular because they had to carry 85 pounds of body armor under their costumes.

Now I still say that this mission would have been a very satisfying national sensationette had it come off. But the midgets developed cold feet. Somebody told them the armor wouldn't stop the really heavy rounds, and that, in Texas, it was an absolutely sure thing they'd be shot.

Even so, I was now really rolling with the *Enquirer*. My interview with a waitress in Billings, Montana, resulting in "Marlon Brando Is the Biggest Cheapskate I've Ever Met," got raves. And by using the *Enquirer*'s Book of Quacks, I found a doctor who said that plain tap water is the best remedy for cataracts. They loved me in Lantana. I was a Yank, yet I kept my socks up.

But I was moving so fast I never had a chance to do anything fun. As the shuttle from Miami would descend for a landing at West Palm Beach airport, I could look down at the people snorkeling and surfing. But I had to rush back to the office to write up a story on "How Vitamin E Can Save Your Marriage." All the previous year I had been working and living outdoors. Now I was roaring around every night with the crazy tryouts and the Brits. I was getting a barroom pallor in Florida.

My decline at Home of the Whoppers began with an assignment to take Lucky to Washington to meet the presidential pups. Lucky, a woebegone mongrel, was the *Enquirer*'s mascot, and had been dragged all over to be photographed with celebrities: "Lucky Meets Lucy," "Lucky Meets Bob Hope." A year or so previously Lucky had met King Timahoe, Nixon's dog, and now the publisher wanted it to meet the puppies of President Ford's dog.

I went to Washington, and for a week pestered Ford's press staff with my ludicrous request. Finally, because I was being such an asshole about it, I got through to presidential press secretary Ron Nessen himself. "Absolutely not," said Nessen. "We won't lend ourselves to this kind of gimmick." Hmph. This Nessen was just a lowly ex-newsman, but now he thought he was better than Lucille Ball. Like a lot of other moralistic people, Nessen isn't terribly bright, and he's been handled by events accordingly.

Right after my conversation with Nessen, I had to rush to New York to interview a famous doctor who had invented a machine that would detect a heart attack five years in advance. His wife, hearing that I had to return immediately to my stake-out at the White House, and finding a chance to take me aside, asked me to deliver a personal letter for her to a high-ranking member of Ford's inner circle.

Yes, knock, knock, it's Mr. Opportunity calling. Sure enough, when I opened the letter in my hotel room it was just as I suspected: a missive to her sweetie, and highly compromising, too.

Now, I should say, in the newspaper biz I had never scrupled about opening desk drawers, nor did I smite my brow too much if my eye happened to light on private correspondence. And, myself, I think it's appropriate to use info thus gleaned for a story, or as leverage to get a story.

But, I wondered, was I now really prepared to use this windfall billet-doux to a middle-aged adulterer as my entree to the White House *so that Lucky could meet the presidential pups?*

I began to suspect that I didn't have the steel for a long career at Home of the Whoppers. In a word, I destroyed the letter and accepted defeat on the Lucky assignment.

Other considerations entered into my decision to quit. For one thing, I wasn't making any money. Like everybody else, my plan had been to grab every cent I could. Yet, like almost everybody else, I was falling deeper and deeper into debt. We were all spending, spending. Nobody was saving for a rainy day. When I went to Disney World and took the ride called Pirates of the Caribbean, it reminded me of the *Enquirer* staff on Friday night at the Oyster Bar. Rape and pillage and a round for the house.

A year before I grinned all night if I found a bar that served 30-cent draft. Now I had to drink Heinekens at a buck a pop, and a restaurant with paper napkins wasn't good enough for me anymore. And the whole thing was made worse by the credit cards and the cash advances. Every time you went out of town you could get a cash advance; so every time you did. I began to think that all the advances and the credit cards were *mine*.

Even Cissy, who is always game and had come to Florida to help me spend money, suggested that perhaps I was going too far. Then the accounting department brought me to heel, and I was shocked. I had pissed away $30,000 in a matter of months. I winced all the more because I knew that accounting hadn't yet received the results of my latest credit spree in New Orleans.

CLEARLY, IT WAS TIME to bow out. I left the day the bill came in for my long-distance credit-card calls. The accountant said he was very concerned. I told him I'd discuss it with him after lunch.

But by 1 P.M. Cissy and I were 700 feet over the shore of Lake Okeechobee, headed north with the few wads of stray cash I had left. I didn't really have a plan, but I thought it would be a good idea to keep a floating address for a while. Then, in Hope, Arkansas, we met this guy who told us about those ghost towns in southern Arizona that could be reached only by four-wheel drive or airplane. You could just move in to any of the old houses and nobody would bother you, the guy said; and with a greasy thumbprint, he stamped the location of the ghost town on my sectional map.

I thought we would be there in two days, but I hadn't counted on the Texas wind. The wind was out of the west at 40 knots, gusting to 55. The little Cessna took a tremendous pounding as we bucked along. Because of the turbulence, I had to slow the plane down to 80, which meant that, with the head wind, our actual ground speed was somewhere around 35 mph. When we looked down at the highway we could see the westbound traffic overtaking us. I had never experienced such a typhoon. At times (although I refrained from mentioning it to Cissy) the plane was not under my control. The stronger gusts would get under the wing, tilt us over 50 degrees, then slew us around to the right. It was disconcerting.

Peering ahead, I made out a tiny crop-duster field on the outskirts of Ballinger. Unhappily, the wind was perpendicular to the dirt runway. I would have to land on a rough field with a strong 90-degree crosswind. My word is good on this: It's tricky business in a little airplane.

When I set up the approach, the nose of the plane was crabbed 45 degrees into the wind; we were sliding toward the runway sideways. The wind, spilling over trees and other obstacles near the ground, had created bone-jarring turbulence; the plane groaned, banged, and grated as we descended. Just over the threshold of the runway I pushed in full down-wind rudder with accompanying full opposite aileron and landed on the upwind wheel, just precisely as it's supposed to be done.

Thank God Cissy was there. Usually, my heroic acts pass unnoticed because nobody's around (although if I fuck up it's SRO). But now I had a witness, someone to whom I could turn in later years and say, "Tell everybody about the perfect crosswind landing I made in Ballinger, Texas, that day when the wind was blowing 90 knots."

I decided that to celebrate I would splurge on a cab to come get us. Then we'd go to the nearest bar where I would buy drinks for everybody while I told what I'd done. When the cab driver arrived he had a quiet chuckle over my invitation to buy the house a round. We were in a dry county.

The wind ·howled a gale for four days, and we were stuck at the Blackstone Motel in Ballinger. Out of prostrating boredom, I wasted a lot of money in this dry little town—I don't know how. But by the time the wind abated, I had run through the wad of money I had left from the *Enquirer*. So that's how I came to take my next job, as a gravedigger at the cemetery owned by the Ballinger Methodist Church.

When telling people about this now, I get the impression they think being a gravedigger was quite the romantic job, that maybe people were lined up for a chance at it. This isn't true. I was the only taker. After all, you dig a grave just like you dig a swimming pool, only smaller.

I would like to be able to claim that in the course of my work I turned up some musty bones that I could philosophize and crack jokes over like you-know-who. But I didn't. In fact, I only dug three graves the entire time I worked there. Mostly I watered the flowers and cut the grass. And the only *memento mori* that crossed my mind concerned my wish for my own marker to be flush with the ground, so the lawnmower could go over it and the dogs couldn't pee on it.

Naturally, I read all the epitaphs, but the only one that was interesting was on the tombstone of Enoch Brubaker: 1844–1929 (if I remember rightly). It was a Latin tag, which, when I got it translated later, turned out to mean, "I was not, I am not, I care not."

By the time we left Ballinger the prospect of the ghost town in the sun-drenched, pristine desert had unlimited appeal. I will not reveal the location of the ghost town, except to say that it's not far from Nogales, which is where we were heading when I noticed the engine was starting to get rough.

We were 700 feet over Tippet, Texas, when the engine blew a cylinder. The fuselage began shuddering violently. I quickly pulled the throttle, perhaps too abruptly, and suddenly it was very quiet. The engine had quit. After trimming the plane for 70 mph, I began studying the ground for landing possibilities, since I knew for certain that within 50 seconds we were going to be there, ready or not.

I spotted the Tippet airport, but I thought I was too far away to make it, and I was right. Our glide ended at a pasture about 200 yards short of the runway; we took a couple of bounces and landed on the concrete, knocking out one of the runway lights.

When the airport mechanic pulled the oil screen, I knew I had serious trouble. The screen was tinged with chunks of metal; one of the cylinders was breaking up. It would cost a grand, at least, the mechanic said, to get my plane flying again.

And this mechanic grinned somewhat sharkishly at me as he delivered the bad news. We both could see who was over the barrel. I sold him the plane for $900, and three days later Cissy and I were back in San Francisco.

It didn't take long to settle back into a hedonistic routine, because it turned out that in my 18-month absence someone had invented hot tubs. Nonetheless, for a while I missed the vividness of my life as an airplane bum. But finally, as it must, the experience faded into a concatenation of grizzled tales that I am only likely to trot out it if I've had a few too many.

I sought America, found it, but in the end was glad enough to toss it back. For every so often I fantasize myself pictured in one of those snapshots tacked on the wall at that fishing lodge in Canada where we stayed. In the fantasy photo, I am smiling vacantly and holding up a fish that is shaped like the United States. "He hooked a 'whopper,' " somebody scrawled in ballpoint.

In any event, I think it's safe now to put a check next to "See America" on my life's itinerary. Except . . . I still keep thinking about that ghost town in Arizona. I know exactly where it is, because that guy's thumbprint is still on my map. And if I had an airplane, I could be there tomorrow.

*October 1977*

part

III

THE

NATURAL

WORLD

# THE BIG BUZZ

*The killer bees are ripping through Mexico and heading for Texas. Arrival time? Next spring. Solution? See your tailor.*

● ▲ ■

ED ZUCKERMAN

Here are the intrepid killer bee researchers, relaxing over a few chilled Carta Blancas from the minibar in their room in the best hotel in Jalapa, Mexico, comparing notes on where they least enjoy being stung.

Orley R. "Chip" Taylor, Jr., a large and jovial insect ecologist from the University of Kansas who has been tracking the killer bees through Latin America for 15 years, has just finished demonstrating the little dance he does when a bee gets into his pants and starts crawling up his thigh. Now he explains that some stings don't matter. "When you're intently working on something, sorting through a colony to find and mark the queen, and you start getting stung on your hands, maybe once a minute—10, 12, 15 times—you just keep going. It doesn't bother you."

Glenn Hall, a sober bee geneticist from the University of Florida, nods in agreement. "Back of your hand, no problem. But the stings on your fingertips are painful."

"The ones I don't like are just *under* your fingernail," says Chip. "Or on the nose here"—he points just inside a nostril. "Your eyes water and you start to sneeze, and you have to stop whatever you're doing."

"Yes," says José Antonio Gutierrez, a hyperactive graduate student at the National University of Mexico. "And when they go in your ears, you try to get them out." He demonstrates by waggling a finger in his left ear.

"I talked to someone who did two autopsies in Tanzania," Chip says, "and there were bees in every orifice—eyes, ears, mouth, nose, anus."

"That's the one that seems to get people," says Glenn, "the anus."

"Right," says Chip, and he issues a mock threat to an invisible foe: "How would you like a bee up your anus?"

Everybody laughs. Ho, ho, say I. Nothing like a little bee humor before an encounter with the killer bees. Of course, these guys have all been working with bees since junior high. (There seems to be a bee-keeping gene that guides certain adolescent boys to the hobby.) These guys *like* bees. They all get stung, all the time, both by the relatively gentle European bees that have been raised in the Americas for centuries, and by the more temperamental African killer bees that have been sweeping north, as much as 300 miles a year, ever since 26 colonies imported for research by one Warwick E. Kerr were accidentally released in Brazil in 1957. Their northernmost column is now on the Mexican Gulf Coast, less than a year away from Texas and just a short drive from our hotel room.

Here we are, on the killer bee front line, relaxing over beer and bee jokes. Chip opens a can of roasted peanuts—which, he notes, taste very much like the sauteed bee larvae he serves when entertaining back home in Kansas. I break the mood by asking about a particularly nasty stinging incident that my pretrip research turned up. I've got a couple of clippings about a University of Miami botany student named Inn Siang Ooi, who was walking in the woods in Costa Rica one day in 1986 when he was unlucky enough to stumble upon a killer bee colony. The sting of an individual killer bee is about as toxic as that of any other honeybee, but killer bees are prone to attack in larger numbers and for a longer time than other honeybees when an intruder threatens—or when they *think* an intruder threatens—their hive.

Chip knows about the incident; several months after it happened, he visited the site, spoke to witnesses. Now, all laughter finished, he tells me and Glenn and José Antonio how Ooi had been climbing on a rock over a cave when he came upon the nest; how the bees attacked and Ooi couldn't run away because the rock face was steep; how his friends threw butterfly nets over their heads and tried to get to him but were driven back by the bees, three of them stung so seriously that they collapsed; how Ooi climbed or fell into a vent in the rock while the bees stung him still; how rescuers heard him moaning but could not find him until they saw one of his feet dangling into the cave below; how rescuers had to wait until dark (when the bees returned to their hive) to retrieve Ooi's body; how it was carried out of the forest in a procession behind a white horse; how it had been stung 8,000 times or, as one report observed, "an average of 46 stings per square inch."

THERE THEY ARE —the killer bees.* On a dry yellow hillside east of Jalapa, Chip has established an apiary of 45 bee colonies. A year ago, shortly before killer bees reached this area, he stocked it (and four others at varying altitudes) with local European bees. Now some of those bees have bred with killer bees, and we have come visiting to see how the apiary has changed.

We arrive at the edge of the apiary—Chip, Glenn, José Antonio, an enthusiastic Mexican student named Felipe Brizuela, and I—and climb out of our van. The morning was cool, but the day is hot. Yellow grasses and bare-limbed trees stretch over the surrounding hillsides. The apiary is in the sun, the hives clustered around short leafless trees with sharp thorns. We are 50 feet away. Figuring 40,000 bees per colony, we are looking at 1.8 million bees. None of them seems to have noticed us.

Good.

The 26 colonies of African bees that escaped in 1957 in Brazil, 7,000 miles south of here, have made ecological history by taking over most of a hemisphere: French Guiana, Surinam, Guyana, Venezuela, Colombia, Panama, Costa Rica, Nicaragua, Honduras, El Salvador, Guatemala, Belize, and now Mexico. They found their niche in the wilds of the American tropics, where European bees never thrived. The Africans were tougher than the Europeans; they could get by on less nourishment and could fly farther—up to 12 miles or more without a rest—to seek out what nourishment there was. They reproduced more prolifically than Europeans; while Europeans stockpiled honey, the Africans used their honey to nurture more bees. Africans sometimes invaded and took over European colonies, killing the resident queens. And when domesticated European queens flew off to mate in areas where Africans lived in the wild, they

---

* A note on nomenclature: Generally, the respectable press has used the term "Africanized bees" for these insects—after, of course, an initial reference to "so-called killer bees" so that readers will know what the article is talking about. Only trashy tabloids use the term "killer bees" all the way through. Now, however, a scientific debate has arisen as to whether the bees are more correctly called "Africanized" or "African." To use one term or the other would amount to taking sides. Therefore, in the interest of objectivity, I feel compelled to refer to the insects as killer bees, except where context requires that they be referred to as "the little bastards."

mated with African drones, and so did their daughters and their daughters'
daughters.

At one time, entomologists expected that this crossbreeding would
result in a diminution of the killer bees' fierceness, a genetic legacy of
their ancestors' lives in Africa, where men and animals routinely raid
hives for honey. But after 32 years of crossbreeding, the killer bees are
as testy as ever. Chip estimates that they have killed between 700 and
1,000 people in Latin America and stung another 70,000 to 200,000
severely enough to require medical attention. Since arriving in Mexico
two years ago, the bees have killed five people, all of whom were elderly
and some of whom had provoked colonies by attempting to capture them
or steal their honey.

The death toll is likely to be lower in the United States, where few
people steal wild honey or capture wild bees. But when the first death
does occur—and some will inevitably occur after the killer bees cross
the Rio Grande sometime around March 1990—it's going to be big news.
(As many as 18 killer bee swarms have already reached the States as
stowaways on cargo ships, but as far as is known, American authorities
have found and destroyed them all.)

American beekeepers are dreading the day. They fear an anti-bee
hysteria that will put many of their number out of business. But the killer
bees themselves will accomplish that; faced with feistier bees than they
have ever worked with before, some beekeepers will close up shop rather
than try to adapt.

Honey production is a relatively minor industry in the United States,
and any honey lost could easily be replaced from the world market, but
American honeybees play another, far more indispensable role: They
pollinate $20 billion worth of fruits, vegetables, and other crops. Some
farmers hire beekeepers to drive truckloads of bees to their farms and
park them there. European bees can be trucked with impunity, but killer
bees are likely to take violent exception to going on the road.

No one knows how widely the killer bees will spread in the United
States. Chip thinks the climate will confine them to the Deep South;
the U.S. Department of Agriculture says they may spread through the
48 contiguous states. The USDA is working on various schemes to
slow or modify the bees. Chip has little confidence in the USDA, but
he is optimistic that the bees *can* be modified in the United States,
where they will encounter large numbers of wild European bees for the

first time. With that in mind, he is working on selecting and positioning European drones to maximize their chances of mating with killer bee queens.

To study mating behavior, Chip has developed a plastic tube (dubbed Chip's Master Mater by his students) that slips over the sex organs of a queen bee. When drones attempt to mate with the queen, they stick to the tube, making them available for scientific scrutiny. To locate "drone congregation areas," Chip has walked the hills of Kansas towing helium-filled weather balloons from which he has suspended sexy queen bees in cages. He has modified old Army radar units to track the flights of drones, and he has experimented with police radar guns. All the while, he has kept up his visits to Mexico to keep an eye on the progress of the killer bees.

Chip hasn't been in this apiary for several months, so he doesn't know what we can expect today. I suit up for the worst in full bee garb: white coveralls, leather gloves, a pith helmet, a mesh veil that attaches to my pith helmet with an elastic band and zips directly to my coveralls, and Velcro straps that seal the bottoms of my pants. The researchers don similar suits, and then we're off, ambling among the bee boxes, which are painted green and blue in cheerful Mexican style.

The researchers set immediately to work. Chip, José Antonio, and Felipe take the covers off bee boxes, shoot puffs from hand-held smokers to subdue the bees, and start pulling out frames. Hanging from each frame is a bee-built wax comb, its individual cells filled with honey, pollen, or wormlike larvae (which are excellent sauteed, as Chip has pointed out). There are also a thousand or so bees on each frame, scurrying from cell to cell on bee business. Chip, José Antonio, and Felipe brush through the bees with their hands, looking for queens.

A bee colony's character is established by its queen, the mother of every bee in the hive. She lays eggs full-time after an early-in-life mating flight during which she copulates—some 40 feet above the earth—with several drones and acquires a lifetime supply of semen; the lucky drones who manage to reach the mating queen literally explode their genitals into her and die.

When a colony prospers and grows full of bees, it "swarms." The queen flies off with 10,000 to 15,000 of her children to find a new home, leaving behind the rest of the colony and several larvae that workers will nourish into new queens. One of the new virgin queens will kill the others, embark on her mating flight, and then return to begin laying eggs, as the cycle begins again.

Some of the queens in this apiary have been here since Chip established it; they are European bees, and so are all of their offspring. But some of the colonies have new queens that have taken their mating flights since wild killer bee colonies moved into the neighborhood, and some of the drones they mated with were killer bees. Some of their children, therefore, are half killer bee. Those offspring are likely to have inherited their fathers' disposition.

Chip, José Antonio, and Felipe are having trouble finding some of the queens in the masses of bees running around on the frames. They pull out frame after frame, virtually disassembling some of the hives. This is just the kind of thing that pisses bees off, and a few fly up to attack the researchers—and me, the innocent bystander. But our suits protect us.

Glenn, meanwhile, is using a squirt bottle to flush larvae out of their cells. He will take them back to Florida, grind them up, and analyze their genes. His work along these lines so far seems to have provided an answer to the puzzling question: Why, after 32 years of crossbreeding with European bees in the Americas, haven't the killer bees been "gentle-ized" by all that European blood?

Because, Glenn has concluded, that European blood ain't there. Genetically, the killer bees at the leading edge of the invasion have shaken off any European influence picked up by their ancestors on the flight from Brazil. The bees now heading toward the Rio Grande, he says, are nearly pure African.

Chip concurs. The African bees, he and Glenn contend, have genetically swamped the relatively few European bees they have encountered. Family lines resulting from African-European crosses have died out in the wild, apparently less able to compete for resources than their pure African cousins.

These findings have been disputed by USDA researchers, who insist that the bees are not African but "Africanized" hybrids. The USDA does concede that these hybrids retain the character traits of their African daddies, so the debate seems a little academic. But it is intense. Chip and Glenn have few kind words for their colleagues at the USDA, which funded Chip's killer bee research until 1981 and then cut him off to move its program in-house; USDA researchers for their part have few kind words for Chip and Glenn. The two sides exchange cutting remarks in the *Bulletin of the Entomological Society of America* and wherever killer bee people congregate for scientific conferences.

ALL THAT SEEMS far away from the apiary, where Glenn gathers more larvae and the others continue to search for queens. Queens that have been in this apiary since the beginning are marked with yellow dots; younger ones are marked with blue or white. The yellow-dot queens definitely preside over all-European colonies. The domains of the other queens are questionable.

Like Colony 47. When Chip opens this box, the bees do not continue about their business like mild-mannered Europeans; instead, a battalion flies up to attack him. They go for his head (rampaging bees are attracted to dark spots like hair, eyes, ears, and mouths) and run across his veil, trying to get inside it.

Mine, too.

"You know what I'd do with these bees in Kansas?" Chip calls out over the angry buzzing. "I'd kill them all." Back in Kansas, he raises gentle European bees. *Those* bees are stinging his ankles (he has forgotten to bring his high white boots). Wincing, he pronounces the colony a "pecky" one.

Glenn, who has been working barehanded—he finds it awkward to manipulate his samples while wearing thick leather gloves—is suddenly stung about 20 times on each hand. He decides that gloves wouldn't be so bad after all.

Chip moves on to other boxes, calling out the colors of the dots on the queens he finds, and I, trying to make myself useful, record them in a logbook. It's difficult to do with gloves on, especially with bees running over the book and my gloves.

As the researchers open more boxes, the attack grows more intense; the bees are stirring each other up. Chip has four bees inside his veil but continues working unfazed. José Antonio is getting stung through his coveralls whenever he bends over and the cloth is pulled taut against his skin. I stand ramrod straight—no taut bee suit on me. Bees are attacking a black pen in my pocket. Angry bees are buzzing all around me, crawling on my veil, fuzzy shapes in front of my eyes and at the edges of my peripheral vision. Bees are defecating on my gloves. The pages of the logbook are smeared with crushed bees.

Felipe has picked up a dead wasp the size of a tennis ball and truly beautiful, an iridescent blue-black. Chip identifies it as a tarantula killer and says it may have been killed by the bees, which are busy stinging the dead wasp as we examine it. Glenn decides to take a picture. The camera pushes his veil against his nose, and a bee immediately stings him in the nostril.

I feel a sharp pain in the top of my head, and I jump. "Yowch!" I remark. The researchers look at me. "Stung through my pith helmet!" I comment. The helmet is mesh.

"We all know the fireman's carry if you fall over," Chip says cheerfully. He opens another box and the bees rush out at him in such an intense wave that he is rocked backward. "That's a new queen," he says. "She mated with some bad boys."

No shit. "Yowch!" The little bastards sting me again. Through the hat again.

I look over at Chip, who has hundreds of bees swarming over his hat and veil. Glenn, José Antonio, and Felipe are under siege as well. The bees are trying to kill us all, and Glenn is taking pictures so that he can remember it. Chip patiently sorts through the bees in the box that exploded at him. He is 52 and has been working with bees for 40 years, with killer bees for 15. Ever since he lost his USDA funding, he has scrounged for grants (he once made a direct appeal to readers of a journal called *The Speedy Bee*) and has forked out $25,000 of his own money to continue his research.

The top of my skull is throbbing. "Tell me again why you do this," I shout to Chip, who is less than 20 feet away but can barely hear me above the buzzing.

"Don't forget," shouts Glenn, "we beg people for money so we can do this."

"It gives intense sexual pleasure," Chip shouts. "It's a secret. We don't tell anybody."

Ho ho. I have had enough. I walk out of the apiary and down a dirt track. Bees pursue me. I walk half a mile, and three or four of them are still bouncing off my veil, trying to sting me in the eye. After another few hundred yards they fall away, and I find a patch of shade under a tree.

DOWN A SHORT SLOPE, trucks are whining up the highway from Veracruz to Jalapa. This is the very route that Cortes took in his cruel conquest of Mexico. This is the route that the Americans took when they invaded in 1847, that the French took in 1862. And now, the killer bees.

I remove my gloves and hat and veil and pull two stingers out of the top of my head. With my pocketknife, I start to scrape stingers out of the narrow cloth strip that borders the mesh in my veil. Many of the stingers trail yellow bee-guts (bees literally pull themselves apart when they sting); one has an entire dead bee attached.

Sitting in the dust, pulling out stingers, I reflect.

I have a long and sorry history with the killer bees. I first encountered them—and Chip—in 1977 in French Guiana, a backwater colony on the northern coast of South America where Chip was doing some of his early research. I was sent down to write a magazine article, and I came home with a hot idea for making a fortune: Why not import and market genuine killer bee honey as a novelty/gift/gourmet item? I did it—sold several thousand bottles—and Killer Bee Honey became briefly famous (in a product review, *Outside* called it "thick, tasty, [and] overpriced"). And I lost my shirt.

What else had I accomplished in the 12 years since I'd last seen the killer bees? I'd done some good work, but I hadn't accomplished some of the things I thought I would have done by now. I hadn't found . . . but you don't want to hear about it. You know how it is. One day you're 28 and tramping around a French Foreign Legion post in South America being attacked by killer bees, and your whole life is ahead of you and you have time to do anything, even sell killer bee honey; and then suddenly you're 40 and everything is starting to look a little familiar, even killer bees, and you measure out your projects carefully, because there are more projects than time. You're older and different. But the killer bees are exactly the same. Glenn's genetic research has established what everybody knows: Creation is constant. Only you and I come and go.

I finish pulling the stingers out of my veil. There are 204 of them—204 of the little bastards tried to get me. They all died, and I'm still here. For the moment.

HERE IS THE PRESS CORPS, descending on the killer bees. Three days after my visit to the apiary, I am back, with colleagues.

"Sarah, dear," calls the *Outside* photographer, "will you come over here?" He is trying to get a picture of Chip being attacked by killer bees, and Sarah, a reporter for the *Philadelphia Inquirer Magazine* is in the way.

The photographer wants to get cracking; for the last two hours he has been moved out of shot after shot by a four-person video crew from a PBS science show, but for the moment the crew is occupied with Glenn a few bee boxes away. This is the photographer's chance to shoot Chip, who is hunched down looking for the queen in a fairly ornery colony. Sarah obliges and moves out of the way, but the bees are being difficult. They are attacking Chip most photogenically, but they are also attacking the photographer's camera, maddened by its blackness. "You've got so many bees on your lens . . .," Chip says dubiously.

Howard Kerr, a nuclear engineer from Tennessee who has shown up in Mexico to promote sales of a killer bee detection device called the Buzzbuster, volunteers to help. He appears at the photographer's side with a piece of cardboard, ready to brush bees away. "Tell me when," Kerr says. The photographer aims. Chip looks up. A bee stings him in the back. Chip yelps. The photographer shoots. The video crew cues Glenn. Sarah and I take notes. The killer bees attack everybody, and everybody is very happy.

Thanks to their impending arrival in the States, killer bees are beginning to be big news. Local television crews from Texas have been trooping through Mexico demanding to be shown the carcasses of cows stung to death by killer bees. One crew, leaving nothing to chance, tossed its own live chicken against a hive and filmed the result.

Our own little media circus began yesterday, in a small apiary behind the Conafrut Research Center, where Howard Kerr—no relation to the Kerr whose bees in Brazil started all this mess—set out to demonstrate his Buzzbuster. Kerr works at the Oak Ridge National Laboratory, where he has lately been employed developing the Star Wars antimissile system. He is also a longtime beekeeper, and during his lunch breaks from plotting the destruction of incoming Soviet nuclear missiles, he used to stroll the woods around the laboratory looking for wild bee colonies. His basic technique—find a bee, see which way it flies, and move in that direction—was slow and uncertain. One day he had a better idea: Why not set out some sweet bee-bait laced with radioactive isotopes, let the bees ingest it, and then track them with radiation monitors? Thinking about it, it finally occurred to Kerr why not.

His next idea was to take sound-detection equipment used to monitor the performance of nuclear reactors and adapt it to recognize the sound of bees. He was working on this when he heard an expert speak on the killer bees. She mentioned that, because they beat their wings about 50 more times per second than European bees do, they sound different. Kerr jumped on this, and he and two colleagues developed a little electronic box that can distinguish the sound of a killer bee from that of a European bee (the sound of European bees makes a green light go on; killer bees produce a red light). Kerr began to consult with Chip Taylor on this project—Chip suggested the name—and Kerr and his colleagues formed a company called B-Tec to market the Buzzbuster.

One day Kerr asked Chip what other kind of hardware might be useful in his research. Chip said he would love to have a device that could track the flights of individual bees. Queens fly off to mate at 14 miles per hour, and it's hard for a 52-year-old entomologist to keep up.

Kerr, eager to help, came up with an infrared transmitter in the form of a microchip that can be glued to a bee's back and tracked with ground-based receivers. He found this project especially interesting because of its similarity to the work he had been doing on Star Wars. Indeed, he's received funding from his lab. "Mathematically," he told me, "the problem of tracking a one-meter-long object [like a nuclear warhead] at 100 kilometers is the same as a one-centimeter-long object [like a bee] at one kilometer. If I can direct a beam that will solve either of those problems, that beam should solve the other."

The microchip, however, is still being tested. Yesterday was the Buzz-buster's day in the sun. Kerr was hoping to sell a few hundred of the things to the USDA, and two officials flew down to see what it could do. The PBS video crew wanted to see, too. So did the reporter from the *Philadelphia Inquirer*, the photographer from *Outside*, and I. We all observed as Kerr grabbed bees and stuck them into a little plastic cylinder attached to the Buzzbuster's microphone. Kerr had a little problem—one of his prototypes had a short circuit—but it was nevertheless clear that the device could tell you when you were in the presence of killer bees, in case the fact that they had just chased your grandmother from Texas to Louisiana hadn't already clued you in.

But today is the day the reporters in town had really looked forward to, when they were to visit an apiary chock-full of killer bees. Ever since the video crew arrived in Mexico, Chip, hoping to inculcate a properly cautious attitude, had been doing his best to scare its members with stories of how other film crews had gotten bees inside their veils, how they'd been stung, and how they'd panicked. This crew's cameraman, a genial and sturdy fellow, had been especially impressed by Chip's account of the cameraman from *National Geographic,* a man renowned as a fearless rock climber, who took a painful sting in the ear, worked for a while unaffected, and then keeled over, unconscious.

Arriving at the edge of the apiary, the crew had suited up with extreme thoroughness. I was envious of their brand-new equipment—nifty nylon coveralls and Velcro spats to cover gaps between their shoes and pants. Methodically, they tucked their pants into their boots, pulled their coveralls over their pants, affixed their spats over their boots and coveralls, and then wrapped tape around their spats. Then they set upon themselves and each other with a passion, taping their zippers, taping their veils, taping their hats to cover every conceivable gap. The cameraman put tape on his face where his veil might be pushed in as he looked into his camera (and promptly sweated the tape off). The sound man put tape on his ears. In an excess of caution, he wore two pairs of pants and a jacket under his coveralls. (He didn't get stung, but he did get seriously overheated.)

In the bee yard, all went well. The researchers opened hives and looked for queens. Glenn extracted larvae for genetic sampling. Howard Kerr listened to bees on his Buzzbuster. The bees attacked everybody. The cameraman got stung twice, but he didn't miss a shot.

As the sun dipped behind a ridge, Glenn stood beside a bee box, pumping smoke from his smoker. The smoke fools bees into thinking the forest is on fire; they rush inside to suck up their honey stores and get too busy to sting. So a beekeeper usually applies smoke before starting to work on a colony. But Glenn was not planning to work on this colony. He was done for the day. He was pumping his smoker—pumping it more than any smoker is usually pumped—because the video crew had asked him to. The smoke looked nice in front of the rosy light from the ridge. It was a very pretty shot.

HERE ARE THE KILLER BEE KILLERS, Pablo Aranda and Manuel Rodriguez, two pleasant and intelligent young men, driving around the state of Veracruz in a white Dodge pickup. They are employees of a joint U.S.-Mexican program designed (according to whom you talk to, and when) either to stop the killer bees, to slow them down, or to do nothing at all.

In 1987, 30 years after the bees started flying toward Texas and three years before they were expected to arrive, the USDA launched an action program. In cooperation with Mexico, the USDA decided to battle the bees at the Isthmus of Tehuantepec, Mexico's narrowest point. It would set out traps to attract and kill migrating killer bees. It would offer bounties (key chains and hats adorned with the program's logo) to peasants who reported the presence of swarms that missed the traps. It would flood the area with European bee colonies and gentle European drones. It would work with local beekeepers to help them keep their apiaries pure. USDA officials announced at first that the program could stop the killer bees, or at least slow them down for ten years.

Before the program could be established in the Isthmus of Tehuantepec, the bees were already there, and it was too late. So the program set up a Bee Regulated Zone (BRZ) to the north. It was divided into two "operational units": one on the west coast around Puerto Escondido, the other on the east coast around Jalapa and Veracruz. (The Sierra Madre mountains keep the bees from moving up the middle of the country.) Nobody talks about slowing the bees down for ten years anymore—a good thing, since the first bees zipped through Veracruz in less than six months—but the program's stated purpose is still to slow the bees . . . somewhat.

Several key elements of the program have never been put into place. The BRZ was never flooded with European colonies because local bee-keepers objected to the competition for a finite amount of nectar and because the program never got the funding to acquire and distribute the bees anyway. But the bee killing has proceeded. In the Veracruz unit, 22,000 cardboard boxes designed to look like good homes to bees have been hung from trees to lure migrating swarms. Each box is checked monthly by one of 25 teams that destroy any bees they find. Between December 1987 and March 1989, the Veracruz teams destroyed 2,500 bee colonies, 500 of them colonies of killers. (Another 2,500 colonies, including 2,000 killer bee colonies, were destroyed in the Puerto Escondido unit.) The program has its detractors, who argue that the number of swarms caught is an insignificant fraction of the number in the area and that, since some swarms die anyway in a process of natural selection, the USDA is not reducing the killer bee population but only substituting its selection for that of nature.

"It's a kill-now, ask-questions-later system," says Chip Taylor. "We're blowing $6 million in a program where we learn almost nothing—it's like stepping on ants."

Pablo and Manuel have some sympathy for these arguments—they have no idea how many swarms they're *not* catching, they say—but it's not their job to worry about that. It's their job to drive around the state of Veracruz day after day, checking 700 bee boxes and killing any bees they find inside them.

So here we are—Pablo, Manuel, and three members of the killer bee press corps—bouncing along a rough dirt road through a steep, rugged canyon with a spectacular waterfall below.

Manuel drives nonstop to the end of the road and the village of Xoltepec, a dusty hamlet of 300 souls where radios play from cinderblock houses and turkeys and chickens scratch for crumbs in the dirt. He and Pablo consult with a peasant beekeeper who has two colonies of tame European bees in rough-hewn hives he built himself; a small boy throws stones at a turkey nearby and other boys set off firecrackers to welcome us to town. Pablo arranges to return another day to give the beekeeper some modern modular bee boxes, and we prepare to depart with two new passengers. José Juan, a shy ten-year-old, wants a lift to the river at the bottom of the canyon, where his mother and sisters are washing clothes, and the village schoolmaster is heading to Jalapa with a large red poster of the Virgin Mary for *his* mother. The boy, the schoolmaster, and the Virgin join the press corps in the back of the truck, Manuel starts the engine, and off we all go, off to kill killer bees.

A quarter-mile down the canyon road, Manuel brakes to a halt, gets out of the truck, ducks under some barbed wire, and walks to a tree from which the first of 29 traps on this route is suspended. He finds no bees. We take off again. He stops and looks again. No bees.

Manuel does find a trap that has fallen out of its tree. He shakes it and finds a large spider. He inserts a fresh capsule of synthetic bee pheromone, the orientation signal that scout bees release when they find a good spot for a hive, then uses a long stick with a bent wire on the end to replace the box in the tree.

In 15 months on the job, Pablo and Manuel have found 45 colonies, 30 of them killers, and the pace is picking up. One day a few months ago, during the wet season, they found eight bee colonies—five of them killers—along this road.

Not today.

Manuel stops and looks. No bees.

We pass an old woman on a burro.

Stop. Look. No bees.

José Juan gets out to find his mother.
Stop. Look. No bees.
The wind blows the schoolmaster's hat off.
Stop. Look. No bees.

FINALLY, HERE WE ALL ARE —researchers, media, killer bee killers, and the killer bees. The bees' presence has been stage-managed. Pablo and Manuel found a colony in a box a few days ago, but they spared it on instructions from their supervisors: Save it for the television crew.

So here are all the human players, bouncing across a dry field in two vehicles, pulling to a stop between the carcasses of two dead horses. We disembark, and Pablo and Manuel lead us all on a long downhill march into the same canyon we have seen before, past rows of mango and coffee trees.

The killer bee swarm is in Box 51, hanging 20 feet up in a spindly tree on the right side of the trail. Pablo and Manuel and José Antonio pull on their bee suits for the benefit of the video crew. (They ordinarily wouldn't bother; migrating swarms and newly established colonies with little honey to protect rarely attack.) They walk toward the tree.

The video crew makes them come back and do it again.

Then the video crew makes them do it again.

A few bees are flying casually in and out of a hole in the bottom of the box, which Manuel now pokes with his long stick. The box drops to the ground. José Antonio cuts it open to take a sample. Bees fly out, but they circle harmlessly. Pablo finds the queen and holds it up for the camera. Then Manuel dumps the entire colony into a black plastic garbage bag.

The coup de grace is delivered off camera. Back at the trailhead, Pablo opens the buzzing bag and pours in water and detergent, a fatal blow. He dumps the dead bees onto the ground near one of the dead horses in an inelegant clump.

One killer bee colony has been terminated.

Down in the canyon, the other killer bees chortle over refreshing drafts of nectar. Tomorrow, they move north.

*July 1989*

# A STAGING OF SNOW GEESE

*The annual migration of white geese at Tule Lake, California, is one of the most awesome and dependable wildlife spectacles in the world—a delicate orchestration of men, birds, and habitat.*

●  ▲  ■

BARRY LOPEZ

I slow the car, downshifting from fourth to third, with the melancholic notes of Bach's sixth cello suite in my ears—a recording of Casals from 1936—and turn east, away from a volcanic ridge of black basalt. On this cool California evening, the land in the marshy valley beyond is submerged in gray light, while the far hills are yet touched by a sunset glow. To the south, out the window, Venus glistens, a white diamond at the horizon's dark lapis edge. A few feet to my left is lake water—skittish mallards and coots bolt from the cover of bulrushes and pound the air furiously to put distance between us. I am chagrined, and slow down. I have been driving like this for hours—slowed by snow in the mountains behind me, listening to the cello suites—driving hard to get here before sunset.

I shut the tape off. In the waning light I can clearly see marsh hawks swooping over oat and barley fields to the south. Last hunts of the day. The eastern sky is beginning to blush, a rose afterglow. I roll the window down. The car fills with the sounds of birds—the nasalized complaints of several hundred mallards, pintails and canvasbacks, the slap-water whirr of their half-hearted takeoffs. But underneath this sound something else is expanding, distant French horns and kettledrums.

Up ahead, on the narrow dirt causeway, I spot Frans's car. He is here for the same reason I am. I pull up quietly and he emerges from his front seat, which he has made into a kind of photographic blind. We hug and exchange quiet words of greeting, and then turn to look at the white birds. Behind us the dark waters of Tule Lake, rippled by a faint wind, stretch off north, broken only by occasional islands of hardstem bulrush.

Before us, working methodically through a field of two-row barley, the uninterrupted inquiry of their high-pitched voices lifting the night, are twenty-five thousand snow geese come down from the Siberian and Canadian Arctic. Grazing, but alert and wary in this last light.

Frans motions wordlessly to his left; I scan that far eastern edge of Tule Lake with field glasses. One hundred thousand lesser snow geese and Ross's geese float quietly on riffles, a white crease between the dark water and the darkening hills.

THE STAGING OF WHITE GEESE at Tule Lake in northern California in November is one of the most imposing—and dependable—wildlife spectacles in the world. At first one thinks of it only as a phenomenon of numbers—it's been possible in recent years to see as many as three hundred thousand geese here at one time. What a visitor finds as startling, however, is the great synchronicity of their movements: long skeins of white unfurl brilliantly against blue skies and dark cumulonimbus thunderheads, birds riding the towering wash of winds with balletic grace, with a booming noise like rattled sheets of corrugated tin, with a furious and unmitigated energy. It is the *life* of them that takes such hold of you.

I have spent enough time with large predators to know the human predilection to overlook authority and mystery in the lives of small, gregarious animals like the goose, but its qualities are finally as subtle, its way of making a living as admirable and attractive, as the grizzly bear's.

Geese are traditional, one could even say conservative, animals. They tend to stick to the same nesting grounds and wintering areas, to the same migration routes, year after year. Males and females have identical plumage. They usually mate for life, and both sexes care for the young. In all these ways, as well as in being more at ease on land, geese differ from ducks. They differ from swans in having proportionately longer legs and shorter necks. In size they fall somewhere between the two. A mature male lesser snow goose (*Chen caerulescens*), for example, might weigh six pounds, measure thirty inches from bill to tail, and have a wingspan of three feet. A mature female would be slightly smaller and lighter by perhaps half a pound.

Taxonomists divide the geese of the Northern Hemisphere into two groups, "gray" and "black," according to the color of their bills, feet, and legs. Among black geese like Canada geese and brandt they're dark. Snow geese, with rose-pink feet and legs and pink bills, are grouped with the gray geese, among whom these appendages are often brightly colored. Snow geese also commonly have rust-speckled faces, from feeding in iron-rich soils.

Before it was changed in 1971, the snow goose's scientific name, *Chen hyperborea*, reflected its high-arctic breeding heritage. The greater snow goose (*C. c. atlantica*)—a larger but far less numerous race of snow goose—breeds in northwestern Greenland and on adjacent Ellesmere, Devon, and Axel Heiburg islands. The lesser snow goose breeds sightly farther south, on Baffin and Southampton islands, the east coast of Hudson Bay, and on Banks Island to the west and Wrangel Island in Siberia. (Many people are attracted to the snow goose precisely because of its association with these little-known regions.)

There are two color phases, finally, of the lesser snow goose, blue and white. The combined population of about 1.5 million, the largest of any goose in the world, is divided into an eastern, mostly blue-phase population that winters in Texas and Louisiana, and a white-phase population that winters in California. (It is the latter birds that pass through Tule Lake.)

The great numbers of these highly gregarious birds can be misleading. First, we were not certain until quite recently where snow geese were nesting or how large their breeding colonies were. The scope of the problem is suggested by the experience of a Canadian biologist, Angus Gavin. In 1941 he stumbled on what he thought was a breeding colony of lesser snow geese, on the delta of the McConnell River on the east coast of Hudson Bay—14,000 birds. In 1961 there were still only about 35,000 birds there. But a 1968 survey showed 100,000 birds and in 1973 there were 520,000. Second, populations of arctic-breeding species like the snow goose are subject to extreme annual fluctuations, a boom-and-bust cycle tied to the unpredictable weather patterns typical of arctic ecosystems. After a series of prolonged winters, for example, when persistent spring snow kept birds from nesting, the Wrangel Island population of snow geese fell from 400,000 birds in 1965 to fewer than 50,000 in 1975. (By the summer of 1981 it was back up to 170,000.)

The numbers in which we see them on their wintering grounds are large enough to be comforting—it is hard at first to imagine what would threaten such flocks. Snow geese, however, face a variety of problems. The most serious is a striking loss of winter habitat. In 1900 western snow geese had more than 6,200 square miles of winter habitat available to them on California's Sacramento and San Joaquin rivers. Today, 90 percent of this has been absorbed by agricultural, industrial, and urban expansion. This means 90 percent of the land in central California that snow geese once depended on for food and shelter is gone. Hunters in California kill about twenty percent of the population each year and leave another four to five percent crippled to die of starvation and injuries. (An additional two to three percent dies each year of lead poisoning, from ingesting spent shot.) An unknown number are also killed by high-tension wires. In the future, geese will likely face a significant threat on their arctic breeding grounds from oil and gas exploration.

The birds also suffer from the same kinds of diseases, traumatic accidents, and natural disasters that threaten all organisms. Females, for example, fiercely devoted to the potential in their egg clutches, may choose to die of exposure on their nests rather than to abandon them in an unseasonable storm.

In light of all this, it is ironic that the one place on earth a person might see these geese in numbers large enough to cover half the sky is, itself, a potential threat to their existence.

THE LAND now called Tule Lake National Wildlife Refuge lies in a volcanic basin, part of which was once an extensive, 2,700-square-mile marshland. In 1905 the federal government began draining the area to create irrigated croplands. Marshland habitat and bird populations shrank. By 1981 only 56 square miles of wetland, two percent of the original area, was left for waterfowl. In spite of this reduction, the area, incredibly, remains an ideal spot for migratory waterfowl. On nearly any given day in the fall a visitor to the Klamath Basin might see more than a million birds—mallards, gadwalls, pintails, lesser scaups, goldeneyes, cinnamon teals, northern shovelers, redheads, canvasbacks, ruddy ducks; plus western and cackling Canada geese, white-fronted geese, Ross's geese, lesser snow geese, and whistling swans. (More than 250 species of bird have been seen on or near the refuge and more than 170 nest here.)

The safety of these populations is in the hands of a resident federal manager and his staff, who must effectively balance the birds' livelihood with the demands of local farmers, who use Tule Lake's water to irrigate adjacent fields of malt barley and winter potatoes, and waterfowl hunters, some of whom come from hundreds of miles away. And there is another problem. Although the Klamath Basin is the greatest concentration point for migratory waterfowl in North America, caring well for birds here is no guarantee they will fare well elsewhere along the flyway. And a geographic concentration like this merely increases the chance of catastrophe if epidemic disease should strike.

THE FIRST TIME I visited Tule Lake I arrived early on a fall afternoon. When I asked where the snow geese were congregated I was directed to an area called the English Channel, several miles out on the refuge road. I sat there for three hours, studying the birds' landings and takeoffs, how they behaved toward each other on the water, how they shot the skies overhead. I tried to unravel and to parse the dazzling synchronicity of their movements. I am always struck anew in these moments, in observing such detail, by the way in which an animal slowly reveals itself.

Before the sun went down, I drove off to see more of the snow goose's landscape, what other animals there might be on the refuge, how the land changed at a distance from the water. I found the serpentine great blue heron, vivacious and melodious flocks of red-winged blackbirds, and that small, fierce hunter, the kestrel. Muskrats bolted across the road. At the southern end of the refuge, where cattails and bulrushes give way to rabbit brush and sage on a volcanic plain, I came upon mule deer, three does and four fawns standing still and tense in a meandering fog.

I found a room that evening in the small town of Tulelake. There'd not been, that I could recall, a moment of silence all day from these most loquacious of geese. I wondered if they were mum in the middle of the night, how quiet they were at dawn. I set the alarm for 3 A.M.

The streets of Tulelake are desolate at that hour. In that odd stillness—the stillness of moonlit horses standing asleep in fields—I drove out into the countryside, toward the refuge. It was a ride long enough to hear the first two movements of Beethoven's Fifth Symphony. I drove in a light rain, past white farmhouses framed by ornamental birches and weeping willows. In the 1860s this land was taken by force from the Modoc Indians; in the 1940s the government built a Japanese internment camp here. At this hour, however, nearly every landscape has a pervasive innocence. I passed the refuge headquarters—low shiplapped buildings, white against a dark ridge of basalt, facing a road lined with Russian olives. I drove past stout, slowly dying willows of undetermined age, trees that mark the old shoreline of Tule Lake, where it was before the reclamation project began.

The music is low, barely audible, but the enthusiasm in some of the strong passages reminds me of geese. I turn the tape off and drive a narrow, cratered road out into the refuge, feeling the car slipping sideways in the mud. Past rafts of sleeping ducks. The first geese I see surge past just overhead like white butterflies, brushing the penumbral dimness above the car's headlights. I open the window and feel the sudden assault of their voices, the dunning power of their wings hammering the air, a rush of cold wind and rain through the window. In a moment I am outside, standing in the roar. I find a comfortable, protected place in the bulrushes and wait in my parka until dawn, listening.

Their collective voice, like the cries of athletic young men at a distance, is unabated. In the darkness it is nearly all there is of them, but for an occasional and eerie passage overhead. I try to listen closely: a barking of high-voiced dogs, like terriers, the squealing of shoats. By an accident of harmonics the din rises and falls like the cheering of a crowd in a vast stadium. Whoops and shouts; startled voices of outrage, of shock.

These are not the only voices. Cackling geese pass over in the dark, their cries more tentative. Coyotes yip. Nearby some creature screeches, perhaps a mouse in the talons of a great horned owl, whose skipping hoots I have heard earlier.

A gibbous moon shines occasionally through a wind-driven overcast. Toward dawn the geese's voices fall off suddenly for a few moments. The silence seems primordial. The black sky in the east now shows blood red through scalloped shelves of cloud. It broadens into an orange flare that fades to rose and finally to the grays of dawn. The voices begin again.

I drive back into Tulelake and eat breakfast amid a throng of hunters crowding the tables of a small café, steaming the windows with their raucous conversation.

BOB FIELDS, the refuge manager, has agreed to take me on a tour in the afternoon. I decide to spend the morning at the refuge headquarters, reading scientific reports and speaking with biologist Ed O'Neill about the early history of Tule Lake.

O'Neill talks first about the sine qua non, a suitable expanse of water. In the American West the ownership of surface water confers the kind of political and economic power that comes elsewhere with oil wells and banks. Water is a commodity; it is expensive to maintain and its owners seek to invest the limited supply profitably. A hunting club that keeps private marshland for geese and ducks, for example, will do so only as

long as they feel their hunting success warrants it. If the season is shortened
or the bag limit reduced by the state—the most common ways to conserve
dwindling waterfowl populations—they might find hunting no longer
satisfying and sell the marsh to farmers, who will turn it into cropland.
Real-estate speculators and other landowners with substantial surface-
water rights rarely give the birds that depend on their lands a second
thought when they're preparing to sell. As O'Neill puts it, "You can't
outweigh a stack of silver dollars with a duck."

The plight of western waterfowl is made clearer by an anomaly. In
the eastern United States, a natural abundance of water and the closure
of many tracts of private land to hunting provide birds with a strong
measure of protection. In the West, bird populations are much larger,
but water is scarcer and refuge lands, because they are largely public,
remain open to hunting.

By carefully adjusting the length of the hunting season and the bag
limits each year, and by planting food for the birds, refuge managers try
to maintain large bird populations, in part to keep private hunting clubs
along the flyway enthusiastic about continuing to provide additional habitat for the birds. Without the help of private individuals, including
conservation groups that own wetlands, the federal and state refuge
systems simply cannot provide for the birds. (This is especially true now.
The Reagan administration has proved more hostile to the preservation
of federal refuges and their denizens than any American administration
since the turn of the century.)

Some birds, the snow goose among them, have adapted to shortages
of food and land. Deprived of the rootstocks of bulrushes and marsh
grasses, snow geese in the West have switched to gleaning agricultural
wastes and cropping winter wheat, a practice that has spread to the
Midwest, where snow geese now feed increasingly on rice and corn. A
second adjustment snow geese have made is to linger on their fall mi-
grations and to winter over farther north. That way fewer birds end up
for a shorter period of time on traditional wintering grounds, where food
is scarcer each year.

As we spoke, O'Neill kept glancing out the window. He told me about
having seen as many as 300,000 white geese there in years past. With
the loss of habitat and birds spreading out now to winter along the
flyway, such aggregations, he says, may never be seen again. He points
out, too, looking dismayed and vaguely bitter, that these huge flocks have

not been conserved for the viewer who does not hunt, for the tourist who comes to Tule Lake to see something he has only dreamed of.

We preserve them, principally, to hunt them.

IN BROAD DAYLIGHT I was able to confirm something I'd read about the constant, loud din of their voices: relatively few birds are actually vocalizing at any one time, perhaps only one in thirty. Biologists speculate that snow geese recognize each other's voices and that family units of three or four maintain contact in these vast aggregations by calling out to one another. What sounds like mindless chaos to the human ear, then, may actually be a complex pattern of solicitous cries, discretely distinguished by snow geese.

Another sound that is easier to decipher in daylight is the rising squall that signals they are leaving the water. It's like the sustained hammering of a waterfall or a wind booming in the full crowns of large trees.

One wonders, watching the geese fly off in flocks of a hundred or a thousand, if they would be quite so arresting without their stunning whiteness. When they fly with the sun behind them, the opaque white of their bodies, the white of water-polished seashells, is set off against grayer whites in their tail feathers and in their translucent, black-tipped wings. Up close these are the dense, impeccable whites of an arctic fox. Against the grays and blues of a storm-laden sky, the whiteness has a surreal glow, a brilliance without shadow.

I remember watching a large flock rise one morning from a plowed field about a mile distant. I had been watching clouds, the soft, buoyant, wind-blown edges of immaculate cumulus. The birds rose against much darker clouds to the east. There was something vaguely ominous in this apparition, as if the earth had opened and poured them forth, like a wind, a blizzard, which unfurled across the horizon above the dark soil, becoming wider and higher in the sky than my field of vision could encompass, great swirling currents of birds in a rattling of wings, one fluid recurved sweep of 10,000 passing through the open spaces in another, counterflying flock, while beyond them lattice after lattice passed like sliding walls, until in the whole sky you lost your depth of field and felt as though you were looking up from the floor of the ocean through shoals of fish.

AT REST ON THE WATER the geese drank and slept and bathed and preened. They reminded me in their ablutions of the field notes of a Hudson's Bay trader, George Barnston. He wrote of watching flocks of snow geese gathering on James Bay in 1862, in preparation for their annual 2,000-mile, nonstop 32-hour flight to the Louisiana coast. They finally left off feeding, he wrote, to smooth and dress their feathers with oil, like athletes, biding their time for a north wind. When it came they were gone, hundreds of thousands of them, leaving a coast once "widely resonant with their petulant and incessant calls" suddenly as "silent as the grave —a deserted, barren, and frozen shore."

Barnston was struck by the way snow geese did things together. No other waterfowl are as gregarious; certainly no other large bird flies as skillfully in such tight aggregations. This quality—the individual act beautifully integrated within the larger movement of the flock—is provocative. One afternoon I studied individual birds for hours as they landed and took off. I never once saw a bird on the water move over to accommodate a bird that was landing; nor a bird ever disturbed by another taking off, no matter how tightly they were bunched. In no flight overhead did I see two birds so much as brush wing tips. Certainly they must; but for the most part they are flawlessly adroit. A flock settles gently on the water like wiffling leaves; birds explode vertically with compact and furious wingbeats and then stretch out full length, airborne, rank on rank, as if the whole flock had been cleanly wedged from the surface of the water. Several thousands bank smoothly against a head wind, as precisely as though they were feathers in the wing of a single bird.

It was while I sat immersed in these details that Bob Fields walked up. After a long skyward stare he said, "I've been here for seven years. I never get tired of watching them."

We left in his small truck to drive the narrow causeways of Tule Lake and the five adjacent federal refuges. Fields joined the U.S. Fish and Wildlife Service in 1958, at the age of twenty-two. His background is in range biology and plant ecology as well as waterfowl management. Before he came to Tule Lake in 1974, to manage the Klamath Basin refuges, he worked on the National Bison Range in Montana and on the Charles Sheldon Antelope Range in Nevada.

In 1975 a group of visitors who would profoundly affect Fields arrived at Tule Lake. They were Eskimos, from the Yukon-Kuskokwim delta of Alaska. They had come to see how the geese populations, which they depend on for food, were being managed. In the few days they were together, Fields came to understand that the Eskimos were appalled by the waste they saw at Tule Lake, by the number of birds hunters left crippled and unretrieved, and were surprised that hunters took only the breast meat and threw the rest of the bird away. On the other hand, the aggregations of geese they saw were so extensive they believed someone was fooling them—surely, they thought, so many birds could never be found in one place.

The experience with the Eskimos—Fields traveled north to see the Yukon-Kuskokwim country and the Eskimos returned to Tule Lake in 1977—focused his career as had no other event. In discussions with the Eskimos he found himself talking with a kind of hunter he rarely encountered anymore—humble men with a respect for the birds and a sense of responsibility toward them. That the Eskimos were dumbstruck at the number of birds led him to a more sobering thought: If he failed here as a refuge manager, his failure would run the length of the continent.

In the years following, Fields gained a reputation as a man who cared passionately for the health and welfare of waterfowl populations. He tailored, with the help of assistant refuge manager Homer McCollum, a model hunting program at Tule Lake, but he is candid in expressing his distaste for a type of hunter he still meets too frequently—belligerent, careless people for whom hunting is simply violent recreation; people who trench and rut the refuge's roads in oversize four-wheel-drive vehicles, who are ignorant of hunting laws or who delight in breaking them as part of a "game" they play with refuge personnel.

At one point in our afternoon drive, Fields and I were watching a flock of geese feeding in a field of oats and barley on the eastern edge of the refuge. We watched in silence for a long time. I said something about the way birds can calm you, how the graceful way they define the sky can draw irritation right out of you. He looked over at me and smiled and nodded. A while later, still watching the birds, he said, "I have known all along there was more to it than managing the birds so they could be killed by some macho hunter." It was the Eskimos who gave him a sense of how a hunter should behave, and their awe that rekindled his own desire to see the birds preserved.

As we drove back across the refuge, Fields spoke about the changes that had occurred in the Klamath Basin since the federal reclamation project began in 1905. Most of the native grasses—blue bench wheat grass, Great Basin wild rye—are gone. A visitor notices foreign plants in their place, like cheatgrass. And introduced species like the ring-necked pheasant and the muskrat, which bores holes in the refuge dikes and disrupts the pattern of drainage. And the intrusion of high-tension power lines, which endanger the birds and which Fields has no budget to bury. And the presence of huge pumps that circulate water from Tule Lake to farmers in the valley, back and forth, back and forth, before pumping it west to Lower Klamath Refuge.

It is over these evolving, occasionally uneasy relationships between recent immigrants and the original inhabitants that Fields keeps watch. I say good-bye to him at his office, to the world of bird poachers, lead poisoning, and politically powerful hunting and agricultural lobbies he deals with every day. When I shake his hand I find myself wanting to thank him for the depth with which he cares for the birds, and for the intelligence that allows him to disparage not hunting itself but the lethal acts of irresponsible and thoughtless people.

I STILL HAVE A FEW HOURS before I meet Frans for dinner. I decide to drive out to the east of the refuge, to a low escarpment which bears the carvings of Indians who lived in this valley before white men arrived. I pass by open fields where horses and beef cattle graze and cowbirds flock after seeds. Red-tailed hawks are perched on telephone poles, watching for field rodents. A light rain has turned to snow.

The brooding face of the escarpment has a prehistoric quality. It is secured behind a chain link fence topped with barbed wire, but the evidence of vandals who have broken past it to knock off souvenir petroglyphs is everywhere. The castings of barn owls, nesting in stone pockets above, are spread over the ground. I open some of them to see what the owls have been eating. Meadow voles. Deer mice.

The valley before me has darkened. I know somewhere out there, too far away to see now, long scarves of snow geese are riding and banking against these rising winds, and that they are aware of the snow. In a few weeks Tule Lake will be frozen and they will be gone. I turn back to the wall of petroglyphs. The carvings relate, apparently, to the movement of animals through this land hundreds of years ago. The people who made them made their clothing and shelters, even their cooking containers, from the lake's tule reeds. When the first white man arrived—Peter Ogden, in 1826—he found them wearing blankets of duck and goose feathers. In the years since, the complex interrelationships of the Modoc with this land, largely unrecorded to begin with, have disappeared. The land itself has been turned to agriculture, with a portion set aside for certain species of birds that have passed through this valley for no one knows how many centuries. The hunters have become farmers, the farmers landowners. Their sons have gone to the cities and become businessmen, and the sons of these men have returned with guns, to take advantage of an old urge, to hunt. But more than a few come back with a poor knowledge of the birds, the land, the reason for killing. It is by now a familiar story, for which birds pay with their lives.

The old argument, that geese must be killed for their own good, to manage the size of their populations, founders on two points. Snow goose populations rise and fall precipitously because of their arctic breeding pattern. No group of hunters can "fine-tune" such a basic element of their ecology. Second, the artificial control of their numbers only augments efforts to continue draining wetlands.

We must search in our way of life, I think, for substantially more here than economic expansion and continued good hunting. We need to look for a set of relationships similar to the ones Fields admired among the Eskimos. We grasp what is beautiful in a flight of snow geese rising against an overcast sky as easily as we grasp the beauty in a cello suite; and intuit, I believe, that if we allow these things to be destroyed or degraded for economic or frivolous reasons we will become deeply and strangely impoverished.

I HAD SEEN LITTLE of my friend Frans in three days. At dinner he said he wanted to tell me of the Oostvaardersplassen in Holland. It has become a major stopover for waterfowl in northern Europe, a marsh that didn't even exist ten years ago. Birds hardly anyone has seen in Holland since the time of Napoleon are there now. Peregrine falcons, snowy egrets, and European sea eagles have returned.

I drive away from the escarpment holding tenaciously to this image of reparation.

*October 1982*

# Secrets of the Stream

*Franklin wanted to tinker with it, Hemingway was obsessed by it—a fast, clear, mysterious canyon of blue water, circling from Florida to Ireland forever*

───────────────── ● ▲ ■ ─────────────────

RICK TELANDER

**I**f I stand on the roof of my house, which I do often these days, I can see the Gulf Stream. I cannot, as Hemingway's alter ego Thomas Hudson did, simply go downstairs and "walk out of the door and down the bluff across the white sand and into the Gulf Stream."

But Hudson lived on Bimini, where the current comes as close to land as it does anywhere, and this is Key West, where there is a reef between the Stream and the land, and where there is a spiritual distance as well between the purity of the water headed north and the decadence of an island spinning off toward moral weightlessness. In Key West there are all-night discos and dope safe-houses and gay baths and a new tombstone in the cemetery that says, "I told you I was sick." There are enough unnatural things in general to make the Stream seem as remote from the island as Mars is from Manhattan; enough unmanly things to make Papa, or Hudson, were either to come back, surely want to break out the old .256 Mannlicher Shoenauer with the 18-inch barrel that Papa kept below decks on the *Pilar* and blow something the Christ to smithereens.

But Key West is as tolerant as it is weird, taking no notice of, say, a man without tools faced seaward on his roof. I am up here now, looking to the south.

Maybe I can't see the Gulf Stream. I have been in it, and I know roughly where it starts—often just beyond Sand Key, which lies seven miles southwest of Mallory Pier, the dock where the tourists go to applaud sunsets. And I can see the southbound freighters that run inside the

Stream to avoid its drag. But the Stream itself is a shifty force, a river of warm water that eddies and whirls and moves its liquid banks from day to day like runoff water weaving over a parking lot.

Sometimes colors are enough to determine where it starts. The shallow tidal flats are green; the open sea gray. The Gulf Stream, though, is blue. At times, depending on the sun and the influx of certain plankton, the Stream can be gold or indigo or even red. But mostly it is blue, incredibly blue, bluer than any paint or tint, a diamond-pure, deepwell, transparent blue that is less opaque, studies have shown, than distilled water.

Good visibility in swimming pool water is about 75 feet. In the reef water of the Keys it can be 100 or 150 feet. But in the Gulf Stream, visibility of 250 or 300 feet is not uncommon. Those few divers who have entered the Stream say they are startled by how much larger the ocean feels, as though the walls of a familiar room have suddenly been pulled back. One Key West diver studying the Gulf Stream recalls distinguishing clearly the prop of his dive boat and thinking nothing of it until he surfaced and found the boat was 400 feet away.

The blue that comes with clarity makes the Gulf Stream easy to spot from an airplane. And the warmth of the water—nearly 80 degrees Fahrenheit in the Straits of Florida between the Keys and Cuba—makes its boundaries readily discernible to temperature-sensitive satellite cameras. (Indeed, fishermen can now get exact readings on the Gulf Stream's daily course from the U.S. Weather Service.)

But just now, from my angle, the lines are blurred. How entertaining it would be if the current could amble up close to shore as it does in Bimini and show its curtain plainly, perhaps tossing some wonder into the torpid lives along A1A. In fact, the Gulf Stream did that once in the mid-fifties—came right up over the Sambos and Eastern Dry Rocks to Smathers Beach on the southeast side of Key West. Don Kincaid, a Key West native and a professional diver and underwater photographer, remembers it well. Just a boy, he waded out to chest depth and straddled the interface between the flats and the Stream, feeling somewhat heroic, he says. "with one foot in green water and the other in deep blue."

THE GULF STREAM has been called the "world's largest river," and in a way it is just that. The current begins in the Gulf of Mexico, where it gets its volume from the buildup of warm surface water that has entered the Gulf through the Yucatan Channel. The water is initially pushed into the Gulf by the prevailing westerlies and by the Coriolis force (the clockwise motion that the earth's rotation gives to bodies of water in the Northern Hemisphere). As this mass of water squirts northward up the coast of the United States and east toward Europe, it carries 25 times more water than all the rivers of the world combined.

The current differs from the water surrounding it not only in temperature and color, but also in salinity, nutrient content, marine life and, of course, speed. In the Narrows of Bimini, where the Gulf Stream is at its narrowest—50 miles wide by a quarter-mile deep—it flows by at a speed of seven miles an hour, nearly as fast as a mountain stream. The flow through the Narrows is about 700 million cubic feet a second, enough warm water, scientists have estimated, to melt the entire Polar ice cap in 40 days were the current to be directed due north.

Not surprisingly, there have been men who have proposed changing the current's route. One of the first of these was inventor-statesman Benjamin Franklin. During the Revolutionary War Franklin proposed deflecting the Gulf Stream waters away from Great Britian in order to plunge the mother country into a new ice age. In 1913 a respected engineer by the name of C. L. Riker presented a plan to the president and Congress of the United States wherein he proposed building a 200-mile-long jetty from Newfoundland out along the Grand Banks to keep the cold Labrador Current from intermingling with the Gulf Stream. Riker claimed the jetty would eliminate fog and icebergs in North Atlantic shipping and at the same time improve the climate of countries near the Arctic Circle.

Though the United States would still like to tap the Gulf Stream's great energy flow (possibly through hydroelectric turbines or heat exchangers), there are fortunately no more plans to bend the current around like an errant piece of copper tubing. Though scientists know precious little about the inner workings of the Stream, they are at least aware that any fiddling with the current could affect the world in countless ways.

The Gulf Stream and the warm winds that blow over it are indeed responsible for the temperate climate in the British Isles as well as much of western Europe and Scandinavia. The Stream is the reason that palm trees (having ridden up from Jamaica) can grow in Scotland; it is why the south of France is far more temperate than New England, though both are at the same latitude; it is why Norway's waters remain ice-free in winter, while the Baltic Sea, far to the south, freezes over each year.

Further, we now know that the Gulf Stream is just part of a vast network of ocean currents that depend on one another for existence. In his book, *The Gulf Stream*, Dr. T. F. Gaskell calls these currents "the great stirrers of the ocean" and explains that it is only through their action that the ocean has been able to absorb and neutralize the tremendous amount of waste we have dumped there.

The Gulf Stream also plays an important role in the nurturing and dispersal of marine life. Though it might seem that a relatively thin jet of water moving through a much larger body of water would soon dissipate and lose its distinctive qualities, that is not the case. If one remembers the old geometry axiom that volume cubes as area squares, it becomes apparent that the edges of the Gulf Stream (the parts that actually touch surrounding water) are a mere fraction of the entire package. Thus, like a traveling zoo moving through strange land, the Gulf Stream can flow along without dispersing—for more than 3,000 miles.

Trapped within the Stream's warm, slightly more saline waters (the result of the heavy evaporation in the Gulf of Mexico and Caribbean Sea) are hundreds of tropical and pelagic fish. (In fact, it was the appearance of so many odd plants and animals on the shores of western Europe that first made Columbus believe there must be land to the west.) Some of the fish in the Gulf Stream are simply riding out their time. A scientist aboard the bathyscaphe *Ben Franklin*, which in 1969 drifted with the current for a month at a depth of 600 feet, reported that a two-inch lantern fish followed the craft from West Palm Beach all the way to Cape Hatteras before being eaten by a ten-inch fish.

Other creatures, though, rely on the Gulf Stream as a sort of conveyor belt toward maturity. Various planktonic and larval animals, some of them as big as car hoods but so transparent that they have been discerned only with the aid of dyes, float with the tide, growing into their adult forms en route. Baby lobsters, crabs, and snails are part of this crowd.

There are certain migratory fish, too—kingfish, tuna, mackerel—that simply disappear into the Gulf Stream and its surrounding waters and reappear at intervals in the Gulf of Mexico or along America's eastern coastline seemingly without rhyme or reason. What they do while out of reach of nets or hooks is not well known. Even a fish as common as the king mackerel, caught for centuries by North American commercial and sport fishermen, becomes a cipher once it moves off Florida's shore and enters the Stream. "Amazingly, we still don't even know where the king mackerel spawns," says Don de Sylva, a professor of marine science at the Rosenstiel School of Marine and Atmospheric Science at the University of Miami.

Also out there, like thoroughbreds in a vast canyon, are the broadbills—sailfish, swordfish, and marlin. It is the marlin, of course, horse-eyed and strong as a jeep, that Hemingway more or less ordained as his own, the true "great" fish.

For Papa, all that was good and noble in the natural world came together in the marlin, and in a man's battle with the fish could be read all that one needed to know of the man. Though Hemingway could be a bastard at sea—once, off the coast of Cuba, he opened fire on a pod of whales with a machine gun—with the great fish, as with bulls in the ring, he grew reverent, almost hallucinatorily solemn. "I loved him so much when I saw him coming up that I couldn't stand it," a character weeps after losing a marlin in *Islands in the Stream*.

And certainly it is Santiago's nighttime war with a marlin in *The Old Man and the Sea*, the two of them alone together, man and beast, far out in the Gulf Stream, that synthesizes Hemingway's vision of man's duty in a dark world. "The fish is my friend, too," the old Cuban says aloud as the gigantic marlin pulls the dinghy out toward the horizon. "But I must kill him. I am glad we do not have to try to kill the stars."

I LOWER MY 15-FOOT MCKEE-CRAFT into the oily water at Garrison Bight, four blocks from home. Since the days of the Mariel boatlift, the formerly free drop now costs three dollars; obviously, the harbor master is going to be ready the next time freedom beckons.

By coincidence, I had shown up at the marina on the first day of the 1980 boatlift, with live shrimp and beer, planning to do some backcountry wandering. I couldn't get my trailered boat near the ramp because of the crowd. Cuban-Americans were running through the parking lot, hands clenching wads of bills, trying to buy or rent anything that might carry them to Mariel.

A man with a wild look in his eye approached my boat. I shook my head. "Nada. No Bueno," I said. My boat is a flats boat, with a push pole and a small engine. He had a bouquet of crumpled fifties in his hand, and he looked like a man who was going to get a boat somehow.

Later I learned that people did try to take boats nearly as small as mine to Cuba. Some of the crafts were found weeks later floating, keels up, drifting in the Stream without survivors.

Though on a calm day the Gulf Stream can be flat as a lake, its potential for sudden violence is legendary. Pilots for the U.S. Navy Oceanographic Office have reported seeing eight- to ten-foot waves in the Gulf Stream while the water at the edge of the current remained unruffled. Because it runs like a river, the Stream must be considered a vector force anytime one sets onto it. Two years ago I went with some friends to a fishing tournament in Havana, which is just 95 miles south of Key West. We ran into some big rollers in the Stream, slowed down, and despite keeping to our plotted course, ended up 30 miles east of the harbor. In Key West there are grocery stores and greyhounds and cute shoppes named for the Gulf Stream, which only makes it more difficult for anyone who goes out in the current to remember the Stream doesn't care about any of that.

DIRECTLY IN FRONT OF ME a poker table, a green sea turtle, heads for the bottom. Now protected, the turtles were once the prized fare of galleons and whaling ships running through the Stream. Flipped onto their backs and stacked on deck like pie tins, the turtles would remain alive for months (with occasional dousings of sea water), serving as warehouses of fresh meat.

Looking back at Key West now, I can see several cigarette boats crisscrossing in front of Mallory Pier. Sleek, gaudy crafts with immense engines, they are good only for crisscrossing and running dope. The Stream plays its part in that area, too. When larger vessels are frightened into dumping their bales off Key West, the packages are often picked up by the Gulf Stream and shuffled up the Keys, so that everyone with a swift boat from Boca Chica to Key Largo has a shot at the goods. A friend of mine found his pair in the mangroves near Coconut Grove and bought a house in South Miami with the profits.

Above me the sky is light blue and the water now a deepening azure. Normally I would not take my boat out into the Gulf Stream, but fair weather is expected all this week. I have plenty of gas, three gallons of water, a chart, a life preserver, a flashlight, a trolling rod, and my friends know exactly where I am going and when it will be time to call the Coast Guard.

In the far south a bank of cumulus clouds rises like a wall. These are the convection currents rising over Cuba.

Just before the Eastern Dry Rocks I notice a group of porpoises running a hundred yards to the left. I aim for them, wondering if they will ride my bow wake as they often do with larger boats. When I am close enough I can hear their aqualung-like breathing and see their grinning profiles. One of them comes alongside and sounds forcefully, drenching me with water. I stop the boat and use a pint of fresh water to clean my sunglasses, figuring that before I could die of thirst because of it, I'll already have been adrift long enough to have died of something else.

After another two miles I reach the first line of flotsam that always spins at the edge of the current, and then I am in the Gulf Stream.

WHEN COLUMBUS discovered America, he was not aware of the Gulf Stream. Nor was Sebastian Cabot aware of it, five years later, when he sailed up the western side of the Atlantic as far as Labrador in 1497. Cabot, however, did notice that the beer in the hold of his ship fermented and turned sour because of an unaccountable warmth below decks (caused, of course, by the high temperature of the Stream). It was not until 1513, when Ponce de Leon described the Florida Current—the swift beginning of the Gulf Stream—that the seafaring world learned of this quick route back to Europe from the West Indies. Captains already knew that by sailing south from Spain they could enter the Canaries Current, which would lead them down the coast of Africa to the North Equatorial Current, which in turn would take them west to the Caribbean. But it wasn't until this century that oceanographers determined that all these currents are tied together in one big 10,000-mile loop spinning clockwise around the North Atlantic Ocean and the Sargasso Sea.

A current shark-tagging program being administered by the National Marine Fisheries Service suggests that some sharks (and perhaps many other fish) actually get in the current and ride it indefinitely. It has been known for years that freshwater eels breed in the Sargasso Sea to the east of Bermuda and then ride the Gulf Stream for as long as five years to reach their new homes in North America, Ireland, Scandinavia, and the Mediterranean. One of the most interesting things about these creatures is that after growing for seven years or so in their freshwater dens, the eels change colors from yellow to silvery black and amass for a return trip to the Sargasso Sea. Hardly any eels complete the journey, however—for two reasons. First, they will not eat en route. And secondly, like many early explorers, they try to fight their way back to the Caribbean against the Gulf Stream's northerly flow, rather than taking the easier clockwise route to the south.

In *The Gulf Stream*, Dr. T. F. Gaskell suggests that it is the eels' hurry to return to their birthing grounds that prevents them from taking the more rational course. I prefer thinking that the eels are testing their limits, that like old sea captains they know what they are doing, enjoy the current, and are happy to die at the wheel.

THE ROLLERS ARE SLIDING below my boat now, sometimes lifting me up high enough so that I can see the base of the lighthouse on Sand Key. The water all around is a deep, unpolluted blue. In fact, the Stream water is so warm and clean that it is not even particularly fertile; the richest ocean waters are the cold ones, like those off Peru and Newfoundland, which rise from the depths and bring with them nutrients from the bottom.

Most of the good fishing in the Gulf Stream occurs right at the edge of the current, where the weeds and debris offer habitat for the small fishes, which in turn attract the bigger ones. I reach overboard and pull in a clump of sargassum weed, the yellow-brown, holly-like plant that serves as home to many Gulf Stream creatures along the perimeter. As I shake the plant, which has small, air-filled sacs for flotation, animals begin to fall on the deck—small shrimp, crabs, something that looks like a snail, odd things that may or may not be alive, parts of a jellyfish.

Below that clump of weed there may have been a biological cone of larger and larger fish leading at great depths to God knows what. The chain of eating is well established in the ocean, and except for those big ones at the very bottom of it, nobody can afford to relax. While on assignment for *National Geographic*, photographer Don Kincaid dived into the Gulf Stream more than 20 times and each time, within minutes, was driven out by sharks. "One thing is certain," Kincaid says. "When man enters the Gulf Stream, he enters the food chain. And he doesn't enter at the top."

Sitting in my boat, I find myself thinking of Winslow Homer's famous painting of the Gulf Stream, the one with the ragged black man (no doubt a Bahamian fisherman) clinging to a makeshift raft in a stormy sea. In the foreground are lunging sharks, and in the distance are a waterspout and a tall ship. Which of these objects is approaching and which is leaving? Or are both the storm and the ship coming or going together?

The picture mesmerizes because it admits the element of whimsy involved in the balance of life at sea. Once when I was in Cuba, I decided to dive overboard and cool off after a morning of trolling in the Stream for Papa's marlin. I plunged into more than a mile of water, opened my eyes for an instant, and shot back into the boat. I had seen only radiant, cavernous blue, but the vision of overwhelming depth, of imminent whimsy, was too much for me.

I am not really in danger out here now, though I suppose I could die from a number of things and it could not be considered unusual. I could end it fast if I were to jump overboard and drown myself purposefully, as a charter boat captain did a few weeks ago, leaving his shocked guests to maneuver themselves back to town. But Key West is far off now; the sun is high and the wind is light. There is a shell of peace awash, and I believe I'll drift for a while.

*February/March 1982*

# A PRIVATE WORD FOR THE HORSE

*He'd rather die than have you take him for a fool.*

● ▲ ■

THOMAS MCGUANE

To represent that I am a horse expert would set my friends upon an ungovernable course of hilarity. As they turn up at the oddest times, I am going to confine my views to those founded in the one unimpeachable attribute I own as an equestrian: the absolute love of those horses that can do something, whether the Amish Standardbreds who pull carts in Central Park and who have learned what most humans cannot learn— parallel parking—or the loyal, swampfooted northernmost draft horses proving again their economy to farming man. As a westerner, I recognize the rarity of the genuine using horse, there at daybreak ready to rope, travel, pack game, drag calves; and make you feel more secure than your own limited senses could, coming down from the hills in complete black-ness, reins loose, feet striking ground you cannot see until that magic pattern of light which is the home place appears, a location long known by this mysterious, careful-footed ally in whose eye you see either your own wishes for blindly reciprocated affection or the immensity of distance humans have come: It is that perilous line of allegiance between ourselves and what we've left behind.

LIKE: GO TO ROCK SPRINGS, Wyoming, and stand in the BLM mustang corrals. Have a real good look at those flared-nostril studs running and whirling with every muscle, every vein in sculptural exaggeration of rage. Go to Flicka. See Flicka plough you way back. Also, his name isn't Flicka. It's Red Desert Number 41019. They found him with his band of mares at a spring. He didn't understand helicopters and this isn't funny to him. His idea of arm's-length is ten miles. A good pony will shorten that up, but a real good one won't shorten it completely. There is that margin of inviolate space: ritual movements with the bridle, blanket, saddle. When a good horse blows up, he doesn't care who you know.

I WOULD LIKE TO MAKE MENTION of my cutting horse, Lucky Bottom 79. He is known as Roan, the horse with the thousand-yard stare. In my opinion, he is one of the most gifted cutting horses in the world; nothing escapes his attention, and when in doubt, he kicks it. The same day that he destroyed his box stall in Fort Worth, he set the highest score in the history of the National Cutting Horse Futurity up till then. He's supernatural. He drags your spurs turning around. He knows what you are thinking. He can kick your rowels loose without changing gaits. He can deceive cattle with his mind. He is, in cutting, the best example of a "trapping horse." When you ride him, you feel his heart pound through the saddle, you feel his hypnotic effect on cows. With your legs, you make spaces for him to run into, carefully remembering that he sees himself as a saddle horse, devoted and reliant on his sense of purpose. When I sent him to Fort Collins for a veterinary checkup, his report said, "Lucky Bottom 79's temperature was not taken as he continually endangered human life." He did not see these diagnostics as part of his sense of purpose. Roan likes iron shoes, a saddle, and something to do. It seemed appropriate to him to savage graduate students who viewed him as a case. To me, he is not a case, but kind and watchful, a beautiful animal with extreme speed, intelligence, and coordination. He'd rather die than have you take him for a fool. He's a horse and you have to know what that is.

HUMAN BEINGS like to wipe out what they don't understand. There's every reason to wipe out the horse. But some atavism, some old dream, has given the horse a stay of execution. His loss might be a reproach we couldn't survive. Horses seem to know something. And we don't know what it is.

When you are first around horses, you are, above all, impressed by their size and strength. Your next impression is of their fragility. It seems you look at a favorite horse and it twists a gut and dies. I recall preparing my favorite mare Dyna Lea for the cutting at the Denver Stock Show. She made one hard turn around and broke into a sweat. A piece of intestine had flipped over, closing the loop. She was dead that day: A brilliant, animated bay mare, who saw everything around her, was converted by one wrong move into something for the Livingston landfill. It's hard to stand that, hard when the truck comes and puts a cable on the back legs you curried down to their fine and magic contours. Life and vitality, what Dyna Lea brought to the dance with her hypnotic speed, disappear with her good mind, leaving some incomprehensible meat-object, almost in mockery. But isn't that how it is with us? The fragility of horses helps us see the difference between what is there in flesh and what is there in spirit. Men who have spent their lives with horses remember those spirits perfectly, and in that distinction lies an intimation of mortality that makes stockmen of every kind powerful company.

"OLD STEEL DUST. What a big-hearted sonofabitch."

Steel Dust is a memory. Jesse James rode a Steel Dust colt. Jesse James is a memory. You and I are that close to being memories. To some people, horses have wings. They took the Sioux out of the Minnesota woods. In Montana's Pryor Mountains they've found horse skeletons with the extra vertebrae of the conquistadors' Moorish steeds, reproachful bones in the hills above pink and blue petrochemical refineries. The U.S. Cavalry lost control of the confiscated hunting horses of the Plains Indians when buffalo appeared on the horizon: The horses struck free and surrounded the bison, their riders vanished from their backs forever. The great scholar of the Northern Plains, the late Vern Deusenberry, said that the principal point of the Battle of the Little Big Horn was that it was the end of the buffalo culture: Cheyenne on foot had about as much to do with the price of beans as a conquistador in a Cartagena counting house: one more pedestrian.

The horses they hunted on must have been very specialized, very specific and personal to their owners. It was the custom to race alongside immense, wide-open-running buffalo close enough to drive a short one-handed spear behind the shoulder. Later a white man's muzzle loader was sawed off to fit between the hand and the inside of the elbow; but the same controlled ride to the quarry had to be made on broken ground, in all weather, and under dangerous conditions. You begin to see that after centuries of this, the Indians of the Plains did not see the immorality of horse-raiding parties. Before the Sioux got horses, they were canoe people. I think they loved the ponies more.

I LIVE IN COUNTRY once belonging to the last buffalo hunters, ones who hunted on horses into the era of Queen Victoria. I can see one travois line from the pasture, and when my neighbor was digging gravel near the end of my road to make cement, he found a yearling buffalo and the remains of a fire.

I raise cutting horses, extremely hot-blooded cow horses, and the brood mares drift over the grounds of the ghost hunters; they circle down along the west fence, grazing through the tepee rings. One wants to think they sense or remember the centuries of hunting horses, travel horses, and war horses picketed here among their owners' smoke-darkened tents, remember them as we remember cousins who have passed away.

Horses are criticized a good deal, much the way sailboats are criticized by the proponents of the outboard motor. Even in Montana, the local gentry have no trouble justifying $4,000 on a snowmobile that will be scrapped in very short order; yet paying that much for a horse is something you wouldn't want to get out. A horse can last 20 years or more if he is cared for properly, an intelligent and gentle science in itself. Admittedly, many horses are to be pitied for the long waits between parades, or the handful of times Dad slings his gut up again to accompany the latest daughter in her quest to become queen of this year's rodeo. Charging up to the line of parents, tries to do a sliding stop and ends up sideways with the pad saddle winding off the horse's withers. Someone says, "That used to be a good horse. Now he just runs on through the bridle." But Dad ran through the bridle years ago. He irrigates on a Honda. Mom gets her petrified wood the same way, and the girls have to try to get their seat back at fair time every year. Finally, when years have passed and Sis has settled down, Mom is tired of rock and Dad has buried his scrap, they each in their way think they've lost their memories. Like a lot of the best things that accompany us through the world, horses aren't *for* anything.

The Sarmations of the ancient Hungarian plains are the only people who seem to have utilized horses fully by modern pragmatic standards: They rode them, ate them, drank their blood, made armor out of their hoofs, and sacrificed them to their gods. These are things Roy mostly didn't do with Trigger.

We've grown more sentimental about our steeds. Napoleon rode his famous Marengo; Buffalo Bill, his white stallion Muson; George Washington, his gray Arab Magnolia; Ulysses Grant, Cincinnati; and Robert E. Lee rode Traveller. What was it about that riderless black horse in John Kennedy's cortege?

The point is, one loves horses for what they are and for what they aren't. Like desert sheiks turning fortunes into hunting hawks, we go broke on animals that will never be pets. A ground-tied horse is a runaway; but the horse that might kick you on the ground will carry you until his heart breaks. Then when you try to pat his shoulder, he spins to look for his band. They're really not people.

*April 1982*

# A CLOT IN THE HEART OF THE EARTH

*Fighting the lost war of the Valdez oil spill*

● ▲ ■

**GRANT SIMS**

Good Friday, March 24, 1989

A quarter of a century ago to the day, big chunks of south-central Alaska shuddered and crumbled in an earthquake that demolished the port town of Valdez and lowered its shoreline by six feet. There was talk that day of sacrifice and resurrection. But what happens today will test that kind of faith. In a flat calm sea, the supertanker *Exxon Valdez* misses a deepwater dogleg in the shipping lanes and wanders into shallow water with 50 million gallons of oil in her hold and an allegedly drunk skipper in command. Or not in command, it seems: Captain Joseph Hazelwood has steered his 987-foot ship onto an incorrect course and gone below.

At 12:04 A.M., the ship lurches. She has snagged on a rock pinnacle about 50 feet below the surface. In the wheelhouse, the crew tries frantically to correct the course, but can't. Impaled, the ship fishtails around the rock fulcrum, shudders, and grinds to a halt as her stern rides up onto a submerged shelf on Bligh Reef.

Bligh Reef: In 1910, the steamship *Olympia* ran aground in foul weather here, and here it perched for a decade—a landmark, a warning, and a popular deck for tea parties on nice afternoons. Otherwise, the reef has never been much of a problem. A few fishing boats have smacked it lightly or snagged a net on it while chasing salmon or herring, but their skippers knew where it was, knew the risk.

The reef juts like a bad underbite off the northwestern shore of Bligh Island in Alaska's Prince William Sound. It was once a place of clear water, of seabirds and sea mammals. Otters lolled around it, dived down into it for crabs and shellfish. Sea lions careened among its barnacles chasing herring or salmon, and sometimes a pod of the sound's 215 killer whales went in after the sea lions.

Captain Joseph Hazelwood won't lose his ship to the reef; neither did Captain William Bligh, for whom it is named. Bligh, the same man who 12 years later was set adrift by Fletcher Christian and the crew of the *Bounty*, was the first white man to anchor off the island, when he served as a navigator under Captain James Cook in 1778. Both Bligh and Cook sailed on to their own tragedies, one to mutiny, one to a knife in the back. Their stories were examined a few years later by the poets Coleridge and Wordsworth, who perused the sea captains' journals and brainstormed the composition of *The Rime of the Ancient Mariner* during a hiking trip through the English countryside. At the core of all tragedy, they decided, is the one mistake that places a man beyond redemption.

Hazelwood has made his mistake, and now comes the tragedy: More than ten million gallons of thick North Slope crude are transfusing the arteries of Prince William Sound. When a grim Officer Michael Fox of the Alaska Division of Fish and Wildlife Protection comes aboard to ask what happened, Hazelwood's face is slack.

"I think you're looking at it," he says.

A VISIT TO ALASKA is an experience as much spiritual as physical. Environmentally, Prince William Sound is only occasionally a friendly place. Its 3,500 miles of ragged shoreline, its ring of icy alps, its frigid seas are as dangerous as they are lovely. Until now, we have gone there not so much because we wanted to rub elbows with beachcombing grizzlies or to swim in water cold enough to kill us in a few minutes, but because it was one of the earth's few remaining islands of innocence. It was a bastion of clean water and misty island distances, of breaching killer whales and loafing otters and red-eyed loons. It had a solitude that triggered primal memories that made us want to beat our chests; if we wanted to yodel, no one would hear.

Within two weeks of Good Friday, black sludge will plug a length of Alaskan shoreline roughly equal to the entire coast of California. Much of the oil is still out there. No one knows how much death will accumulate beyond the thousands of birds and mammals killed during the first week after the spill. We suppose that Prince William Sound will be around for the long haul; it may someday recover. But its innocence is forever lost, a victim of our complacent greed.

From Valdez and nearby Cordova, 600 fishermen normally ply the waters of the sound for salmon, herring, halibut, and Dungeness crabs. For them, and for the others who live there, it was that corruption of innocence that was the hardest to endure. What you and I have visited, they have nurtured. They fought the pipeline, they fought the terminal and the supertanker traffic, and they sued, time and again, to fight the practices that allowed 40 lesser spills and leakages into the sound over the past 12 years.

For five days after North America's worst environmental catastrophe, the fishermen stood ready to help but were frustratingly excluded as official efforts steadily lost ground. When their chance finally came, they had to settle for winning a few tiny but critical battles in a war they knew had already been lost.

This is a small part of the story of those five days.

In Cordova, 70 miles south of Valdez, Rick Steiner is awake but still lounging in his underwear when the phone rings at 7 A.M. He answers and listens. "Holy shit!" he says, and is on his feet, pulling on jeans, sweater, and sneakers. Within minutes he is out the door, heading for his office on the creaking Cordova dock.

Steiner, a 36-year-old assistant professor of fisheries for the University of Alaska's Marine Advisory Program, is stationed in Cordova as the maritime counterpart of a Corn Belt county agent. Most of the town's fishermen think of him simply as the guy on the dock who either knows the answer or will find out. They like his real-time credentials. He is a fisherman. He owns a 43-foot seiner, the *Buddy*; has crewed long months on draggers, trollers, long-liners, and gill-netters; and has had his leg crushed by a 700-pound crab-pot in the Gulf of Alaska. He is an expert on salmon, herring, and halibut, as well as on ocean currents, killer whales, sea lions, and otters. He is six-foot-four, with a stride that he says varies according to what he's running from. Before moving to Cordova, he was the university's marine advisory agent in the Eskimo village of Kotzebue, where the locals called him *Ivalu*, which means sinew. He looks like a skinny Viking, with unkempt blond hair and a full beard, all of it framing an almost constant smile and crinkling blue eyes.

Today Steiner is not smiling. His territory—which ranges along more than 4,000 miles of the world's most pristine coastline—has just suffered the worst oil spill in the continent's history. Steiner gets to his desk and starts collecting as much information as he can by telephone. As he talks, he looks down at the water below his office, where an otter he has watched for three years floats on its back, cracking open a crab. The news over the phone doesn't get any better. He sees one knot of fishermen gather, then another. Abruptly he stands and goes outside to plug into the dock talk, then heads down to the union hall three blocks away.

The offices of the Cordova District Fishermen's United are quiet. Steiner finds four people there, all apparently in a state of shock. CDFU Executive Director Marilyn Leland is listening to someone on the phone. The other three will eventually wind up with Steiner in the Valdez command post: Jack Lamb, David Grimes, and Jeff Guard.

Blocky, clean-shaven Jack Lamb, father of three, is the only married man among the four. A former salmon gill-netter who now owns and operates a 66-foot tender, the *Poncho*, he has lived in Cordova for 26 of his 43 years. He has one artificial leg. Generally Lamb is conventional, but he has panicked more than one skipper by nonchalantly dangling his prosthesis over the gunwale to absorb the shock of collision between his tender and vessels that come alongside.

Jeff Guard, 30, is the quartet's angry young man. This, he says, has been his winter of discontent. Until the oil spill, he has been going at it tooth and nail with the timber industry, which he says is priming Prince William Sound for clear-cut logging like they've done down in the Tongass. Guard says he's just a fisherman who was never involved in politics until he found out what they're planning to do to the woods up here. "And now this," he says. "Prince William Sound is being raped on both sides of the waterline."

David Grimes, 35 years old, six-foot-two, wears his brown hair in a ponytail. He has blue eyes and a tanned, chiseled face. Outdoors he wears thongs, indoors he's usually barefoot. A native of the Missouri Ozarks, he is fresh back from wandering the jungles of New Guinea, where tribal girls sang as they patted flour cakes on rocks, boys chanted to the rhythm of dugout paddles, and Grimes carried a penny whistle to mimic the call of the bird of paradise. He is a salmon and herring fisherman, a wilderness guide, a river runner, a mountaineer, and a musician. He is an articulate gypsy. Above all, he is a spiritualist. To him, Prince William Sound is a Gaian heart—the clear, plankton-rich Gulf of Alaska water pulsing into the southeast side of the sound, swirling through the tidal valves, feeding the higher forms of life, and flushing out through the Montague and

Knight Island straits on the southwest. To him, the oil spill is a clot in this remarkable heart.

In the union hall, Lamb stands glowering at a wall chart of Prince William Sound, Grimes and Guard beside him.

"Anything new?" asks Steiner.

"You tell us," says Lamb.

"I hear there's nobody out there. Nobody's cleaning it up."

"That's what we hear," says Grimes.

Lamb rattles a sheaf of papers—the Alyeska Pipeline Service Company's oil spill emergency contingency plan, required by the state of Alaska. "They say they can contain any spill within 50 miles in 12 hours. This one's only half that far."

Guard gives the chart a hard poke at Bligh Reef, then sweeps his hand along a path of seaward currents, past the dozens of islands, the hundreds of bays and fjords between the reef and the open sea of the Gulf of Alaska. "If no one cleans it up, man, we're done for."

For an hour they talk possibilities. In terms of both commercial fisheries and salmonid biology, this is precisely the worst time of year for an oil spill. Tens of millions of herring—a $12 million annual fishery—will be schooling into the sound next week to spawn in shallow water. In addition, early April is when hundreds of millions of salmon fry migrate from spawning streams into saltwater estuaries, where they feed for three or four months before moving out to sea. Steiner lists the ways that oil can kill them: ingestion of oiled prey, intake of petroleum compounds through the gills, disruption of homing instincts. The fishermen understand. The salmon fry are their seedlings, the stock for a $120 million annual harvest.

"It's not only our livelihood," says Grimes. "It's our home. It's our life."

Steiner nods. "I'm going to have to go take a look," he says, and abruptly heads out the door and down to Gary Graham's Cessna 206 floatplane.

At 10 A.M., 45 miles to the northwest, the Cessna banks around Bligh Island toward Valdez Narrows, and suddenly the sea, for at least three or four miles to the north, is a black-and-purplish bruise. Just below, like bubbles coming up, five sea lions bob and dive, bob and dive, sending iridescent pink swirls through the oil.

At the apex of the spill sits the *Exxon Valdez*, listing. There is a tug beside her, and another tanker, the *Baton Rouge*, lies a quarter of a mile off, blowing huge white plumes of water as she deballasts her holds to make room for the millions of gallons of oil that remain in her stricken sister. Nine hours into it, there is no oil spill containment equipment— no barges, no skimmers, no oil-absorbent booms, no suction pumps. And—Steiner searches up through the narrows toward the port of Valdez—no such equipment is on the way.

SATURDAY, MARCH 25

The spill has now spread to nearly 50 square miles: seven miles long and seven wide. Exxon divers say that at least eight of the ship's 14 tanks have been punctured and that an estimated million barrels of oil—42 million gallons—remain on board. Exxon tried to start pumping the oil into the empty holds of the *Baton Rouge* but had to give up when the pumping system sprang a leak. Now salvage experts, marine specialists, and news teams are racing to Valdez from all over the world. Doris Lopez, a small, fiery woman usually seen with a baby on her hip, says in a commercial radio interview that Valdez fishermen have had their boats standing by, ready to help, since dawn. "Why isn't anybody doing anything?" she asks. Also on the radio, Dennis Kelso, commissioner of Alaska's Department of Environmental Conservation (DEC), calls the spill the realization of everyone's secret nightmare. Alyeska's response, he says, is "inadequate and unacceptable."

Back in Cordova, Steiner has been up all night, talking to fishermen about what they might do if things get really bad. Many of them are down at the docks right now, gearing up their boats to help fight the spill. But all night, Steiner had this feeling of disbelief, a refusal to accept the possibility that Alyeska and Exxon wouldn't have it all mopped up by the end of the day. Now that possibility is sinking in.

On the 70-mile hop to Valdez, he flies over the spill again. It is bigger now, much bigger, and expanding into the southwest. It appears to cover about half the distance to Naked Island, 20 miles out. The island and its surrounding islets are rookeries for throngs of kittiwakes, murres, cormorants, and puffins. And beyond those first small isles—Steiner really doesn't want to think beyond them right now—are thousands of miles of island and fjord shoreline that flank some of the richest marine habitat in the world.

In alp-rimmed Valdez, the Cessna taxis to a dock 30 yards from the plate-glass windows of the Westmark Hotel coffee shop, and Steiner steps forth into chaos. His intent has been simply to locate the oil spill containment headquarters and learn the plan so that he can take some word back to Cordova's 500 fishermen and their 1,500 dependents. What he finds is that Exxon has rented the hotel's second floor, which now bustles with company personnel setting up computers, consulting charts, thumbing through manuals, and keeping people out. Downstairs, federal scientists, mainly from the National Oceanic and Atmospheric Administration and its branches, are doing pretty much the same. Steiner thinks about joining them, until he realizes that they've shown up to watch, not to do. The Alyeska Pipeline Service Company, which is supposed to be overseeing the containment efforts from its massive Alaska Pipeline terminal on the other side of the bay, seems to have no presence in Valdez and won't answer telephone inquiries.

Steiner walks a few blocks to the state building, where the DEC has quadrupled its staff in a day. He talks with Larry Dietrich, the department's director of environmental quality. The DEC, explains Dietrich, is essentially a research and regulatory agency. "We'll be doing everything we can," he says, "but right now we don't have anything to clean up the oil *with!*"

Steiner has heard enough. Cordova has about 500 fishermen, Valdez about 100. Most of them have boats and all would be willing to attack the slick with Kleenex if they had to. Steiner telephones Cordova. "Don't ask," he says to Grimes. "But listen—I think you better get over here."

SUNDAY, MARCH 26
The slick has spread to 100 square miles. Exxon crews have recovered only 3,000 of the 240,000 barrels spilled. Governor Steve Cowper declares Prince William Sound a disaster area. An investigation team from the National Transportation Safety Board is on its way.

The population of Valdez, normally 3,000, is about to double. The sky over the town has begun to swarm; looking out her dining room window, 13-year-old Gina Queddeng counts 12 helicopters in a matter of minutes. Teams from publications and networks arrive hourly. All the hotels are full, so local residents start renting out rooms at $50 a bed.

The four men from Cordova have rendezvoused in the closed-for-the-winter bunkhouse of Sea Hawk Seafoods, just outside town at the east end of the bay. They've been drinking coffee far into the night, and when Exxon schedules its next press conference at the civic center, they head for it in no mood to trifle.

They'll be even more sour an hour later. Frank Iarossi, president of the Exxon Shipping Company, admits that the spill is now beyond control, at least by mechanical means. His firm, he announces, now plans to use a combination of laser-ignited fires and chemical dispersants.

"What bothers me so much is the violation of trust," says Valdez Mayor John Devens. "I remember them telling us over and over when they wanted to locate the terminal here that they would be ready for any contingency."

"We don't have that problem," says Guard. "We never trusted the sons of bitches in the first place."

Steiner is concerned about the use of fire and dispersants. Smoke from test burns yesterday inflicted severe nausea and headaches on the 100 residents of the native village of Tatitlek. And the soaplike dispersants themselves are toxic, he says—maybe as damaging to the environment as the oil itself. What's more, says Steiner, "the dispersants don't get rid of oil, they just break it down into droplets. To the environment, it's the same dose of poison in a smaller pill, which means that smaller critters die first. For some people it's out of sight, out of mind. But the reality is that if the oil gets into shrimp, it gets into whales."

As they leave the conference, Lamb stops abruptly on the sidewalk. "I'm not going to go back and tell our people that they just have to sit back and watch the show again," he says. "It's time we did something."

The foursome, along with Sea Hawk Seafoods boss Ray Cesarini, return to the seafood plant. They talk among themselves and telephone their fellows in Cordova. Some want to blockade the Valdez Narrows with their boats to stop all tanker traffic to the pipeline. Others are more concerned with trying to save three hatcheries in the path of the slick. If the oil coats the spawning estuaries and destroys the natural salmon run, the hatchery stock will be all the fishermen have left to reseed.

OUT IN THE SOUND there is no moon. Photographer Roy Corral stands on the deck of the *Pagan*. While the fishermen are ashore politicking, Steiner has asked him to be their eyes, to help document the spill. It is his first night out and he hasn't yet seen the oil, but he can smell it, feel it sliding past the throbbing hull. Skipper John Herschleb and his crew feel it, too. When they left Valdez, the water hissed and lapped, and the wake swirled with the biophosphoresence of blooming plankton. But now they have sailed into what looks like a black hole. It neither emits nor reflects light. Corral, the crew, and the boat's only other passenger, *National*

*Geographic* photographer Natalie Fobes, stand silent, as if listening for life, but the oil slides by dead against the hull.

After a while the sky begins to dance a slow dance of green and blue-green swirls, fringed with a violet reflection that ripples over the snows of the 5,000-foot peaks rising sheer from the waters of the sound. Herschleb anchors the *Pagan* in a small cove off Disc Island. Corral sleeps on deck; when he awakens, he sees the oil. It is thick and sludgy. Two red snappers ride belly-up on the surface. Corral sees no other dead wildlife, but as the *Pagan* leaves the cove he watches a small flock of murres trying to lift off ahead of the hull. They flap and flounder, and beyond them, five sea otters are frantic. Oil-soaked, they are having trouble staying on top. They pop up through the oil, swimming violently, rolling, trying to scrape their thick coats clean. Then they sink.

MONDAY, MARCH 27

Overnight the winds have raged at up to 73 miles per hour, smearing oil 30 miles out into the sound. Planes can't fly to see just how far it has gone, but word crackles in via fishing vessel radios that the eastern ends of several islands have been hit hard, with oil coating shoreline spruces to a height of 30 or 40 feet. The gale has whipped the oil and water into a froth, which the oilmen call mousse, that can double the volume of a slick. Exxon announces that the stranded tanker has shifted 12 degrees in the wind. Of the million barrels left aboard after the spill, 120,000 have been pumped into the *Baton Rouge*, with 880,000 left to go.

Steiner and the three fishermen, up all night, have decided to hold a press conference of their own.

"It wasn't exactly a press conference as much as it was an education forum," Grimes will recall later. "We were tired of hearing Exxon tell these nightly bedtime stories to the nation about the harmlessness of biodegradable oil." The press had realized that the locals were angry and the fishermen out of work. They weren't going to hear about that from Exxon, and they weren't going to hear about how oil kills fish, other animals, and aesthetics.

They hold the conference early, right after the news people have eaten breakfast, and it works. The phone at Sea Hawk Seafoods starts ringing off the hook with interview requests. That evening, millions of people will begin to see news features on how oil kills.

Monday afternoon, a coincidental meeting finally catapults the sound's 600 fishermen to the front line. It happens when Lamb and Grimes drop by the state building "to raise Cain" with the DEC. They are peeved about a report that Exxon has sprayed oil dispersant illegally in a herring catchment area.

Says Lamb: "We were standing around jabbing charts and saying how we thought things should be, when Larry Dietrich wanders in and listens for a while."

Dietrich, one of the DEC's two top officials on the spill, has just been told by an angry Governor Cowper to sidestep Exxon, get creative, and *do* something. In Lamb and Grimes, he creatively sees several hundred fishermen who have boats that can corral oil with strings of floating booms, deliver crews and absorbent cloth to shoreline cleanup sites, haul hardware, and shuttle cages of oil-tainted wildlife.

"You fellows have a minute?" Dietrich asks. "We'd like to get you involved in a group on this thing."

Five minutes later he has the two fishermen behind closed doors. "Listen," he says, "we're going to try to do something. What do you think it should be?"

Lamb goes to the chart of Prince William Sound—there's one on most walls in town these days—and points out the three hatcheries at Port San Juan, Esther Island, and Main Bay. "We have to protect where the most salmon are," Grimes says. "If we save these, in a worst-case scenario we could reseed the natural environment from the hatchery stock."

At midnight, Lamb, Grimes, and Steiner—along with Riki Ott, a marine biologist and a board member of Cordova District Fishermen's United—are ushered into the presence of the oil spill brass: Exxon Shipping President Iarossi, DEC Commissioner Kelso, Coast Guard Admiral E. Nelson, Jr., and their respective lieutenants.

Kelso, of course, knows that the fishermen are coming; but the oil executive and the admiral at first "looked at us like, 'Who are these nobodies?' " says Grimes. "Then pretty soon Jack is telling them how the water flushes in here and flushes out there, and I'm telling them how the sound is a Gaian heart, and Rick and Riki are giving them some impressive biology, and they're leaning forward in their seats to see the chart better, and they start asking us questions . . ."

In the odd late-night lucidity, the fishermen and the bureaucratic muscle realize together that there is no way to halt the spreading slick.

"That shouldn't stop us from acting, though," says Steiner. "What we have to do is focus on something else, something that is based on a probability of success. We can *defend* with success if we put all our effort into a few key defenses: here at the hatcheries, here at the herring catchments of Herring Bay and Snug Harbor, here along the northwest shore of Montague Island, and at the mouths of a few escapement streams."

"When there's nothing you can do," says Grimes, "you're freed from limitations. You can go for it."

When the meeting ends at 3 A.M., Dietrich pulls the Cordovans aside. "OK, folks, you're in. You tell us what you need and somebody'll get it."

Steiner and Grimes are too exhausted to drive back to Sea Hawk Seafoods, so after everyone else leaves they stretch out on the DEC's kitchen floor. For half an hour it's quiet. Then Grimes asks the darkness, "You know what happened in there?"

"They put us in charge," says Steiner.

"We walk in like bums off the street," says Grimes.

"In the same clothes we've worn for days," says Steiner, "and they put us in charge."

Simultaneously, the two men start to giggle. They won't be able to stop.

"Listen, Admiral," says Steiner through his tears. "I'll tell you what I want."

"Yessir, yessir," says Grimes in the admiral's voice.

"And Frank," says Steiner to the memory of Iarossi, "we need booms. Lots of booms and lots of helicopters."


AT FIRST LIGHT, Roy Corral beaches the *Pagan*'s skiff on Ingot Island. The oil ashore is deep, more than a foot deep in depressions, and has been splattered by high winds up among the rocks and spruce. Ashore, he sees no life, no death. There is only the sticky silence, broken by the chugging of the *Pagan* out in the bay, where crew members Ian Payne and Torie Baker work to contain a patch of sludge within the loop of an absorbent boom. Then Corral realizes that one of the oil-covered rocks he is looking at is not a rock at all. With a stick, he lifts the body of a cormorant that looks as if it has been dipped in molasses. He scans the beach. It is covered with lumps, some obviously rocks, some now obviously not.

After a while he climbs up to a high grassy point from which he watches and photographs flock after flock of floundering seabirds, families of otters, small herds of blackened sea lions on rocks, the futile efforts of Payne and Baker against a mere drop in a wasteland of oil. When he finally lowers the camera and walks away, he knows that he will be a rabid environmentalist for the rest of his life.

TUESDAY, MARCH 28
On the fifth day, the lost war starts. The slick from the *Exxon Valdez* oil spill is now estimated at 500 square miles. Exxon, the Coast Guard, and the state of Alaska snipe at each other over whose fault it is that the oil wasn't contained within hours after it leaked. Only about 5,000 of the 240,000 spilled barrels have been recovered, but Dietrich tells the press that, frankly, no one is really trying to recover oil now. "We're beyond that," he says. "All effort is now in the defense of very sensitive areas."

Across the street from the state building, at Prince William Sound Community College, the state has taken over a couple of buildings for a wildlife rescue center. A few oiled otters, ducks, and seabirds have been brought in, but not many boats are out looking for them yet because winds in the sound remain high.

At 6 A.M., after two hours of sleep, a small group of fishermen gathers at the DEC offices. Those "very sensitive areas" Dietrich is talking about are theirs: the three hatcheries and the few most important bays in the herring and salmon fisheries.

"We walk in and they say, 'Here's phones,'" says Grimes. "'Here's tables and stuff.' They give us a courtroom, and we convert it into an office. Someone comes in and tosses us the keys to a van. Stan Stephens Charters opens up their yacht so we can use their computer."

The fishermen go to work. Lamb parks his briefcase on the judge's rostrum and telephones Cordova. Until today, only 15 fishing boats have been officially employed in the cleanup effort. Before the day is out, another 80 vessels will have headed from Cordova into the sound, without their skippers knowing whether there will be anything for them to do when they get where they're going. Their main tools will be floating containment booms, which can be linked together and stretched across bay mouths or towed in a loop between boats to drag oil. Exxon has dispatched only about a mile of the booms into the sound so far, and they're all in constant use by the boats already at work.

Within the next few days, Exxon and the fishermen will locate more than 260,000 feet of booms—about 50 miles' worth—throughout North America, Europe, Scandinavia, and the Middle East. When Exxon hesitates to pay the transportation bill, the Cordovans will recruit the Coast Guard to fly the booms in.

They also find enough additional boats to swell the defense fleet to some 200 vessels—plus skimmers, tugs and barges, "supersuckers" that vacuum 8,000 gallons per minute, generators, portable living quarters, floodlights for night work, food and clothing, and skiffs for shoreline cleanup. On their behalf, the state commandeers two of its own passenger ferries to anchor near the hatcheries as floating bases for research and cleanup efforts.

At the fishermen's request, a big Sikorsky Skycrane goes whapping off across the sound with the heavy stuff, and smaller Bell helicopters make dozens of daily trips, ferrying light supplies, researchers, photographers, writers, video crews, politicians, and delegates from probably every major conservation organization in the world. Semis loaded with North Slope oil gear come tearing the 800 miles down the still-frozen highway from Prudhoe Bay.

In the windowless courtroom, the fishermen live what Steiner has come to call the absolute nightmare of trying to juryrig a war. "It's a war driven by equipment rather than planning," he says. "It's not like you can say, 'Let's draw what we need from some vast inventory'; you have to say, 'Look what I've found, let's ship it out there and see if somebody can use it.' "

Exxon says it will pay the bill, and the Cordovans run it up into the millions. The whites of their eyes are vein-laced from sleeplessness, but they stay wired; it's a heady atmosphere.

But underneath, says Grimes, is an "enormous grief and anger" that occasionally drags them into a pit. Steiner's girlfriend, Claudia Bain, is a therapeutic masseuse, a toucher, and she coaxes people into corners for back rubs when she senses tempers close to the edge. This night, when all the hatchery reports are bad and countless animals are dying out there in the darkness, she herds the group back to Sea Hawk Seafoods, insisting that they get some sleep.

Instead, they pick up a fifth of Old Bushmills and sit on the floor, drinking until they cry. They sing. They read poetry, or rather Grimes reads poetry, a long one first, a ballad by Irishman Michael Coady that he copied from the wall of O'Connor's Pub in Dodin, County Clare: "The tiding old sea is still taking and giving and shaping," he intones. "The gentians and violets break in the spring from the stone./The world and his mother go reeling and jigging forever,/In answer to something that troubles the blood and the bone."

JOHN HERSCHLEB, skipper of the *Pagan*, slumps in the wheelhouse of his boat. He has heard that the 15 or so fishing vessels trying to protect the sound's hundreds of miles of threatened shoreline have been dubbed "the mosquito fleet," and that's what he feels like. He feels desperate and strong, like he should be able to do something. "But there's such a futility to it all," he tells Corral.

Corral goes ashore on Knight Island. Six waterfowl have beached themselves and are trying to preen, but when he tries to work close enough for photographs, they flush back into the sea, into the oil. He grimaces. He won't do that again.

Along the beach he finds two dead loons, a scoter, a merganser. Over a small rise he sees a frozen waterfall, an icicle-walled cliff irresistible to his photographer's eye. He shoots it until, shifting to another vantage, he comes across a deer carcass and bear tracks and scat. Uneasy, he retreats over the rise and sees a bald eagle, its golden talons oiled black, lifting off the beach, leaving behind the half-eaten body of an oil-smothered bird.

Corral goes down and looks at the wet red against the wet black. He knows that no one can really feel what has happened here unless they come out into the sound, into the sensuousness of it.

He needs a break. Three helicopters have landed down the beach, and he bums a ride back into Valdez. On the way, riding high, he sees the oil from the air for the first time. Ahead and below is a single boat, towing a length of floating containment boom. For perspective, he holds his right hand at arm's length and measures between thumb and forefinger. The boat is a quarter of an inch high. Then he spreads his arms as wide as they will go, but he can't measure the oil.

ULTIMATELY, THE FISHERMEN'S DEFENSE saves the hatcheries and helps protect some of the bays and spawning-stream estuaries. In the meantime, however, the oil slick grows to 750 square miles, then to 1,000, then to 2,500 and beyond.

In what Grimes calls a heart of the earth, there is a clot. The fishermen have no way of knowing whether the shoreline, the wildlife, or the fisheries will recover. The answers are probably years and hundreds of millions of dollars in the future.

"I guess the satisfaction is in knowing that we've done what we could," says Lamb. "This is our home. I don't know how we could have stood it if we couldn't have fought."

Grimes has found himself looking at life much differently the past couple of days. He has sensed the shiftings, from outrage to resistance to concession to faint hope. He looks to the future and wonders whether the ripple from Prince William Sound will jolt us, help us realize just how much killing power we have in our complacency.

"For those of us here," he says, "life has taken on an utter clarity, because in the face of something like this you have to drop all the white lies of your life and know who you are."

It is two o'clock of another morning, and Grimes is exhausted, almost unconscious. "The world may lose a last best place," he says.

Steiner scratches his beard. "Iarossi says he's going to polish every single rock."

"It won't be the same rock," Grimes replies. "Even if you scrape off every drop, it won't be the same rock."

"Well, we'll hold him to it anyway."

"Yeah." As if sleepwalking, Grimes barefoots over to a cassette player on the floor and puts in a tape he made during his New Guinea trip. He stands there for a while, listening to the song of the girls patting flour cakes onto the rocks, the chant of the boys to the rhythm of their dugout paddles, and the fluting call of a bird of paradise.

"Life is music," he says, "and we have to sing the song we are."

Then he crawls under the magistrate's table, stretches out full length, and falls asleep.

*June 1989*

# AMONG THE GRIZ

*It's autumn in an obscure corner of Glacier
National Park, and the great bears are
checking into the Grizzly Hilton.*

● ▲ ■

PETER MATTHIESSEN

Some years ago, in Tucson, Arizona, I met a hairy, husky man named
Douglas Peacock, who wished to talk almost exclusively about grizzlies.
Peacock had noticed my dust-jacket endorsement of a book by a noted
grizzly biologist ascribing the swift decline of bears in Yellowstone to
arbitrary actions by the National Park Service, in particular the sudden
closing of the backcountry refuse dumps on which bears had depended
in their late summer wanderings for 80 years. Inevitably the hungry
animals, drawn to the smell of cooking and fresh garbage, investigated
campgrounds they had previously avoided, bringing about the first fatal
grizzly attacks that had occurred in Yellowstone in decades. The subsequent removal or killing of more than half of Yellowstone's grizzly population outraged conservationists across the country.

Citing my exasperated quote on Frank Craighead's book *Track of the
Grizzly*, which I thought should make Americans as "mad as hell," Doug
Peacock commented, "I was mad, too. Madder 'n anybody."

In 1968, when he encountered his first grizzly while backpacking in
Yellowstone, Peacock had recently survived the Tet Offensive in Vietnam
and like many combat veterans, was unable to adjust to civilian life. "I
almost didn't talk for two whole years," he says, "except 'fill 'er up' or
'gimme a beer.' I was subject to recurrent waves of suicidal impulses and
grief and had to crawl back out into the woods like a wounded animal.
I was too angry, and I always went armed, even slept with a gun under
my pillow. I was dangerous.

"In those years, walking the mountains by myself, I watched a lot of bears, and they saved my sanity. A few years later, when I realized bears weren't around much anymore, I got mad."

In Peacock's opinion, the park's mismanagement of bears shared many characteristics with the Vietnam War—blunders, bureaucratic deceit, cover-ups, phony statistics, even an obscene "body count"—and it served as the focus for a rage which, as he acknowledged, was already in place. By 1973, an estimated 150 to 200 hungry bears had been destroyed or otherwise eliminated from an estimated population of about 300, with the numbers still in sharp decline. By 1975, Peacock's first year as a full-time observer, the grizzly was belatedly granted federal protection as a threatened species, yet "nuisance animals" were still being eliminated from Yellowstone and from Montana's Northern Continental Divide Ecosystem, which includes Glacier National Park, the Bob Marshall Wilderness, and the surrounding mountain forest. These two beleaguered ecosystems contain the last viable grizzly populations in the Lower 48. Today, Peacock says, Yellowstone's remnant population has been dart-gunned, tranquilized, tagged, lip-tattooed, transported, killed, or otherwise meddled with to such a degree that adult and unmarked wild bears are hard to find.

MY OWN EXPERIENCE with *Ursus arctos horribilis*, the "horrible bear," of the awed early explorers, began in the late summer of 1957 at the Trout Creek Dump, far back off the road in Yellowstone's Hayden Valley, where the grizzlies rose on the sage horizon just at twilight and chased off the black bears making free with the park garbage. Within the hour, by the light of fires, 37 grizzlies brawled and roared, rearing up and hurling burning barrels. Since then I have seen this imposing creature near Mount McKinley, in Alaska, and in Canada's Northwest Territories, east of Ross River. My sightings, however, had been made from the safety of a car or light airplane, whereas this man Peacock had for the past ten years observed on foot the dread quadruped that he affectionately calls "Ol' Grizzer." In his early years, his observations were hampered by a dearth of bears and a plenitude of humans. Then, in 1976, he stumbled on what he was looking for while serving as a fire lookout in Glacier Park. In a remote habitat that Peacock had all to himself, *Ursus* was numerous year after year, with nary a *Homo* in sight.

Though Doug invited me to witness this splendor for myself that very summer, our bond was not so mutual as he imagined. Those huge silvertips of the Hayden Valley, shambling and sniffing around my old Ford convertible with its torn canvas top—doubtless wondering whether the human contents, plucked out squeaking like a marmot, might not prove more wholesome, if less tasty, than the feast of offal all about—those hordes of hungry *horribilis* were gone, thanks to the Park Service, but they'd left an impression by no means forgotten. I had also perused quite recently an entire book devoted to grizzly attacks on my own species, and what with one thing and another, I neglected to accept Doug's invitation for an outing with the bears for about six years. Then in the spring of last year, Peacock and I, corresponding in regard to the death of Edward Abbey, discussed an expedition along a wilderness Alaskan coast. I had been warned by doctors that, due to old injury, I could no longer count on my right leg for heavy trekking. On the other hand, it was a mere three-hour climb to his bear paradise in the northern Rockies—a place he calls the Grizzly Hilton—and I decided it was now or never. Never still seemed like a pretty good idea, but now seemed better.

Not long afterward, I received a package in the mail containing a peculiar mace-like canister with the likeness of an aroused grizzly on one side and instructions for use of the contents—a drastic chemical mix based on hot pepper—on the other. The accompanying note was signed by a writer named Joe McGinniss, who apparently had acquired this item in the course of research for a book on Alaska. Having heard about my proposed excursion from a mutual friend, he wrote in part, "I hope to Christ you will not have occasion to use this. It has been proven effective in black bear encounters. Against grizzlies, field tests have been hard to come by. If it succeeds only in pissing off, not driving off, the bear, feel free to write to the manufacturer expressing your dissatisfaction."

CLUTCHING MY CANISTER, I head west late in the month of August. In the Salt Lake City airport I admire a handsome black-and-gold T-shirt emblazoned with the legend BEAR WHIZ BEER—ONLY BEER THAT GLOWS IN THE DARK and portraying, at no extra cost, a bear taking a golden leak into the night. From the Great Salt Lake the plane flies north over the desert into Idaho and on across the Bitterroots to northwestern Montana, where DP, as it seems easiest to call him, meets me at Kalispell. We drive up the Bad Rock Canyon of the Flathead River, northwest of the Hungry Horse Dam—names I work in here to convey a sense of this hard-bitten country.

In the distance rises a weathered range of mountains, and the bear man points to a high knob on the ridge line, scarcely within the western boundary of the great park. "Nobody ever goes up there but me," he says with satisfaction, "because as these northern Rockies go it's low and brushy and unscenic, with no mountain goats or bighorn sheep, and plenty of mosquitoes. They don't even bother to fight fires there. All it's got is bears." In 1967 the south end of this range burned over in a forest fire, and ever since, a bounteous huckleberry crop in late August and early September has burst forth on its opened slopes, even when other berry sites are poor. Here the bears convene, and they are wild: He has never seen a tagged animal among them.

DP carries his shoulders high on a broad chest and takes small steps as if setting himself for combat. Though both self-critical and touchy, he has a warm smile, kindly eyes, and such pronounced mannerisms as thumb-twiddling, compulsive tooth-brushing, and pushing his hair back and forth across a sunburned, balding pate. In Vietnam he served two tours in the Green Berets as a medic attached to native *montagnard* guerrillas, and one of his men, betrayed to the Vietcong, was beheaded because he was DP's friend. Seeking to avenge him, DP killed the wrong man, which still upsets him. By the end of the Tet Offensive he had had all the blood and killing he could handle, and in 1968 he was sent home, deeply sickened and full of hatred for the U.S. war machine, which he links—with justice, in my view—to the corporate right wing and its flunkies in the White House, with their ongoing looting of our nation's resources. DP, in fact, is an ardent supporter of the radical Earth First! movement (he is the prototype of Hayduke, a character in Ed Abbey's *The Monkey Wrench Gang*) and perceives himself, not entirely romantically, as a social outlaw. "I am presently on the lam because of the Dave Foreman [head of Earth First!] arrest in Arizona," he had written in a letter that May from Yellowstone, where he was hunting black morel mushrooms near Slough Creek.

DP's PROUD NAME as a troublemaker at Yellowstone has spread to Glacier, where in 1988 he obliged recalcitrant park officials to bring legal action against a helicopter pilot who was shuttling camera-clicking tourists over DP's study area and harassing the sow bears and cubs. At this season, with bears bent upon huckleberries snuffling in from all directions, the area is off-limits to park visitors; as his truck radio informs us, its only brushed-out trail—several miles down the high ridge from our destination—is now closed. We don't bother to apply for the camping permit we will not be granted.

Not wishing to appear gimpy and timid, with a yellow streak glowing like Bear-Whiz Beer through my Gore-Tex raingear, I am somewhat embarrassed by my concealed weapon, but it turns out DP has also brought a pepper gun, and also feels sheepish. We assure each other that these items are presents that we would never have thought to acquire for ourselves.

In the bar where we invest in a bottle of Jim Beam, I am told by pretty Sue the Barkeep, "You'll have an interesting trip, all right, with Doug." His activities in the park, so he believes, are closely monitored by rangers on the lookout for infractions. Not wishing it known where we enter the woods, he parks his truck in a public lot, where a kind confederate picks us up for delivery to a highway siding a few miles away.

DP is still cautious; we don't wish to be stopped. Once we shoulder our packs, he waits for a broad silence between sight and sound of traffic, then trots across the highway into the alders. In a few minutes we pick up the shadow of an ancient trail by which we will climb into the mountains.

Alder brush gives way to evergreens as our grown-over path, kept open by moose and bears, climbs toward the west. Grouse, moose, and elk are plentiful, to judge from sign, but bear scat is very old and sparse, and we stop just once, when a cracking in the chest-high brush warns us to give some mammal larger than ourselves the right of way. "Mostly black bear in the forest anyway," DP whispers; he is not much interested in this lesser animal. The black bear is essentially a forest dweller, whereas the great silvertip (its nicknames derive from the "grizzle" of silver tips on its thick fur), before man drove it to its last redoubts in alpine meadows of the Rocky Mountains, was typically an omnivore of open country.

We cross and recross a mountain stream and fill up our canteens with cold, fresh water. From that point on, every few feet, DP stops to listen. "Grizzers love this creek; they like to bed down here," he murmurs softly. He does not raise his voice again. "If the bears have arrived, they'll be plentiful from here on up."

We traverse a mountain meadow. Under the last steep ascent to the high ridge, in a dark, damp wood crisscrossed by bear trails, a canteen marks the site of his old camp. It is just five in the afternoon, so we dump our packs quickly (we can make camp later) and climb higher, to a break in the evergreens from which we may observe the huckleberry slopes across the canyon. A black bear rummages on the lower slope, close to the trees (black bears climb to escape grizzlies, which have been known to kill and eat them). Higher up, where the berry bushes are already set afire by first frosts, a big brown grizzly is browsing. Along the ridge are a grizzly sow and cub, both creamy blond.

We are delighted to find bears so soon, but weather is coming swiftly from the west. Soon there is thunder and light rain, then a cold downpour, as cloud smoke shrouds our view. Descending—it is nearly dusk—we have some trouble locating our packs in the thick brush and deadfall. Night is falling, and bear paths wind everywhere. "Just crawling with 'em," DP mutters, frustrated. By the time we find our packs and pitch the tent, we are drenched through by cold, heavy mountain rain, and dark has come.

DP likes to travel light, foraging off the countryside the way his bears do. He has neither pot nor pan, not wishing to attract stray bears with haute cuisine. All he has brought are hard farina he calls tsampa and some ancient trail mix—shards of mummified fruit, musty cereal, dead raisins—stored in tripled plastic bags to withhold from the bears its faded, mousy odor. Tired and wet, we warm ourselves with bourbon, served straight up, from a canteen. With fistfuls of tsampa this makes an acceptable meal.

"These wild bears are the least dangerous ones," he assures me, once we are squashed cozily into his small tent. "A mother griz will always try to move her cubs away unless you come on her so close she thinks you threaten them, and even then she may content herself with a bluff charge to scare you off. The only really dangerous bears are the ones that have habituated to the smell of man—campgrounds and garbage and also too much handling, as in Yellowstone. A bear like that may become predatory, and he's the one you have to fear at night. There's no real reason to have trouble with bears in the daytime, not if you move carefully, know what to look and listen for, when to give warning, and when to back off. But at night . . ." He takes a slug of bourbon.

DP describes his first experience with grizzlies in that late summer of 1968 in Yellowstone. He was camped by a hot spring some distance from the road when, hearing strange snufflings, he peered out of his tent and saw a grizzly sow with two cubs at the wood edge 50 yards away. Though the bears paid him no attention, he climbed a lodgepole pine in terror. Since that day he has spent two decades studying grizzly behavior, and most grizzly biologists would grant that this untrained loner has had more experience with wild grizzlies—bears that have never been exposed to human company—than anyone alive. (His book about it all, *Grizzly Years*, has just been published by Henry Holt.)

Years ago, on the ridge above, DP was seriously threatened by a large male grizzly that prowled around his tent all night despite his hasty bonfires, and he says he never sleeps much in bear country. Most fatal encounters in recent years have occurred at night, when a predatory bear drags a human denizen out of a sleeping bag. It was two completely separate fatalities on the same stormy night in August 1967 here in Glacier—both young women, neither in a tent—that inspired the Park Service to close its dumps. Since then, says DP, six more humans have been killed by bears in Glacier and three in Yellowstone; four of these victims were dragged out of tents or bags.

"When I'm alone," DP admits, "I keep twigs and paper handy for a bonfire, I lie in the very middle of the tent, and I don't sleep much." Since this night is too wet for bonfires, and since both occupants must lie pressed to the tent walls, we make do with a discussion of our bear deterrent. "I don't come in here armed," DP sighs, "so I guess it's nice to have *something* to fall back on. Lets you sleep a little." But in inexperienced hands, he adds, the canister would probably be more dangerous than effective, bolstering false confidence when what is needed is alertness and experience with bear behavior. Pepper in the snout or eye at the wrong moment might provoke a curious grizzly that might otherwise have gone its way in peace. "Sooner or later," he says, "someone will get hurt or killed using one of these, and it won't be the bear."

WE GET SOME SLEEP, albeit fitful. In the cold dawn we drag on wet pants and socks and soggy boots and, without a fire or warm food or coffee, trudge off through the dripping bushes, alarming the squirrels and nutcrackers and Steller's jays.

Climbing the steep slope, we warm up quickly. Near last night's lookout lies fresh bear scat, and on the low end of the spur that we will climb, bear sign has increased. Forging through thick cover in the imminence of large hidden animals of uncertain disposition reminds me, not altogether happily, of days spent with certain field biologists in Africa. At one point I stop to check the temperature of some fresh scat, which seems a bit too toasty for my liking.

DP, rolling like a bear through chest-high huckleberry, stops every little way to listen for warning growls and rumbles, and he speaks in sparse, inaudible whispers. In fact, we are moving so quietly and carefully that I wonder whether we are giving the bears fair warning. A hearty rendition of the Marseillaise might do nicely, or perhaps Miss Cyndi Lauper's "Girls Just Want to Have Fun." It is not in precaution, however, that my partner is whispering, but in consideration of the bears, who should not be chivied from their rightful territory by our racket.

Eventually we emerge from the deep cover onto a bony ridge of argillite and subalpine fir. The firs are broken by scatterings of spruce and larch and the pretty white-bark pine, which in certain years provides rich mast for grizzlies. Though not profuse, huckleberry—a red-fleshed low-bush *Vaccinium* resembling the eastern blueberry—is everywhere. On the northern mountainside that we observed last evening, three large, solitary grizzlies can be seen, dark brown and black.

"This is perhaps the wildest region in all the Lower 48," Doug whispers happily. "Grizzlies, black bears, cougars, coyotes, wolverines and fishers, deer, elk and moose, bighorn sheep and mountain goats, even a few wolves and woodland caribou."

Weak sun seeps slowly through the overcast. The silence is enormous. Below, in a valley that runs east toward the Livingston Range and Grinnell Glacier, lie thick, broad rivers of cloud and fog. Beyond, under fresh snow, rises Almost a Dog Mountain. (In the so-called Baker Massacre in January 1879, the Blackfoot warrior Almost a Dog was crippled for life and lost his parents, wife, and a little daughter who was shot dead by soldiers as he tried to carry her to safety.) A few miles north of here, near Camas Creek, begins the 400-square-mile home range of the Camas wolf pack, one of two packs formed from the "Magic Pack," which in 1986 and again a year later raised the first litters of wolf pups recorded in the West in 50 years.

We continue up the narrow spur, which ascends in steps to the main ridge of the mountains. A hundred feet below our vantage point, the green-and-black water of a tarn sparkles silver in the wind but shows no life. All around it, like dropped sticks, lie silvered skeletons of forest fire. DP humps out of his pack and gazes around him. "There are very few bears in these mountains in the early summer," he says, "but they always turn up this time of year, right here especially. I once identified 71 different bears in a six-week period in berry season."

Leaving our gear, we reconnoiter farther, moving slowly now, peering and listening. "If you are seeing *any* bears, there are sure to be quite a few more, and a lot nearer than you think," DP mutters, "so it's a very good idea to locate them as best you can, not take them by surprise." As he speaks, we locate the bears he has already heard moving, a dark-chocolate female with one cub, near a small rock face on the brushy slope above the tarn. The bears, perhaps a hundred yards away, are browsing for berries, unaware of us. "That little cliff is her security against marauders," DP whispers. "Very serious, solitary bears come through this place, and I give them plenty of room, but that young female with her cub is a lot more dangerous if you come on her too suddenly, too close. She's already spooky enough about big bears."

We traverse a small saddle where bears cross the spur on their way from one ravine to the other. It was here, one late September day, that a huge black grizzly, attacking every bear that crossed its path, chased a sow and cub uphill to this small saddle, where the desperate mother, with horrible snarls, fought the boar to a standstill as her cub escaped. Then she backed off, leaving the big male (one DP calls "the baddest bear in the mountains") in an ugly temper. All of this took place in front of Peacock, who had been about to cross the saddle when the running bears stopped him short. It was close to dark, and snow was falling. Cut off on this narrow spur from his camp high up on the ridge, he had nowhere to go.

Getting Peacock's scent, the male bear reared up on its hind legs, exhaling in a violent sniff, as if trying to clear the man-stink from its nostrils. Seeing the man perhaps 20 yards away, it dropped to all fours and moved toward him with quick short steps, ears back, popping his jaw and slobbering, poised for the charge.

In his pack DP had big black trash bags, which he held outstretched to enlarge his silhouette ("I wasn't sure that it would help, but I knew it couldn't hurt"). With this scarecrow effect, he held his ground, bags flapping in the wind. He kept the bear in the corner of his eye as he gazed off across the tarn, trying to "talk Ol' Grizzer down" with expressions of friendship and soft, meaningless imprecations. Fifteen feet away, the bear halted, undecided, then wheeled and went off, down into the bowl.

"If a bear hasn't got your scent and hasn't seen you," DP advises, "you can back off carefully, but once he sees you, you had better stand dead-still. Let him be dominant. Look off to the side and avoid eye contact, because he'll take staring as a confrontation, just as men and dogs do. Running or trying to climb a tree is the worst thing you can do, because flight excites his instinct toward predation. A bear can run at over 40 miles per hour and stand and reach high up into a tree, so if he's close enough to attack you in the first place, you're not going to make it up your tree even if it's already picked out. And when he has you, he's apt to do more harm than if you lay down and play dead. Subadults may only make a bluff charge, then take off. If the bear keeps coming, just curl up and wrap your arms as best you can to protect your neck and head, and take your licks; you may get away with a big bite in the hip or shoulder."

Recalling that black griz in the dusk, DP becomes excited, and his rising voice spooks the chocolate sow and her cub, which hasten diagonally uphill toward the ridgetop. Twenty years after Vietnam, DP still travels close to rage or tears, and now he curses his own heedlessness and offers the departing bears heartfelt apology. "This is your country, not mine," he says. "I'm sorry."

A big red-brown bear that has been digging under a dead tree beyond the tarn now wanders down to the green-black pool and on into the bushes. Almost immediately it is replaced by a black silvertip that emerges just below us to forage for berries on the near side of the pool. Pale sunlight illuminates the grizzled muscle hump, or roach, on his heavy shoulders, and his bowlegged gait identifies him to DP as the playful, eccentric male he knows as Happy Bear. Soon this bear, too, is gone into the bushes.

For an hour and a half the slopes are still as the bears go into cover in the heat of midday. They will reemerge when mountain shadows fall across their beds. I lean against the shiny trunk of a dead tree. A goshawk, a fine blue-gray male, hunts along the spur at my own eye level, on the lookout for grouse or migrating robins or perhaps the mixed flock of Bohemian and cedar waxwings that have been fussing in the white-bark pines.

IN EARLY AFTERNOON a solitary grizzly comes downhill to the tarn and picks its way out on a dead log, its long ivory claws so valued by the Indians flashing like signals in the sun. It stands awhile, mouth hanging open, as if drinking in the clear, sad mountain light. "See that?" DP whispers. "A bear that's tense and wary keeps its mouth closed." Soon the animal slips gracefully into the water and swims the length of the pond, leaving a rolled wake of chocolate mud. It enters the thick brush directly below us.

On the opposite slope there soon appears a large silver-gray female, blackpointed on its ears, muzzle, and paws—what DP refers to as panda markings. He is excited because she leads three cubs, all panda-marked, of a warm pewter color. Three-cub litters are uncommon among bears —in 20 years in this range DP has seen only one other. Perhaps scenting one of the big bears, the sow leads her cubs in single file up through the firs—"Look at the bear train!" DP murmurs—to a secure place behind the rocks.

Soon there comes a cubbish squawl and squabbling over the teats, followed by an eerie sound like a mix of moaning wind and sputtering motor. "Puttering," Doug says, delighted by my evident mystification. Apparently this sound originates between the bear's throat and its diaphragm, and is also made by nursing cubs, according to DP's friend Doug Seus, who trained the large Kodiak for the recent film *The Bear*. DP glances over to where I sit against my silver tree. "Really," he says. "It's true. And he says bears puttering in their sleep get extremely cross when interrupted."

The bear family, reappearing, remains in sight all afternoon, never more than sprinting distance from the rock face. It takes advantage of the big male's snooze to play and forage, and for a while the triplet cubs regale themselves by freeing rocks from the steep slope and letting them roll and bound and crash down to the pond's edge. Gradually they descend toward the water, where DP feels certain they will swim and play, but then the female lifts her head to catch a scent—not ours—and herds her cubs closer to the incline.

Browsing on huckleberries, we cross the saddle and climb to the ridge meadow where DP established his first camp years ago. Here we flare two mule deer, which bound into wind-stunted spruces before pausing to gaze back at us.

We descend once again to our first lookout, spooking what looks like the young grizzly that had swum the tarn and scaring it back over the ridge. Again DP curses our species and our meddlesome presence. He has grown more and more sensitive to the disruption brought by man, and has given up filming bears entirely; making his visits briefer every year.

The panda-marked triplets are back wandering and sniffing, sending boulders rolling down the steep slopes of the bowl as if trying to raise a great splash in the silent tarn. It is wonderful to sit in sunlight against these silvered snags, watching bears so intent upon bear life not a hundred yards below. In the cool that falls with the dusk shadow in the mountain bowl, the gray panda-marked bears snuffle and grunt among the timbers.

AT DAYBREAK we roll over in the tent. The sky is overcast and the day dark, and without further ado we doze right off again. When we get up and break camp the mountain sun is looming through the fog. "By the time we get up there," DP says, the bears will be going to cover after early feeding."

We shoulder packs and walk down to the meadow by the creek, where we study the broad north slope with binoculars. There is no sign of ursine life, but from the woods along the creek, perhaps 40 yards away, come the deep hooting of the great gray owl, the racket of squirrel, jay, and flicker, and the crack of limbs. "Bear moving," DP murmurs. "Oh, they love this place!" He hikes his pack higher on his shoulders. "We'd better give him room. This is probably as close to a bear as we've been on this whole trip—one that we knew about, anyway."

In happiness we head on down the valley, recounting the rare day before, when we observed 18 wild bears, all but two of them grizzlies, without a single disagreeable encounter. DP is still fretting because of the two that we disturbed and thinks it just as well to leave "before this place draws the attention of the bureaucrats and they send in their rangers and biologists to screw things up. Most of these people are just plain scared of grizzlies, so they cook up some stupid research program that involves darting the bears. They can't just study bears as they are, and let them go their way in peace.

"These Glacier bears are the wildest left, including the grizzlies in Alaska," he continues. "Not one of the 18 we saw yesterday showed ear tags or any other evidence of contact with human beings. All they know of man is an occasional whiff along the trails." What encourages him most are the number of new cubs (we counted six) in proportion to adults and the fact that the bears all seemed relaxed, which may suggest that the bear-buzzing by helicopter has ended.

In his first years here, DP stayed an average of two weeks, with plenty of opportunity to study the effect of helicopter visits, sometimes three or four in a single day. The flights, with all their roar and wind—another disturbing echo of Vietnam—would specialize in hovering over baby bears. "No female with young can habituate to that damned thing," he says, disgusted. After a few years of buzzing, the number of family groups declined, as did what DP terms "play activity," which is very pronounced in cubs and relaxed adults.

Yesterday and the day before, DP instructed me to get under a tree if a helicopter came, not only because we were not supposed to be here, but because he wished to photograph it without being seen. We did hear a helicopter in the distance, but none had passed over this small, unscenic range hunting for bears. "They tell me he's given it up now," reports DP of the pilot. "Says he's found Jesus."

Moving swiftly to keep warm, we hike on down the forest valley, crossing and recrossing the creek, pushing through chest-high *Menziesia* and high-bush huckleberry, serviceberry, salmonberry, and thimbleberry; devil's club, corn lily, and heavy bracken. We pass bear-ripped trees in a wild redolence of evergreens and mountain minerals and earthly fartings.

APPROACHING THE ASPHALT ROAD two hours later, we listen for cars before emerging from the woods. I hide the packs back in the trees across the road while DP hitchhikes the four miles to fetch his truck. Doug relishes his role as a woods "outlaw," and when we are safely in the truck and heading for West Glacier and hot coffee, he pounds the steering wheel in sheer exuberance. Before entering the forest he seemed subdued, and in the realm of grizzlies he spoke only in a whisper, but now he celebrates our successful adventure in a joyful shout: "Enemies of the American Fucking Way of Life!" The sudden volume startles me, and it does not subside much at the café, where DP's loud and foul denunciations of bureaucracy turn every head.

"Whatever happened to the silent mountain man?" I ask to cool him down a little. He laughs and swears and laughs some more, excited as ever. To say the least, DP has been inspirited by his beloved bears, and I, too, feel blessed by the proximity of such creatures, blessed by the mountain silences and light and birds, and blessed anew, this morning, by hot coffee.

Before visiting his friends' house near the Flathead Forks for a hot shower and dry clothes, we spend an hour hunting through warm pine woods for chanterelle mushrooms. Gathering bags of these cool, golden things that push through the sunny needles, together with puffballs and bolitas, polybores and rousselles, brings back lost childhood. The tension of days in the fastnesses of grizzlies is ever so subtly replaced by a soft, weary languor of well-being and a gratitude for overflowing life—almost more life than I feel able to contain.

In the fine fair weather of the next few days we travel southward, cooking up chanterelle stews with friends and fly-fishing the rivers all the way to Moose, Wyoming, still attended by the spirit of the bears. Near Livingston, where the Yellowstone Plateau rises in its dark parapets off to the south, a black bear, its fat fur lustrous in the sun, lopes straight toward us across a broad, wheaten bench of the Gallatin River as if bringing us tidings of the clan. "First time I ever saw a bear from this damn freeway," Peacock says. The bear wheels at the sight and sound and rollicks back across the bench toward the Shining Mountains.

*September 1990*

# THINKING ABOUT EARTHWORMS

*Take a break. Get out of the noösphere.*

●  ▲  ■

### DAVID QUAMMEN

Somewhere between the ages of 30 and 40 each of us comes to the shocking realization that a lifetime is not infinite. The world is big and rich, options are many, but time is limited. Once that dire truth has revealed itself, everything afterward becomes a matter of highly consequential choices. Every hour of cello practice is an hour that might have been spent rereading Dostoyevsky, but wasn't; every day of honest work is a day of lost skiing, and vice versa; every inclusion is also an exclusion, every embracement is also a casting aside, every *do* is also a *didn't*. Then presto: Time is up, and each *didn't* goes down on the mortal scroll as a *never did*. Yikes, why is he punishing us with this platitudinous drivel? you may ask. It's because I've just spent the entire first week of my 39th year thinking about earthworms.

Now I ask you to give the subject ten minutes. That figure includes a small margin, I hope, for divagations concerning television, the Super Bowl, the philosophy of Teilhard de Chardin, the late space shuttle *Challenger*, and other closely related matters, not the least of which is the far-ranging curiosity of Charles Darwin.

DARWIN SPENT 44 years of his life, off and on, thinking about earthworms. This fact isn't something they bother to tell you in freshman biology. Even Darwin himself seems to have harbored some ambivalence over the investment of time and attention. In an addendum to his autobiography, written not long before he died, he confided: "This is a subject of but small importance; and I know not whether it will interest any readers, but it has interested me." The interest had begun back in 1837, when he was just home from his voyage on the *Beagle*, and it endured until very near the end of his life. He performed worm-related experiments that stretched across decades. Finally, in 1881, he wrote a book about earthworms, a book in which the words "evolution" and "natural selection" are not (unless I blinked and missed them) even mentioned. That book is titled *The Formation of Vegetable Mould, Through the Action of Worms, With Observations of Their Habits.* By "vegetable mould" he meant what today would be called humus, or simply topsoil. It was his last published work.

Darwin seems to have found something congenial about these animals. "As I was led to keep in my study during many months worms in pots filled with earth," he wrote, "I became interested in them, and wished to learn how far they acted consciously, and how much mental power they displayed." Among his typically methodical observations of wormish habits was the following: "Worms do not possess any sense of hearing. They took not the least notice of the shrill notes from a metal whistle, which was repeatedly sounded near them; nor did they of the deepest and loudest tones of a bassoon. They were indifferent to shouts, if care was taken that the breath did not strike them. When placed on a table close to the keys of a piano, which was played as loudly as possible, they remained perfectly quiet." It's an image to be inscribed on all human memory, I think, as an antidote to pomposity and aloofness: Charles Darwin, alone in his study with a tin whistle and a bassoon and a piano, trying to get a rise out of his worms. Under the category "Mental Qualities," he stated, as though regretfully, "There is little to be said on this head. We have seen that worms are timid." Later in the book, though, he described some experiments—designed to distinguish instinct, in their leaf-gathering behavior, from judgment—that inclined him to credit them with "a near approach to intelligence."

But what mainly concerned Darwin was the collective and cumulative impact of worms in the wild. On this count, he made large claims for them. He knew they were numerous, powerful, and busy. A German scientist had recently come up with 53,767 as the average earthworm population on each acre of the land he was studying, and to Darwin this sounded about right for his own turf too. Every one of those 53,767 worms, he realized, spent much of its time swallowing. It swallowed dead plant material for its sustenance, and it swallowed almost anything else in its path (including tiny rock particles) as it burrowed. The rock particles were smashed even finer in the worm's gizzard, mixed with the plant material and the digestive juices in its gut, and passed out behind in the form of "castings." The castings contained enough natural glue to give them a nice crumb structure, characteristic of good soil, and were also biochemically ideal for nurturing vegetation. Collectively, over years and decades and centuries, this process transformed dead leaves and fractured rock into the famous and all-important vegetable mould. But that wasn't all.

At least some of those species of earthworm had the habit of depositing their castings above ground. A worm would back tailfirst out of its burrow and unload a neat castellated pile around the entrance. As a result, Darwin recognized, soil from a foot or more underground was steadily being carried up to the surface. In many parts of England, he figured, the worm population swallowed and brought up ten tons of earth each year on each acre of land. Earthworms therefore were not only creating the planet's thin layer of fertile soil; they were also constantly turning it inside out. They were burying old Roman ruins. They were causing the monoliths of Stonehenge to subside and topple. On sloping land, where rainwater and wind would sweep their castings away and down into valleys, they were making a huge contribution to erosion. No wonder Darwin concluded: "Worms have played a more important part in the history of the world than most persons would at first suppose."

His worm book sold well in the early editions—by one account, it was a greater commercial success for him than *On The Origin of Species.* Nowadays it is generally ignored by everyone except soil scientists—who themselves nod to it devoutly but don't seem to take its contents too seriously. Sometimes these scientists mention that Darwin rather overstated the role of worms, while he underestimated such other soil organisms as bacteria, fungi, protozoa, and subterranean insects. *The Formation of Vegetable Mould, Through the Action of Worms* is nevertheless a readable volume, mild and affable and modest in tone, containing a few curious facts and some telling glimpses of the author's fastidious methodology. But the most interesting thing about the book, in my view, is simply that this particular man took the trouble to write it. At the time, evolution by natural selection was the hottest idea in science; yet Charles Darwin spent his last year of work thinking about earthworms.

AND THANK GOODNESS HE DID. That sort of stubborn mental contrariety is as precious to our planet as worm castings. It is equally essential that some people *do* think about earthworms, at least sometimes, as it is that *not everyone* does. It is essential not for the worms' sake but for our own.

More and more in recent years, we are all thinking about the same thing at the same time. Electromagnetic radiation is chiefly responsible; microwaves, macrowaves, dashing and dancing electrons unite us instantly and constantly with the waves of each other's brain. We can't step out into the yard without being bonked by a signal that has come caroming off some satellite, and when we step back inside, there's Dan Rather, ready with the day's subject for thought. One day we think about an explosion in the sky above Cape Canaveral. Another day we think about a gutshot pope. On a designated Sunday in January we gather in clusters to focus our thoughts upon the Super Bowl. Occasionally we ponder a matter of somewhat less consequence, like the early returns from the New Hampshire primary or the question of who shot J. R. Ewing. Late in the evening we think about what Ted Koppel thinks it's important we think about. Over large parts of the world we think quite intently about the World Cup soccer final. My point is not that some of these subjects are trivial while others are undeniably and terrifyingly significant: My point is that we think about them together in great national (sometimes global) waves of wrinkling brows, and on cue. God himself has never summoned so much precisely synchronized, prayerful attention as Mary Lou Retton got for doing back flips. And maybe God is envious. Of course now He too has his own cable network.

The Jesuit philosopher and paleontologist Pierre Teilhard de Chardin gave a label to this phenomenon. He called it the noösphere, and he considered it just wonderful. Teilhard's noösphere ("noös" being Greek for mind, and the rest by analogy with lithosphere, biosphere, atmosphere) was the ultimate product of organic evolution, the culmination of all nature's progress toward man and perfection: a layer of pure homogenized mind enwrapping the planet, hovering up there above us as "the sphere of reflexion, of conscious invention, of the conscious unity of souls." It was prescient of him, I think, to have shaped this idea back at a time when even radio was an inestimable new toy. But in my heartfelt opinion, his enthusiasm was misguided. Too much "conscious unity of souls" is unhealthy—probably even pernicious. It yields polarized thought, in the same sense that a polarized filter yields polarized light: nice, neat alignments of attention and interest (which is different from, but a step toward, unanimity of opinion), with everyone smugly in agreement that such-

and-such matters are worth contemplation, and that the rest by implication are not. Such unity is a form of overall mental impoverishment.
For just one particular instance, it tends to neglect earthworms.

You will have sensed by now that I am a self-righteous crank on this
subject. I believe that unanimity is always a bad thing. The prospect of
all five billion of us humans getting our alpha waves into perfect synch
appalls me. My own miniscule contribution to the quixotic battle—the
battle against homogenization of mind, the battle to preserve a cacophonous disunity of souls, the hopeless fingers-in-ears campaign of
abstention from the noösphere—lies chiefly in not owning a television.

Pitiful, I know. It sounds like the most facile sort of pseudointellectual
snobbery, I know. It is backward and petulant, and I am missing lots of
terrific nature documentaries on the high-minded channels, I know. It's
grim work, but somebody's got to do it. Anyway, I am not at all opposed
to television; I am merely opposed to the notion that *everybody* should be
dutifully, simultaneously plugged in. Maybe someday, for some unfore-
seeable reason, society will have need of a person who has never seen,
say, a video replay of the space shuttle explosion. If so, I'll be ready. It's
a personal sacrifice that I've been quite willing to make.

On the other hand, so as not to sound too tediously righteous, I want
to confess that I did watch the Super Bowl this year, on a friend's set,
thereby merging for two hours my somnolent brain with those millions
of somnolent others. It was a sublime waste of time, and I'm glad I did
it. Next year I won't.

YOU YOURSELF can join in the good fight without even unplugging your
television. Just take a day or an hour each month to think carefully about
something that nobody else deems worthy of contemplation. Break stride.
Wander off mentally. Pick a subject so perversely obscure that it can't
help but have neglected significance. If everyone else is thinking about
the sad and highly visible deaths of seven astronauts, think about the
Scottsboro Boys. If everyone else is thinking about the Super Bowl, think
about a quiet little story called "The Loneliness of the Long-Distance
Runner." If everyone else is busy despising Ferdinand Marcos (as well
they might), devote a few minutes of loathing to Fulgencio Batista. Or
think about earthworms.

Think about the Australian species of worm, *Megascolides australis*, that
grows ten feet long and as big around as a bratwurst. Think about *Lumbricus*

*terrestris*, familiar to soil scientists as the common European earthworm and to generations of American boyhood as the night crawler, nowadays gathered at night by professional pickers on Canadian golf courses and imported into this country for a total value of $13 million per year. Think about how hard it is to tell front from rear, especially so since they can back up. Think about the curious reproductive arrangements of earthworm species generally, hermaphroditic but not self-fertilizing, so that each one during the act of mating provides sperm for its partner's eggs, while receiving back the partner's sperm for its own eggs; now imagine having a full sister whose mother was your father. Think about the fact that these animals can regenerate a lost head. Think about the formation of vegetable mould, and the relentless swallowing, digesting, burrowing, and casting off of waste by which earthworms topple and bury the monuments of defunct civilizations, while freshening the soil for new growth. Think about how sometimes it's the little things that turn the world inside out.

*June 1986*

# THE WOLVES' STORY

*Somewhere in Montana, Canis lupus is*
on the run.

● ▲ ■

RICK BASS

They say you're not supposed to anthropomorphize—to think of animals as having feelings, as being able to think—but late at night I like
to imagine that the wolves have saved themselves once again and that
they are killing. That another deer has gone down in a tangle of legs,
tackled in deep snow; that the deer (or moose calf or young elk) is still
warm, steam rising from the open belly.

They devour the whole animal, eating everything, even the snow that
soaks up the blood.

This often happens at night. They often catch their prey from behind,
but sometimes they'll dart in and grab anything—the nose, the face, the
neck—they can get without being kicked. The prey flounders, and it's
over. The wolves swarm onto it with their teeth, long legs, and—I have
to say this—great hearts.

I like to imagine one group of wolves in particular, a pack that found
its way from Canada down to Montana a few years ago. There were at
least three, two males and one female, and they were one of the first
packs to appear in that part of the United States in decades. They settled
near the town of Marion, 60 miles south of the Canadian border in the
northwestern corner of the state, and it wasn't long before they created
a stir. Wolves were back. And no one was quite sure what to do about
it.

SIXTY YEARS AGO, humans killed the last wolves in Montana and the
American Rockies. And we behaved badly doing it: shooting them, setting
them on fire, leaving them strychnine-laced carcasses to eat. Some of it

was the work of ranchers; the rest was accomplished by the federal government's predator-extinction programs in the 1920s. The logic was simple: A domesticated country like ours was no place for predators; it was fine for sheep and cows and deer and elk and other plant eaters, but not for wolves.

And so they disappeared. Those that weren't exterminated fled to Canada, which was wild enough and big enough to provide wolves with the two things they need most: food and room to hide from humans. There were still a few places in the American West that fit those requirements, but as the wolves must have sensed, there were many more hideouts up north. Canada has always had wolves, and most have stayed there. But as years went by and the wolf population grew to as many as 50,000, some wolves began coming south again, feeding on the sprawling deer populations in the United States. Today there are wolves, or at least rumors of wolves, in Montana, Idaho, Washington, North Dakota, Michigan, Wisconsin, and Minnesota. They're testing us once more, pressing against the edges of our civility, seeing if this time they'll be allowed to stay.

Perhaps they will. A small population of red wolves has already been reintroduced to North Carolina's Alligator River National Wildlife Refuge. And in the Southwest, U.S. Fish and Wildlife Service officials are working to return the Mexican wolf, or lobo, to its historic range in New Mexico, Arizona, and Texas. But the wolf that seems to most belong in the American landscape is the gray wolf, *Canis lupus*, and nowhere is the battle over its return being waged more fiercely than in the northern Rockies, especially around Yellowstone National Park, just 300 miles through the woods from Marion.

Montana Senator Conrad Burns has predicted that if wolves find their way to Yellowstone, specifically to its crowded campgrounds, "there'll be a dead child within a year." Montana Congressman Ron Marlenee has said that wolves are "like cockroaches in your attic—nobody wants them." But environmentalists, naturalists, even some Park Service people think Yellowstone is an incomplete wilderness without the wolf and that the park's herds of deer and elk need something—disease or winter or predators—to thin their numbers. These people are becoming increasingly vocal about the wolf's return and how that might affect its status on the endangered species list. Should wolves arrive in Yellowstone on their own, they will be fully protected, at least in theory, from ranchers and other angry citizens living beyond park boundaries. (There's a fine of up to $100,000 and a one-year jail term for killing a wolf in Montana, but to date it's never been enforced.) If, however, we actively relocate wolves to Yellowstone—bringing them in helicopters and trucks—they will be considered guests, an "experimental" population. Their protection under the Endangered Species Act could then be relaxed, permitting stockmen to kill any wolf that wanders from the park and threatens domestic animals.

The wolves themselves may have decided the matter already. Given that they have been known to travel as many as 124 miles in a 24-hour stretch, any Montana wolf could be in Yellowstone within a week if it had a mind to.

THE MARION WOLVES were in Montana for several months before they were officially "discovered." Ranchers and other residents near town said they'd been hearing wolves for some time but hadn't reported their suspicions for fear that livestock and land-use restrictions might be placed on the area. But the Marion wolves were better than most at staying hidden. They were edgy and wise to human behavior. They pushed their range right up to a cattle ranch in an area called Pleasant Valley, where they began to establish a new home territory. The pack roamed the valley through the fall of 1988, feeding on deer and elk, keeping out of sight deep in the forest. On some of those autumn nights, people around Marion could hear their howls rolling across the cold, snowy hills. But nobody would say for sure that the howls came from anything wilder than a local sheep rancher's herd dogs.

After a long courtship two of the Marion wolves mated in the early months of 1989, and at least three pups were born in early April. That same month one of the adult Marion wolves, a male, went down to a rancher's bullet while allegedly trying to get into a sheep pen. Later that summer another wolf was seen among the same rancher's livestock, and the U.S. Fish and Wildlife Service, the agency in charge of all animals protected by the Endangered Species Act, decided to relocate the pack to Montana's Bob Marshall Wilderness, 250 miles north of the Wyoming border. "We need to develop credibility among ranchers," said Steve Fritts, coordinator for Fish and Wildlife's Northern Rockies Wolf Recovery project. "We need a reputation that we'll do something if there's livestock depredation on account of wolves."

The pack was to be given what's known as a soft release. A temporary holding pen was built at a secluded spot in the Bob Marshall Wilderness. There the wolves would be allowed to acclimatize to their new home while being fed dead deer and elk. (The foundation of all wolf-relocation theory is that a wolf, once released, will hit the ground running, trying to return to familiar surroundings. A newly dug den in which the female plans to give birth or a wire fence are the only two known restraints.) But as the release plans were being refined, the Wyoming Farm Bureau and the state of Montana, led by Governor Stan Stephens, stepped in, demanding a stop to the relocation. Stephens said the feds could release the wolves, not in the Bob Marshall Wilderness, but up near the Canadian border in Glacier National Park. The Farm Bureau's interest in the matter was obvious: There was Wyoming livestock only 250 miles to the south of the Bob Marshall Wilderness. But Stephens's interest may have been even more obvious: While big-game hunting is not allowed in Glacier, it is allowed in the Bob Marshall Wilderness, and because a healthy wolf will eat as many as 15 deer in a winter, it was in the interest of human hunters—who may also be registered voters—to keep wolves out. So, on September 14, 1989, what remained of the Marion pack—a black female, two of the three pups she was known to have birthed, and an old tooth-worn male—was airlifted from Pleasant Valley and dumped in Glacier National Park in what is called a hard release.

The four wolves ran immediately in four directions. One pup headed straight up into the park's rockiest, most game-barren country and quickly starved. The other pup starved two days later. The tooth-worn male fled only 20 miles south before stopping, exhausted, outside a cattle ranch. When the Fish and Wildlife Service had trapped him back in Marion, one of his legs had been damaged, and now it had turned gangrenous. Barely able to walk, he was just camping out at the edge of the woods, watching those cattle and slowly starving to death. Finally, a Fish and Wildlife biologist had to destroy him.

The mother—the black female—was the luckiest, the fleetest, and the most apt to survive. She swam across the narrow Hungry Horse Reservoir, then headed down the eastern side of giant Flathead Lake. One night she went right through the town of Bigfork. Her path, though, was blocked by five-mile-wide Flathead Lake, so instead of heading north and west, she was forced south along the shore.

One day in early October, an old woman living outside Missoula spotted the black female resting in her backyard in the shade of an apple tree. By now the wolf had been on the move for almost a month. "Hey, wolf," the old woman called out. "I see you."

The wolf just stared back at her. "I see you, wolf," the woman kept saying, but the wolf just lay there, watching.

Wolf biologists speak with certainty of wolves having "search images," a seek-and-destroy mentality that brings to mind smart bombs: computerized coordinate grids flashing in the wolves' brains as they weave through the woods. Biologists say wolves are so loyal to these search images that they may run right through a herd of elk or cattle in the pursuit of a single deer.

And so it was with the black female trying to get back to Marion. For months she pushed south, then northwest, rarely stopping except to eat and rest. But on her way she bumped into another lone wolf—a big gray male—in Montana's Ninemile Valley, a beautiful, narrow basin tucked between the Bitterroot and Rattlesnake mountains, and she stopped moving. The two wolves mated in late winter, and the female dug a hillside den next to a cattle ranch belonging to Ralph and Bruce Thisted, tall, lean brothers in their midsixties who'd been living in the valley for 53 years.

In April, the female gave birth to six pups—three gray and three black—and she guarded them while her mate hunted fawns and dragged them back to the den, which was within yards of the Thisteds' pasture.

The Thisteds lived in a house overlooking a clearing where the black female played with her new litter, and the brothers spent hours watching the pups swarm and lick their mother. Then, in mid-June, the Thisteds stopped seeing the black female. Two weeks later, a fisherman found her radio collar at the bottom of a creek several miles from the den. Her carcass was never discovered. I remember reading about her and the Ninemile pack in the local papers almost every day during the summer of 1990, and to those nonranchers who were following the wolves' story, the news of the black female's death lingered long after she was gone. It was as if she were still traveling, still hunting.

The gray male, the loner, was left to raise the pups by himself. He spent every day playing with them in the meadow, chasing them, and showing them how to hunt mice. By the end of the summer they had grown to almost adult size and were beginning to wander beyond their pasture.

Then, in the predawn hours of September 1, the big male was struck and killed by a car on Interstate 90, 15 miles from the den. There are photographs of him lying there on the shoulder of the road, and it is odd to see that kind of motionlessness imposed on an animal whose existence is tied to the fact that it never stops moving.

THE FISH AND WILDLIFE field biologist for the Ninemile area is Mike Jimenez, a 44-year-old man with dark hair, dark eyes, and a constant smile. He's tireless and affable, both in and out of the field, taking strangers' phone calls at his home at all hours, patiently answering reporters who want to know the Ninemile pack's whole story in 25 words or less.

For the next three nights after the male's death, Jimenez went out into the Thisteds' pasture and howled.

The pups howled back with great eagerness. "It was like, 'Dad's back!' " Jimenez says.

As a matter of courtesy, the Fish and Wildlife Service contacted its state counterpart, the Montana Department of Fish, Wildlife, and Parks, and said it intended to feed dead deer to the orphaned pups for about six weeks, long enough to launch them into full, self-supporting adulthood. The pups still had their milk teeth and had not yet been on a real hunt. In the days following their father's death their scat contained nothing but seeds, grasshoppers, and traces of baby mice.

But the state officials balked. "The MDFWP indicated they were not supportive of a long-term feeding program for the pups," says Ed Bangs, leader of the Montana Wolf Recovery Project. "They did not support killing deer to feed the pups."

Finally, after some negotiating, the state allowed Jimenez and Bangs to feed the pups road-killed deer, and on September 4, 1990, Jimenez placed two animals near the pups' den. Because the pups' milk teeth couldn't break through the hides, Jimenez opened each deer's belly with a knife. The next day he added a third deer. Then he began driving up and down the roads around the Ninemile in his truck, searching desperately for more and dropping them off in the pasture as if he were Papa Wolf, the name the Thisteds had taken to calling the big gray male.

The plan was to allow the pups to feed on these road kills until the start of hunting season in late October. At that point, the federal biologists hoped, wounded deer—hunters' gut-shot and butt-shot "mistakes"—

would be staggering around the woods, easy prey. There would be gut piles in the forest, too, mounds of bloody entrails where successful hunters had field-dressed their kills.

So at least in theory the wolves would have little trouble finding food during deer season. The question was, could they teach themselves to find and bring down healthy animals? There were no cases on record of orphan pups surviving in the wild, and though tales are told in many cultures of orphaned humans being saved by wolves, the stories have never been told the other way.

Then on September 6, two days after the state agreed to the road-kill plan, K. L. Cool, director of the MDFWP, sent a letter to the federal biologists asking that the plan be scrapped—a 180-degree change in position. Cool expressed concern that road kill would carry the scent of humans and cars and so might attract the pups to the interstate. As if it were an afterthought, he added, "Wolves have the capacity to dramatically affect hunter opportunities in this state."

Fish and Wildlife complied with Cool's request, and Jimenez responded by obtaining deer dissected in a federally managed research project at the nearby Lee Metcalf National Wildlife Refuge. He was improvising like mad. Because the carcasses were often dragged off by bears, he had to chain them to a pipe driven into the ground. If the pups saw him, he'd fire a gun over their heads to keep them wary of humans. As the pups grew, Jimenez spread the deer out in different positions, even propping them up in a running pose, so that the wolves might get the idea that they should attack standing animals.

The Thisteds, entranced by what was happening in their pasture, started recording the pups on video. Ralph would climb into the loft of the hay barn and wait for daylight. Sometimes his hands would get so cold that they'd shake, and the footage reflects that. On tape, though, there's no mistaking the pups; they are delightful, rolling and playing with each other. One pup climbs on top of a charred stump while another stares in wonder, clearly awed by this god-puppy above it. The god-puppy then leaps down on its sister or brother, a great slam-dunk from heaven, and they play tag around and around the stump.

There was one black pup that spent more time chasing magpies away from the deer carcasses than he or she spent feeding—clearly a dreamer. "We called that one Puppy," Ralph Thisted says, almost shyly. "Anytime there was a bird flying by, it would chase it."

The video shows Puppy always staying away from the other five pups, a loner already. And then one day Puppy disappeared, as did one of its siblings. Those two were never seen again.

"I miss them," says Bruce Thisted. "I could have watched them forever."

A MONTH BEFORE hunting season opened in October, the federal biologists decided to watch the Ninemile pack more closely. They were pessimistic about the pack's chances, certain that at least some of the pups would get shot. They trapped two of the wolves—a black female and a gray male—and fitted them with radio collars. After that, the wolves grew much more wary and nocturnal. Night after night Jimenez and the Thisteds sat in the barn loft, drinking coffee and watching the pups through field glasses.

Then, shortly after the start of hunting season, the pups left the meadow, went into the woods, and stayed there for several days. It was a promising sign. "They may have killed a hunter cripple," said Ed Bangs at the time, "or they're feeding on a gut pile."

Once the pups left their spot in the woods, the biologists moved in to see what had happened, but no carcass was found. "It's the greatest thing about studying them," Bangs says, stroking a handlebar mustache that gives him the look of a circus lion tamer. "Even if you have a radio-collared wolf, it's still mysterious. Sometimes they might as well be magicians."

Jimenez and Bangs tracked the wolves all through the hunting season, and in November Bangs made these notes in his field journal: "The pups have grown into full-size adults. The pack seems to be relying less and less on the deer provided for them. Fresh scats are found containing ungulate hair, indicating that the wolves are obtaining deer on their own. Some of these could possibly be hunter cripples."

By this time the pups had stopped eating the deer Jimenez was leaving for them. (He quit placing carcasses on Thanksgiving Day.) It appeared that the pups had developed a head-on taste for fresh meat. And judging from the movements of the two collared wolves, the pack was starting to expand its home range—from shy three-mile puppy walks, to five-mile trips, to seven-milers, then ten.

By now the snow was down, and Jimenez could follow them. It was as if a door had swung open; he could read where the pack had gone, what it had done.

On December 23, Jimenez found what he was looking for. There was blood in the snow, and the wolves had left a chase trail—there were tracks everywhere. For the first time, Jimenez could say for sure that the Ninemile wolves had taught themselves to hunt. All four of them were going to spend Christmas with fresh meat in their bellies.

"It was like when your kids go off to school for the first time," Jimenez says, laughing. "You know, when they get on the school bus by themselves. Yeah, we were tickled."

One month later, Jimenez found the remains of another deer that the wolves had killed and eaten, along with urine scent marks that indicated pair-bonding, one of the highly social early phases of wolf mating behavior. There was also blood in one of the scent marks, indicating a female in estrus.

Jimenez was amazed. "Physiologically it's possible for wolves to mate at a year old, but it's never been seen in the wild," he told me. "Wolves in the wild don't generally mate before their third year." It made me think that the pack somehow knew it had to hurry things, to write its own rules.

Jimenez kept finding those scent marks, his mind running fast, optimistic calculations. If the female was pregnant, and if she had six pups, all of which survived, there could be at least ten wolves in the Ninemile come April, maybe a dozen if the two pups that disappeared from the Thisteds' had survived.

"I got caught up in it," Jimenez says. "It's hard not to. The goal is to recover the population. The problem is that you do it through individuals—and when you deal with them continuously, it's real tough not to get involved. You're trying to stay objective and do the research, and at the same time there's a growing emotional attachment that you try to avoid."

The Thisteds, though lifelong ranchers, couldn't avoid their growing attachment to the wolves, either. "We had spent all those days and nights taking videos," Ralph says, "and we knew when the wolves' howling schedule was. Those wolves became a part of this valley."

IN MARCH, I went with Jimenez into the Ninemile woods to track the wolves—or rather to see where they'd been. We found a place where someone had dumped part of a deer carcass; judging from the tooth-scoring on the bones, Jimenez noted, the wolves had been feeding on the remains.

We followed the wolves' tracks through the forest. They crossed each other like braided river currents, like streams of desire and hunger. We felt the wolves all around us, saw their fist-size paw prints in the snow, but heard nothing, not even wind in the trees. Deer stood on a bluff above us and looked down calmly, as if we had come to visit them.

"I wonder if they've figured it out yet," Jimenez said, looking up at the deer. "That predator image, the realization that during this season it's the wolves that are hunting them, not humans."

We watched for ravens circling in the sky, a cue that might tip us off to a kill site, but saw none. The wolves, Jimenez surmised, were traveling, looking around, pushing. From the perspective of someone who wants to see wolves return to Montana, that restlessness may prove the key to their survival. The greatest thing that much-harassed black female from Marion did was travel.

Jimenez told me that each lone wolf (each "disperser," in scientific terms) that pushes into Montana is a pioneer for the future. As the animal moves through the forest, marking trees and rocks with urine, it leaves a trail that other wandering wolves might pick up and use for expansion and recolonization. No biologist can say how keen wolves' noses are, and no one really knows how good their hearing is. But once you look into their eyes you know there's something else—a blazing, furnace-hearted need to move, hunt, survive. Wolves are going to stay around, and most important, wolves are going to find other wolves.

"You think they'll get to Yellowstone before they're reintroduced there?" I asked.

Jimenez laughed. "People used to think they'd never get to Missoula or to the Bitterroot Valley, south of there. So they may. They just may."

WOLVES OFTEN LIKE TO GO for an extra-long ramble in late March, right before they dig their dens and settle in to give birth. The whole pack goes on this end-of-winter road trip. Scientists may find some evolutionary advantage to this behavior, but I prefer to think that the wolves know they're going to be cooped up with pups all summer and simply want to head out for one last good time.

The black Marion female made such a trip after arriving in the Ninemile and meeting up with her big gray male. An aircraft pilot saw her and the male and a third adult wolf (which hasn't been seen since) about 40 miles south of home—way over on Lolo Pass—in late March of 1990, but within the next couple of days she and her mate were back in the

Ninemile, digging their den for what would become the orphan pack.

In March of this year, the four Ninemile orphans did the same thing. They left their valley (with the collared female possibly pregnant) and strayed into new territory. Just two weeks earlier, they had passed within five feet of a sick, downed cow but made no attempt to kill it. Once outside their home range, however, they entered a rancher's pasture near Dixon, Montana, and killed two yearling steers weighing 450 pounds apiece.

"They got nervous," Ed Bangs says, "and when they came into that rancher's pasture, it was all new."

Wolves are going to kill livestock; after all, they're predators. But how many? And when, if ever, is it acceptable? In the West, the chronic livestock-killing wolves have historically been cripples whose wounds forced them to cross too far into human territory. In Minnesota, where most wolf-predation data has been collected, healthy wolves that prey on livestock often do so only after eating a dumped carcass. One taste of beef, it seems, and a new search image comes onto a wolf's screen.

Bangs won't speculate as to why, but after killing the steers, the orphans only partially consumed them. Until then, the Ninemile pack had confined its carnivorous tastes almost exclusively to deer. (In the fall, Jimenez had dropped another unfamiliar food, two dead bighorn rams, near the wolves' den, and the pack had been too frightened to even approach them. Finally, after several days, they worked up the courage to nibble at the carcasses before abandoning them.) Now they were familiar with the taste and scent of beef. Would they kill again?

No one waited to find out. In accordance with the deal struck between Fish and Wildlife and the MDFWP, federal Animal Damage Control personnel immediately helicoptered to Dixon and darted all four wolves with tranquilizers.

It wasn't a neat operation. When ADC workers went to gather the downed animals, one of the uncollared ones, a gray male, escaped. Still under the effect of the tranquilizer, he was able to rise and drag himself into the woods while the ADC people chased him.

That wolf got away.

There may never be a wilder wolf than that one. He has escaped traps, darts, helicopters, and people, and if he's learned his lesson he'll stay away from cows. He may take one or two, or even three or four a year, but he'll be one tough animal to catch.

When the news came out about the dead steers, a flood of hysterical rumors swept across Montana. For a while the story was that the wolves had killed two skiers, not steers, and callers from all over the state jammed the 911 emergency lines with reports of wolf sightings.

Ed Bangs pleaded for calm. "Everyone needs to relax a little," he told one reporter. "People have said they heard wolves, or they saw wolves chasing horses, or they saw them alongside roads. It's a classic response to the cattle depredations. People are getting excited."

The biggest tragedy of the wolf capture was that the young black female, the one thought to be pregnant, wouldn't be able to make a den in her hard-earned home, the safe, familiar Ninemile. She'd have to give birth to homeless pups, not an altogether unfamiliar story for her bloodline.

"It's a bad deal, but it's life," said Bangs. "Even if we lose them all in the next few years, it will be but a minor setback for wolf recovery. They're still coming back. I've said that all along."

Jimenez's heart, however, had been touched a little deeper. He talked about how terrible it had been to see the black female in the kennel, waiting to be released.

"I kept thinking we had gotten nowhere," he said. "I kept looking at her, in the same cage where we'd had her mother, and it was like nothing had changed. It was kind of eerie. It makes me question whether we really can help the wolf."

"There's that one that got away," I reminded Jimenez. "That's going to be a good, wild wolf."

"Yes," Jimenez said. He paused; he sounded tired. "I know the state of Montana's big enough for wolves. I just wonder if the people can be big enough."

After eight days in captivity, the three captured pups were set loose in Glacier, not far from where their mother had been released.

"They hit the ground running in all different directions," Jimenez told me later. One went south into the Bob Marshall Wilderness. Another went there too, then came back to his release site. The female went into the Swan area, where her mother had gone, and shortly afterward her radio-collar signals disappeared. She could have been denning, staying underground, or she could have been poisoned or shot.

And the fourth wolf, the one that wasn't caught? "We're living on thin ice," Jimenez said at the time. "People see him, but it's real hard to know. I get reports that he's in two different places at the same time.

"I've been chasing down some other reports we've got from down in the Bitterroot. I've been spending time there, trying to see if the wolf rumors are real. It's hard to tell yet. I've got some tracks and things like that, but they're at the size where it's either a smallish wolf or a large dog."

I tried to pick up Jimenez's spirits, noting how wolves seem to be able to follow precisely where other wolves have been—how they can find those scent stations with a near-mystical ability—and that if some wolf lover wanted wild wolves in Yellowstone, for instance, he could collect urine from someone's pet wolf and set up scent stations every ten miles or so, walking south from Canada along the Continental Divide, blazing a trail to the vast herds of nearly domesticated Yellowstone deer and elk.

"Yeah," Jimenez said, "biologists have joked about that possibility."

He smiled for a moment, then said, "They just follow each other. Nobody ever gave them that kind of credit. But just when you begin feeling good about the future, you spend some time talking with ranchers who are really negative on it, and you realize, boy, it's still an uphill battle."

FOR THE THREE relocated Ninemile orphans things ended badly. Two— a male and the possibly pregnant female—were shot by ranchers. (The female didn't have pups with her when she was found.) The other female wandered over the Continental Divide and killed a couple of lambs; she was recaptured and sent to Wolf Haven, a captive wolf facility in Washington State, where she'll spend the rest of her life in captivity.

Still, by midsummer of 1991, Jimenez had his good nature back. Maybe it was because he had another wolf to watch. A new wandering female —a three-year-old that had split from a pack in Glacier—was following the trail left by the original Marion female, the mother to the Ninemile wolves. This newest wolf had moved down through the Swan Valley, past Bigfork, over to Missoula, and into the Ninemile Valley. She seemed to be following her predecessor's exact steps, showing up in the Thisteds' pasture to lie down not ten yards from where the black female used to lie.

"She's been kind of bouncing around," Jimenez said, "in and out of the Ninemile—checking out the valley. And almost immediately she found another wolf; it's big and gray, and judging by its size we think it's a male."

What if these two wolves pick up the orphan pups' scent and follow it to Dixon? What will happen if they come to the spot where the steer kills occurred, the spot where the Ninemile pack's scent ends, where the pups were darted and lifted out by helicopter?

What if the big gray wolf that's traveling with this new Glacier female is one of those four orphan pups—the one that got away?

Will he howl, when he gets to that spot where the scent stops?

How could he not?

*October 1991*

# Rime of the Ancient Porcupine

*In the bad winter of 1939, the unholy deed was done.*

● ▲ ■

TIM CAHILL

This is a tale of murder most foul, of a crime against nature and man, of instant retribution. It is a tale for those who would believe that there are more things invisible than visible in the universe, and nonetheless true for the fact that it happened in the ancient times, which is to say, about 1939. It is a tale of storm blast and wondrous cold, of snowy cliffs and ice as green as emerald, a tale, in short, of a bad winter in the north country. The ice then, we might conjecture, was here, the ice was there, the ice was all around. It cracked and growled and roared and howled, as Samuel Taylor Coleridge would have it, like noises in a swound— which is a swoon—something unconscious, a frigid, brittle dream. However, this tale is no dream, but a true and locally well-known story. In the bad winter of 1939, the unholy deed was done. It happened no more than three miles from my house, tucked away in a pocketed groin of the Absaroka Mountains.

To understand the nature of the crime, however, it is first necessary to know a bit about the porcupines of the northern Rockies. They can be pestiferous animals. Sometimes called quill pigs, porcupines are actually large rodents. Vegetarians all, they enjoy the tender layer of tissue beneath the bark of living trees. When especially hungry, or perhaps in a destructive mood, porcupines may completely girdle and kill a tree. They have been known to splinter used ax-handles and canoe paddles for the salt and oil they contain.

Porcupines also relish rubber. A friend of mine once parked his car at a mountain trailhead. When he returned after a week of backpacking, he found that the car wouldn't start. Some animal had gnawed through the rubber on his generator coil, shorting it out. My friend decided to wait until morning to walk the ten miles down the old logging road to the main highway and hitchhike ten more miles into town for a replacement. That night, camped by the car, he heard a satisfied scratching and a moist munching under the hood. It was, of course, a porcupine, and the beast regarded him balefully, its large nocturnal eyes glinting in the glare of the flashlight. My friend levered the porcupine off his engine block with a long branch he was saving for his fire. He might have hammered the animal to death with the same branch, but that is not done, not here in the northern Rockies.

It took a full day to get back with the part he needed. He replaced the coil, and since he was already a day late for work, he drove the car hard down the logging road. About three miles from the main highway, the temperature gauge pegged at high and steam began spurting out from under the hood. My friend was more than a little irritated to discover that in his absence the porcupine had returned and eaten a hole through the underside of his bottom radiator hose.

We have more than our share of porcupines out here at the Poison Creek Ranch. About once every six months, one of my dogs, to its detriment, tries to eat a porcupine. The dogs kill skunks with great regularity, and they return to the house with their heads held high, proud and malodorous. But when they've been quilled by a porcupine, they skulk about outside the front door, afraid and ashamed to come in for the doctoring they need.

The porcupine does not run from a dog. He will, instead, present his backside. My dogs, like a man who continually burns his mouth on the first piece of pizza, do not learn from history. They suppose an animal's arsenal is invariably located about the head, since that is so in their own species. The porcupine does not throw his quills but drives its powerful tail into the dog's mouth, leaving dozens of barbed and needle-like quills in the dog's tongue, and in the roof and bottom of its mouth.

The quills, which are modified hairs, range in size from half an inch to three inches. Since they are barbed, the quills will, with time, work their way into the dog, eventually reaching the brain and killing it. For that reason, every quill must be quickly and carefully removed. I do this with needle-nose pliers I bought especially for the operation. You want to roll the dog onto its back, under a bright light, get its mouth open, and pull out the quills. The dogs are never enthusiastic about this operation, and one of them once blackened my eye with a front paw trying to push me away. These days, I put a quilled dog into a large burlap sack, which I tie around his neck. It takes half an hour of intense and sweaty struggle to stuff a pain-crazed 80-pound dog into a gunny sack.

I could, I suppose, wait for a fresh snow, track the porcupines, and blast them into eternity with the 12-gauge, but, as I say, that is not done in the northern Rockies. Since the days of the mountain men here, porcupines have been sacrosanct. Like the albatross in the old poem, a porcupine is considered a pious beast of good fortune, and for very practical reasons. A man or woman lost in the mountains hereabouts can usually find and kill a porcupine. In winter, especially, they show up as dark lumps in the crotches of bare trees. They do not run from man and may be killed with a branch or even a stone. The flesh, especially that of the tail, is rich and fatty, and the calories it contains may sustain a man for days. Of course, rabbits may be easily trapped, but their flesh is lean, its calories quickly burned away. There are documented tales of men who have eaten several rabbits a day while lost, men who died of what is known as "rabbit starvation."

So porcupines are slow-moving, ambulatory sources of food for the lost and injured, and that is why the killing of such a beast in any but the most dire circumstances is considered a dangerous and wanton act capable of generating the worst of luck. And in the bad winter of 1939, in the dismal sheen of the snowy cliffs, no more than three miles from my house, a man committed that very crime; and like the albatross in the old poem, the porcupine was avenged and death fires danced at night.

The man had built a wooden frame house, and he set it up on blocks so that he would not have to dig a foundation. As the long white mountain winter set in, the man discovered a major flaw in the design. Various small animals took to living under the house for shelter and warmth. Every night there was a commotion of yips and squeaks and howls. Every night, the sickly-sweet fragrance of skunk drifted up into his kitchen. The fellow was having trouble sleeping and eating, and as the drifts piled up over his windows and darkened the rooms, as the terrible psychic weight of cabin fever descended upon him, he developed a fanatical hatred for the squabbling things that lived under his house.

And so it happened that this man found a huge porcupine one dreary winter day. It was sitting on the lowest branch of a bare and icy tree, and the man who built his house on blocks looked upon that particular porcupine as the disturber of his sleep and the despoiler of his appetite. Perhaps he chuckled as he dug out the kerosene and matches. Quickly, he doused the porcupine, struck a match, and tossed it onto the animal, which erupted into a colorless flame. In its agony of fire, the porcupine ran to where it lived, ran to the area under the house. The flaming porcupine, this dying animal, set the wooden house aflame. It burned to the ground in a matter of hours.

The tale is true and can be verified. In my mind's eye I see that man, standing there thigh deep in a drift, shivering in an icy wind and looking mournfully at the last glowing, gloating embers smoldering away in the ashy puddle where his house used to be. It was a long and bitter trek to the nearest shelter, and I like to think that this man, who set a porcupine afire, walked like one that hath been stunned and is of sense forlorn. A sadder and a wiser man, I imagine, he rose the morrow morn.

*April/May 1981*

part

IV

THE
**W**ORLD
OUT
THERE

# CLUB DENALI

*Adrian the Romanian, the Honeymooners, and the Throbbing Members think they can tackle North America's highest peak. How hard can it be?*

● ▲ ■

JON KRAKAUER

**B**efore they'll let you climb Mount McKinley, the rangers who oversee mountaineering in Denali National Park make you sit through a tape-and-slide presentation depicting the perils of venturing onto the highest mountain in North America, in much the same way that the Army, before granting off-base passes to new recruits, shows them films depicting the ravages of VD. The ten-minute Denali show runs heavily to images of thundering avalanches, storm-flattened tents, hands deformed by horrible frostbite blisters, and grotesquely twisted bodies being pulled from the depths of enormous crevasses. Like the military's movies, the Denali show is graphic enough to make even the thickest skin crawl. But as a tool for promoting sensible behavior, it would appear that it's just as ineffective.

Take, for example, the case of Adrian Popovich, better known as Adrian the Romanian. A few years ago, Adrian—a loud man in his mid-twenties, with darkly handsome features and a volatile temper—somehow managed to flee his homeland, one of the Eastern Bloc's more cheerless satellites, and find his way to the western United States. He had done some climbing in Romania, enough to realize that he had a natural gift for it, and upon his arrival in America decided to pursue the sport seriously. Toward that end he spent most of his days hanging out at the "Rock" in Seattle—a 30-foot concrete escarpment on the University of Washington campus, where swarms of steel-fingered, Lycra-clad young men and women hone their 5.13 moves and engage in spirited bouldering duels. Adrian developed into one of the hotter climbers at the Rock, and it fanned the flames of his ambition: He announced that in the spring of 1986 he would solo McKinley and thereby become the first Romanian to stand atop the highest peak in North America. Upon hearing this, cynics were quick to point out that the challenges of McKinley were somewhat different from those posed by even the gnarliest routes on the Rock. They further noted that it was impossible, in the strict sense of the word, to "solo" a climb while in close proximity to some 300 people, that being the number of other climbers Adrian could expect to encounter on the route he intended to try. Adrian, however, was not about to be dissuaded by such niggling.

Nor, upon arriving in Alaska in May of last year, was he to be dissuaded when, in the course of registering for his climb, a mild-mannered Park Service ranger named Ralph Moore suggested that it was suicidal to attempt McKinley without a tent, or a shovel to dig snow caves, or a stove, all of which Adrian lacked. Without the latter to melt snow, Moore queried, just what did Adrian intend to drink during the three weeks it typically takes to climb the mountain? "I have money," Adrian replied, as if nothing could be more obvious. "I will buy water from other climbers."

Adrian was shown the grisly slide presentation; he was apprised of the fact that McKinley had killed more climbers than the Eiger; it was explained to him that by the time he was only halfway up the 20,320-foot peak he could expect to find conditions more severe than those at the North Pole, with temperatures of 40 below zero and winds that howled at 80 to 100 miles per hour for days and sometimes weeks at a stretch; he was given a booklet, which cautioned, among other things, that on McKinley "the combined effect of cold, wind, and altitude may well present one of the most hostile climates on Earth." Adrian's reaction to these caveats was to propose angrily that the rangers mind their own business.

Moore, who had no authority to keep Adrian off the mountain (and whose responsibility it would be to rescue him or retrieve his body should either action be called for), ultimately resigned himself to the fact that nothing was going to persuade the hotheaded Romanian to abandon his plans. All the ranger could do was try to see that somebody loaned Adrian a stove and a tent, and hope luck turned out to be on the guy's side.

It did, at least in the sense that Adrian didn't die. He actually managed to make it all the way to 19,000 feet without falling into any hidden crevasses or getting frostbite. But he had been too impatient in his ascent to acclimatize thoroughly, and he let himself become seriously dehydrated as well, thus violating two of the most fundamental rules of self-preservation at high altitude. As he plodded alone, gasping at the thin, frigid air, he began to feel increasingly nauseated and dizzy, and began to stumble.

Adrian was experiencing the onset of cerebral edema, a deadly swelling of the brain brought on by ascending too high, too fast. Terrified by what was happening to him, finding it harder and harder to think clearly or stand up, he nonetheless succeeded in dragging himself back down to 14,300 feet, whence he and another would-be soloist—a Japanese whose feet were so badly frostbitten that all ten toes had to be amputated— were evacuated by airplane to a hospital in Anchorage. When he,was handed a bill for his share of this risky air rescue, Adrian refused to pay, leaving the National Park Service to pick up the tab.

THE MOUNTAIN that officially bears the surname of our 25th president (an appellation that is largely and pointedly ignored by climbers in favor of Denali, the peak's Athabascan name) is so big that it beggars the imagination. One of the largest landforms on the planet, McKinley's hulking massif occupies 120 square miles, and its summit stands more than 17,000 vertical feet above the rolling tundra. Mount Everest, by comparison, rises a mere 12,000 feet from the plains at its base.

McKinley's bitterly contested summit was first reached in 1913 from the north by a party led by Hudson Stuck, the Episcopal archdeacon of the Yukon. It took 19 years for the peak to be climbed again, but in the ensuing decades approximately 5,000 have joined the Reverend Stuck. Along the way, McKinley has seen some memorable feats and personalities.

In 1961 the great Italian alpinist, Ricardo Cassin, led a team up the elegant granite buttress that bisects the mountain's steep south face, an impressive enough achievement to prompt a congratulatory cable from President Kennedy. In 1963 seven brash Harvard students (among them *Outside* contributing editor David Roberts) took a route directly up the center of the 14,000-foot, avalanche-swept Wickersham Wall, an act so bold or foolish that, 24 years later, it still hasn't been repeated. In the seventies and eighties, such bonafide heroes as Reinhold Messner, Doug Scott, Dougal Haston, and Renato Casarotto visited McKinley and left challenging new lines in their wakes.

Most people who attempt McKinley, it is safe to assume, do not do so seeking the solitude of the great outdoors. There are currently more than 20 routes to the summit, but an overwhelming majority of those who attempt the mountain do so by a single line, the West Buttress, a route pioneered by Bradford Washburn in 1951. In 1987, in fact, nearly 700 of the 817 climbers on McKinley thronged to the "Butt," as it is affectionately known. During the peak climbing months of May and June, while nearby faces and ridges are often empty, lines of climbers cover the West Buttress like ants. So many people try the route, Jonathan Waterman writes in *Surviving Denali*, that at the higher elevations where gale-force winds regularly scour all fresh snow from the slopes soon after it falls, climbers must "select cooking snow very carefully from among the wasteland of brown turds. . . . Fortunately, sometimes below 15,000 feet, snowfall will cover the excrement, the bodies, the trash, and the jettisoned gear."

The typical McKinley climber drops, on average, between $2,000 and $3,500 (a sum that rises to as much as $5,000 if he climbs with a commercial guide service, as 40 percent of McKinley climbers do), and subjects himself to three weeks of exceedingly cruel and unusual punishment. He does so not in order to commune with nature, but because he (or she: perhaps 10 percent of McKinley climbers are women) wants very badly to add the pinnacle of North America to his trophy collection. And by ganging up on the West Buttress—the easiest way up the mountain—he hopes to stack the odds in his favor as much as possible. Most years, McKinley still wins about half the time. Some years it does even better. Last April and May, for instance, Park Service records show that six out of every seven climbers on the mountain went home in defeat. One of them was me.

THINGS BEGAN WELL ENOUGH. Just 14 hours after pulling into Talkeetna—the comfortably seedy, dirt-street hamlet carved out of dense stands of spruce and alder 60 miles south of the mountain that is the time-honored point of embarkation for expeditions to McKinley—I was in a plane bound for base camp. I expected to have to wait the customary three or four days for flying weather, as I had the last time I'd flown into the Alaska Range, 12 years before, and was thus pleasantly surprised to find myself quickly shoehorned into the back of a small red Cessna owned by ace pilot Doug Geeting. Forty minutes later I was delivered intact to Kahiltna International Airport, a rutted-snow landing strip on the lower Kahiltna Glacier.

Exactly 13,320 vertical feet above the airport, and 15 circuitous miles to the north, the summit of McKinley glistened brightly in a flawless sky. To be torn from the security of the Fairview tavern in Talkeetna and dropped into a landscape of vertical rock and avalanching ice that dwarfed the human form into utter insignificance was rather disquieting, but every 15 minutes another Cessna or Heliocourier would buzz out of the sky to disgorge a load of climbers onto the glacier. The swelling ranks beside the landing strip went a long way toward softening the shock of the inhospitable new surroundings.

Thirty or 40 tents, dug into the slope above the landing strip, housed an army of climbers who were hooting and yelling at one another in at least five languages as they inventoried supplies and packed their loads for the climb ahead. Rob Stapleton—a tall, dour man hired jointly by the competing glacier pilots to live at Kahiltna International and try to maintain some semblance of order—shook his head at it all, and speculated that some of the folk around him were headed for trouble. "It's amazing," he opined, "how unorganized and fucked-up a lot of the groups already are by the time they get here. Too many of these guys are operating on about 90 percent energy and 10 percent brains."

This collective energy, misplaced or not, was a welcome antidote to the unrelieved drudgery of the slog from the airport up the lower glaciers, a 7,000-foot elevation gain that most parties take a week to cover. I had come to Alaska alone, but as I skied up the Kahiltna each day, I would inevitably be absorbed by one or another genial, motley procession—a seemingly endless line of climbers, trudging stoically upward with teetering, 100-pound loads that brought to mind scenes of the Klondike gold rush. That first week the weather was all you could ask for: At night the air had a wintery bite, enough snow fell to make for some memorable after-dinner powder skiing, and the days were generally filled with sun.

Occasionally a knot of climbers, already having met defeat, would pass in descent, offering warnings of sledgehammer winds and hellish cold above 14,000 feet, but those of us on our way up maintained a smug conviction that conditions would be different by the time we got up high. Even after encountering two Scotsmen whose teammate had just been helicoptered off the mountain after taking an 800-foot tumble, and two other climbers on their way down after nearly dying from high-altitude edema—first a Yugoslav, then a Pole, both with Himalayan experience—the optimism of those fresh off the Cessnas remained unshakable.

When registering climbers for McKinley, the rangers ask that each party provide them, for record-keeping purposes, with an official expedition name. The expeditions with whom I shared the mountain chose such official designations as "The Walking Heads," "Fat Rod," and "Dick Danger and the Throbbing Members." Upon pulling into the large camp at 14,300 feet that climbers use as a launching pad for assaults on the upper peak, I threw my pack down near a couple of Throbbing Members, who were in a heated argument with another climber.

"I tell you something, big guy," the non-Member spat contemptuously, "in my country you do that, they line you up and shoot you!" I had no idea what the discussion was about, but there was no mistaking that heavily accented voice, which I'd heard ranting similarly on many occasions at the Rock in Seattle: Adrian the Romanian was back on McKinley. You had to admire the guy's nerve, I thought: The rangers were still fuming about being stiffed for his last rescue bill.

Adrian, however, had had plenty of time to mull over the debacle of the year before, and was determined not to fail again. "All winter, it is all I can think about." he explained. "It make me crazy." Though he had again come alone, this year he had assembled a full arsenal of top-of-the-line gear, including not one but two tents, and had double-carried enough food and fuel to 14,300 feet to stay on the upper mountain for two months if need be, an approach that reflected a far more enlightened view of acclimatization.

He had, in fact, already been up to 19,000 feet on two occasions and had prudently turned around both times because conditions were less than perfect. I tell you something," the new Adrian was now in the habit of admonishing anyone he could buttonhole, "this is a very big mountain. You make one little mistake, it really kick your ass." From the looks of the way the camp was dug in, by the time most people had reached 14,300 feet they were starting to believe it.

The "camp" was in reality a full-blown tent city with a population that fluctuated between 40 and 120 as parties came and went. It spread out across the edge of a desolate glacial plateau. To one side, the upper ramparts of the mountain soared in a single sweep of granite and snow and gleaming blue ice, culminating in the summit more than a vertical mile above; to the other side, the flat shelf of the plateau ran for several hundred yards before breaking off abruptly in a clean, 4,000-foot drop.

To prevent their tents from being ripped from their moorings and blown off that drop, climbers had taken to placing their shelters in deep bunkers surrounded by massive snow-block walls. The walls lent the camp a battlefield air, as if a barrage of incoming artillery was expected at any moment. Carving such bunkers is a formidable chore, so when I found a good, deep one that had recently been vacated, I immediately laid claim to it, even though it was located next to the camp's continually busy communal latrine: a plywood throne, completely open to the elements, that had an inspiring view, but left tender flesh dangerously exposed to the full brunt of a windchill that regularly dipped below minus 70 degrees.

The opposite side of camp, the high-rent district, was distinguished by a complex of igloos, bombproof dome tents, and propane-heated Weatherports that served as the offices and residences of Dr. Peter H. Hackett and his staff. Every summer since 1982, Hackett—a lean, laconic, tired-looking climber/physician who is the world's foremost authority on high-altitude pathology—has set up shop at 14,300 feet to conduct research into the mysterious ailments that afflict humans at altitude. He comes here, he said, because he can always count on finding a reliable supply of very sick climbers to study: "Lots of people on McKinley don't know what they're getting into, and climb too fast, and become seriously ill. Fresh guinea pigs are always staggering in the door." At least a dozen of these guinea pigs would now be dead were it not for the ministrations of Hackett and his team.

Hackett was quick to emphasize that "we never perform experiments on walk-in patients that we wouldn't perform on ourselves." At that very moment, for example, his research partner, Rob Roach, was in the process of testing a new, blue-colored medication for altitude sickness. From the green cast to Roach's skin, and the blue vomit splattered over his white vapor-barrier boots, it appeared that the new drug was less than completely effective.

Hackett's team, I later learned, not only received no remuneration for their lifesaving labors, but—having failed to obtain funding in both 1986 and 1987—met most of the project's expenses out of their own pockets. I asked one of the doctors, Howard Donner, why they volunteered to spend their summers in such a godforsaken place. "Well," he explained as he stood shivering in a blizzard, reeling from nausea and a blinding headache while attempting to repair a broken radio antenna, "it's sort of like having fun, only different."

THE WEST BUTTRESS of McKinley, it is often said, has all the technical challenges of a long walk in the snow. That is more or less true, but it's also true that if you should, say, trip on a bootlace at the wrong moment during that walk, you will probably die. Between 16,000 and 17,000 feet, for instance, the route follows the crest of a knife-edge ridge that features a 2,000-foot drop on one side and a 3,000-foot drop on the other. Furthermore, even the flattest, most benign-looking terrain can be riddled with hidden crevasses, many of which are big enough to swallow a Greyhound bus, no problem.

Not that a crevasse has to be huge to be dangerous. In February, 1984, Naomi Uemura—the renowned Japanese mountaineer and explorer—disappeared after making the first solo winter ascent of McKinley. It is widely believed that he met his end in one of the relatively small crevasses that split the broad slope between the camp at 14,300 feet and the knife-edge ridge at 16,000. Indeed, last spring a pair of newlyweds from Denver almost ended their honeymoon (for reasons known only to them, they had decided to spend it on McKinley) in one of those same slots.

The Honeymooners—the name under which the expedition of Ellie and Conrad Miller was officially registered—were camped with Adrian the Romanian and three other expeditions in a crowded, poorly protected tenement of a bunker that happened to be next door to mine at 14,300 feet. On May 16 the Millers climbed to 17,200 feet to cache a load of food and fuel for a later summit push. That evening, they were descending to their camp at 14,300 when Conrad, who was in the lead, suddenly broke through a thin snow bridge and found himself plummeting through space, "ricocheting like a pinball" between the walls of a narrow but very deep crevasse. The slope above was fairly steep, and the force of Conrad's fall jerked Ellie off her feet and pulled her toward the hole. Moments before she, too, would have disappeared into the crevasse she managed to dig in the pick of her ice axe and bring them both to a stop.

Dangling 50 feet below the surface in the blue twilight of the crevasse, Conrad first made a quick examination of his trousers to see if his sphincter had let go (it hadn't), then checked for broken bones (there were none). Then, with Ellie tugging on the rope from above, he slowly front-pointed up one of the vertical walls of the slot. As he struggled back onto the surface, he was gripped with the conviction that had he gone all the way to the bottom, still hundreds of feet below, "the last thing I would have seen would have been Uemura's frozen corpse."

Both Conrad, a 36-year-old architect, and Ellie, a 28-year-old retail clerk, were badly shaken, but they were also very determined to get to the summit of McKinley, and on May 18—despite the ongoing storm and the forecast of an even bigger one at any moment—they headed back up to 17,200 feet, intending to recover their cache, hang tough until the weather got better, and then make a dash for the top.

But the storm, which grew worse that day, proved to be considerably more severe and of considerably longer duration than the Honeymooners had reckoned. Temperatures at 17,200 feet dropped to minus 50, and gale-force winds raked the peak for more than a week, driving the windchill well down into triple digits. Not only was climbing out of the question, so was sleeping; Conrad and Ellie were reduced for the most part to lying in their tent with all their extra clothes on, praying that their shelter didn't blow apart at the seams. (Indeed, shortly before the Honeymooners arrived at 17,200, a dome tent—one of the sturdiest made—had done just that, exploding in the middle of the night and leaving its three occupants in a very bad way.)

The gale that blasted the upper peak was terrifying to behold, even from the relative safety of 14,300 feet. Whenever the wind lulled at the lower camp, a much deeper, wilder, wailing roar—like the scream of a jet engine opened to full throttle—could be heard coming from the ridge 3,000 feet above. At the onset of the storm, most of the 20 or 30 climbers camped at 17,200 immediately bailed out and battled their way down to 14,300, but not the Honeymooners.

EARLY IN THEIR STAY at 17,200, Conrad and Ellie spied the entrance to an ice cave. Thinking it had to offer more secure accommodations than their tent, Ellie went to investigate. It turned out to be a T-shaped affair carved deep into the slope, with a 15-foot-long entrance tunnel that led to a perpendicular main tunnel at least twice that length. It was, without question, infinitely more stormproof than the tent, but the briefest tour of the premises convinced Ellie that she'd rather take her chances out in the maelstrom.

The inside of that cave, she says, "was incredibly grim: really dark and damp, and extremely claustrophobic. The place was a hellhole; it was absolutely hideous. There was no way I was going to move into that thing."

The tunnels were only four feet high, garbage littered the floor, and the walls were stained with God only knew what. Most disturbing of all, though, were the creatures Ellie found inhabiting the subterranean gloom.

"There were seven or eight very strange guys in there, she says. "They'd been in the cave for days, and had long since run out of food. They'd been just sitting there, shivering with all their extra clothes on in the suffocating air, breathing these thick stove fumes and singing theme songs from TV shows, getting stranger and stranger. I couldn't get out of there fast enough."

The cavemen, as it happened, were members of two separate expeditions. One of them—a trio from Arizona and Ohio called the Crack o' Noon Club—had actually been in there only a day or so. The other and decidedly stranger group had been in the cave for the better part of a week. It turned out to be none other than Dick Danger and the Throbbing Members.

The Members—a.k.a. Michael Dagon, Greg Siewers, Jeff Yates, and Stephen "Este" Parker—were four tough, arrogant, in-your-face Alaskans in their late twenties and early thirties. They possessed very little in the way of mountaineering experience, but they had done their homework and were bent on bagging the summit of McKinley at almost any cost. Dagon—Dick Danger himself—had sworn off red meat and alcohol for a year to prepare for the expedition, and had trained and schemed so obsessively that his wife had left him.

The Members, it seems, had first arrived at 14,300 feet on May 9; a day later, Yates came down with pulmonary edema—a mild case, but a gurgling, wheezing, potentially life-threatening case nonetheless. Most climbers would have promptly retreated, but the three healthy Members left Yates to recover for a day at 14,300, carried a cache of food up to 16,000 feet, and returned to 14,300 for the night. The next morning, having decided that Yates wasn't getting any worse, all four headed up onto the knife-edge ridge to establish a high camp in preparation for a summit bid.

When the Members arrived at 17,200 feet on May 13, they took up residence in their tents in a poorly built bunker, alongside the sturdier bunkers of a half-dozen other expeditions, including a party of Park Service personnel led by ranger Scott Gill, a group led by a seasoned Alaskan guide named Brian Okonek, and a SWAT team on vacation from Montreal. At the time, the Members figured they had enough food for three days, maybe four if they stretched it. By the 18th it was still storming, and the food was almost gone.

To complicate matters, that afternoon ranger Gill received a weather report over the radio predicting that an even nastier storm front—the forecasters were calling it "a major three-day storm"—was due to slam into the upper mountain within a matter of hours. When a voice cut in over the radio to ask just how major, the person relaying the forecast replied with a macabre chuckle, "Well, major enough so that when it hits, everyone who's above 15,000 feet is going to die."

"All of a sudden," Yates says, "it was like, 'Wow, maybe we'd better be getting out of here.' " He reports that other teams "started booking down right away, but it took us three hours to pack up, and by the time we'd gotten under way the storm was on us for real. Right away we lost the trail in the whiteout. The wind was so bad that someone in the last party to leave camp ahead of us had to abandon his pack to keep going. By the time we were two rope lengths away, it was obvious we weren't going to make it, so we turned around and headed back up to 17,200."

At that point, says Dagon, "we figured we were in deep shit." They reerected their tents and anchored them to the slope with snow pickets and an elaborate web of climbing rope, but feared that the rising gale would still rip the shelters right off the ridge. It was at that point that Brian Okonek, secure enough inside his thick bunker, told them about the ice cave. He had built it, he said, during a bad storm in 1983 and it saved the lives of 18 climbers.

The intervening years had plugged Okonek's cave full of drifting snow, and it took the Members, assisted by another expedition called 5150, six hours of digging—during which all four Members received frostbitten fingers and toes—to reexcavate it. Once they were all moved in, however, they took a perverse liking to cave life: Despite frostbite and lack of food, they resolved to wait out the storm, no matter how long it took, and then go bag the summit.

LIFE AT 14,300 FEET, meanwhile, was undeniably better than the wretched existence of those dug in at 17,200, but it was not without its hardships. Trapped in camp but relatively free of the storm that raged above, we residents of 14,300 initially bided our time cheerfully enough—flying kites, skiing the crusty powder on the protected slopes immediately above camp, practicing ice climbing on nearby serac walls. But as the storm dragged on—and food, fuel, and energy began to flag—a collective depression settled over our embattled city.

When word came over the radio in the medical tent confirming rumors

that five well-liked climbers had been killed in avalanches on the neighboring peaks of Mount Foraker and Mount Hunter, the air of gloom
deepened further still. People took to staying in their miserable little
bunkers day in and day out, bickering and shivering inside their tents,
emerging only to visit the latrine or shovel out from under the snowdrifts.
"It was your idea to come on this damn expedition," I overheard someone
in a nearby tent whining to his partner. "I told you we should have gone
rock climbing in Yosemite!"

As the storm continued, trade in critical supplies became brisk and
cutthroat. Expeditions with an abundance of some particularly valuable
commodity like toilet paper, cigarettes, Diamox (a medication to prevent
altitude sickness), or Tiger Milk bars found increasingly favorable rates
of exchange. I had to trade away an entire half-pound of Tillamook cheese
to secure three Diamox tablets. Adrian, who had an enviable hoard of
food, was able to ease the interminable boredom by renting a Walkman
from a hungry American climber for the ridiculously low rate of one
pemmican bar per day.

In the midst of those dark days I began to see Adrian's fiasco the year
before in a different, more sympathetic light. I was forced to admit that
on this, my first trip to Denali, I too had grossly underestimated the
mountain. I had listened to the ranger's warnings; I had heard no less
experienced an alpinist than Peter Habeler pronounce that McKinley's
storms, "are some of the worst I have ever experienced"; I knew that
when Dougal Haston and Doug Scott had climbed McKinley together
just six months after standing on the summit of Everest, Haston had said
they'd been forced to draw "on all our Himalayan experience just to
survive." And yet, somehow—like Adrian in 1986—I hadn't really believed any of it. This was reflected in the corners I'd cut: I'd brought
along a pitiful ten-year-old sleeping bag and a bargain-basement tent, and
had neglected to pack a down jacket, overboots, a snow saw, or any snow
pickets. I figured the West Buttress to be a farmers' route; I mean, how
challenging could a climb that succumbed to more than 300 freds and
hackers a year possibly be?

Plenty challenging for the likes of me. I was continually miserable, and
frequently on the brink of disaster. My tent was starting to shred even
in the relative calm at 14,300. The unceasing cold caused my lips and
fingers to crack and bleed. At night, even wearing every article of clothing
I had, it was impossible to stave off violent shivering attacks. Condensed
breath would build up an inch of frost on the inside of my tent walls,

creating an ongoing indoor blizzard as the walls shook in the wind, and anything not stowed inside my sleeping bag—camera, sunscreen, water bottles, stove—would freeze into a useless, brittle brick. My stove did in fact self-destruct from the cold early in the trip; had a kind soul named Brian Sullivan not taken pity on me and lent me his spare, I would—to paraphrase Dick Danger—have been in deep yogurt.

The storm reached a new level of violence on the morning of May 21. That evening, however—despite a forecast of high winds and heavy snowfall for at least five more days—the sky cleared and the wind quit. By the following morning it was 30 below and a few small lenticular clouds had reappeared over the summit of Foraker, but it was still calm and otherwise clear, so I packed a light rucksack and accepted an invitation to join a four-man party led by Tom Hargis—a Himalayan veteran who had made the second ascent of notorious Gasherbrum IV in 1986—to attempt a one-day 6,000-foot push for the summit. As I pulled out of camp, Adrian took a look at the sky, let out a cackle, and yelled, "Good luck, dude: You sure going to need it! I think maybe I find you up there later, frozen like fish!"

By the time we reached the start of the knife-edge ridge, two hours after setting out, the breeze had risen to 20 knots, and clouds were starting to obscure the sun. Upon reaching 17,000 feet an hour later, we were climbing in a full-blown blizzard, with near-zero visibility and a 40-knot wind that froze exposed flesh in seconds. At that point, Hargis, who was in the lead, quietly did an about-face and headed down, and nobody questioned the decision. After surviving the West Ridge of Everest and Gasherbrum IV, Hargis was apparently not interested in buying the farm in pursuit of the Butt.

WITH THE RETURN of the storm on the 22nd, the Honeymooners finally threw in the towel. That afternoon they stumbled into camp at 14,300 feet, completely whipped but with an astounding bit of news: The strange guys in the cave had made the summit.

One by one, other parties had gradually abandoned their fortified encampments at 17,200, but Dick and the Members had hung tough. Further excavations in their shelter had revealed just enough old cached food—some ancient but edible oatmeal, a little chocolate, a can of tuna and another of kippered herring—to sustain them. When their stove had started to malfunction, they mooched melted snow to drink from their original cave mates, the 5150 expedition.

5150 was a team of four Alaskans who took their name from a Van Halen album, and their inspiration from regular inhalations of Matanuska Thunderfuck, a legendary strain of Cannibis sativa cultivated in the 49th state. The 5150 crew boasted, in fact, that they had consumed more than a hundred joints of the potent weed between Kahilma International and 17,200 feet. Even this, however, was not enough to prevent one member from becoming extremely hypothermic after only a day in the cave, so his teammates attempted to revive him by upping his intake further still. "It was kind of pathetic," Mike Dagon says. "They kept telling him. 'It's gotten you this far, it can get you the rest of the way, too.' But when the guy still hadn't warmed up after two days in the cave, the 5150 boys decided to make a break for it and bailed out."

The departure of 5150 and the functioning stove might have had dire consequences for the Members, but no sooner had 5150 moved out than the Crack o' Noon Club moved in. The Nooners also proved to have a working cooker, and were no less generous with it.

"Mornings in the cave," Dagon admits, were real depressing. I mean, you'd wake up and some guy'd be snoring in your face, there'd be nothing to eat, and all you had to look forward to was another day of staring at each other in an ice hole. But we managed to keep it together pretty well. To kill time we played trivia games, or talked about the food we were going to eat when we got down, and Este taught us the theme songs from 'Gilligans Island' and 'I Dream of Jeannie.' "

Then, on the evening of May 21, the gale suddenly abated. Dick and the Members were frostbitten, severely dehydrated, weak from hunger, stupid from the altitude, and sick from breathing the carbon monoxide put off by the stove. But they also subscribed to the "no guts, no glory" school of alpinism, and figured the mountain might not see clear skies again for another month. They did their best to ignore their infirmities, and all but Greg Siewers—the only experienced climber among them— mobilized to make an assault on the summit. At 9:30 P.M., in the company of the Crack o' Noon Club, they emerged from their burrow and started upward.

The Members moved painfully slowly in the bitter night air, and were soon left behind by the three Crack o' Nooners. At 18,500 feet, just after midnight, Dagon lost one of his mittens while trying to repair a mechanical ascender he was using on a short piece of fixed line. A few minutes later, Yates says, "Mike told me his hand was cold, and I looked down and saw that it was bare, but Mike didn't seem to realize it. I didn't know how long it had been like that, but I could see he was in trouble and starting to lose it bad. I took his hand and shoved it inside my jacket."

When Dagon's hand had warmed up, a spare mitten was produced, and the Members continued upward until 5:30 A.M., at which time they'd reached the base of the final headwall at 19,000 feet. There they had to stop again, this time for a full hour, to warm Dagon's hands and feet on Yates's and Parker's bellies. "Este told Mike that he was going seriously hypothermic, that we should go down," says Yates, but Mike said no way, not when we were that close, and he reached deep and found the strength to keep going up the last thousand feet."

As they made their way up the summit ridge, they could see the graceful spires of Mount Huntington and the Mooses Tooth poking surrealistically out of a thick layer of clouds blanketing the Ruth Glacier, a distant 13,000 feet below. "I knew in an abstract, intellectual sort of way," says Yates, "that it was a beautiful view, but I couldn't get myself to care about it: I'd been up all night; I felt totally strung out; I was just too tired."

At 9:20 on the morning of May 22, the Members finally stood on the summit of McKinley. The pinnacle of North America, Mike Dagon reports, consists of "these insignificant bumps on a rounded ridge, with one bump rising a little higher than the others. That's all. It was incredibly anticlimactic: I guess I expected there to be fireworks, and music playing in my head or something, but there wasn't anything like that. As soon as we got there we turned around and started down."

Within minutes after the Members topped out, the layer of clouds they'd first seen hovering over the Ruth had climbed the 13,000 feet to the summit: The 16-hour window of good weather had slammed shut. For the next six hours they fought their way back through a whiteout to 17,200. Only a trail of bamboo tomato stakes, stuck into the snow every ropelength on the way up by the Crack o' Nooners, enabled the Members to make it back to their cave, which they did after 18 straight hours of climbing. Once in the cave, the Members were pinned down for two more foodless days, but on May 24 they finally managed to struggle down to 14,300, where Rob Roach and Howard Donner labored over their frozen digits in the medical tent for several hours.

BY DEMONSTRATING what could be achieved with bullheaded determination and a high pain threshold, the Members—one of only a handful of expeditions to make the summit in May—should have inspired the rest of us at 14,300 to suck it in a little harder and take our own best shot at greatness. By then, however, I was running low on Fig Newtons, and had developed a powerful thirst for something more than melted snow, so on May 26 I packed my tent, locked down my ski bindings, and bid my comrades-in-arms adieu.

As I shouldered my pack to go, Adrian looked wistfully off to the south toward Talkeetna, and started muttering about how the weather didn't really look like it was going to improve anytime soon. "Maybe," he thought out loud, "the best thing is for me to go down like you, climb McKinley next year instead." But a moment later he turned his gaze back toward the peak and set his jaw. As I poled off down the glacier, Adrian was still standing there, staring up at the summit slopes, conjuring up images, I have no doubt, of the glories awaiting the first Romanian to climb McKinley.

*December 1987*

# SHIVA WINKED

*Being a reverential account of wildwater rafting in the foothills of the Himalayas*

● ▲ ■

TIM CAHILL

"Ah," N. N. Badoni said, "your master will not seek you. You will seek your master. I believe you are seeking your master even while you deny this to me and to yourself."

A day before, rafting on a river that drops out of a snowfield in the Himalayas, I had been thrown out of a boat and into a rapid, where I spent some time tumbling underwater in nature's frigid spin-and-rinse cycle. This was followed by a fast rush through a couple more downriver rapids that featured numerous unpleasant collisions with boulders of varying size and unvarying solidity. The successive impacts necessitated some predictably unsuccessful attempts to breathe underwater. My life did not pass before my eyes, but somewhere in the middle of the third rapid, cartwheeling along ass over teakettle, caroming off the rocks, the phrase "holy shit, this is serious" began ringing through my mind. It was high noon, and even deep underwater, I could see the bright mountain sun above. It shimmered on the surface of the water, nuclear bright, and I fought toward it, feeling the surface retreat from me even as I swam. It was like a bad dream, a real tooth-grinder, and I longed to rise to the light, to breathe, to break through to the other side.

Now, 30 hours later, sitting in a hotel restaurant, there was a lingering congestion in my lungs, and I felt as if someone had taken a baseball bat to my entire body. N.N. Badoni, a sweet-shop owner in this north Indian town of Dehra Dun, suggested I might consider my swim a religious experience. N.N. was an avid trekker and a devout Hindu.

I am not much of a fan of the Hindu religion, associating it as I do with the pestiferous weenies known as Hare Krishnas, whose panhandling presence in U.S. airports results in such mind-boggling exchanges as:

"We're giving away copies of this book. It's 5,000 years old."

"5,000 years?" Stunned disbelief. "It looks brand new."

My experience thus far with holy types in India, I told N. N., made the Krishnas seem like a class act.

N.N. agreed that some of the holy men who populate the subcontinent like rats in a granary were undoubtedly transparent frauds and despicable money-grubbers. Still, he felt there were teachers of spiritual distinction, teachers who did not come to you. They were men you searched for in your soul. And when you found them, you would know. He mentioned a pair of swamis, now deceased, whose teachings had enriched his life.

I nodded politely, and N.N. bought me another beer. He was of the priestly Brahmin caste and did not, himself, drink. N.N. had provided research for Garry Weare's book, *Trekking in the Indian Himalaya*, and had spent many years studying the Garhwal region to the north, where I had just been. Located in the lush Himalayan foothills that rise above the blistered plains of northern India, the Garhwal is considered the Abode of the Gods and is replete with Hindu pilgrimage sites: Gangotri, near the source of the sacred Ganges River; Yamunotri, where pilgrims boil rice in the hot springs below the temple of the goddess Yamunotri so they may eat the "food of the gods"; Kedarnath, the divine resting place of the god Shiva; and Badrinath, the home of the god Vishnu. The Garhwal is the holiest and most sacred area in all of India.

I had been rafting the Tons, one of the innumerable glacier-fed rivers of the Garhwal. It is a little-known tributary of the Ganges, and at its source are the snowfields of a 20,720-foot mountain called Bandarpunch, the monkey's tail. The Tons is considered holy to Shiva, one of the most complex of the Hindu gods. Shiva blows hot and cold: He is at once Shiva the Beneficent and Shiva the Avenger. In the homes along the Tons there are small altars where candles burn below bright, printed posters of the ambiguous god. Here is Shiva carrying, in his four hands, a trident, a deerskin, a drum, and a club with a skull at the end; Shiva with a serpent around his neck; Shiva wearing a necklace of skulls. The streak of blue in his hair represents the Ganges, for it is Shiva who brought the Holy River to earth, breaking its fall from heaven by allowing it to trickle through his matted hair. Shiva is usually depicted with a third eye in the middle of his forehead. When the eye is closed, Shiva is pacific and the figure symbolizes a search for inward vision. When it is open, Shiva the Wrathful rains fire and destruction upon the earth.

Such tales of the gods, N.N. said, aren't necessarily the literal truth of the creation. They are a way of *thinking* about creation, life, and the meaning thereof.

It is a commonplace observation that India, and northern India in particular, has been a hotbed of innovative spirituality since the dawn of civilization. Hindus, Moslems, Jainists, Sikhs, Buddhists, and Christians exist side by side, and all react one upon the other so that over the centuries it has become religion—colorful, earnest, variegated—that defines the country. Indians, as a people, are intoxicated with religion, and even a visitor of sharp and jaundiced opinions is likely to be tumbled willy-nilly in the torrent of spiritual concerns.

N.N. was right, of course. My little swim in the Tons had been an exercise in perceived mortality. Food for compulsive thought. I couldn't, for instance, shake this terrifying religious image of Shiva as I'd seen him in the posters: Shiva the Pacific, the inward-looking; suddenly the third eye snaps open and there is piercing fire, nuclear white and final.

I thanked N.N. for the beer and the conversation and hobbled off to my room. When you begin to imagine strange three-eyed gods winking at you, it's time to regroup, reconsider, change your religion, even finish the last beer and go to bed.

DELHI IS THE CAPITAL of India, and its administrative center, New Delhi, is often described as a city of gardens. Unfortunately, I had come to this otherwise graceful place at the worst of times, which is to say, during the month of May. Afternoon temperatures rose to 110 degrees and would hold there for another month until the cooling rains of the monsoon. Dust, fine as talc, floated over everything and colored the sky a dull, whiskey brown. In the countryside, whirlwinds swept over the baking plain, and at a distance, it was impossible to tell the sky from the earth.

Delhi's heat in May can try men's souls. In 1986, on May 13, a man named Gupta killed his wife because he believed she had been sleeping with another man named Gupta. Eight persons—members of a wedding party who had asked for some water at a temple—were injured in a fracas with temple keepers, who believed the water would be used to mix alcoholic drinks. A civil servant who had not been promoted at the dairy board left a note excoriating his superiors, then killed himself.

There was Santa Ana tension in the still-burning air of the city, but May and June are also months of snowmelt in the Himalayas, the months the foothills erupt in wildflowers, the months most auspicious for a pilgrimage to the cool beauty of the sacred Garhwal.

SIXTEEN OF US were camped in a lush meadow by a wide eddy in the Tons River, in the Abode of the Gods. There was the scent of rhododendron in the air, and the temperature, at four in the afternoon, stood just shy of 80 degrees. The river valley was narrow, 400 yards across, and the hills rose steep and spirelike on either side, obscuring a glittering ridge of the high Himalayas to the north. There were leafy alders in the meadow. Deodar cedars, similar to lodgepole pines, forested the higher slopes. In geological terms, it was a young river valley, and the Tons, fed by spring snowmelt, was running high and fast.

It was our first day on the river, and Jack Morison laid it out for his nine paying passengers. Jack is the president and chief guide of White Magic Unlimited, a rafting-and-trekking business out of Mill Valley, California. He had made the first descent of the river six years ago. His original plan, when his company was just starting out, had been to raft the more well-known Yamuna River, of which the Hindu scriptures say: "No mortal mocks her fury; no mortal stops her onward flow." But the Yamuna struck Morison as a pretty tame ribbon of water, about Class II whitewater ("rapids of medium difficulty with clear, wide passages"), and he didn't think American mortals would be willing to travel all the way to India for a gentle float trip. Hiking east, however, over an icy ridge, he came upon the Tons. It was his dream river, a river he could build his company around.

As Jack spoke to our group, local people from the nearby village of Mori gathered about. The children came first, followed by old men, and finally, by the men who seemed to hold positions of authority in the village. They wore clean Western-style clothes in subdued colors. The women did not come into our camp; they sat up on the hills in tight little groups, and occasionally the wind would carry the tinkle of giggles down into the meadow where we sat.

This would be the fourth time the river had ever been run, Jack said. The trip was really a "commercial exploratory," which meant that there would be a lot of time spent scouting the rapids ahead and deciding on strategy.

There was plenty of water, but what set the Tons apart from other big-water rivers Jack knew—he mentioned the Bío-Bío in Chile and the Zambezi in Zambia—was the "consistency" of the whitewater. "It's one rapid after another," he said, "almost 80 miles of Class III and IV and even Class V rapids. The whitewater sections are separated by a hundred yards or less of flat water, which is probably moving at five or seven miles an hour." Class V rapids are defined as having "extremely long, difficult, and violent rapids that follow each other almost without inter- ruption . . . plenty of obstacles, big drops, violent current, and very steep gradient. . . ." The obstacles and drops on the Tons meant the rafts would have to do a lot of evasive maneuvering in heavy water. It was a very "technical" river.

The major danger, of course, was that we would be thrown from the rubber rafts, or that the rafts would flip. A person might be held down for some time in a major hole, might be thumped up and down in a circular motion—"Maytagged"—but to be swept through several con- secutive rapids would be even worse. "On most rafting rivers," Jack said, "there will be a quiet pool at the end of a rapid." On the Tons, however, the rapids were closely linked, and even the strongest swimmer could be dragged from one rapid to another. "The water is cold," Jack said. "It's all spring snowmelt now, and the longer you're in it, the more it saps your strength. Swim too many rapids, and you'll be too weak to make it to the bank. If you go in, do everything possible to get out after the first rapid."

Such was the nature of our pilgrimage.

A MAN FEELS A FOOL. Here I was, sitting under an alder in the meadow, trying to read a book titled *Hindus of the Himalayas* and getting absolutely nowhere because I was surrounded by a hundred or so Hindus of the Himalayas who wanted to know what I was reading.

Gerald Berreman's book on the region's ethnography says that plains Brahmins consider the hill people to be rude bumpkins. They live in this most religiously significant area of India, but according to Berreman, they engage in "frequent meat-and-liquor parties . . . are unfamiliar with scripture, largely ignore the great gods of Hinduism, marry across caste lines," and do other things that made me think I'd enjoy their company.

I read that passage to a man named Ajaypal Rana, who declared it "blasphemy." His tone was mild, unconcerned. He might just as well have said the passage was "interesting" for all the passion in his voice. I read on. "Says here that people 'conceal these activities' and 'project behavior indicating adherence to the accredited values of society.' "

Mr. Rana smiled and asked if our rubber rafts were filled with helium.

"Just air," I said. My friend seemed disappointed at the technological poverty of this arrangement.

THE NIGHT WAS JUST COOL ENOUGH for the thinnest of sleeping bags, and I had laid mine out under one of the leafy alders, in a field of calf-high marijuana and mint. The breeze felt like velvet, and the stars swirled above in the clear mountain air. Far to the south the sky flickered blue as heat lightning shimmered over the baking plain of the Ganges River.

We had talked for several hours, the Hindus of the Himalayas and I. Some were men with obvious physical handicaps, but they were teachers or farmers or tailors. There were no beggars among the hill people.

Which had not been the case in Delhi. The heat, pounding down from above and then rising up off the concrete, kept battalions of beggars working feverishly. There was no shade, no place to sit, and so the horribly mutilated hopped or rolled or lurched along, hands (or whatever passed for hands) out, beseeching looks on their faces. The novelist and travel writer V. S. Naipaul, a West Indian Hindu who has written two brilliant books about his travels in India, the land of his grandfather, found the sheer numbers of beggars particularly distressing. In *India: A Wounded Civilization* he wrote: "The very idea of beggary, precious to Hindus as religious theater, a demonstration of the workings of karma, a reminder of one's duty to oneself and one's future, has been devalued. And the Bombay beggar, displaying his usual mutilations (inflicted in childhood by the beggar-master who had acquired him, as proof of the young beggar's sins in a previous life) now finds, unfairly, that he provokes annoyance rather than awe. The beggars themselves, forgetting the Hindu function, also pester tourists; and the tourists misinterpret the whole business, seeing in the beggary of the few the beggary of all."

There had been, in Delhi, a young man, naked but for a white loincloth. He was lean and dark, starkly muscled, and his right leg had been amputated just above the knee. He saw me—an obvious tourist—across a wide boulevard choked with the chaotic late-afternoon traffic that, in India, is a form of population control: That day, in Delhi alone, three died in accidents and 17 were injured. The man came for me, threading his way nimbly through the cars, hopping on one bare foot and a crutch fashioned from the branch of a tree. I was amazed at his dexterity, at the athletic fluidity of his movements.

The beggar reached the sidewalk, and just for a moment I saw triumph in his face, and a kind of joy. But as he fell in to hop-step beside me, the light died in his eyes and he stared fixedly with a wet and pathetic spaniel-eyed beggar's gaze. "Alms," he said.

I am a man who habitually doles out spare change to winos, seeing, I suppose, the possibility that I might, one day, total my karma and find myself sitting in an alley behind a tattoo parlor swigging muscatel from a bottle in a paper bag. But this idea of the sins of the previous life resulting in the mutilation of children by beggar-masters and misery pimps . . . I would not, I decided, perpetuate this system. I would not, as a matter of principle, give money to these beggars.

"Alms," the one-legged athlete moaned.

I stared through him and silently chanted the mantra that makes beggars disappear. "You are invisible . . ."

He hopped along by my side for three blocks—"you are invisible"— then peeled off and made for the other side of the street, playing picador with the taxis.

I kept replaying the encounter in my mind, and it was keeping me awake. His misfortune wasn't his fault. Giving him money, the penny or so he wanted, would it be such a sin? I thought it would be like standing on the brink of hell and tossing in a wet sponge.

THE FIRST DAY out of Mori was the easiest: rapids without a lot of rocks. It is a romantic conceit, but I had rather hoped that the villagers, who gathered by the hundreds to see us off, might regard us with awe. "Crazy, brave fools, risking watery death for naught but glory . . ." That sort of thing.

As it was, we had severe competition from a band of Gujars, semi-nomadic Moslem herdsmen who arrived that morning. I heard them driving their cattle along the trail above our meadow, and saw them in the pale light of false dawn: fine, tall people with aquiline features shouting and laughing on the hillside. The women wore intricately patterned pant-and-tunic combinations, and covered their heads with scarves of bright red or green. The older men dyed their beards red. All the males, men and boys, wore red skull caps embroidered with golden thread and topped with a red pom-pom on a braided stalk.

There had been Gujars among the Hindus the night before, but this was a special group. Their clothes were finer, brighter, the women wore more bangles, their cattle were fatter, and their dogs were bright-eyed and well fed. They were, I learned later, show-biz Gujars.

The group, about 18 of them, set up in a meadow not far from us, and the people of Mori abandoned us for the Gujar show, which was undoubtedly more interesting than watching people load rafts all morning. The Gujars had with them several dusty Himalayan bears, sometimes called moon bears for the white or orange-yellow crescent on their chests. The bears were controlled by a long rope that ran through the nose and out the mouth, but they seemed to respond to verbal commands. There was "sleeping bear," who lay on his back with his paws in the air; "smoking bear," who sucked on a six-foot-long stick of bamboo; "disco bear," who danced; and "hugging bear," who gently embraced a local child. The people of Mori laughed, threw coins to the Gujars, and strolled back to watch us cast off.

And so we paddled out of the eddy, caught the current, and went spinning down the Tons—crazy brave fools who would risk watery death, but who were, demonstrably, no more interesting than your basic dancing bear. The Gujars had stolen our thunder and destroyed a romance. "Stupid damn hats," a man paddling beside me said. "Makes 'em look like nitwits."

TWO DAYS LATER we hit Main Squeeze, the first really nasty rapid. It was hellishly technical. The river narrowed down to 30 feet, and, naturally, a bridge spanned the Tons at the point of its greatest fury. The water thundered between rock walls in wildly irregular waves that clashed, one against the other, throwing spray ten feet into the air. Just before the bridge the river rose up over a rock—a "domer"—then dropped four feet into a hole. The hole was six feet long, and at its downstream end a wave four feet high curled back upstream.

We wanted to hit the hole dead on, power-paddle into the curling wave, punch through, jog right to avoid the tree trunk that served as a pylon for the bridge, duck under the bridge—Jack Morison said he'd never seen the Tons so high—then hit hard to the right. About ten feet past the bridge, the river widened to 50 feet, but a rock 30 feet wide cut the Tons into two ten-foot channels. The left channel was shallow and rock-strewn. We would need to pull hard to the right as soon as we passed under the bridge.

There were seven of us in the paddle boat: three on each tube with paddles, and Jack Morison manning the oars from the frame in back. Jack called out orders—"paddle right"—and muscled the bow into the line we'd chosen. We spent two hours scouting Main Squeeze, and we ran it in 30 seconds.

By now, those of us in the paddle raft (the rest of our group were in oar-steered rafts) were getting cocky, impatient with all the scouting Jack thought necessary. We were a strong team, and we worked well together. Why couldn't we just "R and R": read the river and run? There was some grumbling about the matter.

A TRIBUTARY I couldn't find on the map—local people called it the Pauer—emptied into the Tons, effectively doubling its volume, just before the town of Tiuni. The river below Tiuni gathered force, and the gradient steepened until the Tons was dropping 100 feet every mile. It was a wild ride. There were, for instance, five major rapids just below the town— at least two miles worth—with no more than 20 yards of flat water in the whole run. Occasionally, we hit a hole out of position and people were thrown from the boat—"swimmer!"—but we managed to right ourselves and scoop up the swimmers without stopping.

A mile downstream from the town, we passed a dozen or so men sitting on the rocks beside a six-foot-high pile of burning sticks. We were paddling hard, dodging rocks and punching through curlers, but there was time enough to see the body on top of the funeral pyre. A yellow sheet covered the corpse to the shins, and flames licked at the bare feet.

The ashes would be dumped into the Tons, and they would flow into the Yamuna, which empties into the sacred Ganges. There, in those holy waters, the soul of the departing might achieve *moksha*: liberation from the cycle of being, from the necessity of being reborn. At the moment, however, the physical body was being consumed in the burning flame of Shiva's open third eye.

ON THE SECOND to last day, the river entered a long, narrow gorge. The cliff walls that rose on either side sported odd, travertine striations that looked like decorations on some alien and inhuman temple. We had come 70 miles, dropped almost 3,000 feet, and the Tons had spent much of its power. There were long, flatwater floats where the river was so quiet we could hear the chatter of monkeys and the call of cuckoos. The land, which upstream had looked like a steeper version of the northern Rockies, now took a more gentle, tropical rhythm. Palm trees grew at the edge of the cliffs, and their roots dropped 80 feet into the nourishing water of the Tons.

There were waterfalls here and there, and once, floating languidly under cobalt skies, we passed through a falling curtain of mist that stretched 100 feet along a mossy, green cliff wall. It was warmer here, 85 degrees, and I raised my face to the cooling water. The sunlight was scattered through that silver curtain—each drop a prism—so for a moment what I saw was a falling wall of color that shifted and danced in the breeze. The mist had the odor of orchids to it, and I wondered then why it was that anyone would want to be liberated from the cycle of being.

THERE WAS BIG TROUBLE the last day. The Tons had lately been so flat and friendly that the last series of rapids were a major surprise and are, in fact, called Major Surprise. I followed Jack and his boatmen as they scouted the noisy water: There was a hole, a pretty good curling wave, a house-size rock, and a small waterfall called a "pourover." We needed to skirt the rock, punch through the hole, and pull left in order to hit the pourover at its shallow end, which would give us a drop of about four feet.

Major Surprise ate us alive.

I recall hitting the hole and punching cleanly through the curler. But we didn't get left, not even a little bit, and the boat rose up over a domer so high that I found myself looking directly into the sky. We tipped forward—the drop was eight feet—and the boat seemed to hesitate momentarily, like a roller coaster at the summit of the first rise. This, I told myself, does not bode well.

The first thing a person notices underwater in the turbulence of a big hole is the sound. It's loud—a grinding, growling jackhammer of unrelenting thunder. You do not register temperature, and if you are being Maytagged, you have no idea where you are. It's like catching a big ocean wave a bit low: There's a lot of tumbling involved, not to mention a sense of forces beyond human control.

The river took my swimming trunks. It ripped the tennis shoe off one of my feet. It sent me thudding against unseen rocks, shot me to the surface dead center in the hole, then sucked me down again and batted me around for a period of time I was never able to calibrate. It didn't seem fair. I couldn't even recall falling out of the boat: The entire situation was unacceptable.

Presently, I came to the surface with the hole behind me. The river ran high, between a large rock and the canyon wall. A person could get wedged in there, underwater. I swam left and suddenly felt myself being hurtled down a smooth tongue of water toward a series of peaked waves of the type boatmen call "haystacks." It was like being sick, like vomiting. After the first painful eruption, you think, good, that's all over. But almost instantly your stomach begins to rise—oh God, not again—and that is the way I felt being sucked breathless into the second rapid.

While I was zipping along underwater, trying to get my feet downstream to ward off the rocks, the other members of the paddle-boat team were enjoying their own immediate problems and proving Jack Morison's contention that we were taking the river entirely too lightly. John Rowan and Martha Freeman were sucked to the right and had managed to pull themselves out after the first rapid. Jack and Billy Anderson held onto the boat, which was still stuck in the hole and being battered by the upstream curler wave. Sue Wilson and Douglas Gow were somewhere out ahead of me in the second rapid.

I surfaced and spotted Gow in the flat water between that second and third rapid. He was ten yards downstream and didn't seem to be swimming at all. His helmet was missing. I thought he might have been Maytagged rather badly, that he might be unconscious, and I am proud to say I swam to the man who needed help. (In point of fact, Gow took off his helmet because it had slipped down over his eyes and he couldn't see.)

"You OK?" I called when I was within arm's reach. Gow practices emergency medicine in Australia and is used to reacting calmly to tense situations. "Fine, thanks," he said, and then—oh God, not again—I was pulled down into the third rapid.

There was, in time, a sense of water moving more slowly. Sunlight shimmered on a flat water surface that seemed to recede even as I swam toward it, but then there was air and a handhold on the canyon wall. Morison and Anderson came by in the boat and fished me out. I lay on my belly on the floor of the raft and spit up a quart of yellow water.

We were somewhere else then, pulled up onto the sand on the left side of the river. Sue Wilson and Doug Gow were gasping on the bank. Someone gave me a pair of swim trunks to wear, though this didn't seem an important matter. I lay on my back, on the floor of the raft, looking at the sun, and there was a moment when it seemed to darken slightly, but I did not lose consciousness. I thought of Shiva's blinding third eye, of a long, lewd wink.

I WENT TO RISHIKESH, the holy city on the banks of the sacred Ganges, just in case.

The river runs through a wide, rocky gorge there, and every day pilgrims by the thousands cross over a suspension bridge that spans the Ganges and leads to the temples and ashrams—to what the guidebook calls "the abode of saints and sages." To get to the bridge, you have to walk down a wide staircase set against a white cement wall. There are large boxes sculpted into the wall, and sitting in these boxes are the most unfortunate, the most horribly mutilated beggars in all of India.

Either they live in these boxes or they are carried to them each morning, because it was clear to me that none of them could walk. As I passed they called out to me, called out in the most theatrically pathetic and heartrending tones: "Alms, alms, ALMS . . ." I made them invisible and crossed the bridge to the abode of saints and sages.

A wide cement walkway ran along the ridgetop, and in the formal gardens on either side, sacred cows grazed on a variety of colorful flowers. Beggars didn't seem to be allowed here, near the temples, but holy men lined the walkway. There were more sadhus and gurus and anandas and babas and bhagwans and rishis and maharishis than a guy could shake a stick at. A man in a white loincloth with yellow sandalwood paste on his forehead offered to bless me for a rupee. I gave him the money, just in case, and he held out his palm to me, like a policeman stopping traffic —which is the kind of blessing you get for the equivalent of eight cents.

Under a tree in the center of the walkway, a thin, dark man lay on a bed of nails, a collection bowl for donations by his side. He wore a skimpy loincloth that revealed a thin appendectomy scar angling up from his groin. Nailed to the tree was a large frame containing four photographs. The first three showed the same man lying on his bed of nails in front of what I took to be various holy places. The fourth was of him reclining in a pile of thorns.

Farther down toward the main concentration of temples I stopped into an herbal medicine shop where, according to a leaflet I was given, they sold "chandra prabhavati," which was said to "cure piles . . . rheumatic pains, gonorrhea, syphilis, and spleen complaints." I asked to buy some mahavringraj oil, which "checks the fallings of hair, invigorates the nerves, and removes brain fag." They were fresh out of mahavringraj oil.

Some earnest young people—three or four Indians and a like number of Westerners—urged me to follow them to their ashram. "Let's go," I said brightly, but something in my attitude—brain fag, maybe—put them off.

There were steps that led down to the holy river, and places along the bank to bathe. A bath in the Ganges is said to wash away a pilgrim's worldly sins. The river was swift and cold, hard to swim in. I got myself out into the current and let it carry me several yards. It felt good, going with the flow like that.

Passing over the bridge again, sinless after my swim, I stopped in front of the boxes in the wall and allowed myself to finally see the beggars. "Alms," they cried, and I gave them alms. I stood there tossing wet sponges into the fires of hell, just in case.

Later that night, in Dehra Dun, I met N. N. Badoni. He told me that the soul seeks its master. I told him about the Tons River.

*September 1986*

# Moments
# OF DOUBT

*He believed in the greatness of risk. Then death
came suddenly, too easily. And it came
again and again.*

● ▲ ■

### DAVID ROBERTS

*When one is young, one trifles with death.*
*—Graham Greene, at 74*

$\mathbf{A}$ day in early July, perfect for climbing. From the mesas above Boulder,
a heatcutting breeze drove the smell of the pines up onto the great tilting
slabs of the Flatirons.

It was 1961; I was 18, had been climbing about a year, Gabe even less.
We were about six hundred feet up, three-quarters of the way to the
summit of the First Flatiron. There wasn't a guidebook in those days, so
we didn't know how difficult our route was supposed to be or who had
previously done it. But it had gone all right, despite the scarcity of places
to bang in our Austrian soft-iron pitons; sometimes we'd just wedge our
bodies in a crack and yell "On belay!"

It was a joy to be climbing. Climbing was one of the best things—
maybe the best thing—in life, given that one would never play shortstop
for the Dodgers. There was a risk, as my parents and friends kept pointing
out; but I knew the risk was worth it.

In fact, just that summer I had become ambitious. With a friend my
age whom I'll call Jock, I'd climbed the east face of Longs Peak, illegally
early in the season—no great deed for experts, but pretty good for 18-
year-old kids. It was Jock's idea to train all summer and go up to the
Tetons and do *the* route: the north face of the Grand. I'd never even
seen the Tetons, but the idea of the route, hung with names like Petzoldt
and Pownall and Unsoeld, sent chills through me.

It was Gabe's lead now, maybe the last before the going got easier a
few hundred feet below the top. He angled up and left, couldn't get any

protection in, went out of sight around a corner. I waited. The rope didn't move. "What's going on?" I finally yelled. "Hang on," Gabe answered irritably, "I'm looking for a belay."

We'd been friends since grade school. When he was young he had been very shy; he'd been raised by his father only—why, I never thought to ask. Ever since I had met him, on the playground, running up the old wooden stairs to the fourth-grade classroom, he'd moved in a jerky, impulsive way. On our high school tennis team, he slashed at the ball with lurching stabs, and skidded across the asphalt like a kid trying to catch his own shadow. He climbed the same way, especially in recent months, impulsively going for a hard move well above his protection, worrying me, but getting away with it. In our first half-year of climbing, I'd usually been a little better than Gabe, just as he was always stuck a notch below me on the tennis team. But in the last couple of months—no denying it—he'd become better on rock than I was; he took the leads that I didn't like the looks of. He might have made a better partner for Jock on the Grand, except that Gabe's only mountain experience had been an altitude-sick crawl up the east side of Mount of the Holy Cross with me just a week before. He'd thrown up on the summit but said he loved the climb.

At 18 it wasn't easy for me to see why Gabe had suddenly become good at climbing, or why it drove him as nothing else had. Just that April, three months earlier, his father had been killed in an auto accident during a blizzard in Texas. When Gabe returned to school, I mumbled my prepared condolence. He brushed it off and asked at once when we could go climbing. I was surprised. But I wanted to climb, too: The summer was approaching, Jock wasn't always available, and Gabe would go at the drop of a phone call.

Now, finally, came the "on belay" signal from out of sight to the left, and I started up. For the full 120 feet Gabe had been unable to get in any pitons; so as I climbed, the rope drooped in a long arc to my left. It began to tug me sideways, and when I yanked back at it, I noticed that it seemed snagged about 50 feet away, caught under one of the downward-pointing flakes so characteristic of the Flatirons. I flipped the rope angrily and tugged harder on it, then yelled to Gabe to pull from his end. Our efforts only jammed it in tighter. The first trickle of fear leaked into my well-being.

"What kind of belay do you have?" I asked the invisible Gabe.

"Not too good. I couldn't get anything in."

There were 50 feet of slab between me and the irksome flake, and those 50 feet were frighteningly smooth. I ought, I supposed, to climb over to the flake, even if it meant building up coils and coils of slack. But if I slipped, and Gabe with no anchor . . .

I yelled to Gabe what I was going to do. He assented.

I untied from the rope, gathered as many coils as I could, and threw the end violently down and across the slab, hoping to snap the jammed segment loose, or at least reduce Gabe's job to hauling the thing in with all his might. Then, with my palms starting to sweat, I climbed carefully up to a little ledge and sat down.

Gabe was now below me, out of sight, but close. "It's still jammed," he said, and my fear surged a little notch.

"Maybe we can set up a rappel," I suggested.

"No, I think I can climb back and get it."

"Are you sure?" Relief lowered the fear a notch. Gabe would do the dirty work, just as he was willing to lead the hard pitches.

"It doesn't look too bad."

I waited, sitting on my ledge, staring out over Boulder and the dead-straw plains that seemed to stretch all the way to Kansas. I wasn't sure we were doing the right thing. A few months earlier I'd soloed a rock called the Fist, high on Green Mountain, in the midst of a snowstorm, and 60 feet off the ground, as I was turning a slight overhang, my foot had come off, and one hand . . . but not the other. And adrenaline had carried me the rest of the way up. There was a risk, but you rose to it.

For Gabe, it was taking a long time. It was all the worse not being able to see him. I looked to my right and saw a flurry of birds playing with a column of air over near the Second Flatiron. Then Gabe's voice, triumphant: "I got it!"

"Way to go!" I yelled back. The fear diminished. If he'd been able to climb down to the snag, he could climb back up. I was glad I hadn't had to do it. Remembering his impatience, I instructed, "Coil it up." A week before, on Holy Cross, I'd been the leader.

"No, I'll just drape it around me. I can climb straight up to where you are."

The decision puzzled me. *Be careful*, I said in my head. But that was Gabe, impulsive, playing his hunches. Again the seconds crept. I had too little information, nothing to do but look for the birds and smell the pine sap. You could see Denver, smogless as yet, a squat aggregation of downtown buildings like some modern covered-wagon circle, defended against the emptiness of the Plains. There had been climbers over on the Third Flatiron earlier, but now I couldn't spot them. The red, gritty sandstone was warm to my palms.

"How's it going?" I yelled.

A pause. Then Gabe's voice, quick-syllabled as always, more tense than normal. "I just got past a hard place, but it's easier now."

He sounded so close, only 15 feet below me, yet I hadn't seen him since his lead had taken him around the corner out of sight. I felt I could almost reach down and touch him.

Next, there was a soft but unmistakable sound, and my brain knew it without ever having heard it before. It was the sound of cloth rubbing against rock. Then Gabe's cry, a single blurt of knowledge: "Dave!"

I rose with a start to my feet, but hung on to a knob with one hand, gripping it desperately. "Gabe!" I yelled back; then, for the first time in half an hour, I saw him. He was much farther from me now, sliding and rolling, the rope wrapped in tangles about him like a badly made nest. "Grab something," I yelled. I could hear Gabe shouting, even as he receded from me, "No! Oh, no!"

I thought, there's always a chance. But Gabe began to bounce, just like rocks I had seen bouncing down mountain slopes, a longer bounce each time. The last was conclusive, for I saw him flung far from the rock's even surface to pirouette almost lazily in the air, then meet the unyielding slab once more, headfirst, before the sandstone threw him into the treetops.

What I did next is easy to remember, but it is hard to judge just how long it took. It seemed, in the miasma of adrenaline, to last either three minutes or more than an hour. I stood and I yelled for help. After several repetitions, voices from the Mesa Trail caught the breeze back to me. "We're coming!" someone shouted. "In the trees!" I yelled back. "Hurry!" I sat down and said to myself, now don't go screw it up yourself, you don't have a rope, sit here and wait for someone to come rescue you. They can come up the back and lower a rope from the top. As soon as I had given myself this good advice, I got up and started scrambling toward the summit. It wasn't too hard. Slow down, don't make a mistake, I lectured myself, but it felt as if I were running. From the summit I down-climbed the 80 feet on the backside; I'd been there before and had rappelled it. Forty feet up there was a hard move. *Don't blow it.* Then I was on the ground.

I ran down the scree-and-brush gully between the First and Second Flatirons, and got to the bottom a few minutes before the hikers. "Where is he?" a wild-eyed volunteer asked me. "In the trees!" I yelled back. "Somewhere right near here!"

Searching for something is usually an orderly process; it has its methodical pleasures, its calm reconstruction of the possible steps that led to the object getting lost. We searched instead like scavenging predators, crashing through deadfall and talus; and we couldn't find Gabe. Members of the Rocky Mountain Rescue Group began to arrive; they were calmer than the hiker I had first encountered. We searched and searched, and finally a voice called out, "Here he is."

Someone led me there. There were only solemn looks to confirm the obvious. I saw Gabe sprawled face down on the talus, his limbs in the wrong positions, the rope, coated with blood, still in a cocoon about him. The seat of his jeans had been ripped away, and one bare buttock was scraped raw, the way kids' knees used to look after a bad slide on a sidewalk. I wanted to go up and touch his body, but I couldn't. I sat down and cried.

MUCH LATER—but it was still afternoon, the sun and breeze still collaborating on a perfect July day—a policeman led me up the walk to my house. My mother came to the screen door and, grasping the situation at once, burst into tears. Gabe was late for a birthday party. Someone had called my house, mildly annoyed, to try to account for the delay. My father took on the task of calling them back. (More than a decade later he told me that it was the hardest thing he had ever done.)

In the newspapers the next day a hiker was quoted as saying that he knew something bad was going to happen, because he'd overheard Gabe and me "bickering," and good climbers didn't do that. Another man had watched the fall through binoculars. At my father's behest, I wrote down a detailed account of the accident.

About a week later Jock came by. He spent the appropriate minutes in sympathetic silence, then said, "The thing you've got to do is get right back on the rock." I didn't want to, but I went out with him. We top-roped a moderate climb only 30 feet high. My feet and hands shook uncontrollably, my heart seemed to be screaming, and Jock had to haul me up the last ten feet. "It's OK, it'll come back," he reassured.

I had one friend I could talk to, a touch-football buddy who thought climbing was crazy in the first place. With his support, in the presence of my parents' anguish, I managed at last to call up Jock and ask him to come by. We sat on my front porch. "Jock," I said, "I just can't go to the Grand. I'm too shook up. I'd be no good if I did go." He stared at me long and hard. Finally he stood up and walked away.

That fall I went to Harvard. I tried out for the tennis team, but when I found that the Mountaineering Club included veterans who had just climbed Waddington in the Coast Range and Mount Logan in the Yukon, it didn't take me long to single out my college heroes.

But I wasn't at all sure about climbing. On splendid fall afternoons at the Shawangunks, when the veterans dragged us neophytes up easy climbs, I sat on the belay ledges mired in ambivalence. I'd never been at a cliff where there were so many climbers, and whenever one of them on an adjoining route happened to yell—even if the message was nothing more alarming than "I think it goes up to the left there!"—I jerked with fright.

For reasons I am still not sure of, Gabe became a secret. Attached to the memory of our day on the First Flatiron was not only fear, but guilt and embarrassment. Guilt toward Gabe, of course, because I had not been the one who went to get the jammed rope. But the humiliation, born perhaps in that moment when the cop had led me up to my front door and my mother had burst into tears, lingered with me in the shape of a crime or moral error, like getting a girl pregnant.

Nevertheless, at Harvard I got deeply involved with the Mountaineering Club. By 20 I'd climbed McKinley with six Harvard friends via a new route, and that August I taught at Colorado Outward Bound School. With all of "Boone Patrol," including the senior instructor, a laconic British hard man named Clough, I was camped one night above timberline. We'd crawled under the willow bushes and strung out ponchos for shelter. In the middle of the night I dreamed that Gabe was falling away from me through endless reaches of black space. He was in a metal cage, spinning headlong, and I repeatedly screamed his name. I woke with a jolt, sat shivering for ten minutes, then crawled, dragging my bag, far from the others, and lay awake the rest of the night. As we blew the morning campfire back to life from the evening's ashes, Clough remarked, "Did you hear the screams? One of the poor lads must have had a nightmare."

BY MY SENIOR YEAR, though, I'd become hard myself. McKinley had seemed a lark compared to my second expedition—a 40-day failure with only one companion, Don Jensen, on the east ridge of Alaska's Mount Deborah.

All through the following winter, with Don holed up in the Sierra Nevada, me trudging through a math major at Harvard, we plotted mountaineering revenge. By January we had focused on a route: the unclimbed west face of Mount Huntington, even harder, we thought, than Deborah. By March we'd agreed that Matt Hale, a junior and my regular climbing partner, would be our third, even though Matt had been on no previous expeditions. Matt was daunted by the ambition of the project, but slowly got caught up in it. Needing a fourth, we discussed an even more inexperienced club member, Ed Bernd, a sophomore who'd been climbing little more than a year and who'd not even been in big mountains.

Never in my life, before or since, have I found myself so committed to any project. I daydreamed about recipes for Logan bread and the number of ounces a certain piton weighed; at night I fell asleep with the seductive promises of belay ledges and crack systems whispering in my ear. School was a Platonic facade. The true Idea of my life lay in the Alaska Range.

At one point that spring I floated free from my obsession long enough to hear a voice in my head tell me, "You know, Dave, this is the kind of climb you could get killed on." I stopped and assessed my life, and consciously answered, "It's worth it. Worth the risk." I wasn't sure what I meant by that, but I knew its truth. I wanted Matt to feel the same way. I knew Don did.

On a March weekend Matt and I were leading an ice climbing trip in Huntington Ravine on Mount Washington. The Harvard cabin was unusually full, which meant a scramble in the morning to get out first and claim the ice gully you wanted to lead. On Saturday I skipped breakfast to beat everybody else to Pinnacle Gully, then the prize of the ravine. It was a bitter, windy day, and though the gully didn't tax my skills unduly, twice sudden gusts almost blew me out of my steps. The second man on the rope, though a good rock climber, found the whole day unnerving and was glad to get back to the cabin.

That night we chatted with the other climbers. The two most experienced were Craig Merrihue, a grad student in astrophysics, said to be brilliant, with first ascents in the Andes and Karakoram behind him, and Dan Doody, a quiet, thoughtful filmmaker who'd gone to college in Wyoming and had recently been on the big American Everest expedition. Both men were interested in our Huntington plans, and it flattered Matt and me that they thought we were up to something serious. The younger climbers looked on us experts in awe; it was delicious to bask in their hero worship as we nonchalanted it with Craig and Dan. Craig's lovely wife Sandy was part of our company. All three of them were planning to link up in a relaxing trip to the Hindu Kush the coming summer.

The next day the wind was still gusting fitfully. Matt and I were leading separate ropes of beginners up Odells Gully, putting in our teaching time after having had Saturday to do something hard. I felt lazy, a trifle vexed to be "wasting" a good day. Around noon we heard somebody calling from the ravine floor. We ignored the cries at first, but as a gust of wind came our way, I was pricked with alarm. "Somebody's yelling for help," I shouted to Matt. "Think they mean it?" A tiny figure far below seemed to be running up and down on the snow. My laziness burned away.

I tied off my second to wait on a big bucket of an ice step, then zipped down a rappel off a single poorly placed ice screw. Still in crampons, I ran down into the basin that formed the runout for all five gullies. The man I met, a weekend climber in his 30s who had been strolling up the ravine for a walk, was moaning. He had seen something that looked like "a bunch of rags" slide by out of the corner of his eye. He knew all at once that it was human bodies he had seen, and he could trace the line of fall up to Pinnacle Gully. He knew that Doody and Merrihue were climbing in Pinnacle. And Craig was a close friend of his. During the five minutes or so since the accident he had been unable to approach them, unable to do anything but yell for help and run aimlessly. I was the first to reach the bodies.

Gabe's I had not had to touch. But I was a trip leader now, an experienced mountaineer, the closest approximation in the circumstances to a rescue squad. I'd had first-aid training. Without a second's hesitation I knelt beside the bodies. Dan's was the worse injured, with a big chunk of his head torn open. His blood was still warm, but I was sure he was dead. I thought I could find a faint pulse in Craig's wrist, however, so I tried to stop the bleeding and started mouth-to-mouth resuscitation. Matt arrived and worked on Dan, and then others appeared and tried to help.

For an hour, I think, I put my lips against Craig's, held his nose shut, forced air into his lungs. His lips were going cold and blue, and there was a stagnant taste in the cavity his mouth had become, but I persisted, as did Matt and the others. Not since my father had last kissed me— was I ten?—had I put my lips to another man's. I remembered Dad's scratchy face, when he hadn't shaved, like Craig's now. We kept hoping, but I knew after five minutes that both men had been irretrievably damaged. There was too much blood. It had been a bad year for snow in the bottom of the ravine; big rocks stuck out everywhere. Three years earlier Don Jensen had been avalanched out of Damnation Gully; he fell 800 feet and only broke a shoulder blade. But that had been a good year for snow.

Yet we kept up our efforts. The need arose as much from an inability to imagine what else we might do—stand around in shock?—as from good first-aid sense. At last we gave up, exhausted. I could read in Matt's clipped and efficient suggestions the dawning sense that a horrible thing had happened. But I also felt numb. The sense of tragedy flooded home only in one moment. I heard somebody say something like "She's coming," and somebody else say, "Keep her away." I looked up and saw Sandy, Craig's wife, arriving from the cabin, aware of something wrong, but in the instant before knowing that it was indeed Craig she was intercepted bodily by the climber who knew her best, and that was how she learned. I can picture her face in the instant of knowing, and I remember vividly my own revelation—that there was a depth of personal loss that I had never really known existed, of which I was now receiving my first glimpse.

But my memory has blocked out Sandy's reaction. Did she immediately burst into tears, like my mother? Did she try to force her way to Craig? Did we let her? I know I saw it happen, whatever it was, but my memory cannot retrieve it.

There followed long hours into the dark hauling the bodies with ropes back toward the cabin. There was the pacifying exhaustion and the stolid drive back to Cambridge. There was somebody telling me, "You did a fantastic job, all that anybody could have done," and that seeming maudlin—who wouldn't have done the same? There were, in subsequent weeks, the memorial service, long tape-recorded discussions of the puzzling circumstances of the accident (we had found Dan and Craig roped together, a bent ice screw loose on the rope between them), heated indictments of the cheap Swiss design of the screw. And even a couple of visits with Sandy and their five-year-old son.

But my strongest concern was not to let the accident interfere with my commitment to climb Huntington, now only three months away. The deaths had deeply shaken Matt; but we never directly discussed the matter. I never wrote my parents about what had taken place. We went ahead and invited Ed, the sophomore, to join our expedition. Though he had not been in the ravine with us, he too had been shaken. But I got the three of us talking logistics and gear, and thinking about a mountain in Alaska. In some smug private recess I told myself that I was in better training than Craig and Dan had been, and that was why I wouldn't get killed. If the wind had blown one of them out of his steps, well, I'd led Pinnacle the day before in the same wind and it hadn't blown me off. Almost, but it hadn't. Somehow I controlled my deepest feelings and kept the disturbance buried. I had no bad dreams about Doody and Merrihue, no sleepless nights, no sudden qualms about whether Huntington was worth the risk or not. By June I was as ready as I could be for the hardest climb of my life.

IT TOOK A MONTH, but we climbed our route on Huntington. Pushing through the night of July 29–30, we traversed the knife-edged summit ridge and stood on top in the still hours of dawn. Only 12 hours before, Matt and I had come as close to being killed as it is possible to get away with in the mountains.

Matt, tugging on a loose crampon strap, had pulled himself off his steps; he landed on me, broke down the snow ledge I had kicked; under the strain our one bad anchor piton popped out. We fell, roped together and helpless, some 70 feet down a steep slope of ice above a 4,500-foot drop. Then a miracle intervened; the rope snagged on a nubbin of rock, the size of one's knuckle, and held us both.

Such was our commitment to the climb that, even though we were bruised and Matt had lost a crampon, we pushed upward and managed to join Ed and Don for the summit dash.

At midnight, 19 hours later, Ed and I stood on a ledge some fifteen hundred feet below. Our tents were too small for four people; so he and I had volunteered to push on to a lower camp, leaving Matt and Don to come down on the next good day. In the dim light we set up a rappel. There was a tangle of pitons, fixed ropes, and the knots tying them off, in the midst of which Ed was attaching a carabiner. I suggested an adjustment. Ed moved the carabiner, clipped our rope in, and started to get on rappel. "Just this pitch," I said, "and then it's practically walking to camp."

Ed leaned back on rappel. There was a scrape and sparks—his crampons scratching the rock, I later guessed. Suddenly he was flying backwards through the air, down the vertical pitch. He hit hard ice 60 feet below.

Just as I had on the Flatiron, I yelled. "Grab something, Ed!" But it was evident that his fall was not going to end—not soon, anyway. He slid rapidly down the ice chute, then out of sight over a cliff. I heard him bouncing once or twice, then nothing. He had not uttered a word.

I shouted, first for Ed, then for Don and Matt above. Nothing but silence answered me. There was nothing I could do. I was as certain as I could be that Ed had fallen 4,000 feet, to the lower arm of the Tokositna Glacier, inaccessible even from our base camp. He was surely dead.

I managed to get myself, without a rope, down the seven pitches to our empty tent. The next two days I spent alone—desperate for Matt's and Don's return, imagining them dead also, drugging myself with sleeping pills, trying to fathom what had gone wrong, seized one night in my sleep with a vision of Ed, broken and bloody, clawing his way up the wall to me, crying out, "Why didn't you come look for me?" At last Don and Matt arrived, and I had to tell them. Our final descent, in the midst of a raging blizzard, was the nastiest and scariest piece of climbing I have done, before or since.

From Talkeetna, a week later, I called Ed's parents. His father's stunned first words, crackly with long-distance static, were "Is this some kind of a joke?" After the call I went behind the bush pilot's hangar and cried my heart out—the first time in years that I had given way to tears.

A week later, with my parents' backing, I flew to Philadelphia to spend three days with Ed's parents. But not until the last few hours of my stay did we talk about Ed or climbing. Philadelphia was wretchedly hot and sticky. In the Bernds' small house my presence—sleeping on the living room sofa, an extra guest at meals—was a genuine intrusion. Unlike my parents, or Matt's, or Don's, Ed's had absolutely no comprehension of mountain climbing. It was some esoteric thing he had gotten into at Harvard; and of course Ed had completely downplayed, for their sake, the seriousness of our Alaska project.

At that age, given my feelings about climbing, I could hardly have been better shielded from any sense of guilt. But mixed in with my irritation and discomfort in the muggy apartment was an awareness—of a different sort from the glimpse of Sandy Merrihue—that I was in the presence of a grief so deep its features were opaque to me. It was the hope-destroying grief of parents, the grief of those who knew things could not keep going right, a grief that would, I sensed, diminish little over the years. It awed and frightened me, and disclosed to me an awareness of my own guilt.

I began remembering other moments. In our first rest after the summit, as we had giddily replayed every detail of our triumph, Ed had said that yes, it had been great, but that he wasn't sure it had been worth it. I hadn't pressed him; his qualifying judgment had seemed the only sour note in a perfect party. It was so obvious to me that all the risks throughout the climb—even Matt's and my near-disaster—had been worth it to make the summit.

Now Ed's remark haunted me. He was, in most climbers' judgment, far too inexperienced for Huntington. We'd caught his occasional technical mistakes on the climb, a piton hammered in with the eye the wrong way, an ice axe left below a rock overhang. But he learned so well, was so naturally strong, complemented our intensity with a heaty capacity for fun and friendship. Still, at Harvard, there had been, I began to see, no way for him to turn down our invitation. Matt and I and the other veterans were his heroes, just as the Waddington seniors had been mine three years before. Now the inner circle was asking him to join. It seemed to us at the time an open invitation, free of any moral implications. Now I wondered.

I still didn't know what had gone wrong with the rappel, even though Ed had been standing a foot away from me. Had it been some technical error of his in clipping in? Or had the carabiner itself failed? There was no way of settling the question, especially without having been able to look for, much less find, his body.

At last Ed's family faced me. I gave a long, detailed account of the climb. I told them it was "the hardest thing yet done in Alaska," a great mountaineering accomplishment. It would attract the attention of climbers the world over. They looked at me with blank faces; my way of viewing Ed's death was incomprehensible. They were bent on finding a Christian meaning to the event. It occurred to them that maybe God had meant to save Ed from a worse death fighting in Vietnam. They were deeply stricken by our inability to retrieve his body. "My poor baby," Mrs. Bernd wailed at one point, "he must be so cold."

Their grief brought me close to tears again, but when I left it was with a sigh of relief. I went back to Denver, where I was starting graduate school. For the second time in my life I thought seriously about quitting climbing. At 22 I had been the firsthand witness of three fatal accidents, costing four lives. Mr. Bernd's laborious letters, edged with the leaden despair I had seen in his face, continued to remind me that the question

"Is it worth the risk?" was not one any person could answer by consulting only himself.

TORN BY MY OWN AMBIVALENCE, studying Restoration comedy in a city where I had few friends, no longer part of a gang heading off each weekend to the Shawangunks, I laid off climbing most of the winter of 1965–1966. By February I had made a private resolve to quit the business, at least for a few years. One day a fellow showed up at my basement apartment, all the way down from Alaska. I'd never met him, but the name Art Davidson was familiar. He looked straight off skid row, with his tattered clothes and unmatched socks and tennis shoes with holes in them; and his wild red beard and white eyebrows lent a kind of rundown Irish aristocracy to his face. He lived, apparently, like a vagrant, subsisting on cottage cheese in the back of his old pickup truck (named Bucephalus after Alexander's horse), which he hid in parking lots each night on the outskirts of Anchorage. Art was crazy about Alaskan climbing. In the next year and a half he would go on five major expeditions—still the most intense spate of big-range mountaineering I know of. In my apartment he kept talking in his soft, enthusiastic voice about the Cathedral Spires, a place he knew Don and I had had our eyes on. I humored him. I let him talk on, and then we went out for a few beers, and Art started reminding me about the pink granite and the trackless glaciers, and by the evening's end the charismatic bastard had me signed up.

We went to the Cathedral Spires in 1966, with three others. Art was at the zenith of his climbing career. Self-taught, technically erratic, he made up in compulsive zeal what he lacked in finesse. His drive alone got himself and Rick Millikan up the highest peak in the range, which we named Kichatna Spire. As for me, I wasn't the climber I'd been the year before, which had much to do with why I wasn't along with Art on the summit push. That year I'd fallen in love with the woman who would become my wife, and suddenly the old question about risk seemed vastly more complicated. In the blizzard-swept dusk, with two of the other guys up on the climb, I found myself worrying about *their* safety instead of mere logistics. I was as glad nothing had gone wrong by the end of the trip as I was that we'd collaborated on a fine first ascent.

Summer after summer I went back to Alaska, climbing hard, but not with the all-out commitment of 1965. Over the years quite a few of my climbing acquaintances were killed in the mountains, including five close friends. Each death was deeply unsettling, tempting me to doubt all over again the worth of the enterprise. For nine years I taught climbing to college students, and worrying about their safety became an occupational hazard. Ironically, the closest I came during those years to getting killed was not on some Alaskan wall, but on a beginner's climb at the Shawangunks, when I nearly fell head-first backwards out of a rappel—the result of a carabiner jamming in a crack, my own impatience, and the blasé glaze with which teaching a dangerous skill at a trivial level coats the risk. Had that botched rappel been my demise, no friends would have seen my end as meaningful: instead, a "stupid," "pointless," "who-would-have-thought?" kind of death.

Yet in the long run, trying to answer my own question "Is it worth it?," torn between thinking the question itself ridiculous and grasping for a formulaic answer, I come back to gut-level affirmation, however sentimental, however selfish. When I image my early 20s, it is not in terms of the hours spent in a quiet library studying Melville, or my first nervous pontifications before a freshman English class. I want to see Art Davidson again, shambling into my apartment in his threadbare trousers, spooning great dollops of cottage cheese past his flaming beard, filling the air with his baroque hypotheses, convincing me that the Cathedral Spires needed our visit. I want to remember what brand of beer I was drinking when that crazy vagabond in one stroke turned the cautious resolves of a lonely winter into one more summer's plot against the Alaskan wilderness.

Some of the worst moments of my life have taken place in the mountains. Not only the days alone in the tent on Huntington after Ed had vanished—quieter moments as well, embedded in uneventful expeditions. Trying to sleep the last few hours before a predawn start on a big climb, my mind stiff with dread, as I hugged my all-too-obviously fragile self with my own arms—until the scared kid inside my sleeping bag began to pray for bad weather and another day's reprieve. But nowhere else on earth, not even in the harbors of reciprocal love, have I felt pure happiness take hold of me and shake me like a puppy, compelling me, and the conspirators I had arrived there with, to stand on some perch of rock or snow, the uncertain struggle below us, and bawl our pagan vaunts to the very sky. It was worth it then.

*December 1980/January 1981*

# GOING PLACES
*Moving targets are hard to hit.*

○ ▲ ■

JIM HARRISON

Everyone remembers those kindergarten or first-grade jigsaw puzzles of the 48 states, not including Hawaii or Alaska, which weren't states when I was a child and perhaps for that reason are permanently beyond my sphere of interest. I'm not at all sure at what age a child begins to comprehend the abstraction of maps—Arthur Rimbaud's line about the "child crazed with maps" strikes home. Contiguous states in the puzzle were of different colors, establishing the notion that states are more different from one another than they really are. The world grows larger with the child's mind, but each new step doesn't abolish the previous steps, so it's not much more than a big child who finally gets a driver's license, certainly equivalent to losing your virginity in the list of life's prime events.

It is at this point that pathology enters: Out of a hundred drivers the great majority find cars pleasant enough, and some will be obsessed with them in mechanical terms, but two or three out of the hundred will be obsessed with going places, pure and simple, for the sake of movement, anywhere and practically anytime.

"You haven't been anywhere until you've taken Route 2 through the Sand Hills of Nebraska," they're liable to say, late at night.

"Or Route 191 in Montana, 35 in Wisconsin, 90 in West Texas, 28 in the Upper Peninsula of Michigan, 120 in Wyoming, 62 in Arkansas, 83 in Kansas, 14 in Louisiana," I reply, after agreeing that 2 in Nebraska is one of my favorites. To handle Route 2 properly, you should first give a few hours to the Stuhr Museum in Grand Island to check on the human and natural history of the Great Plains. If you don't care all that much about what you're seeing, you should stay home, or if you're just trying to get someplace, take a plane.

There is, of course, a hesitation to make any rules for the road; the main reason you're out there is to escape any confinement other than that of change and motion. But certain precepts and theories should be kept in mind:

- Don't compute time and distance. Computing time and distance vitiates the benefits to be gotten from aimlessness. Leave that sort of thing to civilians with their specious categories of birthdays, average wage, height and weight, the number of steps to second floors. If you get into this acquisitive mood, make two 90-degree turns and backtrack for a while. Or stop the car and run around in a big circle in a field. Climbing a tree or going swimming also helps. Remember that habit is a form of gravity that strangulates.

- Leave your reason, your logic, at home. A few years ago I flew all the way from northern Michigan to Palm Beach, Florida, in order to drive to Livingston, Montana, with a friend. Earlier in life I hitchhiked 4,000 miles round-trip to see the Pacific Ocean. Last year I needed to do some research in Nebraska. Good sense and the fact that it was January told me to drive south, then west by way of Chicago, spend a few days, and drive home. Instead I headed due north into a blizzard and made a three-day back-road circle to La Crosse, Wisconsin, one of my favorite hideouts. When I finished in Nebraska, I went to Wyoming, pulled a left for Colorado and New Mexico, a right for Arizona, headed east across Texas and Louisiana to Alabama, then north toward home. My spirit was lightened by the 35 days and 8,000 or so miles. The car was a loaner, and on deserted back roads I could drive on cruise control, standing on the seat with shoulders and head through the sunroof.

- Spend as little time as possible thinking about the equipment. Assuming you are not a mechanic, and even if you are, it's better not to think too much about the car over and above minimum service details. I've had a succession of three four-wheel-drive Subaru station wagons, each equipped with a power winch, although recently I've had doubts about this auto. I like to take the car as far as I can go up a two-track, then get out and walk until the road disappears. This is the only solution to the neurotic pang that you might be missing something. High-performance cars don't have the clearance for back roads, and orthodox four-wheel drives are too jouncy for long trips. An ideal car might be a Saab turbo four-wheel-drive station wagon, but it has not as yet been built by that dour land without sunshine and garlic. A Range Rover is a pleasant, albeit expensive, idea, but you could very well find yourself a thousand miles from a spare part.

- A little research during downtime helps. This is the place for the lost art of reading. The sort of driving I'm talking about is a religious impulse, a craving for the unknown. You can, however, add to any trip immeasurably by knowing something about the history of the area or location. For instance, if you're driving through Chadron, Nebraska, on Route 20, it doesn't hurt to know that Crazy Horse, He Dog, American Horse, Little Big Man, and Sitting Bull took the same route when it was still a buffalo path.

- Be careful about who you are with. Whiners aren't appropriate. There can be tremendous inconveniences and long stretches of boredom. It takes a specific amount of optimism to be on the road, and anything less means misery. A nominal Buddhist who knows that "the goal is the path" is at an advantage. The essential silence of the highway can allow couples to turn the road into a domestic mudbath by letting their petty grievances preoccupy them. Marriages survive by garden-variety etiquette, and when my wife and I travel together we forget the often suffocating flotsam and jetsam of marriage.

If you're driving solo, another enemy can be the radio or tape deck. This is an eccentric observation, but anyone under 50 in America has likely dissipated a goodly share of his life listening to music. Music frequently draws you out of where you belong. It is hard work to be attentive, but it's the only game in town. D. H. Lawrence said that "the only true aristocracy is consciousness," which doesn't mean you can't listen to music; just don't do it all the time. Make your own road tapes: Start with cuts of Del Shannon, Merle Haggard, Stravinsky, Aretha Franklin, Bob Seger, Mozart, Buffett, Monteverdi, Woody Guthrie, Jim Reeves, B. B. King, George Jones, Esther Lammandier, Ray Charles, Bob Wills, and Nicholas Thorne. That sort of thing.

If you're lucky, you can find a perfect companion. During a time of mutual stress I drove around Arizona with the grizzly bear expert Douglas Peacock, who knows every piece of flora, fauna, and Native American history in that state. In such company, the most unassertive mesa becomes verdant with possibility.

- Pretend you don't care about good food. This is intensely difficult if you are a professional pig, gourmand, and trencherman like I am. If you're going to drive around America you have to adopt the bliss-ninny notion that less is more. Pack a cooler full of disgusting health snacks. I am assuming you know enough to stay off the interstates with their sneeze shields and rainbow jellos, the dinner specials that include the legendary "fried, fried," a substantial meal spun out of hot fat by the deep-fry cook. It could be anything from a shoe box full of oxygen to a cow plot to a dime-store wig. In honor of my own precepts I have given up routing designed to hit my favorite restaurants in Escanaba, Duluth, St. Cloud (Ivan's in the Park), Mandan, Miles City, and so on. The quasi-food revolution hasn't hit the countryside; I've had good luck calling disc jockeys for advice. You generally do much better in the South, particularly at barbecue places with hand-painted road signs. Along with food you might also consider amusements: If you stop at local bars or American Legion country dances, don't offer underage girls hard drugs and that sort of thing. But unless you're a total asshole, *Easy Rider* paranoia is unwarranted. You are technically safer on the road than you are in your own bathroom or eating a dinner of unrecognizable leftovers with your mother.

- Avoid irony, cynicism, and self-judgment. If you were really smart, you probably wouldn't be doing this. You would be in an office or club acting nifty, but you're in a car and no one knows you, and no one calls you because they don't know where you are. Moving targets are hard to hit. You are doing what you want, rather than what someone else wants. This is not the time to examine your shortcomings, which will certainly surface when you get home. Your spiritual fathers range from Marco Polo to Arthur Rimbaud, from Richard Halliburton to Jack Kerouac. Kerouac was the first actual novelist I ever met, back in 1957 or 1958 at the Five Spot, a jazz club in New York City. I saw him several times, and this great soul did not dwell on self-criticism, though, of course, there is an obvious downside to this behavior.

- Do not scorn day trips. You can use them to avoid nervous collapse. They are akin to the ardent sailor and his small sailboat. You needn't travel very far unless you live in one of our major urban centers, strewn across the land like immense canker sores. Outside this sort of urban concentration, county maps are available at any courthouse. One summer in Michigan's Upper Peninsula, after a tour in Hollywood had driven me ditzy, I logged more than 5,000 miles in four counties on gravel roads and two-tracks, lifting my sodden spirits and looking for good grouse and woodcock cover (game birds literally prefer to live in their restaurants, their prime feeding areas). This also served to keep me out of bars and away from drinking, because I don't drink while driving.

- Plan a real big one—perhaps hemispheric, or at least national. Atrophy is the problem. If you're not expanding, you're growing smaller. As a poet and novelist I have to get out of the study and collect some brand-new memories, and many of our more memorable events are of the childish, the daffy and irrational. "How do you know but that every bird that cuts the airy way is an immense world of delight closed to your senses five?" asked Blake. If you're currently trapped, your best move is to imagine the next road voyage.

I'm planning a trip when I finish my current novel, for which I had to make an intense study of the years 1865 to 1900 in our history, also the history of Native Americans. I intend to check out locations where I sensed a particular magic in the past certain culverts in western Minnesota, nondescript gullies in Kansas, invisible graveyards in New Mexico, moonbeam targets in Nebraska, buffalo jumps in Montana, melted ice palaces in the Dakotas, deserted but well-stocked wine warehouses in California. Maybe I'll discover a new bird or animal. Maybe I'll drive up a gravel road that winnows into a two-track that stops at an immense swale, in the center of which is a dense woodlot. I'll wade through the bog into the woods, where I'll find an old, gray farmhouse. In this farmhouse I'll find all my beloved dead dogs and cats in perfect health, tended by the heroines in my novels. I'll make a map of this trip on thin buckskin that I'll gradually cut up and add to stews. Everyone must find his own places.

*June 1987*

# BOB VERSUS THE VOLCANO

*He was called to climb Ararat, most holy of mounts. No one told him, however, about the test-in-the-wilderness part.*

● ▲ ■

### BOB SHACOCHIS

*And then I passed on further into Great Armenia, to a certain city called Erzurum, which had been very rich in old time, but now the Tartars have almost laid it waste. In this country there is the very same mountain whereupon the ark of Noah rested. This I would willingly have ascended, if my company would have waited for me. However, the people of this country report that no man could ever ascend the mountain because they say it pleases not the Most High.*
—The Journal of Friar Odoric, A.D. 1330

**W**ell-trampled Erzurum, one of history's doormats, seemed more than ever resolved to its continued existence, being rather conspicuously fortified. Alongside an airstrip, a village of camouflaged bunkers housed fighter jets. Stuporous conscripts dozed in the sun, manning antiaircraft guns mounded like anthills throughout the arid no-man's-land of the plain. On the outskirts of town, Turkey's entire Third Army was encamped, charged with the security of the eastern provinces. In NATO's dossier of the Apocalypse, here was a vital front-line unit, its troops rotating along a border nervously shared with some major spooks—the Soviet Union, Iran, Iraq, and Syria—each an ancient and sometimes modern enemy, brother, slave, subject, or ruler of the Anatolian peoples of Asia Minor.

The needles visible on the horizon were either minarets or missile sites—easy for a non-Muslim Westerner like myself to confuse, given the times. This part of the world was nobody's idea of a playground, and my journey coincided with another questionable piece of adventurism: Saddam Hussein's surprise trek into Kuwait. Waiting in Erzurum's airport for my luggage, I tallied up the previews to see what I was working with so far: The Middle East. Impending full-scale war. Overwhelming military presence. Alleged Kurdish terrorist activity. A reputedly conservative and xenophobic Islamic city smack in the middle of what is one of the most earthquake-prone venues on earth.

Such facts had been nicely titillating back home in Tallahassee, but the truth was I felt relief to finally be here on Marco Polo's Silk Road, since I was traveling under the strange impression that I had been called to this land. *Called*—not like a godstruck novice or the Son of Sam; more like a delinquent summoned to the tax collector's office. I had the queer feeling that something big was up and that somehow I had a role to play, perhaps as a stableboy to the Four Horsemen. One doesn't argue with intuitions of destiny, one buys a plane ticket and a bottle of Kaopectate. The date was September 7. Two more days and the calendar would provide a most portentous serial: 9/9/90. On that day I would be on Agri Dagi—Mount Ararat, the Big Doggie—attempting what Friar Odoric had counseled against on the premise of annoying God.

BY ANY ACCOUNT I was a vice-ridden sinner and ill-conditioned to do what I had never done before: climb a dormant volcano-cum-mountain, especially a 16,945-foot one, higher than any peak in Europe or the contiguous United States. I found the friar's words not only provocative but an implicit challenge, meant only for me, because 9/9/90 would also be my 39th birthday, the starting gate of my 40th year, crisis time for any nicotine-fouled, under-exercised, previously able-bodied ex-surfer loathe to wander far above sea level without a chairlift. Something definitely was up, some lure irresistible to the disposition of my mortal self. I could smell it. Something not too dressy, like Reckoning, or Enlightenment.

I had not come unprepared. In my rucksack I carried an emergency library of the soul, should I have reason to call upon the wisdom of the prophets: a portable World Bible, accommodating all faiths including fire-worship; a paperback edition of the Koran; a scholarly survey of biblical sites in Turkey, the "other" Holy Land; the newest translation of the Gilgamesh epic, in case I encountered heavy rains. And since an American should not go anywhere in the eastern Mediterranean Diaspora without that most pertinent of testaments, *The Innocents Abroad*, Mark Twain's travelogue through the Ottoman Empire, Europe, and North Africa, I had that, too.

Of personal effects, my toilet kit bulged with Nicorette chewing gum, to prevent me from becoming deranged and inadvertently killing somebody should I elect to stop smoking. I also had with me my new, first-ever pair of hiking boots, broken in by walking the dog to the park. What I lacked, however, were crampons and an ice ax, two items rumored to be convenient atop the glacier-bound summit of the Big Doggie. But I had never seen such equipment in my life, and neither had the Florida outfitters where I shopped. Come back in January, they had said, amused, and we'll sell you a sweater. In all other aspects of the preparation, I was either uninformed or ignorant and considered both states to be the mother of adventure.

So here I was in Erzurum, where the road to Mount Ararat began. Erzurum had a reputation for being somber and severe, a city "never recovered from winter," and though no one thought to disparage its tenacity by calling it lovely, the negative image seemed unjustified, even if Erzurum did have the only university campus in existence where wolves were a lingering security problem.

I had thrown in my lot with a robust band of mostly German alpinists. Erol, our courier from an Istanbul agency called Trek Travel, ushered all 17 of us onto a *dolmus*, the Turkish word meaning "stuffed" and referring to grape leaves, aubergines, and mini-buses. We were outward bound for Dogubayazit, a four-hour drive east, the staging area for any ascent of the Dog. We slalomed through an army convoy onto the scorched pastures of the valley, the higher landscape a geological punishment—rocky, sunburnt, and unyielding. But not infrequently would we top a rise and be treated to a golden vista of bulgar wheat or men harvesting green lakes of hay. The horizon would pour into a gorge, then split open again into a vastness daubed with the parched wheels of sunflowers. Whatever watercourse cut through the distance was described by perfect lines of Lombardy poplars or hairy clumps of willows. The farther we went, the more the land's few resources were given over to nomads, their flocks out beyond, muzzling the scrub.

I had never been among Germans before or traveled anywhere with a single one, so I knew no better than to be glad about it and, for the most part, was. Wolf, a physician from Bavaria, spoke English. White-haired Rudi was an Austrian, splendid to look at, with a profile you could pledge allegiance to and the personality of Kurt Waldheim, circa 1943. There were 12 others, all of them middle-aged, and all had wasted their youths by interminably scaling the Alps and whatever else got in their way. I was, and would remain, the only pilgrim.

Perhaps because of the echoing chill of *Midnight Express*, the gringo hordes continue to bypass Asia Minor, which is a shame, but not for me, since I occasionally see Americans in Florida and get my fill of them there. Besides, there were two others on the bus: Rob of California and Chris of Michigan. Rob, my junior by ten years and a ringer for Superboy, chiseled out a living as a photographer. Chris was an economist for the state government in Lansing. I found his company agreeable, mostly because he was smaller than I and because he was the only other fool on the expedition who had come this far in life without scaling a mountain. Chris and I mulled over the prophesies of Nostradamus, particularly those predicting that, on or near the second millennium, a charismatic Antichrist (Gorbachev) would reunite the world (Europe), Babylon (Iraq) would be back in business, and mankind could kiss its butt good-bye, as these events would culminate in the Last Judgment, for which we were wondering if we had front-row seats. In the Christian mythology of the Second Coming, the Big Doggie had been approximately targeted as Ground Zero.

For reasons other than salvation, though, Mount Ararat has been off limits to foreigners (except NATO snoops) for most of this century. Only since 1982 has the mountain been officially open; no one can set foot on it without first obtaining written permission, a months-long process requiring a daunting 72 signatures. This absolute triumph of red tape explained why Erol was among us and why we clung to him. Trek Travel was one of the very few outfits with a knack for expediting the formalities. Erol's assignment was to escort us all in a piece to Dogubayazit and deliver us to our mountain guides.

Chris and I, brother greenhorns, compared notes we had culled from the available literature. We were most encouraged that the books unanimously emphasized one needn't be an experienced mountaineer to achieve the summit, though they allowed the climb was strenuous and demanded great stamina. We asked Erol to bolster our courage with a little pep talk, and he fortified us with good information. Trek Travel had succeeded in marching 98 percent of its customers to the summit. If our group was representative of the whole, this was heartening news, implying that the majority of Ararat trekkers were well sunk into middle age, and that the mountain was cake.

In Erol's experience, the worst incident to unfold on Ararat had

occurred last July, when a trekker—a German trekker, it so happened
—somehow concealed a hang glider in his baggage. The packers hauled
it unaware to base camp, whereupon the German flew down to Dogubayazit on the day of the World Cup soccer finals, in search of a TV.
"If the soldiers had seen him," Erol explained soberly, "they would have
shot him out of the air. They wouldn't have known what it was they
were seeing."

I asked what the soldiers were doing on Ararat anyway.

"They are guarding the camp against terrorists."

But what was this bull about terrorists—there were none, not this
far north anyway. Yes, Erol conceded, but the soldiers didn't know that.
"Whatever you do," he told us solemnly, "don't go outside camp after
dark."

"THE GREAT PROVOCATION," Wolf pronounced from the veranda of our
hotel in Dogubayazit, assessing Ararat in the early morning light. It wasn't
just big; you could forget big. The surrounding tableland, flat as a Nebraska
cornfield, swept the eye across an uninterrupted horizontal right into a
dead stop, whereupon a mountain as perfect and unreal as a child's
rendition, a great breast of mountain that had nurtured the very roots
of civilization, heaved abruptly more than 13,000 feet straight off the
plateau. Without outlying foothills to interfere with its immensity, the
mountain, skull-capped with dazzling ice, was startlingly exposed, as if
it had no other choice than to be naked and divine. I looked at it and
felt the awful undertow of attraction.

We were quite a party now—46 of us—having rendezvoused with
two other Trek Travel groups. One had come, like us, from Erzurum.
The other had been hiking a week, gaining unfair advantage, in the Taurus
mountains.

Erol came to notify us of a delay: Our permit awaited its final signature,
which it would receive automatically once the commander of the local
garrison remembered he had something to do today. As we kicked around,
waiting, I noticed that Chris seemed aloof and unwell. As we mustered
in the parking lot, our documents secured, our gear collected, he bailed
out, citing reasons of health and personal scheduling problems that con-
flicted with Armageddon. I was sorry to see him go, since I had hoped
we might launch our alpine careers together, humiliation being a state
best enjoyed with a comrade.

Off I drove with Rob and the Germans and Rudi. We raised a terrible train of dust, bouncing across the plain toward road's end on the hem of the mountain. I was a bit apprehensive about our drop-off point at the tiny Kurdish village of Çevirme, having been forewarned by a guide-book not to violate anyone's *namus* and cause a ruckus. Eyeballing women was strictly out. Pointing cameras at Kurds was also an offense, so I figured that Rob, who couldn't restrain himself, would be beheaded within minutes and that our arrival would result in a flurry of diplomatic gaffes.

I shouldn't have worried. Our appearance on the central pasture of Çevirme was the signal for the population to throw their touchy sense of honor to the wind. They scrambled forward to cull baksheesh and bonbons and to beg for *fotoçek.* Actually, the behavior of the villagers was exemplary, considering they were being invaded from outer space. I retreated to a stone wall fencing a sugarloaf stack of hay and smiled at three prepubescent Cleopatras who judged me satisfactory material to stare at. For reasons of epic length, I was smitten; these were Noah's granddaughters.

It would be unkind of you not to let me say a few words about that ancestor we share. Fundamentalists and frauds, maverick archaeologists, even a former astronaut all have mounted expeditions up the Dog to prowl around its ice cap, hoping to chip out a hatch cover from the old boat. Which would certainly be a miracle.

The story of Noah can rightfully be called the seminal myth of recorded history, the sequel to the Garden of Eden. Something devastating did happen; one winter's snowfall probably was extreme, the spring thaw likely coincided with heavy rains and astronomical tides, the rivers rose, inundating the lowlands. But not to the preposterous level of 16,945 feet, the present height of Ararat, which last erupted in 1840, vaporizing its old cap and, presumably, anything stuck up there.

The Old Testament version is derived from ancient Mesopotamian myths, anyway. The Mesopotamian prototype allegedly landed near the flood plain of the upper Tigris River, the same region where the Hebrew scribes probably intended to run their Noah aground. But Genesis, which properly set the patriarch down "upon the mountains of Ararat," was misinterpreted almost immediately. The mountains became one mountain, and Ararat, "a land far away," became the Big Doggie itself. By A.D. 70, Josephus was swearing the ark was up there in plain view, and Marco Polo reported the same stirring news 12 centuries later, though neither man had seen the ark himself, relying on the accounts of others.

Standing in Noah's front yard, I told myself, all right, it doesn't matter, since I preferred Noah as a metaphor for starting over anyway. Behind the Kurdish girls, atop the stone wall, lay a horse, or rather what was left of one, a long ivory chain of neck vertebrae still posted to their hideous skull, the macabre buck-toothed laugh rudely suggesting the distinction between Noah fact and fiction. The irony moved me along.

Called back to the ranks, we were introduced to our Kurdish guides, Halis, Sandwich (or so the Germans pronounced his name), and Ahmet. We crammed bag lunches into our daypacks while the staff loaded the more substantial gear into a Soviet four-wheel-drive Niva. Led by Halis, a rather arrogant sort with the impersonal eyes of a warrior, the Taurus Mountains bunch filed out the back of the village, disappearing into the rising folds of land. I quick-stepped to their rear, anxious to get going, though I properly belonged to Ahmet.

Fortunately, the day's agenda was cushy, a genteel stroll up past the 9,500-foot mark, and the weather was excellent, hosted by a magnanimous sun. Our collective mood was jubilant, even a shade romantic, and already the elevation was handing out rewards. The guides handled us well and were true professionals in their trade, having undergone years of rigorous training and apprenticeship as shepherds. The Europeans attacked the grade in stacked formation, unrepentant tailgaters with the playfulness of mules. This was the poetry of plodding; I found it inspirational, yet every tenth step I seemed to lose the 11th, slacking off until I had been inducted as an honorary member of the Sandwich contingent. I did what I could to enjoy it until eventually I filtered back through the column, alone for a while before being reunited with my own tribe, who welcomed me with indifference.

Ahmet, however, was pleased to see his lost lamb. He was older than Halis, and clearly wiser, but not a leader. He possessed a sad tenderness, in contrast with the mountain. For 90 seconds we cultivated a warm friendship, until he had exhausted his English vocabulary and I had exhausted myself. "Cigarettes," I confessed, pounding my chest, mock-coughing. Ahmet brightened. He pulled a pack from his shirt pocket and offered me one, which I declined, but he lit one for himself, raising his chin toward the impossible summit and squinting down at me. "Cigarette . . . no problem," he struggled to explain. "Ararat . . . no problem."

This was exactly my attitude, though I could afford it only in spirit. Among my company I was the slowest, the preordained last, eating the troops' dust until I was alone. Every five minutes I stopped to suck air like a vacuum cleaner. I felt fine, but my lungs lacked capacity, and everyone's physical superiority was in dramatic contrast to my own self-inflicted limitations. Repeatedly I lost sight of the procession weaving into gullies, behind crags, but the path was unmistakable and, as I slugged it out in my solitude, it was gratifying to imagine I had embarked on a quest. Noah had been 600 years old when the Almighty enlisted him in the navy. I had come to Ararat to learn, on the eve of my 40th year, just how much stuffing I had left in me. The trek was not pure, but then neither was I. I sat down on a basalt throne and, plucking what I thought was wild mint, raised a stinging nettle to my nose.

BASE CAMP was dug in atop a scraped knuckle of ground; above us, Ararat remained the same, monolithic and undiminished. Dinner was set and the field cook stuffed us with a variety of tasteless carbohydrates. I had a beer and was instantly drunk. I lit a cigarette—my sixth of the day, compared with my usual 50—and was simultaneously stoned. Ahmet and I sat leg against leg and chatted like two retarded brothers. The sun set and took the world with it. Out in the dusty central plaza of our bivouac, the staff smashed up packing crates and built a modest campfire. The Europeans meditated upon the lambent flames for a minute, then burst into beer hall songs. The clock eased back several eons, and the darkness muted our many voices, made every gesture meaningful, and offered us the illusion that we were a tried and tested community, which felt nice, as illusions often do.

The next day dawned cold and clear—9/9/90, my birthday, and I fully expected to die, choking either on chemical gas or Nicorette gum or both. As I understood the plan, our objective for the day was to acclimatize to the altitude, promenade up to 13,800 feet, where the high camp was situated, eat lunch, exclaim about how damn high and cold it really was, retreat back down the slope to our feathered nests, and rejoice, each according to his abilities. My own version of the plan was more ambitious: I had vowed to forsake smoking the entire day and night, breaking a 20-year record.

When Ahmet saw me at breakfast, he beamed, all bright and cheering rays. "Bob! We go! No problem!" He shook a cigarette from his pack, tempting me back into the brotherhood. I had no alternative but to flee, slipping in with Halis's veterans. Hands-on, the first and lasting impression of Ararat was of a volcanic dreamscape where a wanderer was forbidden to ask for forgiveness. Massive basalt bombs peppered its flanks in all directions, fanned out like black huts at the lower altitudes but increasing in density the higher we went, until we were picking our way through huge tumbled galleries, the rocks sharply edged like broken lumps of glass. Where there were no rocks, there were baked meadows of field grass, rasping in the wind. The mountain was overgrazed, not by livestock, but by the macrocosm. Instead of the expected bears and wolves and wild boars, I could do no better than a ladybug and a half-dozen honeybees. Ararat was theirs.

I began to falter, and soon drifted back among Sandwich and his ducklings, all in a row, stabbing one another with their ski poles. I pulled over to let them pass. "Good day," I bowed. "Lovely morning, eh? *Auf Wiedersehen.*" Those who spoke English pecked at me, vicious health harpies, and those who didn't made do with cold neglect. I had not announced my birthday because being celebrated, I feared, would interfere with my growing dignity as a scapegoat. Accordingly, I fell back some more, and there was Ahmet.

"Ahmet, are you following me? I can feel you breathing down my neck."

"Bob! Bob! Bob! We go. No problem. We smoke. It's good."

My conversations with Ahmet were intensely soothing. When I looked up from my feet to speak again, though, there was Rudi glowering at me, and when I looked up the next time, I was alone on Ararat, tracking bootprints through an illicit solitude. I had never *seen* silence of such uncompromised scope, the altitude abstracting the valley and composing the panorama of the horizon into a Euclidean sampler, all swooping, slanting masses, planispheres and primary shapes, glimmering in the thermals. It was as fine a birthday present as I'd ever received.

I stayed with the trail until midafternoon, when I caught sight of high camp, still, at my speed, an hour ahead, and then turned back down. To my surprise, Ahmet was waiting for me, clearly set at ease to see he wouldn't have to go and fetch me. He clapped me on the back and we descended, dropping into another twisty, close-walled gully, so steep our strides grew longer and longer as gravity put the idea into our heads to race. Ahmet whooped and accelerated out of sight. I braked to a stop, red lights blinking. I had thought prudence and good judgment and flexibility would keep me out of hot water, but no one had told me going up was easy compared with going down. All the unpaid bills started coming due. My return took hours, and it infused weariness right into my marrow. I fell four times, controlled slides through the gravel that sucked out from under me, my legs too weak to fight.

Back in camp, off-duty soldiers were cooling out in the community tent, paying rapt attention to a broadcast from a transistor radio. From our quartermaster, I purchased a bottle of water and joined them at the table. We shook hands, and I asked them to aim high if they should see me sleepwalking. Erol was there, so I had asked him for the news from Iraq and Saudi Arabia—were they still on the map? The soldiers said screw the news, screw Iraq; they were listening to a soccer game. I finished the water and begged for hot tea. My flesh throbbed in its cells.

I asked Erol to tell Ahmet I wanted to discuss a few things with him. It was done. Ahmet peered keenly into my face, without expression, then spoke rapidly to Erol, who translated. "He says, 'What do you want to know?' "

"I want to find out the history of the Kurds."

Ahmet studied me and gave me the most piercing look of betrayal I have ever received. And yet I didn't get it. He spoke again to Erol, waited for the translation, and left. Now even Erol seemed oddly without humor.

"Ahmet says he is sorry, but he knows nothing about the history of the Kurds."

What a damn vacant fool I was. The Kurds had been gassed in Iraq, massacred in Iran; Turkey was the one relatively safe haven they occupied in the world, and even here they were under the thumb, however lightly it pressed. The inviolable mountains near the Iraqi border were a Kurdish stronghold and in fact supported an armed (but largely inactive) independence movement. And although Kurds held elected seats in parliament, the Kurdish language remained banned in all public forms. Essentially, at an expense I had no ability to calculate, I had just asked Ahmet to jeopardize his employment and maybe make a tour of his own in the police stations.

Erol, no dummy, shrugged it off. Nobody wanted the camp contaminated by politics, where it had no place, no use, no point. I felt wretched, then infinitely worse as Erol explained they had summoned another guide up the mountain from Dogubayazit. He spoke English and would be assigned to me alone. Oh, the ignominy, to be coddled with my own guide! And, as my composure failed, he introduced himself—Bulent, a

Turk from the Sea of Marmara—and as he talked on, I impolitely cradled my head on the table, with no desire whatsoever for palaver. He gave up on me and walked away.

I HAD NOT SMOKED YESTERDAY, nor would I today, and I was swaggering a bit after breakfast, because I knew I had high camp nailed. Bulent quickly asserted his own approach to the way things were done. While the Kurdish guides folded their hands over the small of their backs, lending a preoccupied, professorial stoop to their walking posture, Bulent favored ski poles to assist his footing. At the gorge above camp, where Halis veered his squad to the right, Bulent led me to the left, politely suggesting I not step on the fragile grass. For the most part, we spoke little but pegged along, Bulent monitoring my progress and condition. When the party halted for lunch, we were right there.

But then I ruined myself again by clambering into the rocks, my stomach churning. After a particularly long pause to catch my wind, I pivoted summitward to discover Bulent asleep on his feet, bent over his poles. The afternoon turned late. On the perimeter of high camp, I lowered myself down onto the rubble, hypnotized by the Dog. Finally I was here, on the threshold of the summit of the beast. Beneath its white mass, the high camp was like a grotto, cloud-shadowed and mysterious, quarried out from the glacier, its palisades of ice streaked with dirt and volcanic debris. Stones plinked out of the frozen face and rolled musically onto the moraine.

As soon as the tent was pitched, a blizzard raged down on us, stretching prodigiously to the valley two miles below. Rob and I scuttled inside. I could not unzip my sleeping bag. I could not manage the zipper on my daypack or my duffel bag. If anybody had inquired about me, I would have to tell them I had keeled over dead. I lay on my sleeping bag, booted and jacketed. It had grown terrifically cold. Dinner was called, but I could not respond. Bulent brought me a cup of macaroni soup, a thermos of tea. Falling through layer after layer of stupefying aches, I landed on a brittle layer of sleep. Bulent was back at 2 A.M., rousing us for the summit.

There were stars above the silvered dome, but not many—no omens good or bad. Rob had defected from Halis's group, and together with Bulent we groped our way forward, Bulent's headlamp dabbing into the unknown. On Ararat, I had not made the acquaintance of steep until now. Executing a tight back-and-forth traverse, we made a zigzag stitch right up over the rocks. If you've humped up the Washington Monument with your throat swollen shut and a clothespin on your nose and a chest cold, that's about what it was like on the first section, at least for me.

We constituted a provisional vanguard. Below, the embers of Halis's raiders bobbed out from camp and formed a beautiful jeweled snake, slithering upward. A crag obscured them, and when they came into view again, they were halfway to us, we could hear their dull clank and puff, and Sandwich was coming on. By the time Ahmet waded into the invisible stream of night, Halis had overtaken us, and we halted to let his company pass. The imagery was powerful, militaristic—the solemn clandestine movement under cover of night, the lowered heads and muffled thuds of bootsteps, the circumspect cones of dim light preceding each individual, the intense sense of mission that prohibited talk or comment, the implicit glory. The operation was pure war-game and uplifting drama, and since we had no sons to give to it, we gave up Rob, who fastened himself like a burr on the tail of a wolf and was gone.

Sandwich filed by. No one exchanged a word. Ahmet filed by and I thought I recognized a radiance from a visible fragment of Ahmet's smile, wishing me well. Twenty minutes later, when we craned our necks, we could see the almost imperceptible backwash of light from the procession above us, then it flicked its tail for the last time, and vanished.

"Bub?"

"Bulent?" Bulent's English was better than he gave himself credit for, but clogged and submerged in the deep bass vowels and glottal stops, irrefutably male, of Turkish.

"Uh . . . how do you feel? Are you sick? Does your head ache? Do you want to stop?"

This discourse became the refrain of our ascent, an Araratian call-and-response: Are you . . . ? No, boss. Do you . . . ? No, boss. Bulent was my Moses, leading me to an elusive promised land, and I hearkened to his command. In the growing light he seemed more trusting of me, permitting himself to ascend out of view. Ten minutes ahead, I'd find him sagged over his poles, dozing.

To tell the truth, I felt like the most persecuted man on the planet, and I had ceased joking with myself about my prospects or the risks. I traveled only in 12-foot sections or less, my lungs extended to full volume with each breath, but the wash of oxygen was missing, and I could not be satisfied. Extended beyond my limits, past ordinary recklessness, I had put myself in a position where anything could happen. I was aware that altitude sickness buried mountaineers no matter their level of experience, that it was most lethal to climbers with a stubborn streak, and that I was a prime but untested candidate for it. I was suffering as I had never suffered, and yet there was an absorbing momentum, an onward press so inexorable that it never crossed my mind to dig in my foot and make it stop, a perpetual motion aspiring onward, but all the while descending within, unseen, like a deep-sea diver.

I pushed on alone for a few minutes. A storm had enveloped the summit, but the first trekkers would be dancing on it by now. I gazed up from my labor and saw Rudi, picking his way down toward me, on the verge of panic. He shouted in my face, thumping the left side of his chest. I understood the words "heart attack." I nodded with lethargic stupidness and he pushed wildly past, bent forward into an invisible gale.

Bulent and I reunited without mention of Rudi; he simply asked if I would be happier back in camp.

"Bulent, do *you* want me to go back?"

It wasn't a fair question at all, and I knew he shouldn't answer it. On his deadpan face his own weariness showed from this frustrating trial of his patience. But the question seemed to make him reconsider the unspoken nature of our pact, and he grinned. We rested for a half-hour, replenished ourselves with liquids, and pressed on.

After this, everything was different between us. Bulent's brow unfurrowed; a bit of excitement married his eyes. For eight and a half hours we'd been clawing the slope together, and now he suddenly had faith in my perseverance. We had become partners. He looked at his wristwatch. There was still time to reach the summit, he said, if I could increase my pace.

He encouraged one more surge from me, which placed me gasping on a ledge. Before I could catch my wind and move, Halis and his partisans blocked the path in front of me, fattened with self-esteem, and I spent three unnecessary steps climbing off to let them pass. I offered congratulations, but no one looked over at me.

I convinced myself to make the next four steps. I made 40 or 50, at glacial speed, before the next group pushed me aside. Sandwich hailed me on the wing; the others glanced sideways, with no fellowship to spare, as though I might jump in their way. This cold shoulder for such hot effort! To hell with false modesty—I'd earned a salute, a nod, *something*.

They have slain the Big Doggie, I cried out in righteousness, emulating Noah in that regard. They have bagged their trophy, and must make room on the shelf.

I trudged ahead and came even with Bulent. From here, the seamless bleak roll of the summit was at hand, and we saw Ahmet's company hiking down its curve. Two hundred feet above us the rockscape terminated for good upon a knoll, with nothing beyond but the glacier. Rob appeared on its crest and bounded down to where we stood. He had been among the first on top in order to make *fotoçek*. "You didn't miss anything," he said, downplaying it for my benefit.

This was too much. I narrowed my eyes down the mountain, down toward the valley where all human endeavor had been rendered microscopic—furious, *furious*. "I put a curse on all of them," I snarled. I condemned them to roam endlessly in search of fatuous triumph, stumbling to keep up with a merciless cigar-smoking guide, spraining their ankles on the bones of sinners that cluttered the trails to Paradise.

"What?" Rob said, his eyes opening wide. "Look, don't worry about them." He told me I was doing great; he was proud of me.

"*Great?*" I snapped. "Phooey. Anyone who wants to climb this mountain can, except for fascist relics in cardiac arrest and diarrhetic junkies." I couldn't help but wonder if tantrums were a little-known symptom of altitude sickness. Noah's sole recorded utterance in the Bible was a curse and a blessing, so there was the mountaineer's precedent.

Bulent and I pressed ahead, atoning for my peccadilloes. I struggled now with a mild headache. Bulent took six more steps and turned to see if I had followed. I hadn't. My pulse roared, I waited for it to calm itself, and we moved on. Ahmet appeared above us on the crest. He threw his arms up when he spotted me and came hopping joyously down the slope as fast as his legs would carry him. From the beginning he had measured me by my own standards. He had studied them as he studied everything, an avid student of all that came his way out here in the remote core of eastern Turkey, and he had not found them wanting—he understood what the mountain was for me. Whatever the price of his tribute and compassion, it was worth it; worth, in fact, more—an Everest or two. He crowed, he embraced me, his face stuck in mine, eyes glistening, nodding emotionally and with exhilaration. "Bob! Bravo! Bravo, Bob!" And then he let me go and was gone to tend his flock.

It was the greatest inducement to endure and do well that a person could expect from heaven or earth, but that was it for me. I had been undermined by Ahmet's goodness. We pressed on, slowly conquering the knoll, and tagged the glacier—16,200 feet. Bulent was very happy. "One hour more. We can do it, we can," he said. "You are so pigheaded. We can."

"Bulent," I said, "I can't." The hour would split slowly and divide into two. There was no chance he could urge me back down before nightfall. I had seen what I could do, and this was it.

AN HOUR ABOVE BASE CAMP, we threw ourselves down in the dust, propped our backs against a single boulder, slept deeply for a few minutes, and awoke to the light melting across the valley like butter, quieting the emptiness. An alpine coolness circulated on the breeze, refreshing and sweet. Bulent conceded I had used good judgment in deciding to turn back, though he still believed we could have made it. Maybe next year, I idly replied. We had become friends, and we sat together in the stunning peace above the plateau and talked as friends do, about our histories, our politics, our loves; about mountains—he wanted me to see the Kaçkar Range, the Little Caucasus, along the Black Sea coast, which he thought the most lovely in all of Turkey. I told him I would—and did, the following week, driving off with Rob to Lake Van, then to Harran, on the border with Syria, where Abraham had once lived; making another predawn climb, this time to the summit of Nemrut Dagi to see the sunrise considered by the ancients to be the most beautiful in the world; then finally to the Black Sea, Bulent's Shangri-La, to marvel at the Kaçkars and wish we were on them . . . but we had run out of time.

As for Bulent and myself, we reached camp at dusk and were enthusiastically received by the company. I was of two minds about our welcome, not so anxious to lift my curse, but in the end I relented and replaced it with the other half of Noah's utterance.

*February 1991*

# VOYAGE OF THE SMITHEREENS

*Gentle reader, know this: Sailing in paradise isn't supposed to be fun.*

● ▲ ■

**CRAIG VETTER**

### A BITTER NIGHT IN CHICAGO . . . GRENADINE DREAMS . . . A CHANCE TO LEARN PORT FROM STARBOARD.

You have to try to imagine the trip the way I did that cruel winter evening in Chicago when Jack and I dreamed it up. We had a nice big *National Geographic* map open on the table in front of us, and there they were—the West Indies, the Windwards, the Grenadines—arching down the blue page from 15 degrees south to 12 degrees south. Just the island names warmed the room: Martinique, St. Lucia, St. Vincent, Bequia, Mustique, Canouan, Union, Carriacou, Grenada. I pictured the big equatorial sun in the big Caribbean sky, felt the big, steady push of the trades riding into the sails of our 47-foot sloop till the beak of the thing was down into the swell like a plow in a furrow, bucking warm spray into my nut-brown face where I stood at the wheel like every Spanish explorer, every French pirate, every English merchantman who ever slid a ship on these perfect turquoise waters, past these green volcano islands, into glassy little bays where huge crowds of coco palms come right down to the beach to meet you, where the natives are so friendly, so gentle, that even when they talk about money it sounds like they're singing.

And on top of all that, my old friend Jack, who'd spent ten years of his life as a boat hobo on these particular seas, had promised he'd teach me the what's-that and the how-to of this big old bareboat, from the pointy front porch to the stubby rear end and every last yo-ho-ho in between.

As a fantasy, the whole thing was—How do you say in the languages

420

of the Caribbean?—perfecto. Magnifique. Smashing. Nobody should have so much fun. Well . . . as it turned out . . . nobody did.

It's a squalid little story, I swear.

## ROOSTERS . . . DOGS . . . THIEVING FROGS . . . AND DRAWERS LIKE THEY HAVE AT THE MORGUE.

There was a waning moon in the warm starry sky when Mrs. Babbs and I arrived at the dock in Rodney Bay, St. Lucia. The *Indies Adventure* was lashed to a pier along with half a dozen other fiberglass rent-a-yachts and she looked pretty good to me. Forty-seven feet is a lot of boat if most of your sailing experience has been on little day sailers. Of course you don't have to make a *life* among five other people on those little boats, either.

But if I didn't yet know the potential for peevishness among otherwise decent people who go cruising together, Jack had said he did. In his many years before the mast he'd seen more than a few pleasure voyages sail straight into the jaws of hell when those aboard discovered they just didn't like one another enough to put up with the relentless intimacy of life on a boat. Jack and I would be fine together, we knew that. We'd been pals for 20 years, we'd traveled together, we'd even shared my small apartment for several weeks. But the rest of the crew was going to have to be chosen carefully, and that night in Chicago, Jack said he thought he'd come up with a mix that was just right. Along with himself, me, and Mrs. Babbs, he'd invited an illustrator friend of his from London named Fran, a boat builder named Buzz, and Buzz's friend Sonny, who would do the cooking. All of them had been cruising before, he said, and Buzz was one of those mellow salts who'd actually made a voyage around the world. A good group, Jack thought. Then he made a quick sketch of the boat, including kitchen, bathrooms, and beds. He and Fran would take the aft cabin, which was the largest on board and had a double mattress and a single. Mrs. Babbs and I could have the fore cabin with its double bed, and Buzz and Sonny would take the single bunks just aft of the salon on the port side.

It all looked fine to me, but that's only because nowhere in any of the hundred sea stories I'd grown up on had anyone bothered to mention that, to an experienced sailor, where you end up sleeping on a boat is more important than a working compass, and that there has probably been more grisly death at sea over the allotment of beds than from storms or scurvy or the division of plunder.

Unfortunately for Mrs. Babbs and me, all the experienced sailors were on board when we arrived. Everybody said hi, then Jack took our bags and led us below. "Here's your cabin," he said, nodding his head into a room that was just slightly larger than one of Houdini's trunks. There was a little built-in wardrobe adjacent to over/under bunks, which had approximately the same quality of light, the same headroom, as those drawers they have in the morgue. Mrs. Babbs, a Chicago woman who grew up in a family of eight in a two-bedroom apartment under the el tracks, looked at me as if she might weep, or maybe kill someone.

"Jack, you don't expect us to live in there for 12 days," she said.

"You'll get used to it," he told her.

"Maybe we could rotate cabins or something," she said.

"Oh, I don't know," he said. "You might get Buzz and Sonny to trade with you now and then . . . we'll see. Meanwhile, don't live out of your suitcases . . . unpack . . . settle in . . . get comfortable." Then he disappeared topside, leaving me with the vague feeling that I'd just been swindled in some sort of nautical bait-and-switch.

Ah, but that first night, as we sat on deck meeting each other, the soft Carib air made everything seem possible. The Big Dipper was low enough and close enough that you could have swung on the handle, and the warm breeze carried that wonderful jungle smell of something green somewhere smoldering. Now and then, one of the roosters in the hills around the bay would screech something about his territory, then another, then a hundred others would take up the argument till every skinny little fish-eating dog on the island felt compelled to come howling into the riot. Then it would die and leave only the chucking of the water against the hull, and the wind-chime tink of the lines on the tall aluminum masts.

The six of us talked about our possible route among the islands . . . maybe north to Martinique, then south toward the bright water and deserted islands of Tobago Cays. Everything depended on the wind, of course, which was usually straight out of the northeast this time of year . . . but you never know. Jack said we were going to have to lock our dinghy to the boat every night because word on the island trotline had it that the filthy French yachties were stealing them, and he and Buzz remembered back to a time in the southern Caribbean when you didn't have to lock anything. Then, at a certain point, Jack put in that all of us were going to have to make some sacrifices, that things were a bit Spartan on a boat this size. We were going to have to be stingy, for instance, about the way we used water: no long showers. Then he added, "This is not The Love Boat . . . this is not a honeymoon cruise." He didn't look at Mrs. Babbs or me when he said it, but he didn't have to, because as it turns out, on a crowded boat, pointy little remarks like that just sort of fly up into the rigging and hang there like signal pennants that finally spell out "bad blood aboard."

Mrs. Babbs and I made our separate beds that night on either side of the wheel, on the long benches in the cockpit, listening to the barking and the crowing and the occasional resonant bray of a single donkey who could out-shout the whole hillside when he got going.

"I didn't come down here," hissed Mrs. Babbs, "to sleep in an airless little closet for two weeks."

"Don't worry," I told her. "We'll work it out." And I thought we would. But that was only because nowhere in any of those goddamn sea stories did Melville or Conrad or C. S. Forester bother to mention that the sea hates an optimist.

## FULL-SERVE PARK-A-YACHT . . . MARLEY MARLEY ALL NIGHT LONG . . . THE SMELL OF ELEPHANT DUNG.

The next morning broke like that fantasy I'd had standing over the map in Chicago: 80 perfect blue-sky degrees with a few puffy clouds on the horizon for effect. We drove into the crowded little port town of Castries to shop for bananas, mangoes, papayas, cinnamon, and paprika, and to change our money into the Eastern Caribbean currency, which is worth about 37 cents to the American dollar. A huge white cruise ship towered over the foot of the main drag looking like something Bugsy Siegel might have built if he hadn't settled on Las Vegas to play out his vision. The disgorged passengers moved in packs along the sidewalks, through the hawk and bustle of the St. Lucians.

We sailed out of Rodney Bay about two that afternoon. Actually we motored out. There's a lot more motoring on a large sailboat than you'd think, because you have to run the big diesel engine two hours a day to keep the batteries charged. Even after we got the sails up and came south onto the light wind along the lee coast of the island, it was hard to tell how much of our four knots was sail and how much was screw, and in the still air below decks while we were under power, it smelled a little like we were sailing an oil rig.

Martinique lay off our stern, its beautiful volcanic hump shrinking against the northern horizon. Jack had made a command decision to skip the French island and take us three hours south, down the coast of St. Lucia, for an overnight at a small deep-water bay that was towered over by two huge rock cones called The Pitons. We spotted them an hour away: beautiful, overgrown pinnacles that could have been brought from Yosemite. About three miles from the anchorage, a long, narrow open boat with an outboard came cutting toward us at high speed. She was flying French, German, and American flags from her gunwales, and the two St. Lucians aboard hailed us with big smiles as they came alongside. They wanted to know if they could help us park in the cove, which was going to take a deep anchor and a bow line to one of the palms on shore. Jack said no, that we ought to be doing this sort of thing for ourselves. The men persisted. How much? Ten dollars, E.C. Oh, all right, Jack told them, and they sped off waving happily, yelling they'd meet us there.

As soon as we got the anchor down, other merchants came alongside offering us marijuana, then fresh tuna, which we bought for dinner. Over the rest of the afternoon, we barbecued the fish on the afterdeck, we swam, and we visited an elephant that was rocking neurotically back and forth under the palm forest above the beach. Buzz and Jack said that the absentee owner of the cove had brought the poor young pachyderm from Africa years before and stranded it for reasons nobody understood.

Just before sunset, Buzz and I rowed the dinghy around the limits of the cove to stretch our arms and backs. We watched as the boat boys escorted ship after ship into the cove and moored them with an efficiency that reminded me of the parking lot at Le Dôme or Ciros. By the time the sun hit the sharp blue horizon, they had 30 yachts anchored cheek by jowl between the rock pinnacles that flanked the cove. A rainbow formed itself to the west. A northbound cruise liner turned to silhouette against the intense red splash of the last of the sun. As we pulled back toward the ship, Buzz noted that Jack seemed very uptight to him, and that the two of them were already into a running antagonism over the finer points of how to sail. He said he thought the best thing for him to do was just to fade into the background and let the captain have his way. I told him the captain's way was getting on my nerves.

We ate dinner at the cockpit table in a wind that was beginning to smell like rain, to the beat of Bob Marley and the Wailers coming out of a huge sound system on shore. The local boatmen were camped around a big yellow fire at the base of The North Piton, which was bouncing the reggae across the cove as if it were coming from the rock itself.

"No woman, no cry," sang Marley as Mrs. Babbs and I made our bed on deck, this time on the space just forward of the mast. Sonny and Buzz had rhapsodized to us about how wonderful it was to sleep topside in the open air, and then had added that tonight they might just try it themselves. But after dinner, when Mrs. Babbs had asked the cook if she and her boyfriend were indeed going to take a turn on deck, Sonny hemmed and hawed, saying they hadn't decided and that she didn't know when they'd decide.

Our berth on the bow turned out to be comfortable enough, though, and for half an hour we lay listening to the languid music as it mixed with the happy jabber of French and German coming from the neighboring boats. Now and then the smell of elephant dung swept by on the stiffening breeze. Then it started to rain. Lightly at first, then a little heavier, and by the time our thin blanket was soaked, I knew it was hopeless. We gathered the mattresses and bedding and took them below. I pitched mine on the floor under the dinner table. Mrs. Babbs slept on a couch.

### THE HORRIBLE TRUTH ABOUT SAILING . . . ROOSTERS IN THE BARNYARD . . . THE WISDOM OF OLD SAM JOHNSON.

I caught Jack in the cockpit first thing in the morning.

"Listen," I said. "You're going to have to work out some sort of cabin rotation."

He went into his little speech about how sacrifices had to be made on a boat, and I told him fine, as long as sacrifice got shared there was no problem. "Fair is fair," I said.

"It doesn't necessarily work that way on a boat," he told me.

"Well it damn well better work that way on this boat," I said, as Mrs. Babbs clambered up the gangway and jumped into the fray. If he'd told her she was going to be stuck in a closet on an airless little bunk bed, she said, she never would have come. Jack looked at the two of us as if he really didn't understand the squall of outrage that had just broken on him; as if we had missed some crucial truth about boats and the sea, a truth so obvious and fundamental that it hadn't occurred to him that he would ever have to speak it.

"Look," he said. "Sailing isn't supposed to be *fun*." He hit the word "fun" as if it were for wimps.

Thinking back, of course, that was the moment at which we should have just spit in each other's eye, said thanks, and scuttled the whole voyage. And actually, we did try to end it. Jack let my stunned silence hang in the beautiful morning air for a few seconds, then said, "I mean if it's going to be like this, I'd just as soon turn around and sail back to Rodney Bay."

"If we can't work it out," I said, "that's just what you're going to have to do."

There was a heavy pause while the implications of our words worked on us.

"Of course we can work it out," Jack said in a tone that called up the original fantasy, and all the planning we'd done, all the warm anticipation that had carried us through the long, cold winter. It couldn't end like this, could it? Barely 12 nautical miles into the cruise? Two old friends standing there in everything that is perfect about the tropics crowing at each other like a couple of roosters at war over some invisible line in the barnyard dirt?

Nothing had been resolved by the time we pulled anchor and struck south on an eight-hour course for Bequia, but at least, I thought, bearings had been taken, positions were known. I spent some of the morning on the fantail watching the wake, thinking that Sam Johnson had been right when he said, "Being in a ship is being in jail, with the chance of being drowned." I think I would have welcomed the threat of drowning that morning; at least it would have broken the sloshing boredom of the day. Truth is, there isn't much to do on a sailboat while you're under way in a light wind. Jack gave each of us a turn at the wheel, but on a straight reach like ours, even that is an uneventful meditation on compass and landmark.

Around noon, Jack got out the sextant and showed me how to shoot the sun with it. It was an academic exercise, since we were never out of sight of one island or another, but I'd always wanted some sense of what it was to steer by the stars, and celestial navigation was one of the things Jack had offered to teach me on the trip. After we'd taken a few sightings, though, he suggested we leave the calculations for later, then slipped back into his funk, whatever it was. When I asked him what was wrong, he said he was fine, just fine, in the tone people get when they don't want to have the conversation you're trying to open. He told me Mrs. Babbs and I could have the aft cabin that night, then went below for a nap.

A wide gray squall brushed us in the last few miles across the channel where the Atlantic and the Caribbean meet between St. Lucia and St. Vincent. The wind came up to about 30 knots, the ship heeled over, got its bow down into the four-foot seas, and for about an hour there was some rodeo to it. Everybody's spirits rose to the action: We trimmed the sails, braced the mast, and then hung on while Jack manhandled the wheel.

"Put another quarter in," I said as the muscle went out of the wind in the lee of St. Vincent, but the high ride was over. We gentled along for another three hours or so, then caught sight of a cruise ship at anchor just outside the mouth of Admiralty Bay, Bequia.

### THE GIRL THEY TOOK TO VEGAS . . . UGLY PEOPLE ASHORE . . . CAPTAIN BLIGH KICKS THE LADLE OUT OF FLETCHER CHRISTIAN'S HAND.

As we came around the headlands, another ship came into view, this one a huge schooner belching smoke out of one of its four great masts.

"Oh no," said Buzz. "Not that abomination . . . that pig . . . that sorry excuse for a ship . . . *Windstar*. We ought to come back after dark and sink her."

As we motored through her shadow, Jack joined in the litany of nautical disgust. It wasn't really a sailing ship, he explained, it was a cruise liner disguised to look like a sailing ship: 440 feet long, four 200-foot masts that double as smokestacks for the huge engines, 74 cabins, the whole thing completely computerized right down to the joystick where the wheel ought to be.

As Jack and Buzz went on about the horridness of the big ship, Mrs. Babbs's sense of kitsch kicked in. "I think it's beautiful," she said. "I bet the beds are *huge*."

A half-hour later we had our anchor down near the head of the bay, and were surrounded on three sides by the palmy hillsides that enfold the thatch and stucco of the little village called Port Elizabeth. Bequia has always been the yachties' favorite among the Grenadines, probably because it is accessible only by boat and has a long maritime tradition back to the days when it was a whaling port. Twenty or 30 ships rode at anchor around us, bobbing on the wakes of the small-boat traffic in the harbor: water taxis, dories selling fruit and knickknacks, shore launches from the cruise ships, even a boat to take you waterskiing.

It was all a bit much for Jack and Buzz. It had been several years since either of them had been to Bequia, and they didn't like the squeeze that had come on the place. "Yeah, it's still pretty," Jack told me when I marveled at the lazy green perfection. "But to me it's like a girl you knew when she was young and beautiful and innocent. Now," he said as we watched a dozen pier boys scrambling and fighting for the bowline of a shore launch, "it's like somebody's taken her to Vegas."

The same theme was echoed that night in a small waterfront restaurant called Mac's. Buzz and Jack had found three old friends in the harbor: an American couple named Bob and Sandy who had lived in Bequia for years, and a photographer from Grenada named Joe. "Speed boats in the bay and ugly people ashore," was the way Bob put the changes. Sandy added that you could actually see a personality change come over the local kids at high season. They worked the bay and the piers like bellboys. "You say hi to some kid you've known for years, a sweet kid," she told us, "and he'll look at you as if to say, 'Not now. I'm working.' Then, come May, the sweetness returns."

Sunset that night was obliterated by *Windstar* as she sat at the mouth of the harbor, her shrouds lit like a Mexican plaza by long strings of bright bare bulbs.

"Gorgeous," said Mrs. Babbs. "I love it."

Jack's mood was not good when he woke from his night on deck. He repossessed his cabin, then took off with the dinghy to visit friends in the harbor, which pretty much stranded the rest of us and left me with the feeling that I was living in a one-car family in Los Angeles.

Mrs. Babbs and I hailed a water taxi and spent the morning on a wild, empty windward beach with Buzz and Sonny. We bodysurfed for a while on the small waves, then Buzz and I sat out of the sun in an abandoned stone building, where he talked about his adventures in the Caribbean among the colorful and generally misanthropic characters who are attracted to sailing. Somewhere in the conversation he asked me why I thought things had grown so brittle on our ship, and I told him I was damned if I knew, but that it didn't seem to be getting any better. He agreed, and when the subject of the water supply aboard the *Indies Adventure* came up, he said he thought Jack's attitude had become a bit strange. I told him I thought "strange" was a kind way to describe it, that the whole thing was starting to remind me of *Mutiny on the Bounty*.

Which it was. Jack had been starchy about our 200 gallons of water before we left the dock, but it had gotten to the point where every time he heard a tap go on for even a moment, he'd yell, "Mind the water, now." Mrs. Babbs and I hadn't even taken a shower since we'd sailed, and as far as I could tell everyone else was using the supply just as carefully. Nevertheless, shortly after we'd sailed out of The Pitons, Jack had gone nuts on Mrs. Babbs as she stood at the sink in the galley. No one had told her that when the engine is running, *all* the water on this boat was hot, and she had opened the tap and given it about ten seconds to run cool. When Jack saw what she was doing, he'd yelled "What's the matter with you? . . . don't do that . . . my God. . . ." And on and on, too long and too loud and too crazy. I stood silent a few feet away, trying to match the outburst with the incident, and feeling very much as if I had just watched Captain Bligh kick a ladle out of Fletcher Christian's hand.

On the beach that morning, Buzz said that Jack had told him that he wasn't going to top off the tanks in Bequia because it cost something like 16 cents a gallon, and, besides that, he just didn't think it was good sailing form to fill up every time you had a chance.

## THE WHINING CONCH . . . THE DEATH OF YO-HO-HO . . . RATS ON A ROPE IN UNION ISLAND.

Mrs. Babbs and I spent the afternoon walking the island, but no matter what stunning panorama, or perfect beach, or great green jungle gully we came onto, the conversation always pulled back to the pissy little details of life aboard our humorless barge.

In a way, I knew the situation was classic: Groups, friends, couples go out camping, river running, sailing, under the cruel delusion that they know each other and can pull together happily, only to come back wishing death and pestilence on one anothers' heads. I've even heard of expeditions hiring psychologists onto their trips to cool hot blood and bandage torn egos. Still, it had never occurred to me that such contentiousness would overtake this trip, in this place. I felt as if I'd traveled to paradise, found a perfect conch, put the shell to my ear, and heard the sound of children arguing over a nickel.

It wasn't all Jack's fault, I knew that. I'd become pretty pugnacious myself when efforts at conciliation had failed, and had even begun looking for trouble. But something about taking on the captaincy of our voyage had turned Jack, my old buddy, a guy who had spent years telling me how he'd chased a disorderly kind of fun across the Caribbean, into somebody I didn't know: a stiff, moody, abrupt character who seemed to have turned back on the original spirit of the enterprise before we even set sail. I tried to talk to him about it, but it didn't work. Instead, he kept telling me that life on a ship wasn't a democracy and didn't include the normal civilities, the manners you could expect on land; and I kept telling him that in close quarters the small courtesies seemed to me all the more important. When it became clear that neither of us was listening to the other, a poisonous silence took up between us.

Mrs. Babbs and I decided to take a hotel room that night to avoid another snarling spat over bunks. We had dinner on board, then, just after dark, as we prepared to go ashore, a local dinghy pulled alongside and the boys in it launched into a sorry version of "Yellow Bird." They finished and asked for money.

"We didn't ask you to sing," Buzz tried to tell them.

"You should have stopped us . . ." they said.

The exchange turned bellicose after that, and when Buzz finally shined a flashlight in their eyes and told them to shove off, one of them raised a large stumpy stick and shouted, "You see this club? I will remember your face. I will remember your dinghy. I take care of you when you come ashore."

I came on deck just as they rowed off, just in time to hear one of them yelling, "We come back later tonight and blow your boat to *smithereens.*"

As their nasty laughter receded across the dark bay, I thought to myself, save yourself the trip, boys, because as far as I can tell this boat is going to blow *itself* to smithereens, and the blast is going to shred every sail and sink every dinghy in this harbor.

In the morning all of us agreed that another day on the island was a good idea, and we pretty much went separate ways. Jack changed his mind and filled the water tanks, then disappeared with the dinghy again. Mrs. Babbs and I walked, spent some time on the beach, and that afternoon found Fran in one of the waterfront bars. She had managed to stay almost entirely apart from the bad feelings aboard, spending long hours alone with her book. When the inevitable subject came up, she said that nothing was much different than it had been the other times she'd sailed with Jack. "It's just the way he is on a boat," she said. "You just have to sort of ignore it. Everyone who's ever sailed with him calls him Captain Bligh. It's his nickname."

We ended the conversation holding out the hope that things might get better, but I didn't believe it, and in a way it was a relief that night when I started yelling at Jack, who started yelling at Mrs. Babbs, who started yelling at Sonny over the music of steel drums at a hotel jump-up in Friendship Bay. Fran and Buzz had stayed on the ship, perhaps because they sensed that the huge billious bubble of acrimony was about to explode, and they were right. It got nasty early. It got cheap and it got low. In fact, it occurred to me several times in the angry free-for-all that fists and feet would have done much less damage than the verbal slash-and-slur that got loose that night. It was amazing: The band played "Down the way where the lights are gay" while the four of us sat there and beat the crap out of each other's spirits.

Exhaustion finally ended the mayhem. Nothing had been resolved. Jack suggested we wait till the next day to make any decisions and I agreed, although it felt like the death of yo-ho-ho to me.

Ah, but these things are never over when they're over, and somehow the next morning everybody was urging everybody to make another try. Jack drew up a rotation schedule for the big beds, and I decided what the hell . . . one more island . . . one more bead on this fool's rosary . . . why not? Who knows, I thought, it might even give me a chance to smooth my neck feathers back down into a more gentlemanly nap, maybe give me time to accept that common points of decency get left on the dock when you cast off, that sailing is supposed to be punishment, not fun.

Yeah, right.

It was four hours to Union Island, and five minutes out Jack made a remark that convinced me that we were going to find about as much union at Union as we had found friendship in Friendship Bay. He spotted a ship he had once sailed on, a lovely sleek clipper, and he said, "I'll bet they're headed for Antigua. I wish I were going with them."

"Well then, get out the goddamn flare gun," I almost said. "Rig the boatswain's chair, hail them on the radio, whatever it takes . . ."

Instead I got out the map, and when I saw there was a small airport on Union, I knew it was just a matter of waiting for the right moment to run like a rat across the next line that connected us to land.

It came around noon, a day later. Mrs. Babbs and I were on the beach, waiting for Jack to pick us up in the dinghy. After a while, Mrs. Babbs decided she'd swim out and get him while I waited with our packs on shore. When she was about halfway to the ship, I saw Jack set out in the little boat, saw Mrs. Babbs wave to him from the water, and watched as he ignored her and made for the shoreline where I stood waving and pointing.

"Was that Mrs. Babbs?" he said as he drifted into the beach. "I saw somebody waving, but I thought, I don't know anybody out here, so I just kept going."

It was an awkward moment, and it grew worse when he suggested that Mrs. Babbs was the problem, that she didn't seem to be a boat person, and that perhaps I ought to consider putting her on a plane and flying her out. I said that sounded like a great idea . . . and that I'd be getting on it with her. Other things were said; hard things, some of them. But finally there wasn't a lot of anger left in either of us. Mostly, I think, we were just deeply relieved to be out from under the grinding failure of what had seemed like such a sunny plan as we stood over that map sailing our index fingers from island dot to island dot unable to imagine the trouble that lay ahead for us in every blue half-inch.

*December 1988*

# My LIFE WITH THE HORROR

## There's nothing funny about motion sickness.
## Really. I mean it.

● ▲ ■

### DONALD KATZ

The second-worst physical sensation I've ever encountered came upon me like a hurricane just a few miles off the coast of Virgin Gorda. I was in the British Virgin Islands to do some deep-sea fishing with a bunch of professional anglers. I remember well the élan with which we wolfed down our breakfast of banana-nut pancakes sodden with heavy maple syrup, and I remember that as we headed out to the marlin lanes as the sun rose, the sea began to churn.

The horror came upon me before anyone had cast a line. As always, it began with a strange idea. How absurd, I thought. Here I am heading out for a bit of rod-and-reeling in the deep blue when all of life as we know it is doomed as of today.

The violent bout of motion sickness that ensued continues to rank very high on my list of remembered agonies in motion, less for its physical intensity than for its terrible and unceasing length. By 7 A.M. I was paralyzed—so spent that one cheek was riveted to the bottom of the cabin, so weak that I couldn't even moan. For the next ten hours—as the day grew hot and steamy above me—the old boys on deck continued to fish, eat innumerable salami sandwiches, guzzle beer, belch, and tell long, derisive stories about other seasick wimps they'd observed over the years.

There are so many other moments, each of them welded forever to my memory. There was my first ride on the Boomerang, an amusement at the now-dismantled Riverview Park in Chicago and clearly invented by a psychopathic sadist. The Boomerang rotated a tiny car so quickly that the very lips of the four children seated inside would roll back to reveal the tops of their gums. The dreaded machine then unleashed the whirling car into a parabolic tunnel, the walls of which bore the results of more than a few riders' neurovestibular responses.

There was the day I spent in 28 feet of fiberglass hell called *Livin' II* —a craft from which I trolled for coho salmon and provided free chum for several hours under a hot sun. There were the times I rode the elevators—vertical coffins, really—in the old Morrison Hotel in Chicago. The elevators stopped short of the desired floor several minutes before your kishkes caught up, and they never failed to make me ill. There was the un-air-conditioned airplane in northwestern China that was missing a cowl over one engine, which actually might have been fine if not for the various farm animals on board that were as sick as I was. I'm not proud to admit it, but there are even rocking chairs of an uncertain arc that have set my gizzards and soul to quivering.

One of my favorite examples of bureaucratic understatement has long been the commercial airlines' decision to refer to the horror of motion sickness on their official barf bags as "motion discomfort." "Discomfort" describes the internal upheaval of motion sickness in the way that "neck ache" describes hanging. The specific feelings that attend a full-fledged case of motion sickness are probably impossible to describe, but what the hell, let's try.

It begins subtly enough with a flickering sense of ennui. You might find yourself sitting in a boat or a plane or a Boomerang car at Riverview, minding your own business, when you realize in passing that you are strangely uneasy about something. You might sigh a few times and notice that you are salivating uncommonly. Then you might feel clammy.

By now you have begun to yawn. This, I've always believed, is your system's way of suggesting that in a perfect world you would be at home in bed, fast asleep, for no organism should have to experience what's about to happen next.

You soon realize that your entire life to this point has been devoid of meaning, and then you actually begin to lose touch with your emotions, your capacity to reason, and most of your motor skills. The demons of motion sickness are now fiendishly disengaging all unnecessary functions to allow you to concentrate every faculty on the appalling sensations that are on their way. Your operative senses become sharpened to everything too loud or too bright. Engine noises seem deafening, and radios scream like air raid sirens. Terrible, noxious odors begin to gallop through your nose in stampede.

You begin to pant. Your skin grows tingly, then numb, then cold as your blood abandons your useless extremities (your throbbing, spinning head, for motion sickness purposes, being an extremity), and flows into your heaving thorax to rally round your heart as if to make one valiant last stand.

A thin coating of sweat covers your entire body, and the world around you begins to resemble a vast emissive basin. You are now approaching the peak of the exponential curve traveled by the symptomology of the affliction. The pain is astonishing: a braying, mocking, undefined sort of pain that makes you yearn for a gunshot wound or a compound fracture . . . anything to distract the mind.

Eventually a centrifugal force begins to emanate from the bonfire in your gut. A private tide then sets out on its inexorable rise toward the blinding light, and finally emerges as an expression of such unbelievable biological urgency that people some distance away will join you in wishing that you had never been born. Finally—and in many ways, worst of all—the horror crosses that delicate membrane that separates transitory sensation from indelible experience. It lodges there in your trauma file forever, ready to be trundled out for future travels so that it can all be recapitulated in great detail once again.

IT'S NOT PRETTY, and as any survivor can assure you, it most certainly is not funny. My casual research indicates that the idea that throwing up is somehow humorous is rooted more deeply in our drinking cultures than in our peripatetic ones. The British, not surprisingly, have created an entire comedic idiom devoted to barfing—"talking to God on the great white telephone" and "driving the porcelain bus" being just two inspired examples. And the men of Dartmouth College have, over time, developed as many variations on the vernacular verb "to boot" as there are Eskimo nouns for snow. But the boozy analogues have nothing at all to do with the feeling of losing it on the road, at sea, in the air, or at the Morrison Hotel.

Precious little cuteness or mirth decorates the awful truth of motion sickness because the sensation is in fact characterized by unmitigated and reverberating horror. There are really only two thoughts that come to the addled mind of the afflicted, and they are both variations on the same theme: You either believe that you are about to die, or you realize from the last time it happened that you can't actually die from motion sickness, and wish only that you could.

Which brings me to the single worst physical sensation I've ever known. It occurred 13 years ago, during a particularly rough winter crossing of the English Channel. Several hours into the trip, a series of gigantic waves began to slowly but powerfully roll the huge ship from side to side. The decks seemed to dip at right angles to the sea when, quite suddenly, it appeared that some universally suggestive wave frequency had been attained, because all at once, several hundred people began to vomit.

The entire ferry turned into an orgy of airborne bile. People fell upon their neighbors, retching uncontrollably. Children screamed and threw up on their mothers. People could be seen grabbing at the boat's paper-thin metallic ashtrays and spewing all over and past the little things, like a great waterfall might overflow a pitched good-luck penny.

I saw an elderly porter trudging through the miasma, seemingly unaffected by the nightmarish scene. He held a whisk broom and a metal dustpan, bending down every so often to dip his pan into one of several raging torrents while giggling strangely to himself. All around him greenish passengers lay on their backs with their eyes open wide like the recently dead.

The bathroom was worse. People crawled pitifully along the floor and a halfhearted fistfight was being waged over who was to be next in a stall. I don't remember how I actually secured a toilet, but I do remember that it was there, on the Southampton-Ostend ferry, through the twilight of my waning consciousness, that I had my one and only waking vision.

Perhaps it was due to the proximity of the Normandy coastline, but I suddenly believed it was June 6, 1944—D day—and I was staggering through the surf toward the beach from a landing craft, my weapon cast into the sea. I was waving wildly to the Germans manning the machine gun nests on shore. "Shoot me!" I pleaded. "Oh God, please shoot me!"

As I faded back to reality and heard once again the sobs and moans outside the cubicle, it came to me that I truly wanted to die. How interesting, I thought. Here was a physical sensation that can render in moments an otherwise happy individual ready and willing to exit his life forever. I clutched the sides of the stall, and wondered: Just what is this secret force and why hasn't it been eradicated by our wizards of science? One of these days, I thought, I'm going to look more deeply into the face of the horror.

Then I passed out.

. . .

MOST EXPERTS AGREE that there are as many kinds of motion sickness as there are means of propelling objects through space. Camel sickness, for instance, is a problem in the Middle East and North Africa, and one that profoundly afflicted T. E. Lawrence. Legend has it that no less a tough guy than Emperor Hadrian lost it atop his elephant. Lord Nelson was famous for suffering regularly through bouts of seasickness, and still managed to become one of the greatest sailors of all time. Charles Darwin, another mariner of note, reportedly came upon his theories of evolution in the Galápagos only because he demanded to be let off the *Beagle* so that he could walk.

Motion sickness has always been one of the most powerful impediments to the successful waging of war, but until recently it was only during war that any thought or research was devoted to the subject. Though 60 to 70 percent of all naval recruits are afflicted during training in boats or planes, the traditional attitude in senior military circles has been that because motion sickness goes away after a few days, a soldier should just tough it out. But these days a big war might not last much longer than a medium-grade case of motion sickness. And some sailors actually don't get over it until they stop moving. My father-in-law's bunkmate on the U.S.S. *Coral Sea* provided evidence throughout most nights of the Korean conflict that some people just can't lick it.

For 40 years it's been understood that motion sickness involves dysfunctions within the sensory systems that help to tell us where we are. A great deal of organic activity goes into telling the brain that you're sitting up straight. There's vision, tactile information from the skin, input from the muscles, and an extremely intricate vestibular response that emanates from a bunch of organs and canals in the inner ear. Those organs and canals are designed to respond to both motion and gravity, and as long as you remain on terra firma, they work quite well.

It is the vestibular response to gravity—or to the lack of it—that has provided the key to what little is really known about motion sickness. And the lion's share of the existing information has been generated by scientists and physicians doing research for NASA. It turns out that a case of motion sickness in space makes a few hours circling La Guardia after the kid next to you has missed his doggie bag seem like mere practice.

Though NASA hasn't publicized the fact, more than half of the men and women in space have suffered through extreme cases of the horror.

During the earliest flights it wasn't much of a problem. Our chimps and the Mercury and Gemini astronauts reported no discomfort. Only the Soviets seemed prone to losing their instant stewed borscht. The Ruskies even had to bring their first woman in space back early because of her space motion sickness, and the great Titov, one of the Soviets' earliest and most popular cosmonauts, reportedly vomited throughout his entire flight.

American astronauts experienced the problem only when they began to move around the larger Apollo crafts. While one of the Apollo astronauts, Rusty Schweickart, was traveling through the chute that connected the command module to the lunar excursion module, his "egress was compromised," as they say at NASA, and the poor guy proceeded to lose a meal right there. He was sick for 50 hours afterward, a torment that in my book should have earned him the Congressional Medal of Honor. From then on, especially after the shuttle flights began, reports of illness came back with every mission. "I began to experience a mild epigastric awareness, and the awareness of salivation," one astronaut recorded after his return. "Then I upchucked after eating a can of stewed tomatoes."

During space motion sickness all of the symptoms appear in overdrive. A couple of victims haven't even had time to get their bags up, and in a state of weightlessness, projectile vomiting takes on a whole new meaning. Many astronauts are so destabilized by the time they return to Earth that they can't walk for a few days. After one Skylab flight, two got badly sick on the recovery vessel.

The first full-time test subject sent aloft to study space motion sickness was the flying senator from Utah, Jake Garn. Though Garn was a military reserve pilot with considerable aerobatic training, and was known for his cast-iron stomach, he still managed to perform awesomely for the sensors tethered to his body and the microphones listening to his bowels. To this day, the wags at NASA speak of measuring the intensity of a space motion sickness episode in "garns."

There have been two shuttle flights with research physicians on board, and the NASA Life Sciences Division has spent more money on motion sickness than on any other research subject. The best academic talents in the field have been contracted, and separate labs have been established at the Ames Research Center in Stanford, California, and at the Johnson Space Center in Houston. I'd heard that scientists in Houston had constructed a rambling complex of gigantic machines that study the relationship between vestibular stimuli and nausea by simulating uncomfortable traveling conditions. The machines were designed as "ground modalities," and if nothing else had been accomplished, NASA apparently had perfected the ability to make people as sick as dogs. It was thus with considerable trepidation, clammy hands, and the faintest flutter in my stomach that I filled out an application to become a test subject.

THE HUGE, high-tech vomitorium that is the neurophysiology lab of the Johnson Space Center exceeded my expectations—and my fears. I was shown a giant steel swing that looked like a cross between a Nautilus machine and some device from the Spanish Inquisition, and a helmet (with an official NFL-style chin strap) that covered your whole head in blackness and bombarded your eyes with whirling images. A terrifying rotating chair—a stainless steel contraption with a green waterproof cushion and Velcro wrist straps—was designed at great expense to revolve test subjects at a constant velocity until they "exhibited symptoms." The floor of most rooms in the lab was covered with indoor/outdoor carpeting, and though it was clear that the scientists and technicians were immune by now, the place smelled of experimental results.

Dr. Mil Reschke, the director of the lab, took me to see the machine employed in the dreaded "sudden-stop" test. "It's a very acute test . . . extremely provocative," said Reschke. "You are accelerated to a constant velocity of 50 revolutions per minute, and you are held there for 20 seconds before being slammed to a stop. You are stopped in less than a second, and then you are started again in less than a second, and it's repeated over and over again until you get sick . . . but hardly anybody makes it past three trips."

The most essential research tool available to the motion sickness scientists of NASA, however, is too big to be housed in the lab. I was there for several days of training for an eventual flight as a test subject on the infamous KC-135, the "vomit comet." A souped-up 707 with padded walls, floors, and ceilings, the KC-135 is designed to go into such powerful climbs over the Gulf of Mexico that a force of two Gs—roughly equivalent to a flying tackle by Refrigerator Perry—is exerted upon its occupants. It flies up along a specific parabola that, at its peak, creates a period of almost 30 seconds of total weightlessness. The KC-135 then descends into a screaming dive of 15,000 feet that exerts two Gs in the opposite direction. I flashed briefly on my day of banana-nut pancakes and deep-sea fishing when I was informed that the KC-135 would travel its gut-wrenching parabolas not once, but many tens of times, before returning to base. It would dive toward the Gulf for four hours while test subjects with government-issue motion discomfort bags attached to their jumpsuits suffered for science in its cabin.

Those who don't get sick describe the flight as one of the most thrilling experiences of their lives. Some do endless somersaults and launch themselves from one end of the plane to the other like superheroes. Those who do get sick don't want to talk about it, though one fellow offered the observation that under microgravity, vomit tends to form before you into thousands of little BBs before attaching to the nearest wall or person when the plane reaches the top or bottom of the dive. During our first lecture as part of the training, the instructors told us that those who failed to hit the bags fitted conveniently below their chins would be required to clean up the plane after landing.

Some 400 civilians and NASA employees are qualified volunteer test subjects in the motion sickness program. Though most people in my training program were engineers or astronauts, a few were space groupies. One of my classmates, Sharline, showed me sensitive poems she'd written about individual astronauts and about spaceflight in general, and she claimed to be more than ready to go up and blow lunch for the Red, White, and Blue.

"How many a ya's gonna fly zero-G?" she barked before class began the second day. A few raised their hands, but the weak response clearly disappointed her.

BECAUSE THE KC-135 is a high performance aircraft, test subjects must go through the same sort of preliminary physiological program and pass the same written examination as fighter pilots and astronauts. For two days our trainers—all of them ex-military fliers of the old school—took turns standing next to the silver space suit propped lifelessly in the corner. They ran through the rudimentary physics of flying at altitude, and taught us a great deal about the substernal pains, the loss of speech, and the feeling of ants crawling under your skin that come with rapid flight. We learned the many symptoms of hypoxia, or oxygen deprivation, at altitude. ("It's different than land-based hypoxia—strangulation," drawled a flat-topped instructor. "Like, you know, in an auto accident when grass and dirt are driven down your windpipe.") We learned how to parachute out of a plane and how to survive in the jungle or on the open sea. "You probably won't need to know this for your flight," said the instructor. "In all these years there's never been a bailout of a KC-135 . . . 'course there have been crashes."

The instructors all hailed from a certain camp within the NASA establishment that appeared to have considerable antipathy for the scientific and medical communities, and for their test subjects. In the macho tradition of the old *Right Stuff* ethic, the instructors held motion sickness researchers in particular disdain, believing that they were only developing tests that would keep perfectly tough fliers on the ground.

For their part, the scientists in the neurophysiology department assumed that more than a few instances of the horror had been covered up by flight crews. During one of the Skylab missions, astronaut Bill "Lead Belly" Pogue got sick, and though the crew saw to discarding the evidence, they forgot about the on-board tape recorder that documented the episode and the cover-up. Pogue had been renowned for being inured to any of the torture devices dreamed up to make people motion sick, but once in space, the lead belly turned molten. The incident speaks to one of the strangest and most baffling things about space motion sickness: Susceptibility to one form of it indicates nothing about vulnerability to another.

Toward the end of our training session, one instructor, Mike Fox, described the basic anatomy of the vestibular system housed in the inner ear. Various canals, sensitive to twisting and turning movements, activate a group of otolith organs that record information about those movements and send it to the brain. Motion sickness, said Fox, probably results from confusing and mismatched inputs emanating from these and other sense organs. The information just doesn't compute.

To demonstrate this supposition, Fox lugged into the middle of the room a steel chair resting on a vertical pole, which in turn was connected to a sturdy, round base. The device was a stripped-down version of the automated rotating chair back in the neurophysiology lab. Then, of course, the bastard picked me from the audience to ride the chair in demonstration of a few simple otolith-displacement tests.

It was all I could do to make it to the front of the room without falling to my knees. Fox gave me one spin, and the bearings on the damned thing were so good that I really took off. He had me close my eyes and point my thumbs in the direction I believed I was spinning.

Then he stopped the chair and sent it the other way. I suspect he didn't twirl me in the opposite direction after each stop, though, because everyone in the class was laughing when I pointed my thumbs. Then—and I will never forgive Mike Fox for this—he told me to make a gesture that seemed simple enough to an early motion-sick individual spinning like a dervish in a stainless steel chair. He told me to tilt my head and touch my ear to my shoulder.

I couldn't believe it. I yelled "A-a-a-a-ah!" like someone falling off a cliff, but I was really thinking, I can't believe it! The sensation rang bells and lit sparklers. The pain was astonishing, as if I'd torn all the muscles in my brain. I saw a white-hot bell rising on one of those carnival test-of-strength machines. It flew up past the Boomerang at Riverview, transcended the horror off Virgin Gorda, and topped out just past the hallucinatory ride to Ostend. The bell rang unbearably as NEW NUMBER ONE flashed on the marquee inside my eyelids.

As I wondered if I had the strength and wherewithal to get my hands up before egesting in front of the class, Fox stopped the chair and ordered me to open my eyes, look at the clock in the back of the room, and tell everyone what time it was. I saw only a black-and-white circular blur careening from one side of the room to the other. It slowed a little and I saw it was a clock, but for another half-minute it rolled around the room as I tried to visually chase it down and read the time. My classmates were hysterical. From the outside, apparently, it looked as if my eyeballs were bouncing in their sockets like pinballs. Who ever said motion sickness isn't funny?

THE ONE SURE THING INDICATED by scientific literature and by doctors working on motion sickness is that nothing much at all is known or understood. They've put rotating chairs in the shuttle and they've poured tens of millions into research, but they still don't really know what it is, who is bound to suffer from it, or how to cure it.

"One thing I can tell you for sure," said one researcher, "this disorder is very . . . depressing."

I'd never thought of it that way, but all in all I liked the idea. (The remark reminded me of the Vatican spokesman's statement after the Pope was shot in St. Peter's Square: "The Papa, he's-ah depressed.")

Most people know that several available drugs modify the symptoms of motion sickness. The ubiquitous sailor's patch loaded up with Transderm-V has actually been shown to help some sufferers of seasickness.

But the drug does have side effects, and most researchers admit they are bothered by not knowing why it works. The active ingredient, scopolamine, was used as a truth serum by the Nazis, and though I've tried it to various effects, I've always felt nervous for fear of ratting on members of the Maquis.

The good old counterculture has contributed at least two possible miracle cures: ingesting huge amounts of ginger until you burp, and using biofeedback to control the sensation. The NASA people won't even comment on the ginger idea, but an entire lab unit at the Ames Research Center has been working on biofeedback and autogenic therapy for ten years.

Though some Houston-based scientists scoff at biofeedback, the general mind-over-matter thesis does have a following. It's known that the driver of a vehicle doesn't get motion sick nearly as often as the passenger does, because the driver's brain is more fully informed of what's coming. One astronaut says he fought off motion sickness by using his "egocentric coordinate system": Whichever way the top of his head pointed was up, and when his crewmates got sick the first time they looked at someone while upside down in the shuttle, he was fine.

Mind over matter has always made a certain amount of sense to me as a layman and a lifelong victim because the one time I beat the horror, I think I *willed* it back into its lair. I was flying across the Rockies toward Denver in a small plane that was falling into every air pocket and catching every updraft the mountains had to offer. Before the roughness set in, I realized that my seatmate was none other than Clint Eastwood. I distinctly remember the interchange between the portion of my brain housing ego, self-esteem, and perception of relative manhood, and the section that wanted to completely embarrass me in front of Big Clint. But the vomit doctors from coast to coast all told me I was mistaken in my mind-over-matter theory. "It's a physiological response," one of them said. "If you were physically bound to experience all the symptoms of motion sickness next to Clint Eastwood, you most certainly would have."

Most experts are skeptical—not only about one another's work, but also about the possibility that they'll discover something new about the horror before their careers end. Neurophysiologists at NASA have motion sickness experiments scheduled for a spring 1990 shuttle flight, but several of them complain that funding has reached a plateau, and that a breakthrough might still be decades away.

Until then, you can try available drugs if you don't mind getting groggy, and also "avoid soda pop before travel, avoid gum, empty your bowels before leaving, eat breakfast [though not banana-nut pancakes], don't drink the night before, get rest, do not have any psychological problems, and try to be real psyched-up." This list was given to me and the other test subjects as we left Houston to await our KC-135 flight. But as my anxiety about the flight mixed with a slightly queasy feeling on the plane home, I realized the tough, old fighter jocks and the scientists had failed to mention one other possibility—just don't go. I actually tried this particular remedy last summer when my cousin Jimmy invited me to spend a weekend on his new sailboat. Jimmy had just purchased the handmade Rolls-Royce of sailing ships—the kind on which Michael Douglas wooed Kathleen Turner in *Romancing the Stone*. But I said no, and sure enough, I didn't feel sick all weekend.

It wasn't really the fear of the physical consequences that made me ponder how much I didn't want to fly in the KC-135. It was just that I wasn't up for feeling like I wanted to die again, not even for the readers of *Outside*. Life has been particularly good lately, and somehow the idea of wanting nothing more than a sudden and painless death seemed to test even the limits of the existentialist's instructions to act and act again into the void.

So I really didn't mind much when a senior NASA official decided at the last minute that even though I was a qualified, trained, and medically certified test subject, I was still a writer—and therefore ineligible under directives spawned by the *Challenger* disaster.

THROWING UP IN A BOAT, car, or space shuttle seems to be such a pedestrian thing, a rote physiological response; something that should be consummately fixable in a world that has mastered the ability to repair an injured heart, attach severed limbs, and allow two-pound babies to grow to be adults. But it seems that the body's programming is simply not designed for certain kinds of movement at certain times. Or, to put it another way, it may be designed *not* to accept certain kinds of situations, as if this were part of a higher plan.

Eight years ago a psychologist working on the problem posited that motion sickness was actually a variant of some ancient survival-response to poison. The body can detect certain poisons and vomit them out most efficiently. This fellow contended—though he didn't say why—that motion sickness was a somewhat similar response. Without a vestibular system, you wouldn't get motion sick, but as with rats—animals that never vomit and can thus build homes in rotating chairs and not care— you couldn't eject poisons, either. Other researchers think the mystery might be part of a larger neurological purpose that once protected early man. From an evolutionary point of view, the animals that stay still, that don't venture forth to eat or to chase mates during disturbing physical events, tend to be the ones that survive. I can certainly attest from personal experience that when motion sickness sets in, you do not want to eat or chase mates. Maybe some primordial impulse rises like an internal fire storm to tell you that thou shalt not have banana nut pancakes before hitting the open sea, shalt not ride the Boomerang, and shalt never, ever again strap thy backside into a rotating chair.

"There is only one sure cure for motion sickness," an old English proverb instructs. "Go and sit in the shade . . . of a church."

*September 1987*

# POSTCARD FROM THE APOCALYPSE

*Kuwait is burning. Wish you were here.*

● ▲ ■

TIM CAHILL

During the occupation of Kuwait, Iraqi soldiers often defecated in the finest rooms of the finest houses they could find. It was a gesture of hatred and ignorance and contempt. Then, in retreat, the Iraqis literally set Kuwait on fire. There was no strategic significance to this, no military advantage for the retreating Iraqi troops. Blowing the oil wells—nearly all the oil wells in the country—was the environmental equivalent of crapping on the carpet.

Because fierce desert winds would carry smoke and soot at least 500 miles in any direction, Iraqi children would breathe carcinogens along with the children of Saudi Arabia and Kuwait. Iraqi farmers would likely suffer acid rain. These Iraqi troops, under Saddam Hussein, had done something that no other animal on earth does: They had fouled their own nest.

The conflagration in Kuwait is madness made visible, madness with possible global consequences.

I had spent the Fourth of July and the two following weeks dashing around the burning oil fields of Kuwait in company with photographer Peter Menzel, attempting to assess the extent of the madness. But this day, toward the end of our stay, was set aside for a long, leisurely drive. The madness, we felt, had soiled us just as surely as the soot and the purple petroleum rain that fell from the drifting black clouds. This rain created lakes of oil that covered acres of desert, and when these lakes caught fire the smoke was thick and blinding, so that directions to various wells had to be quite specific as to roadside landmarks: "Turn left at the third dead camel."

I myself particularly wanted to forget the three dead Iraqi soldiers I had had every reason not to bury. They were still out there in the desert, near the Saudi border. The wind covered them with sand. And then, after a time, it uncovered them.

So: Why not spend the day in pursuit of recreational diversion? Peter and I would climb Mount Kuwait. Go to the beach. See the emir's gardens. Maybe even take in a drive-in movie. Think about things a bit.

MOUNT KUWAIT sits in an area of newly formed oil lakes, south of the oil town of Al Ahmadi, past the distinctive Longhorn fire, and a few miles off the Burgan road. Because we envisioned a long day, and because the summer temperatures in the desert often exceeded 120 degrees Fahrenheit, it was a good idea to start early.

At 3:30 in the morning the air felt cool, about 85 degrees, and the streets of Kuwait City were empty. The traffic lights worked, but there was no traffic. It was a great place to run red lights, which I count as a fine activity.

A gentle breeze from the north had swept the sky clear of smoke. The city center might have been Miami, except that businesses and homes were abandoned, windows were broken, and the major hotels all showed evidence of recent fires. There were streaks of soot on most of the buildings. In March the city had been covered over in a thick shroud of smoke, and when the spring rains came they fell black and soiled all they touched.

By July, the fires in the oil fields south of the city had been beaten back dozens of miles. More than 200 fires had been "killed," and the best estimates had another 500 still burning. Fire fighters were working from the north with the prevailing winds at their backs, and Kuwait City was seldom inundated by smoke. Some days were whiskey brown; others were bright and blue and hot.

The outskirts of the city looked like Phoenix, where futuristic divided and elevated highways ran over single-story poured-concrete houses. We exited the freeway and plowed down a two-lane blacktop toward the oil fields. There was a mound of sand and a sign in English that said ROAD CLOSED. As journalists, we assumed the sign did not apply to us.

Levees of sand kept ponds and lakes of oil from consuming the road. The oil lakes seemed to glow, silver-red, with the light from the fires on the southern horizon. After a few miles, the shimmering in the distance separated itself into individual fires: great plumes of flame that dotted the flat desert landscape. The shapes of the plumes themselves had become familiar landmarks. Some looked a bit like Christmas trees; some geysered up every 30 seconds; some lay close to the ground and seemed to burn horizontally. Not far past Al Ahmadi, the most distinctive of the fires howled out of control. Two plumes shot out along the ground—one to the west, one to the east—and each turned up at the end. The fire fighters, most of them Americans from Texas, called this one the Longhorn fire.

It was close to the road, and the western plume was directed at passing vehicles like a pyromaniac's wet dream. Here the moonless night was bright as day, only the light was red, flickering, hellish. A 20-mile-an-hour wind carried inky billows of smoke to the south, but along this road and others in the oil fields the winds sometimes sent impenetrable clouds of gritty soot rolling over passing vehicles.

Not far from here, on April 24, a small Japanese sedan had swerved off the oil-slicked road and into a burning oil lake, killing two British journalists. The driver had apparently been disoriented by the smoke and falling soot. Two other vehicles, a pumping truck and a tanker, had apparently followed the tracks of the sedan into the flames. At least one fire-fighting crew had passed by the three vehicles without raising an alarm: Burned-out cars in burning oil lakes are a common sight around Al Ahmadi. Those who finally recovered the bodies had seemed unaffected when they described the horror, but they mentioned it a lot, especially to journalists who assumed written warnings didn't apply to them.

The sun finally rose, a sickly orange color that I could look directly into without squinting, and in the near distance a rocky butte about 300 feet high, the highest piece of ground in all the oil fields, appeared. It took, by my watch, a little over two minutes to stroll to the top of this bump that oil workers had long ago named Mount Kuwait. It was supposed to be a joke, the name, like calling a bald-headed guy Curly.

The whole world smelled like a diesel engine. There were fires burning in all directions, more than 30 at a count, and they thundered belligerently. The lake below was burning in streaks and ribbons, with the flames hanging low over a mirrorlike surface that was unaffected by the wind. The ground was black, the sky was black, the drifting clouds were black, and only the fires lived on the land.

What I was seeing, it seemed to me, was the internal-combustion engine made external.

The country of Kuwait sits atop a vast reservoir of oil, 94 billion barrels of known reserves. This reservoir is two miles deep in places, and the oil is under tremendous pressure. Drop a pipe deep enough into the ground and oil erupts to a height of 30, 50, 70, 100 feet. Wells are capped with valve assemblies, the oil is transferred to gathering centers, then piped to sea terminals for export. It is used in internal-combustion engines around the world.

Iraqi troops had wired nearby wells to a single detonator. These wires still lay across the black sands. The explosions—dynamite directed downward by sandbags—had blown the caps off the wells and ignited the gushing oil.

Kuwait, on this day in July, would lose about $100 million worth of oil. That was the generally agreed upon figure, though the effects of the fires on the people and on the environment had yet to be coherently assessed. Toxic metals, released by combustion, will surely contaminate the desert soil and the sheep and goats and camels that graze there. Many of these food-borne metals might then cause brain damage and cardio-vascular disorders in humans.

Meanwhile, a month earlier, a National Science Foundation team, flying over the burning oil fields, had said that environmental damage was a "concern" and not a crisis. Environmental Protection Agency experts measured pollutants common to American cities—the results of internal combustion—and decided, mostly from planes flying 20,000 feet over the choking hell below, that the air quality was not deadly. Further, the flights proved that while plumes rose thousands of feet, the fires weren't propelling the heavy smoke high enough into the atmosphere to cause worldwide climatic change.

Still, in April, about five million barrels of oil a day had gone up in flame. Black rain had fallen in Saudi Arabia and Iran; black snow had fallen on the ski slopes of Kashmir, more than 1,500 miles to the east. And no one had yet measured pollutants peculiar to this crisis: a class of carcinogens called polyaromatic hydrocarbons generated out of partially burned oil. Standing on the summit of Mount Kuwait, my own assessment was bleak. The desert, here in the oil fields, was both dead and deadly. It was a sure vision of the environmental apocalypse.

By the time we scrambled down Mount Kuwait, the sun was higher in the sky. A purple petroleum rain had fallen while we'd been climbing, and the evidence could be seen as pinpricks on the windshield. Peter fired up the Land Cruiser, but it was hard to hear the internal-combustion engine over the roar of the surrounding external combustion. I thought about those unburied Iraqi soldiers out near the Saudi border; one of them had been decapitated. In the gathering heat, the oil on the windshield now turned a streaky red, so that it looked like dried blood.

ON THE WAY to the emir's gardens, deep in the southern oil fields, we saw a brown Land Rover, coated in black, gummy sand, parked by the side of the road. American fire fighters drove Ford and Chevy pickups, Kuwaiti oil executives drove Mercedes. The Land Rover, we knew, had to belong to our friends in Royal Ordnance, a subsidiary of British Aerospace. Composed mostly of former British military explosive experts, RO had won the contract to dispose of explosives in this area of the fields.

When Iraqi troops blew the wells, they sometimes salted the surrounding area with antipersonnel mines to sabotage the fire-fighting effort. But what RO was mostly finding were the universally feared Rockeyes that had been dropped by American pilots onto Iraqi positions. A Rockeye is a metal cylinder, maybe three feet long. When it is dropped it splits apart, releasing 247 six-inch-long rockets designed to explode on impact. The deadly submunitions look like fat lawn darts. All over, all across the black desert sands, there were Rockeye submunitions buried about three inches deep. Sometimes the pilot had dropped the Rockeyes too low to the ground; sometimes the submunitions had hit very soft sand. In any event, RO estimated that between 30 and 50 percent of the submunitions were still live. They were black with oil and could be identified only by their three fins. Usually there was a blackened Rockeye cannister nearby.

Our RO friends had the dirtiest, meanest job in the fields. Whereas the fire fighters who followed them worked with the north wind at their backs, which meant that they often had blue sky overhead, the RO teams worked in heavy smoke in the midst of the fires, looking for explosives within a 150-foot radius of a burning well.

Three teams of ten apiece were now walking the hellish landscape. I could just make them out through the shifting clouds of soot that blotted out the desert sun. They were illuminated, in silhouette, by a nearby plume of fire some 80 feet high. They walked with their heads down, very slowly, looking like a precision drill team of very depressed men. The Rockeyes were marked with red-and-white tape fluttering at the end of a metal stake driven into the sand.

Later that day another man would come through the field, stopping at each of the markers. He would dig a hole next to each of the Rockeyes, place a wad of plastic explosive in the hole, string a long wire, and detonate the deadly submunitions from a safe distance.

Now, however, Lance Malin was standing by the Land Rover, coordinating the three teams currently walking the sand. The process of locating and destroying live ammunition was called explosive ordnance disposal, or EOD, and I knew it amused Malin that American fire fighters were using the acronym as a verb: "Has this area been EODed?"

He was talking to a man wearing heavy leather gloves. There was a large spiny-tailed lizard, about two and a half feet long, dangling from the man's index finger. The RO men had found a lot of these lizards, known locally as dhoubs, stuck in the sand and too weak to free themselves. They took them back to their headquarters in Al Ahmadi and fed them bits of apple until they regained their strength and snapped at anything that moved. Finally, the lizards took a ride in one of the Land Rovers and were released in the relatively pristine northern desert.

The RO men had no choice. They had to rescue the lizards. They were British.

Malin stowed this particular dhoub in the Land Rover and asked if I had been to the big mine field that RO was working near the Saudi border.

A couple of days ago, I said.

"The Iraqi corpses still there?"

We admitted that they were. Right where everyone had left them. Unburied. For five goddamn months.

THERE WAS NO ONE at the guard station that flanked the entrance to the emir's gardens, a weekend retreat for Kuwait's ruling family. It would have been cruel to station a man there. Fire-fighting teams had not yet reached the large walled compound—they were working far to the north—and the fires burning on all sides kept the area shrouded in heavy smoke no matter which way the wind was blowing. It was, at ten o'clock on a desert morning, dark as dusk, and the temperature under the smoke stood at 80 degrees. It was 105 in the sun.

We drove through a shallow pond of oil at the entrance and onto a circular driveway fronting a modest group of buildings. There was a children's play area nearby: teeter-totters and monkey bars coated in oil. On the ground were the oily remnants of a cow that had been slaughtered, presumably for food, by occupying Iraqi troops. There were other black cowlike shapes on the ground, interspersed with the corpses of several large birds, presumably from the compound's aviary. The largest and highest plume of flame I saw in Kuwait—I estimated its height at 200 feet—boomed and thundered just beyond the north wall.

This fire was a smoker, and it had formed a lake that abutted the eight-foot-high wall. Where there were breaks in the blackened cinder blocks, tongues of oil seeped into a low-lying palm orchard. These small rivers were burning and running down irrigation ditches, where they lapped at the tree trunks.

My boots were caked with a black, sandy muck so that I walked in a clumping, stiff-legged manner, like Frankenstein's monster. Visibility was limited to about 15 feet, though I could see, through the falling soot, the large fire and half a dozen others leaping above the north wall. I moved toward them, careful to avoid stepping on the nubbly tracks of coke, a rocky, coallike by-product of the burning oil. In some places the coke was several feet deep, but it was also possible that the coke could be mere scum over a burning stream below. Crack the coke, I thought, and the entire track could reignite.

Presently I saw a man-size break in the wall and moved toward it through the swirling, granular darkness. The inferno beyond lit the break with a shifting, red-orange light, and I could feel the heat on my face like a bad sunburn. Everything that wasn't burning was black: the earth, the familiar shapes of the trees, the animal carcasses that littered the place. This was ground zero for the largest man-made environmental disaster in history. It was a perfect vision of hell.

I moved through the break in the wall and stopped. The next step would put me in the burning lake, which was throwing up the thickest, grainiest smoke I had yet encountered. It blinded me and made my eyes water. Despite the bandana I wore over my nose and mouth I found myself choking, and then I was coughing in fits that bent me over at the waist.

It was a sudden misery, and yet something that lives in my soul—some compelling, god-awful urge—found this horror grotesquely enthralling. It is the same urge, I think, that drives us to observe the destructive effects of a hurricane or tornado, an avalanche or flood. We shudder deliciously in the face of incomprehensible forces, in the wake of events that insurance companies call "acts of God."

But this was an act of Man, which made it a palpable evil: madness made visible in flame.

I fled back into the black gardens, clumping over the burning trenches, coughing uncontrollably as tears streamed from my eyes.

ON OUR WAY BACK NORTH to the Al Ahmadi drive-in we decided to stop and see how Safety Boss was doing on its fire. Safety Boss Ltd. is a fire-fighting crew out of Calgary, Canada. The other three outfits fighting the fires—Boots & Coots, Red Adair, and Wild Well—were all from around Houston. All were experienced pros, good teams that worked well to-gether.

Safety Boss—I loved the name—hadn't been in the business nearly as long as the other companies, but the Calgary group thought its men worked safer, harder, and dirtier than anyone else. This was a matter of constant argument. Every fire fighter thought he worked harder, safer, and dirtier than anyone else.

Safety Boss had started on this new well yesterday and thought it would have it under control today. That was fast: I had watched some other fire fighters work two full weeks to extinguish a particularly nasty smoker.

The road here was a newly plowed lane—sandy white against the oily desert—built in part through an oil lake that was showing a bit of ripple under a freshening afternoon wind of about 40 miles an hour. The wind had swept the area clear of smoke, and the sky was clear. We drove past burned- and bombed-out Iraqi tanks, armored personnel carriers, bunkers, and ammunition depots. Every half-mile or so we passed a Rockeye cannister. Red-and-white RO marking tape waved on metal spikes, in-dicating that the field to the south hadn't been fully EODed.

It was pleasant to breathe fresh air again after the burning oasis we had just visited. In March the town of Al Ahmadi had looked much like the emir's gardens, and doctors there had been treating a large number of respiratory complaints. Now, with the fires beaten back around the town, the air was still smoggy, but at least you could see through it.

One foreign industrial-health specialist at the hospital in Al Ahmadi had shown me a chart indicating that sulfur dioxide levels had dropped to the point where they were hardly measurable. A Kuwaiti chemist had argued with the man: The industrial-health specialist was measuring known pollutants, the by-products of internal combustion; how could he—how could anyone—know what toxic substances were being released by all the external combustion surrounding the town?

The chemist was one of the few Kuwaitis I met who seemed concerned about the level of toxins in the air. People in Al Ahmadi, for instance, having undergone months of smoky dusk at noon, now lived under mostly blue skies. The air was breathable, it had no odor, and things could only get better. So they seemed to think. The chemist believed that it would be years before anyone knew for certain just how badly the Kuwaiti people had been poisoned.

Safety Boss was now just up the lane. We turned, as we had been instructed, at the third dead camel, which was a rounded, camellike lump of tar lying on its side and baking in the sun. Arranged to the north of a 70-foot-high plume of flame were a few three-quarter-ton American pickups, a backhoe with an 80-foot-long shovel, two water tankers, an 18-wheel pumping truck, a huge crane, and a bulldozer with a tin shed on top to protect the operator from the heat. There was also an 18-wheel mud truck, an indication that Safety Boss thought it would have the fire out momentarily. Mud trucks are called in just before a fire is killed.

The plume of flame billowed orange and black against the blue sky above and the smoke to the south. I had spent days staring at such plumes. They were transfixing. You couldn't be near them and not stare. They were hell's lava lamps.

Two man-size backless tin sheds had been erected a hundred feet or so from the fire. Large hoses ran from tanks of water, through the pumping trucks, and up to the sheds, where they were mounted on tripods like heavy high-power rifles. There was a man in each shed, working the hose through a rectangular slit in the front of his enclosure.

A crew foreman gave me a hard hat and permission to walk up to the sheds. I had a scientific thermometer to measure the heat near the fire, but it was useless. At one o'clock in the afternoon it was already 122 degrees. The thermometer pegged at 125.

One of the men had his hose trained on the arm of a backhoe that was chopping away at what had been a seven-foot-high mound of coke at the base of the well. The coke accounted for the curious shapes of the fires, bending and twisting the flame as it accumulated. It was necessary to clear the wellhead of coke before it could be capped.

The concussive stress on the backhoe, combined with the heat, often resulted in broken shovels. This one was digging close to the wellhead, and one of the hoses was trained on its dinosaur head, keeping it cool.

The backhoe swung around and deposited another shovelful of steaming coke on the ground 80 feet from the well. Because this coke, even 80 feet away, could reignite the well once it was extinguished, the bulldozer quickly pushed a mound of sand over it.

The fellow manning the water monitor in the shed where I stood was spraying the fire. My completely useless thermometer said 125 degrees. It was hotter than that. There was no talking above the jet-engine howl of the fire, and though I wore earplugs I could feel the sound reverberating in my chest. The ground literally shook under my feet.

The billowing plume of fire looked as fierce as any burn I had seen, but it had already been beaten. When the backhoe finished its work, one man trained a stream of water at the wellhead. About 15 minutes later the fire went out. But only at the wellhead. The geyser of oil above it was still burning. And then both hoses started putting the fire out from the bottom of the geyser up.

When the plume had been killed to a height of perhaps 20 feet, it reignited from below. The hoses started again. It only took a few minutes for the fire to surrender at the wellhead. When the hoses had beaten it up to the 20-foot level, one held steady, right there, at the point where the fire wanted to reignite. The other worked its way up the wavering plume and when the fire was out to a height of 30 feet the whole thing died, puff, like that, revealing a gusher of rusty black oil shooting 70 feet into the air.

In the relative silence I heard the *crump-crump-crump* of a controlled RO explosion to the south. A few hundred yards away, in the smoke, another depressed drill team was wheeling slowly around a nearby burning well.

The Safety Boss crew moved back behind its trucks. Only two men would work with the damaged wellhead. It was the most dangerous job for a fire fighter. The first order of business was to remove the wellhead. There were bolts to be loosened—bolts that had been fused by explosives and fire—but sparks from power tools could turn the gusher above into a massive fireball. The men used wrenches and hammers made of a special alloy that didn't spark, and they worked in a downpour of oil. The black pool they stood in was hot and burned their feet so that every few minutes they jumped away from the wellhead and let the men with hoses spray them down.

Half a dozen men hooked a series of hoses to the mud truck and ran the line toward the well. A new wellhead was lowered onto the gusher with a crane. Two men with ropes directed its fall, then bolted it into place. Oil erupted out of the new wellhead as before, but this assembly had a pipe projecting from its side.

The hose from the mud truck was screwed onto the side pipe. At a signal, the mud man began pumping a mixture of viscous bentonite and weighty barite into the well. This "mud" had been formulated to be much heavier than oil, and it was pumped into the well under extremely high pressure. The gusher dwindled to 30 feet, to 20, to ten, and then it died, smothered in mud.

No one shouted, and no one shook hands. These men had been working since five in the morning. It was now past two in the afternoon, and they were ready to move out, to get on to the next well.

The only break the Safety Boss crew had had all day was a brief catered lunch. A few of the men had chosen to eat several hundred yards away, near a bombed-out Iraqi tank. There were always interesting things to be found in the tanks: live ammunition, helmets, uniforms, diaries, war plans, unit rosters, oil-smeared pictures of Saddam Hussein.

Near this tank, the crew had found a black, man-shaped lump of tar lying on its back with black clawlike hand raised in death. Graves details had long ago buried all the dead they could find but hadn't been able to work their way through the choking smoke of the oil fields, over land that had yet to be EODed. The Safety Boss crews, which were working farther south than the other companies, were always finding bodies: the bodies of men who had fought for oil and died for oil and finally, horribly, been mummified in oil. The Safety Boss crew had buried this soldier on its lunch break. They had buried him where he fell and driven a stake into the ground to mark his final resting place. They always buried the dead they found.

A HUGE BOMB CRATER graced the entrance to the Cinema Ahmadi Drive-In, which was baking in the heat under relatively blue skies. Surrounded by a high, white cement fence and featuring an immense screen, it was perhaps the most luxurious and high-tech drive-in on earth. Every speaker post featured a thick hose ending in a device that looked like something that might be used to clean draperies but in fact provided air-conditioning for each car. Occupying Iraqi troops had ripped the gadgets off each and every post so that the place as a whole looked like an explosion in a vacuum-cleaner factory.

The theater was otherwise empty except for a few late-model American cars that had been stripped of their tires. The doors were open and the windshields had been smashed. The wind, now gusting to 50 miles an hour, was the only sound inside the world's most luxurious drive-in theater.

In the refreshment stand, behind a broken window sporting an advertisement for Dr Pepper, I found a number of Iraqi helmets, uniforms, grenades, rifles, and ammunition clips. The troops had defecated in the projection room, which they had also thoroughly trashed. Dozens of reels of film had been methodically cut up into four-inch pieces. That would teach those Kuwaitis, all right: Rip out their air conditioning, crap in their projection room, and cut up their film! Ha!

I held one of the film strips up to the light: a lovely Arab woman was comforting a sick old man. Other strips featured other lovely Arab women in family situations: cooking, eating, tending children.

These gentle family films hardly seemed appropriate for a postapocalyptic drive-in. This was *Mad Max* territory, this was *Road Warrior* turf. Australian director George Miller's vision of postnuclear desolation—depraved individuals driving a disparate variety of vehicles powered by internal-combustion engines and battling each other for . . . well, for oil—seemed, in this place, less a B-movie triumph than a sagacious prophecy.

Scenes from just such a movie were being played out in the Burgan field every day. Caravans of odd vehicles moved slowly through the darkness at noon, their headlights pathetic against the swirling smoke. Sometimes they were illuminated by the flickering light of a nearby fire: a few pickups, an 18-wheel mud truck festooned with valves, a bulldozer with a metal enclosure, a huge backhoe . . . all these vehicles, most of them like nothing seen anywhere else on earth and all of them moving against a backdrop of fire, deeper into the blackness, into the smoke and soot and falling purple rain.

THE POSTAPOCALYPTIC TOWN OF DUBIYAH, 45 minutes south of Kuwait City, was a fenced-off vacation community for mid-level Kuwaiti oil executives. Iraqi troops had thought to make a stand here, and the beaches were very obviously mined. I could see a number of Italian-made mines about the size and shape of flattened baseballs littering the sand. They were designed to maim, to tear a man's leg off at the knee. It takes several men to care for one wounded soldier. The mines, which didn't kill, were therefore militarily efficacious. A few weeks earlier, a Kuwaiti teenager, ignoring the posted signs, had strolled out onto the beach and lost a leg for no military reason whatsoever.

Now the town was deserted. The wind had swept the skies clear of smoke, but the sea itself, washing up onto the mined beaches in sluggish waves, was covered over with a faint rainbow sheen of petroleum. Dead fish rotted on the beach next to the mines.

Sometime in mid-January, Saddam Hussein's troops had purposely spilled an estimated six million barrels of oil into the gulf. The spill was actually a series of releases, with main dumping on January 19 at Sea Island, a tanker-loading station not far from Dubiyah. Prevailing winds had carried the massive slick south, sparing Kuwait. Saudi Arabia took the brunt of the spill, and its beaches had become heavy mats of tar. The glaze of oil here, off Dubiyah, had come from the petroleum rains, from rivers of oil that had flowed from the fields to the sea.

Closer to where I stood, the beach that fronted the deadly sea was decorated with a double row of concertina wire, and behind the concertina wire was a trench reinforced with cement blocks that stretched for miles. There were houses three rows deep beyond the trench. They were blocky cement buildings with faded lawn chairs and tattered umbrellas on concrete patios. Most of them were undamaged, except for those that fronted antiaircraft guns, which had been deployed about every half mile along the beach. Each and every gun had been destroyed. Some were mere heaps of shredded metal. The houses behind the guns had taken some corollary damage. They were, in fact, piles of rubble. All the other homes were intact, undamaged but for a broken window or kicked-in door. And there was no one there, not a soul in this town that must have housed thousands of people. It felt as if the apocalypse had met the Twilight Zone at Kuwait's last resort.

I stepped through broken floor-to-ceiling windows and invaded any number of these houses. Dozens of them. Everywhere it was the same. At least one room was completely full of human excrement. Sometimes every room was packed with the stuff.

Peter and I, being journalists, felt compelled to quantify the mess. I don't know why, really, but that's what we did.

"I got 34 piles in here," Peter yelled.

"Seventeen in the kitchen," I shouted, "and 24 in the laundry room."

We examined the condition of the piles.

"These guys," I said, "weren't healthy."

And then it occurred to us that maybe the soldiers had been scared. Maybe they'd shit in these houses because they were afraid to go outside during the bombardment. Maybe the odor, at least here in Dubiyah, wasn't so much contempt as fear.

Someone had drawn on a wall in red Magic Marker. There was an idyllic scene of an Arab boat, a dhow, floating in a calm lagoon. Near that, on the same white wall, was another drawing in another hand: a man and a woman staring at one another with a large heart between them.

Iraqi soldiers, I knew, had been allowed to listen to only one radio station: 20-20 news straight from the mouth of Saddam Hussein himself. Those who disobeyed could be disciplined or killed. Kuwaitis who had talked with Iraqi soldiers before the bombardment said that the occupying troops had no idea that forces were massing on the Saudi border, for they weren't hearing that news on their single radio station. What they didn't know would kill them. And poison their world. They defecated in bathtubs and drew pictures of men and women in love on the wall.

I thought about the day we had driven to an oil field near the Saudi border. There the Iraqis had installed a mine field that stretched from horizon to horizon. They had marked it off with a pair of concertina-wire fences. Presumably only portions of the field were heavily salted with mines, and the fence had been built to give the advancing troops pause. On the Kuwait side was a deep pit, which was, I suppose, meant to contain oil that could be set afire.

The allied troops had easily punched through the mine field, and there was a cleared road over the oil pit and through the fence. I could see rounded antitank mines, about the size and shape of home smoke alarms, scattered around beyond the fence. They were a beige color, hard to see in the sand until my eyes adjusted. Then I could see dozens of them.

There were three corpses in Iraqi uniforms alongside the road. Presumably they had lain there for at least five months. It was 118 degrees, the wind was blowing a low-level sandstorm, and the dead men were partially covered in sand.

Someone—the Saudis, I was told—had decapitated one corpse, and the head lay on the man's lap in an obscene position. The lower portion of the face was all grinning bone, but the upper portion of the head, protected by hair, was intact. The skin was desiccated, a mottled yellow. I have seen mummies in museums and in the field. This scene, these corpses, were five months old and already looked like ancient history.

Peter and I were alone, and we thought to bury the corpses, as was the custom. We had equipped our Land Cruiser with a shovel to dig ourselves out of the sand. Still, I didn't want to dig a grave in a mine field.

We discussed the possibility of putting the dead men in the back of our vehicle and driving to a place where we could dig. But the idea of having that desiccated, grinning head rolling around in the back was distressing.

"We could just leave them here," Peter said. "To illustrate the horror of war."

Which is what we told ourselves we were doing as we drove off into the desert, leaving three men unburied in contravention of Muslim and Christian custom. I felt mildly guilty about this and knew that I should feel very guilty about it, so I ended up feeling very guilty about feeling mildly guilty.

I was still thinking about those dead men as I stepped carefully through the chalets that fronted the oily beach.

"Oh, man," I heard myself shout as I moved into one of the grander chalets. It had a fine view of the mined beach and the dead fish and the glittering petroleum sheen that was the sea. And in one big room, in front of the broken picture window, there were well over a hundred remnants of the men who had invaded this land. Souvenirs of ignorance, all in fear-splattered piles.

Outside, not far away, contaminants released by the howling fires were poisoning children; they were creating acid rains that would kill crops so that people could starve in the name of oil; they were spawning rivers of flame that ran to the sea and killed what lived there; they were throwing 3 percent of the world's carbon dioxide into the air, intensifying the greenhouse effect that would bake the earth in drought before an alternative to the internal-combustion engine could be found. It was the beginning of the end, the environmental apocalypse, and here I was, in the oblivion of the Last Resort, thinking about the unburied dead and counting crap.

*December 1991*

# COSTA RICA, THE TWIG SYNDROME, AND THE WORLD RECORD THAT GOT AWAY

## When fishing and travel mix too well

● ▲ ■

### RANDY WAYNE WHITE

Despite heavy rain, fruit bats were hitting on yellow poppers, those Styrofoam lures some people learn how to make by reading fly-fishing magazines. Rudy Dodero, an excellent caster, would haul the popper off the water, shoot line into the jungle darkness, shoot again on the forecast, and let the popper swing into the lights of the dock where the river current boiled in an oleaginous slick.

"See? Es coming now, man. I strip eet in slow, real slooow, make it splash. See 'em? Hear them fruit bats pooping?"

Peeping; that's what I think Rudy meant.

Into the annulated haze came these shadowy creatures, little rats on wings vectoring wildly toward the lure. I ducked, reasoning that fruit bats may not be attracted to artificials, but vampire bats might be. (Actually, they were probably *Noctilio leporinus*, the fish-eating bats of Central America—not that I would have recognized a fish-eating bat had I landed one.)

There was a grunt, a moment of mad thrashing, and I looked up to see Dodero, one of the most knowledgeable fly-fishermen in all of Costa Rica, silhouetted by dock lights against a scrim of silver rain, back arched, rod bowed, smiling as his line flew heavenward—an inspiring sight.

This was at Río Colorado Lodge on the Caribbean coast of Costa Rica, a comfortable outpost 14 miles from the Nicaraguan border. Río Colorado is considered by many to offer the best tarpon and snook fishing in the world—something that one who's made his living as a fishing guide in Florida for the last nine years should not admit. The lodge is located on a river that flows from the jungle right into the Caribbean. No roads, no towns, no barrier islands, just this river and a bunch of lagoons making a straight shot into the sea; a confluence of wilderness water to which predatory fish come unimpeded, ready to feed. If you want to be certain of catching a large fish on fly rod, then you book the three-day package at Río Colorado Lodge ($745 for double occupancy: rooms, meals, drinks, guide, and in-country travel all included).

I did not come to Costa Rica to catch tarpon (a jumping fish that commonly weighs more than a hundred pounds and looks like a giant chrome-glazed herring) or snook (a smaller game fish, wedgeheaded, with a black lateral stripe like something dreamed up in Detroit), so I had not booked the three-day package. I had come to Costa Rica specifically to fish for Pacific sailfish on fly rod; in fact, planned to try and beat the world record, the one held by Stu Apte, the famous fly-fisherman who in 1965 landed a 136-pound Pacific sail on 12-pound tippet. That I had found my way to the Caribbean coast, where there are no Pacific sailfish, and that I was now standing in the rain watching the manager of Río Colorado Lodge play a flying reptile, were, I suppose, illustrative not only of Costa Rica's charm but also of the peculiar lunacy that embraces one just beyond the portals of many exacting sports.

"Reptile?" said Dodero looking over his shoulder, the fly line still describing high, wild patterns. "Where you learn that crazy thing? Bat es no reptile, man."

Oh.

This was in May, right on the front edge of Costa Rica's rainy season. The rainy season, which lasts through November, is not considered the ideal time to tour a country in Central America, but it happens to be when the fishing in Costa Rica—always good—is at its very best. Why this was of concern to me, why fishing is still the nucleus around which I plan every trip, mystifies my friends almost as much as it continues to mystify me. In late April I had celebrated my 1,800th career fishing charter by attending taco night at a bar on Sanibel Island, and before leaving for Costa Rica, had guided more than a hundred trips during a four-month period, a withering schedule of being on the docks before light and finishing at the cleaning table just before dark. It is this marathon of wind and water, plus the Florida tourist rush, that produces in the operators of fishing vessels a phenomenon known as Twig Syndrome, or Guides' Disease, a psychological distemper with a whole bunch of un-attractive symptoms: Snapping like a dry twig is one, and maybe leaving your boat to go on a fishing vacation is another. Now I was witnessing a couple of new symptoms, I thought, watching Dodero out there in the rain, grinning into the darkness. The poor guy had a case of it himself —and no wonder, holed up 12 months a year with a beautiful wife and a wonderful son in this paradise of rain forest and wild monkeys, dealing with interesting people and fishing every day.

"Nice-looking bat, Rudy."

"Sí. Not so bad, huh?" He loosened the drag abruptly, giving slack, then watched as the creature dropped the hook, fluttered for a moment, and banked off toward wherever it is Central American bats go after having the bejesus surprised out of them. "Clean release. Nice an' clean. He's a happy theeng, no? Happy to be free." Dodero was reeling in the line now, making the lure splash in transport, and I looked on in mild fear that something else would swoop down out of the sky and eat it.

"Yeah, Rudy, that's one happy bat."

"Es not a reptile, though. Bat es a mammal, man." He was checking the lure, clicking his tongue at the fang marks, saying as he did, "You want to catch reptiles, turtles and snakes 'n' theengs, you got to use streamer flies. White es good; sometimes red. Not poppers, though; reptiles won't hit poppers. 'Cept for frogs, maybe."

Oh.

Fun and beauty exact their toll.


THERE MAY BE ULTERIOR MOTIVES intertwined in this passion of mine for fishing distant lands. Judge for yourself.

Understand first that a rod strapped to your back serves as more than just a device by which you can yank unfamiliar fish from unfamiliar waters. As a stranger without motive in a strange place, your presence is often viewed with mistrust if not outright suspicion. Carry a fishing rod, though, and people who normally wouldn't stop to give you directions will drop everything to give detailed misinformation and lie about the local angling. Women will sometimes even offer food, assuming—too often correctly—that you haven't caught anything and probably won't. Also, I always choose a country where the fishing is supposed to be superb, yet has enough local character so that the fishing really doesn't matter so much once you get there. I settle upon a place I would like to see, then spend evenings after my charters with books and maps, doing research while I tie the prescribed flies beneath the reading light in my office. This is called armchair fishing, a fantasy sport discouragingly more productive than the real thing. Before leaving for Costa Rica, I had tied and packaged 40 leaders and 40 big streamer flies, rehearsing this scene as I did: Me on the stern of a boat, a record-shattering sailfish at my feet, hands blistered, sweat pouring, blithely waving away the crew's appeals that I rest, yelling up to the fly bridge, "Swing her around for another pass, Julio! Might as well break the record on eight-pound while we're out here." Silly stuff like that.

But the passion to fish often begins to ebb shortly after arrival, usually at a speed directly influenced by the number of other things there are to do. Beer and hammocks sometimes play a role, too. Remember that I usually take these trips immediately after the spring charter marathon: a time when Twig Syndrome is in full blossom, and the pressure to put fish in the boat has rendered even the best of fishing guides a jelly blob of neuroses and bad language. In the grip of this malady I once went to Little Cayman Island to fish for bonefish on fly, but ended up doing a bird count. I went to Belize to fish for permit, but spent most of my time in the back of a pickup, happily riding through the rain forests of Guatemala. I went to Cuba to fish for anything, but ended up scuba diving twice a day. I went to Ireland with a salmon rod, and caught nothing but the flu, which with great persistence I tried to cure by stopping in every country pub my bicycle happened to come across. That I sometimes don't catch the fish I originally seek is not surprising; that I no longer pretend to care is beginning to worry my friends.

But this was my third trip to Costa Rica. All frivolities should have long since been dispensed with. I had planned and researched and tied these beautiful artificial lures in preparation, and had even contacted a magazine—this magazine—and laid my intentions clearly on the line: I was going to try to set the new International Game Fish Association world record on Pacific sailfish. In other words, I was determined. In further words, I had a written contract.

So I landed in San José, Costa Rica, on a Thursday, with sincere intentions of being at one of the isolated billfishing camps on the Pacific coast by Friday night. Come Saturday, though, I was still in San José roaming the streets, getting lost, dickering badly in the marketplaces, and generally having a very good time.

San José is as different from most other Central American cities as Costa Rica is different from other Central American countries. First off,

San José has one of the lowest crime rates in the world for a major metropolitan area. It's clean, too. You fly in through clouds and there, surrounded by mountains, is this great glittering city looking maybe a little bit like Atlanta, but without the freeways and yuppie housing. Then, you walk out early and the *tienda* keepers are washing the sidewalks, and kids with pretty faces are holding hands on the way to school; there are fruit carts on every corner, the smell of sliced mangoes and pineapples mixing with the mountain air and the bakery smell of the morning. The boundaries of the city, this metropolis of 800,000, seem to draw in then, and it becomes a personable and reasonable place, not nearly so large as it actually is. Men and women smile at you; passersby shake your hand as you ask directions, then shake it again once you're thoroughly confused. It is a noisy, cheerful place, a city of country markets, ornate architecture, and Spanish formality. The people take great pride in the way they dress, and neither wearing shorts nor drinking beer in public is acceptable— unless you're an American, in which case misbehavior is not only expected, but greeted with wry looks, as if to say, "Ah, those crazy gringos . . ."

Anyway, it's one of the few cities where I'm tempted to linger, and I did. It was at the Key Largo, a bar where world expatriates and some of the most beautiful women in Costa Rica sometimes meet for pleasure and business (respectively), that I met Archie Fields, the owner and president of Río Colorado Lodge. Fields, a huge, articulate man in a guayabeara shirt, was saying, "So, why just fish the Pacific coast? I can fly you up to my place; fish for tarpon or snook, the best in the world."

There was this really stunning brown-eyed girl smiling at me from across the room; and a man named Jack, wearing a silk scarf and one of those French kind of caps, was singing "Satin Doll" with a jazz band backup; and I think I told Fields I didn't want to catch tarpon and snook because I had Guides' Disease, only I'm not sure if he knew what that meant.

"You can fish for the jungle fish, then," he said. "Guapote and machaca—you don't have those in Florida. They hit like bass and fight like tarpon. And you'll be our guest; won't have to pay for a thing."

This girl, whose name turned out to be Teresa, was winking now, and people were dancing because Jack had asked them to. I think I told Fields about my determination to set the world record on Pacific sail, but I'm almost certain I didn't tell him I'd always tried to avoid fishing resorts because most of them cater to Americans and seldom have much in common with the country in which they operate. Not only that, there was a question of ethics. No journalist with integrity accepts a freebie.

Fields said: "You can spend a couple days on the Caribbean. Head over to the Pacific later and get your sail." Then he leaned forward as if to share a secret. "If you really want to see this country, I can stick you in a boat, take you 70 miles upriver through some of the most beautiful rain forest in the world, have them drop you at the lodge."

So much for integrity. I left for Río Colorado the next morning.

I CAUGHT THE BOAT in Moin, just east of Limón, after a drive through the mountains that lie between San José and the Caribbean—a car trip of remarkable beauty through cloud forests with silver rivers that roll toward valleys in the far distance. Then it was seven hours aboard, traveling a watercourse of rivers and canals northward that is the only means of commerce along Costa Rica's wilderness Mosquito Coast. The JUNGLE ADVENTURE sign atop Fields's open boat gave me pause at first, but then the forest began to crowd in, the river narrowed, and soon the method of conveyance no longer mattered. The canopy trees of the jungle— tropical moist forest by definition—grew and joined, 150 feet high, and the understory growth filled in, absorbing light, so that it seemed we were traveling through sheer, green canyons of tangled vines and bright flowers. Then the jungle would thin abruptly, coconut palms and banana thickets would appear, and there would be a few bamboo huts with pigs rooting beyond the swept lawns and with clothes dangling on the line, and children would come running toward us, grinning. Behind, dugout canoes would thrash on our wake.

Far to the north, only about 25 miles from the Nicaraguan border, we entered Tortuguero National Park, a preserve (inspired largely by the work of Archie Carr of the University of Florida) to protect the green turtle, which annually lays its eggs along the 22-mile stretch of beach there. The rain forest beyond, the most spectacular we had seen, is protected, too—and to Costa Rica's credit. Even so, Costa Rica's un-protected natural resources suffer from the very things that make the country attractive to travelers: nearly 40 years of political stability, and a much longer history of middle-class majority rule—a social oddity among the bitter caste fighting that keeps the rest of Central America in endless turmoil. Because Costa Rica is stable, outside corporations have invested here with confidence, including several American fast food chains that now consider Costa Rica their major source of cheap beef. To increase production, corporations, individual ranchers, and Japanese logging contractors are expanding pasturage by leveling the rain forest at a phenomenal rate. It is said to take 15.2 square meters of pasture land to produce just a single quarter-pound hamburger patty, and it comes down to trading one of the world's greatest natural wonders for Big Macs and Whoppers. Riding a boat through the heart of it all, it seemed particularly nauseating to think that, at the present pace of destruction, 80 percent of Costa Rica's rain forests will be gone by the end of the century.

RÍO COLORADO LODGE is a series of cabins connected by roofed boardwalks, all built on the edge of the Río Colorado and raised on pilings so that it seems you are staying on a huge raft, or maybe in a tree house. Lodge capacity is 24, but there were only about a dozen other guests when I arrived, most of them fishermen, but a few had come just for the river trip and to see the wildlife. I gravitated toward the latter group not because I don't like fishermen—I do—but because I don't like the specific brand of ego-brittle, blood-sport, name-dropping, would-be Hemingways that the former group seemed to be, heart and soul.

Sitting in the bar that first night with a nice couple from Boston, we overheard this conversation:

"I'd always thought the African elephant was dangerous until I came up against my first Cape buffalo. For my money, they're the most dangerous game going." (Pause for effect.) "I had to kill three of them just to be sure." (Laughter.)

Second man: "Yeah, but for action, you ever go shooting down in Colombia? They got this valley south of Bogotá that the farmers plant. I killed 466 dove there in one day. A *single* day. I'd of killed more, only my gun broke."

Third man: "'Course, we carried $5,000 worth of shells with us—not everyone can do that."

No kidding, they said all that. It seems unlikely to me that lodges like Río Colorado get a steady flow of these people, probably because they show up so rarely on my charter boat. One of the great myths of chartering is that the people you take out are drunken boobs who pay big money to offend and to make fools of themselves. Just the opposite is true. Most of the people I take out are nice, some have become close friends over the years, and the fly-fishermen invariably know more about the sport's finer points than I do. But when you do get a bad group, it's almost always made up of blow-dried nimrods who pack the Gold Card in their wallets and gonads on their sleeves. That one of these jerks was a newspaper fishing writer from New Jersey, a guy who hung with the highfliers by trading free advertising for free trips, didn't do anything to buoy my spirits—especially because I was now doing exactly the same thing. The one bright spot that first night was that it had begun raining nonstop with no end in sight, and there was the very real possibility I wouldn't have to fish at all.

But then I met Rudy Dodero. Dodero, in his late twenties, was just back from playing soccer, and it looked as if fisticuffs had been involved. ("In theeese jungle we don't have soccer teams, we have soccer *armies*.") While he cleaned off the mud and blood, he outlined his life as freely as if I were his analyst—and it all revolved around fishing: fishing as a child growing up in Costa Rica, skipping school for fish tournaments, fishing on his honeymoon, now fishing on his time off from a job that was fishing. Some might have interpreted all this as extreme dedication, but I saw it for what it was and couldn't have been happier. After meeting Dodero, casting for bats seemed the natural progression on a path mutually shared. It was, in fact, a little bit like coming home.

NOT ONLY ARE THERE BATS and fish in Costa Rica, but there are 820 species of birds—more than in the United States and Canada combined—plus a long list of Central American mammals and reptiles. This is all the more attractive because Costa Rica is a tiny country, smaller than West Virginia, and the zones of fauna demarcation—while they vary greatly and change abruptly—are never more than a few hours from one another. On a busy day you can watch iguanas and howler monkeys on the Pacific coast, fish for rainbow trout in the central mountains (some are more than 12,000 feet high), see quetzals in the cloud forests, then travel down into the Caribbean lowlands to look for three-toed sloths and American crocodiles.

I saw my first three-toed sloth during the car trip from San José to Moín, a pathetic, oil-stained creature crossing a busy highway. This animal moved into traffic with such mechanical resolve, like a windup toy with dying batteries, that it seemed less like a living creature than road kill on the hoof. I turned away and couldn't look back.

I had seen a number of other native species at the zoo in San José, but it was on the Río Colorado that the diversity of the country's wildlife hit me full force. Fishing for machaca, we would run far upriver, cut the engine, then drift along a solid forest wall, casting poppers toward the bank. The silence would grow, then slowly freshen with sound: water dripping from the giant elephant-ear leaves, the woodwind cry of a bird, a distant grunt followed by the frantic chatter of creatures unseen and unknown—all of this echoing for a moment, then quickly absorbed by the forest. Even with no wind, there was the steady groan of limbs and vines, the sound of the jungle itself, as if it were growing as you watched, and might, if you lingered, entangle and then consume you.

Spider monkeys would sometimes come rustling through the canopy, whole families of them, flushing parrots and green-billed toucans as they traveled to see the intruders who had come by boat. The females would stay to the rear, sometimes with babies clinging to their backs, while the males cautiously swung to the outer ledge of forest, their startlingly human eyes peering out. On the banks, turtles and crocodiles sunned themselves, and I saw several more sloths in the lower trees, each looking like a hairy, squint-eyed child. The most striking creatures amid all this activity, though, were the butterflies. They would come fluttering into the river gloom, catch a stray ray of light, and burst into bright flames of iridescent lavender or gold, then veer back into the shadows, the light still clinging to their wings.

To me, this was the best fishing: being on the river in silence, the familiar weight of fly rod in hand, each cast serving as a kind of conduit by which you are not only linked to the quarry you seek, but, in moments of absolute concentration, rendered a legitimate extension of the river itself.

There were other good moments at Río Colorado. One night I crossed the fence separating the lodge from the village beyond, and went to mass, for it is my habit while traveling to attend whatever church is available. My reasons for doing this are more social than spiritual, for there are no strangers in a small church, and as an outsider you are credited with virtues not normally ascribed to you by friends who know the truth. On this night, though, I'd gotten the time wrong because of my terrible Spanish, and no one was there. I left money for the candle I'd lit, then sat in the plywood chapel and watched as the village kids poked their noses over window sills and around corners, giggling at this silly gringo to whom, only a few hours earlier, they had so carefully explained the church schedule. Couldn't these Americans get anything straight?

Back at the lodge, though, things weren't quite so pleasant. Some of the fishermen were upset because of the constant rain and angry because the fishing, under these less than ideal conditions, wasn't as spectacular as they'd hoped. Sure, they'd each had tarpon strike, but their group had landed only one. Where was the constant action they'd read about in the fishing magazines? Most of the anger was aimed at Dodero, and the fishermen were taking sly, invidious avenues to vent it. That night at dinner, Rudy's wife asked one of the men if the diamond in his ring was real. Slightly offended, the man held the ring to the light, recited the karat weight—the stone was the size of a goiter—and said: "But I got a good deal; it only cost me 16."

It was a trap; I knew it. But there was nothing to do but listen. "Sixteen hundred dollars?" asked Rudy, amazed that someone could afford to pay so much for a ring, but a little uncomfortable, too, because Costa Rica is a poor country and open talk of big money is obviously a subject of embarrassment.

The man bored in. "No, $16,000. I have a friend who's a jeweler if you're interested."

Rudy and his wife winced visibly. He had told me what his salary was, and it would take him three years to make that much money—a fact the man with the ring had to at least suspect.

Despite all this, Dodero and his staff remained models of diplomacy, but I knew the complaining and the baiting had to be taking a toll—for it was already wearing on me, a kind of sympathetic response. The rain wouldn't stop, and the men weren't landing enough fish, and it was everyone's fault but their own. It is exactly this pressure to control the uncontrollable that is the spore of Twig Syndrome, and I was feeling the familiar roll of stomach and abdominal tightness that, under different circumstances, I might have written off as nothing more than liver disease. Even worse for Rudy, this was all happening in plain view of a journalist—me.

I left the next day, insisting I had to get on with my quest for a world-record Pacific sail. But this was an excuse, a fiction that, if not dropped upon my arrival in San José, I had certainly abandoned now.

TELL SOME PEOPLE you're going to Central America to fish, and you get this weird look, like maybe next time it will be mushroom hunting in Libya. Isn't it dangerous? they want to know. Don't the contras maintain bases in Costa Rica? The week before my arrival, there had been an explosion outside the U.S. Embassy and the newspapers were filled with it. When I got back to San José, I decided to go to the embassy and ask just how dangerous it was roaming around this country. Costa Rican national guardsmen (Costa Rica dissolved its army in 1948 and funnelled the money into education) gave me hard stares as I approached, and I passed through the door to find a U.S. Marine looking at me through bulletproof glass. Behind him, hanging on the wall, was a flak jacket, an M-16, and a large photograph of a smiling Ronald Reagan.

"You want to know about the explosion, sir? Went off across the street. Broke some glass, that's about all. It was just a grenade."

"Just a grenade?" I felt silly that I'd even asked.

The Marine had short blond hair and big arms with veins showing— the kind of guy you like to see on the other side of something bulletproof. "Right. Just a grenade. That's about the only trouble we've had. The State Department advisories tell you to use common sense around the Nicaraguan border."

"So it's safe to travel anywhere else in the country?"

The Marine almost showed some emotion. "I don't know. You going by plane or driving?"

It was a point worth making. Put these kindly, mild-mannered Costa Ricans behind the wheel of a car, and some kind of bizarre personality transformation takes place. They become aggressive, wild, filled with a crazy faith in life after death. Various sources rate Costa Rica second or third in the world in per capita traffic accidents, and it seems a point of honor with them to someday be first. It's not the roads. The roads are generally very good and well maintained. It's the driving habits of the people, and I have no explanation for it. If you go to Costa Rica, forget about the contras and the Sandinistas—watch out for the Toyotas.

Riding on a crowded bus from San José to the Pacific, I saw fast rivers that certainly held trout, forests growing green in the mountain clouds, but all I could think of were these cars we kept meeting head-on as we passed slower vehicles on hills and curves. I pictured the police rooting through the inevitable carnage, finding my two beautiful fly reels—a handmade Sea Master and a big-game Fenwick—and kicking them into the ditch as nothing more than gold-plated cylinder heads.

Puntarenas, a Pacific port town dirty by Costa Rican standards, seemed almost pristine on arrival, a place where you might stumble off a bus and kiss the good earth. I got an inexpensive hotel room (the farther you get from San José, the cheaper everything is), then made the rounds of the fishing docks, looking for a boat to charter for sailfishing. Strangely, once shed of the pressure to fish for sails, it suddenly seemed like a fun thing to actually try. But the few boats operating were already booked, and the ones not booked were broken-down. I could have gone on up the coast to fishing resorts like Tamarindo Beach or El Ocotal, but that would have required a decision with hard edges and a certainty of purpose I not only lacked but didn't want very much. Instead, I settled on the Peninsula of Nicoya, a remote shoulder of mountains and wilderness beach that extends far out into the Pacific and where, it was said, whales came in close to shore and, in certain isolated areas, there were no sport-fishing boats of any kind.

PENINSULA OF NICOYA: abrupt green hills with birds of paradise and bananas growing wild, the swept lawns of isolated villages connected by one-lane dirt roads more often traveled by horses than by cars. I stayed on the southeastern cusp of the peninsula, Bahía Ballena, at La Hacienda, a cattle ranch reminiscent of television's Ponderosa, but with the ocean out front and the mountains at its back.

Several years ago the owner of La Hacienda decided to build a few guest rooms, and now it has become a kind of bunkhouse-style hotel. The main house is constructed of heavy wood and red tile, with broad porches, hammocks, and grounds so perfectly kept that it's as if someone had transported a botanical garden to the seventh fairway of the Augusta Country Club. There are the hedges of hibiscus, in big red bloom, where hummingbirds compete with bees, and there are the coconut palms and mango trees with iguanas the size of dachshunds blinking beneath, and everywhere else you look there is nothing but water and vegetation and empty beach—unless you lean from your hammock enough to see the corrals, and then you can watch the cowboys branding or maybe doing rope tricks.

I fished there. I'd get up before sunrise, climb on a horse, and ride down the beach, a fly rod braced against my thigh like a Winchester. As the beach is the most convenient means of travel between the village of Pochote, three miles north, and the village of Tambor, three miles south, there were occasionally other solitary horsemen with whom to exchange waves, a pleasant thing in lonely country. I'd cast for a couple of hours, watching for the spout plumes of whales, then ride back, the sound of surf, the clatter of parrots, the eerie grunt and grumble of howler monkeys wild in the pale light.

At such times, La Hacienda seemed to be the best of Costa Rica, for it afforded all those small intersections for which we travel—primitive backcountry and unaffected people—and there was the fishing, too, another form of intersecting, and with similar ends: to touch for a moment those kindred things of which you can never truly be a part. And sitting on the porch one night at La Hacienda, reading by generator light, I was hardly even tempted when bats came vectoring down—fruit bats, maybe—called by the lamp's citreous glow in which, turning, I could see my fly rod against the rail, its golden reel glittering like something electrical, or something alive . . .

*December 1986*

# PERMISSIONS
• ▲ ■